THE ULTIMATE GUIDE

TO

DOROTHY DUNNETT'S

THE GAME OF KINGS

AN ILLUSTRATED ENCYCLOPÆDIC RESOURCE OF
TRANSLATIONS, AND HISTORICAL, LITERARY,
MYTHOLOGICAL, MUSICAL, AND POETIC REFERENCES
IN THE ORDER IN WHICH THEY APPEAR

LAURA CAINE RAMSEY, J.D.

THE GAME OF KINGS
DOROTHY DUNNETT © 1961, 1989

QUOTED TEXT USED WITH PERMISSION

THE ULTIMATE GUIDE TO DOROTHY DUNNETT'S *THE GAME OF KINGS*

LAURA CAINE RAMSEY, J.D.
© 2015

CONTRIBUTORS:
JAIME JACOBS
ELIZABETH RAMSEY
VICTORIA SACCENTI
GAYLYNN LATIMER
MARIA ELENA ALONSO-SIERRA

LYMONDGUIDES@GMAIL.COM
WWW.LYMONDGUIDES.BLOGSPOT.COM
P.O. BOX 782, WEXFORD PA 15090

ISBN: 1478260335
ISBN: 978-1478260332

Table of Contents

Acknowledgments: 4
Author's Note: 5

Acknowledgments

First and foremost, my gratitude and an all-encompassing *merci beaucoup!* to my children, Gordon, Elle, and Sophie, for their love and understanding in allowing me the sheer indulgence of exploring the depth of *The Game of Kings*. To my mother for her love, and to my father for always encouraging an intellectual challenge.

Thank you to my editor and contributor, Jaime Jacobs, for her invaluable knowledge, insights, and exemplary editorial skills. Thank you to Liz Ignatuk for her unerring eye. Thank you to my contributors: Elizabeth Ramsey, Gaylynn Latimer, Victoria Saccenti, and Maria Elena Alonso-Sierra. Thank you to Linda Gillard, Marta Farensbach, and Julia Hart, for their guidance and assistance. And thank you to my dear friends who share a love of literature, without whose support and encouragement this book would not exist.

Thank you to my on-line community of readers at the Outlander Book Club, and our team of moderators who devote themselves to creating a community where one can foster an intelligent, thoughtful, and caring dialogue. We invite and encourage readers of all genres to join in our discussions covering a wide range of books, including *The Lymond Chronicles* and *The House of Niccolò*.

Thank you to Vivienne Schuster, Dorothy's literary agent, for permission to use the quotes from *A Game of Kings*. Thank you to the groups and organizations who keep Dorothy's work alive:

The Dorothy Dunnett Society (www.dunnettcentral.org)
www.dorothydunnett.co.uk
Marzipan Yahoo Group
Game of Kings Yahoo Group
www.outlanderbookclub.freeforums.org
The National Library of Scotland

Thank you to the National Library of Scotland for access to the Dorothy Dunnett archives housed in their facility in Edinburgh. Thank you to Pam Keeling for her devotion to diligently and painstakingly cataloguing the files. There is a wealth of information in the archives; I encourage everyone to make the effort to access this treasure trove.

Thank you to Elspeth Morrison for compiling the *Dorothy Dunnett Companion I* and *Dorothy Dunnett Companion II*. Ms. Morrison's works contain something mine can never obtain: information directly from Dorothy herself.

And, of course, a deep bow of humble gratitude to Dorothy Dunnett. I wish we could have met.

Author's Note

The Ultimate Guide to THE GAME OF KINGS *by Dorothy Dunnett* is an encyclopædic resource of historical, literary, mythological, and poetic references used within the book, along with a compendium of translations, in the order in which they appear in the text. An understanding of the complexity of the references illumines the conversation and expressions of the characters. Often, the entire poem or reference is cited, often just a small section; the text dictated what was necessary to include.

The Guide follows the page numbers of the Vintage edition currently marketed by Random House, as this is the most widely available edition. The Index provides where a reference can be found on a text page. With the advent of e-readers, it may seem archaic to follow physical page numbers, but this is the most comprehensive and clear way to follow the chronology of references. Each entry includes the text page number from the Vintage edition, an italicized line from the book, followed by the explanation of the reference.

The book took a little over two years to research and compile, which included two trips to Scotland. During my second trip I had the pleasure of attending the Annual General Meeting of the Dorothy Dunnett Society and spending time poring over the archives housed in the National Library of Scotland. End-notes marked with a 'D' (i.e. [1/D]) indicate a note from a file in the archives. Serendipitously, I finished the book on the 90th anniversary of Dorothy's birth. I cannot think of a greater homage.

Why create a book of references almost as large in scope as THE GAME OF KINGS itself? A love of learning, a knack for research, and a quest for knowledge. It was fascinating to step into Lymond's mind and mine its vast capacities. What I gained was a genuine feeling of awe for Dorothy Dunnett's breadth of knowledge, her unparalleled skill at writing, and her ability to weave an intricate story which changes and shifts each time it is read. It isn't a static piece of literature, but a breathing, living expression. It is my hope illuminating the work of this national treasure of Scotland will give rise to a new generation of readers. Fifty years after its initial publication, THE GAME OF KINGS remains relevant, worthy of attention, and a joy to read.

For my Dad

THE GAME OF KINGS

Opening Gambit: Threat to a Castle

Title Page from the 1493 Florence edition of
The Buke of Ye Chess by Jacobus de Cessolis

First your chess game shall be meticulously made
And seen after the proper moves
Of every man in order of his king
And as the chess game shows us his moves
Right so it may be to kingdom and to crown
The world and all that is therein ought lie
The chess game may his form signify.[1]

From *The Buke of Ye Chess* by Jacobus de Cessolis, meaning one's substance may be shown by how one plays the game. An opening in chess is termed a 'gambit' when the first player is prepared to sacrifice a pawn in order to gain an advantage and quicken development of the game. The term is derived from the Italian word *gambetto*, used to describe a wrestling move where the contender gives his opponent an apparent advantage for the purpose of tripping him up. It is a feint; an attempt to deceive.

The opening quotes for each of the chapters in the book are either from *The Game and Playe of the Chesse* by William Caxton (c.1415-1492) or the book from which it was derived, *The Book of the Customs of Men and the Duties of Nobles,* also known as *The Buke of Ye Chess,* by Jacobus de Cessolis (c.1250-c.1322). Written in the 13th century and first printed in 1473, *The Buke of Ye Chess* used the game as the basis for a series of sermons on morality. Neither book illustrates play or player improvement, but uses the chessboard and pieces to 'allegorize a political community whose citizens contribute to the common good'[2].

In his prologues to *The Game and Playe of the Chesse*, first published in 1474, Caxton frames the text as more concerned with the 'moral instruction of an entire community than with that of a single ruler'[3]. His entreaty is to all those who read the book to follow the precepts appropriate to their social role, be it king, queen, bishop (judges), knights, and rooks (the king's emissaries); or tradesmen, doctors, notaries, and blacksmiths. 'This new metaphor for social order reimagines the king as a member of the kingdom; the realm is no longer a reflection of royal will but rather a complicated matrix of different affiliations in which the king is one piece among many.'[4]

Introduction of the Art of Printing:
Caxton Reading the First Proof-Sheet from His Printing Press, 1474,
from a painting by E.H. Wenhurt.

011   ...*the* Sea-Catte *reached Scotland from Campvere...*

Campvere, a fortified seaport of the Netherlands on the island of Walcheren, was once of considerable commercial importance as all goods sent from Scotland to the Netherlands were held there until sold. The Scots in Campvere formed a separate community and were given the privilege of being governed by Scots law.

011   ...*was being rowed on a warm August night over the Nor' Loch...*

The Nor' Loch, part of the natural defence of Edinburgh, was used as a smugglers' route, and for the punishment of crime. Some 300 witch trials by dunking were held at the loch. It was drained in 1759 and is now the Princes Street Gardens.

Edinburgh Castle sits upon volcanic Castle Rock with the city trailing down toward the Palace of Holyroodhouse, which stands at the bottom of the Royal Mile in Edinburgh, at the opposite end to Edinburgh Castle. The 'Castelh-Mynyd-Agned' or *Fortress of the Hill above the Plain,* pre-dates the city of Edinburgh, and was the nucleus around which the city grew. A favourite residence of David II, he began building David's Tower in 1367. During the reign of the Stewart Kings, the castle became a palace. James I, upon his return to Scotland after captivity in England, built the Parliament House (now the armoury) and private apartments, and it remained a residence of the kings and queens of Scotland. During the reign of the 'chivalrous and splendid'[5] James IV, Edinburgh was celebrated throughout Europe as the scene of 'knightly feats'[6]; chevaliers came from all countries to participate in the royal tournaments. After the death of James IV at Flodden, the castle was used mainly as a fortress, prison, and barracks.

Edinburgh Castle, before the Lang Siege of 1573

Holyrood Abbey was founded in 1128 by King David I. While hunting in the royal forest of Drumselch, on the outskirts of the city of Edinburgh, he was attacked by a enraged stag when 'an arm wreathed in a dark cloud and displaying a cross of dazzling brilliancy'[7] came between them. The stag fled, and David returned to the castle. During the night in a dream he was advised, 'as an act of gratitude for his miraculous deliverance, to erect an abbey...upon the spot where the miraculous interposition took place'[8]. The Abbey of Holy Rood was one of the richest and most opulent religious establishments in Scotland, and was used for coronations, marriages, baptisms, and funerals of the Scottish monarchs.

Interior of the Chapel Royal of Holyrood House, 1687

The foundation of the Palace of Holyrood was laid about 1501 by James IV, and became the chief seat of the Scottish sovereigns. The abbey and palace sit outside of the ancient city limits; it was a pleasant, grand, luxurious house within parks and gardens, and the site of celebrations and revelry.

The Royal Palace of Holyrood House by J. Gordon Rothiemay, 1647

On 14th August 1543, the treaty between Regent Arran and Henry VIII was ratified in Holyrood Abbey, promising the marriage between the infant Queen Mary and young Prince Edward. The Scottish parliament repudiated the treaty in December of the same year, prompting Henry VIII to attack Scotland, with the order to sack Holyrood House. The English army, under the command of the Earl of Hertford (later, Protector Somerset), invaded Scotland in the spring of 1544, and both the abbey and the palace were burned; the choir and transepts of the abbey were destroyed, and the baptismal font was carried away. The abbey and the palace were quickly repaired, but in late September 1547, the English again pillaged the abbey, stripped it of its bells, and 'committed every species of outrage'[9].

Bird's-Eye View of the English Attack on Edinburgh and Holyrood, 1544

The Battle of Flodden Field (9 September 1513) was fought in Northumberland between an army of 30,000 Scots under King James IV, and an English army of 32,000 English under the Earl of Surrey. The conflict between the two nations began when King Henry VIII entered into a league against France; in response, James declared war on England to honour the Auld Alliance with France. The battle began around 4 o'clock in the afternoon and was decided in little more than an hour. Towards the end of the battle, the Scots formed themselves into a ring of spearmen while the English, with arrows and bills, maintained their attack. Two arrow wounds and a gash of a bill ended the gallant life of King James IV, and all of his division were killed.

Amongst the 10,000 slain were twelve earls, thirteen lords, and five eldest sons of peers. 'Scarce a family of eminence, but had an ancestor killed at Flodden, and there is no province of Scotland, even at this day, where the battle is mentioned, without a sensation of terror and sorrow.'[10] One mounted knight was able to steal away from the battlefield to tell Edinburgh the King was dead and the battle lost. The English victory was so nearly a defeat, with the loss of 4000 men, Surrey was unable to continue the war with much continued vigour. Despite its grave and disastrous results, the battle made no permanent modification in the relations between England and Scotland.

Flodden Field

The Messenger from Flodden

Edinburgh, c.1575

After the defeat at Flodden in 1513, Edinburgh began building a wall around the city; it was completed in 1560. The Flodden Wall was approximately 1.2m (4') thick and up to 7.3m (24') high.

After King James V refused to join King Henry VIII's break from the Roman Catholic Church, a furious Henry mobilised troops against Scotland, and in 1542, the Scottish army came to a terrible defeat at the Battle of Solway Moss. King James died just days after the battle, leaving his infant daughter, Mary, as sovereign in the care of her mother, Mary de Guise. In July 1543, the Treaty of Greenwich was signed by the Regent of Scotland, James Hamilton, 2nd Earl of Arran, promising Queen Mary to Prince Edward and a union of Scotland and England. As many within Scotland favoured an alliance with France, the Scottish Parliament later rejected the treaty. This led to the Anglo-Scottish conflict which became known as the War of the Rough Wooing, as King Henry VIII attempted to kidnap the queen and force her marriage to his son.

Major hostilities began with an attack on Edinburgh in 1544. The Scots won a victory at the Battle of Ancrum Moor in 1545, followed by a period of peace until May 1546, when clashes renewed and then escalated in the spring of 1547. King Henry VIII died on 28 January 1547, leaving his young son Edward VI as King. The boy's uncle, Edward Seymour, 1st Duke of Somerset, acted as Regent on his behalf. *The Game of Kings* opens in September 1547, on the eve of the battle of Pinkie Cleugh. The English are (yet again) attempting to kidnap young Queen Mary (age 5) and force her marriage to King Edward VI (age 10).

Battle of Solway Moss
24 November 1542

Solway Moss by J.M.W. Turner, 1816

When Henry VIII of England severed ties with the Roman Catholic Church, he asked his nephew, James V of Scotland, to do the same. James ignored the request and refused to join Henry at a meeting in York. A furious Henry mobilised troops against Scotland and sent an army across the Tweed, where villages and farmsteads were burned and laid waste. James responded by raising an army of 10,000 under Lord Maxwell, who marched toward the western border.

James, suspicious of the loyalty of his nobles, gave secret orders to Oliver Sinclair to take chief command of the army once it reached English soil. When the army reached the banks of the Esk at Solway Moss, the army was halted and Sinclair was raised on platform to read the royal commission. The army loudly and violently protested, and most of the chiefs refused to serve under him. During the ensuing confusion, several loyal peers attempted to restore order.

At this most inopportune moment, the English commanders Thomas Dacre and Jack Musgrave with a small force of 300 horse, were watching the border for movement of the Scots army. They seized on the opportunity of the state of confusion and charged with lances levelled. Taken by surprise, the Scots scattered, some becoming entangled in Solway Moss, where many drowned. Only twenty men were slain, but 1200 were taken prisoner, including the Earls of Cassilis and Glencairn, the Lords Somerville, Maxwell, Gray, Oliphant, and Fleming, the Masters of Erskine and Rothers, and Home of Ayton.

James, who was not present at the battle, withdrew to Falkland Palace ill with fever. He died two weeks later at the age of thirty-one, leaving behind a six-day-old daughter, Mary, Queen of Scots. After the death of James V, the hostages were returned to Scotland after signing a pledge to assist Henry VIII in furthering the English cause.

James V of Scotland
1512 - 1542

The son of King James IV of Scotland and Margaret Tudor of England, James V was only seventeen months old when his father was killed at the Battle of Flodden. His minority was a troubled period caused by several factors: the rivalry of the pro-English faction and the pro-French faction; the intrigues of Henry VIII; private quarrels amongst the aristocracy; and open war between the Hamiltons and Douglases. In 1524, when James was just thirteen years old, he was placed at the head of the government. In 1525, Archibald Douglas, 6th Earl of Angus, seized custody of James and held him for three years, exercising power on his behalf. James escaped from Angus's care in 1528, and took control of the government; Angus was removed from power and his family was forced into exile in England.

James, 'the king of the commons', travelled around Scotland disguised as the *Gudeman of Ballengeich*. He was a lute player, a patron of poets and authors, and employed foreign artisans and craftsmen to enhance the prestige of his Renaissance court. James spent a large amount of his wealth on building and restoring Stirling Castle and the palaces Falkland, Linlithgow, and Holyrood.

In support of the alliance between Scotland and France, James married Mary de Guise, daughter of the Duke de Guise, with whom he had three children: James, Robert, and Mary; both of his sons died in infancy. The French marriage solidified his pro-Catholic and pro-French position, but angered his uncle, Henry VIII. Two plots to murder the king were discovered, and he foiled Henry's attempts to kidnap him. After James refused to meet Henry at York, war broke out between the two countries. The Scots won a victory at the Battle of Haddon Rig in August of 1542, but suffered the serious defeat of Solway Moss in November of the same year. James became ill shortly after the battle and died just days after the birth of his only surviving child, Mary.

Mary de Guise
1515 - 1560

Mary de Guise was the queen consort of Scotland, the second spouse of King James V and the mother of Mary, Queen of Scots. She was a member of the powerful House of Guise, a prominent family in 16th century French politics. At age eighteen, she married Louis II, Duke of Longueville. In 1535, she gave birth to her first son, Francis. Her husband died in 1537, leaving Mary a widow at the age of twenty-one.

In 1537, to further the interests of the Franco-Scottish alliance against England, James V sought a second French bride. The recently-widowed Henry VIII of England, in attempts to prevent this union, also asked for Mary's hand. Given Henry's marital history – banishing his first wife and beheading his second – Mary refused the offer and married James.

James and Mary had two sons, James Stewart, Duke of Rothesay (b.1540) and Robert (b.1541); both died in 1541. The third and last child of the union was a daughter, Mary, born on 8 December 1542. King James died six days later, making the child Mary queen regnant of Scotland.

The government of Scotland was first entrusted to James Hamilton, 2nd Earl of Arran. Henry VIII of England wished the infant Queen Mary to wed his son, Prince Edward. This led to internal conflict in Scotland with those who preferred alliance with France, and led to an English invasion, later termed the Rough Wooing.

Mary, Queen of Scots
8 December 1542 - 8 February 1587

Mary, Queen of Scots, the only surviving legitimate child of King James V of Scotland, was only six days old when her father died following the Battle of Solway Moss. During her minority, Scotland was ruled by regents. James Hamilton, 2nd Earl of Arran, next in line to the throne, ruled on her behalf until 1554, when Mary's mother succeeded him.

Henry VIII of England took the opportunity of Arran's regency to propose England and Scotland be united through the marriage of Queen Mary and his own son, Prince Edward. The Treaty of Greenwich was signed on 1 July 1543, when Mary was just six months old, promising the marriage of Edward and Mary. It was Henry's wish Mary should move to England where he could oversee her upbringing.

Feelings among the Scottish people towards the English changed when Cardinal Beaton rose to power and began to push a pro-Catholic and pro-French agenda. The Treaty of Greenwich was rejected by Parliament, which caused Henry VIII to begin his Rough Wooing, designed to impose the marriage of his son and Mary. This consisted of a series of raids on Scottish and French territories and other military actions.

James Hamilton
Duke of Châtellerault and 2nd Earl of Arran
c.1516 - 1575

James Hamilton, 2nd Earl of Arran and Duke of Châtellerault, was next in line to the throne after the infant queen by his descent from James II. After the death of James V, Arran was chosen governor of Scotland during Mary's minority. A man of great wealth, Arran was 'genial and tolerant...but in public affairs indolent and vacillating in the extreme'[11]. Described as foolish, weak-minded, and timid, Arran was friendly to the Reformers and inclined to England and agreed to the proposed marriage of Edward, Prince of Wales, to Queen Mary, which the Scottish Parliament ratified as the Treaty of Greenwich on 1 July 1543. The pro-Catholic, pro-French factions led by Cardinal Beaton and the Queen-Dowager, however, were successful in having the Scottish Parliament break the marriage treaty in December 1543. Henry VIII reacted by sending an army into Scotland to take Leith, burn Edinburgh, and ravage the Lothians. Arran quickly changed allegiance and joined the pro-French faction in resisting the English invasion.

After the defeat at Pinkie Cleugh, Arran gradually lost control of the government, seeing the reins slip into the stronger hands of Mary de Guise. She convened a council at Stirling where it was resolved to appeal to France for assistance against the English, foreshadowing the marriage of Mary to the Dauphin of France. Arran, who had hoped for an alliance between Mary and his eldest son, James Hamilton, Master of Hamilton, agreed to the French proposal after receiving a judicious amount of French gold and the grant of the duchy of Châtellerault.

Edward Seymour
1st Duke of Somerset, 1st Earl of Hertford, 1st Viscount Beauchamp of Hache
1506 - 1552

Edward Seymour, 1st Duke of Somerset, was Lord Protector of England in the period between the death of Henry VIII in 1547 and his own indictment in 1549. Edward was the eldest brother of Jane Seymour, Henry VIII's third queen consort. Somerset was a skilful soldier, which he proved on expeditions to Scotland, specifically the burning of Edinburgh in May 1544. When Governor Arran joined forces with Cardinal Beaton and the Queen Dowager, Henry VIII was thrown into a paroxysm of rage. On the eve of fusing the two countries via the marriage settlement of Prince Edward and Queen Mary, the defection of Arran had ruined all, and revenge drove Henry to seek to chastise a people who had now added mockery to their refusal of his overtures[12] by sending an army into Scotland to devastate the country. Seymour was sent to burn Edinburgh...

> *...and so deface it as to leave a memory for ever of the vengeance of God upon "their falsehood and disloyalty," do his best...to beat down the castle, sack Holyrood House, and sack, burn and subvert Lythe and all the towns and villages round, putting man, woman and child to fire and sword where resistance is made; then pass over to Fifeland and extend like destruction there, not forgeting to turn upside down...St Andrews...sparing no creature alive, especially such as be allied to the Cardinal, and, if the castle can be won destroying it piecemeal. By a month spent thus this journey shall succeed most to the King's honor, the army's surety and the saving of expense. He shall take order with the Wardens on the Marches to burn and destroy to the uttermost, not leaving Jedworth behind if it may be conveniently destroyed.[13]*

Edward VI
King of England and Ireland
1537 - 1553

The son of King Henry VIII of England and his third wife, Jane Seymour, Edward VI was crowned King of England and Ireland at the age of nine. A Regency Council, led by his uncle, Edward Seymour, 1st Duke of Somerset, reigned on his behalf. He was the first English monarch raised as a Protestant.

Henry VIII signed the Treaty of Greenwich on July 1, 1543, sealing a post-Solway Moss peace with Edward's betrothal to the seven-month old Queen Mary. The Scots were in a weak bargaining position after the defeat, and Henry, seeking to unite England and Scotland, stipulated Mary be handed over to him and raised in England.

The Scots repudiated the treaty in December 1543, renewing their alliance with France. An enraged Henry ordered Edward's uncle to invade Scotland, and Seymour responded with the most savage campaign ever launched by the English against the Scots.

012   *...parting the flat waters of the Nor' Loch like an oriflame...*

An oriflamme (Latin, *aurum*, gold, + *flamma*, flame) was a banner of red or orange-red with two or three points attached to a lance. Preserved in the abbey of St. Denis, Paris, it was carried by the King of France in war as the special royal ensign. In heraldry, it is a blue flag charged with three golden fleur-de-lis.

012   *In a small room in the High Street...*

The High Street is one of a succession of streets in Edinburgh which make up the Royal Mile, flowing from Edinburgh Castle at the peak to Holyrood Abbey at the foot, in the order of Castle Esplanade, Castlehill, Lawnmarket, High Street, Canongate, and Abbey Strand. The High Street included the Tolbooth (the former center of administration, taxation, and justice), St. Giles Cathedral, and the Mercat Cross. The Netherbow Port divided High Street from the Canongate.

High Street, Edinburgh

Netherbow Port from the High Street

Netherbow Port from the Canongate

012 *The swimmer, collared with duckweed, grounded, shook himself...*

Duckweed is an aquatic plant which floats on, or just beneath the surface of, still or slow-moving fresh water bodies.

013 *'I am a narwhal looking for my virgin.'*

A narwhal is a whale with a long tusk; here, it refers to a unicorn. According to legend, if a virgin is led to a place where a unicorn was seen and left there, the unicorn, upon seeing her, will run to her, rest his head in her lap and fall asleep. This was how the unicorn was frequently captured and killed. The unicorn was sought after by kings who wanted to display it as a symbol of power.

Virgin & the Unicorn, detail of fresco by Domenico Zampieri, c.1602

013 *'I have sucked up the sea like Charybdis and failing other entertainment will spew it three times daily, for a fee.'*

In Greek mythology, Charybdis was a sea monster, once a beautiful naiad and the daughter of Poseidon and Gaia. She took form as a huge bladder of a creature whose face was all mouth, whose arms and legs were flippers, and who swallowed huge amounts of water three times a day, and thrice daily threw it up again, creating whirlpools.

013 *'Shy,' said Lymond with simplicity, 'as a dogtooth violet.'*

A Dogtooth Violet (*Erythronium,* also known as Fawn Lily, Trout Lily, Yellow Snowdrop, and Adder's Tongue), is a small, herbaceous flowering plant of the lily family. The graceful, nodding, bell-shaped flowers are bright yellow and appear in shady wooded areas by the hundreds in the spring.

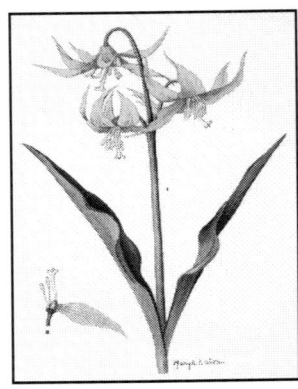

013 *In his tall house in Gosford Close...*

Gosford Close was located on the west pavement of what is now George IV Bridge, and stood directly east of Old Bank Close. In addition to the mansion of Mungo Tennant, the close included the town mansion of the abbot of Cambuskenneth, a building of considerable size with beautiful Gothic carvings, which 'may serve to remind us how little idea we can form of the beauty of the Scottish capital'[14]. The mansion of Hume Rigg of Morton was thus described as having a spacious dining and drawing-room, 'indeed, more so than those of any private modern house we have seen. The lobbies were all variegated marble, and a splendid mahogany staircase led to the upper storey. There was a large green behind, with a statue in the middle, and a summer-house at the bottom.'[15] The neighbourhood was the 'favourite resort of the most fashionable and distinguished among the resident citizens, and a perfect nest of advocates and lords of session'[16].

Gosford Close

014 *In the gratified presence of their host, Sir Walter Scott of Buccleuch...*

Sir Walter Scott
1st of Branxholme, 3rd of Buccleuch
1495 - 1552

Sir Walter Scott, 1st of Branxholme, 3rd of Buccleuch, succeeded his father while still in his minority. For nearly fifty years, 'Wicked Wat' held the family estates and engaged in several perilous adventures. Described as stout as Hercules, he was an active, enterprising man of fearless character, who, as a border chieftain and 'an inveterate enemy of England'[17] often made raids across the border.

A 'gallant and active warrior'[18] Scott led a body of men in the Battle of Flodden and was knighted on the field. In 1526, the young King James V enlisted Scott's help to free himself from the control of the Douglas faction led by Angus. Scott led 600 lances to intercept the king and his train but was defeated by Angus's forces near Melrose. The Scotts were driven off, pursued by the Kerrs. During the pursuit, a rider in Scott's service killed Kerr of Cessford, which led to a bloody feud between the Kerrs and Scotts. Scott was exiled for his role in the affair. After the overthrow of the Douglases, Scott was pardoned and made a chief advisor to the king in opposition to Angus.

After the death of James V, Scott opposed the marriage of Queen Mary to Henry VIII's son, Prince Edward, and became active in the wars with England. In 1545, Scott joined Arran and Angus against the invading English at the Battle of Ancrum Moor, leading a contingent in a rout of the English forces.

Scott had two sons by his first wife, Elizabeth Carmichael: David (d.1544) and Sir William Scott of Kincurd. In a short-lived attempt to resolve the Scott-Kerr feud, Sir Walter married his second wife, Janet Kerr, daughter of Andrew Kerr of Ferniehurst. They had no children. In 1543, he married his third wife, Janet Beaton (b.1519). They had 5 children: Grizel, Janet, Margaret, Walter, and David.

Signature of Sir Walter Scott of Buccleuch, c.1519

Saint Columba (521-597 AD; Gaelic, *Columcille'*, 'dove') was an Irish monk of royal lineage. A dispute over monastic possessions forced his banishment from Ulster in 563 AD and brought him to exile with twelve companions. They settled on the island of Iona, Scotland, and brought Christianity to the Picts. His evangelical mission became a centre for literacy and diplomacy, and he founded several churches in the Hebrides. While chanting the 45th Psalm, St. Columba's voice was 'preternaturally strengthened so as to be heard like a thunder-peal above the din and clatter by the which the Pictish magicians tried to silence his evening prayer under the walls of the Pictish palace'[19].

St. Columba by John R. Skelton

014 *...Tom Erskine...was a son of Lord Erskine, who was head of one of the families nearest the throne...*

Thomas Erskine
Master of Erskine
(died c.1551-1552)

Thomas Erskine, Master of Erskine, was the second son of John Erskine, 4th Lord Erskine, a Scottish nobleman and member of the distinguished Erskine family. In the family lineage, Mary Erskine was married to Sir Thomas Bruce, brother of King Robert I, who knighted her brother, Sir William de Erskine. Under David II, Sir Robert de Erskine held several high offices; his son, Sir Thomas Erskine, was the governor of Stirling Castle. For several generations the family was entrusted with the keeping of the heirs apparent to the Scottish crown during their minority: Alexander, 2nd Lord Fleming, had charge of James IV, while John, 4th Lord Erskine, was charged with the keeping of James V, and also the infant Queen Mary after her father's death.

Thomas Erskine was commendator to Dryburgh Abbey between 1541 and 1547. His tenure was marred by strife along the border, and the abbey and town were ransacked by an English army of 12,000 in September 1544. The Scots retaliated the next year under the command of the Earls of Home and Bothwell, and the abbots of Dryburgh and Jedburgh, and crossed into Northumberland and burned the village of Horncliff. This was the first time in the history of Dryburgh Abbey the head of the religious community acted as a feudal chief and a man of war.

In late 1545 or early 1546, Erskine was captured by the English *en route* to Rome when his ship, the *Lyone*, foundered off the coast of Dover. He was held captive in London in early 1547, prompting Mary de Guise to write on his behalf calling for his release. After his older brother, Robert, was killed at the Battle of Pinkie Cleugh, he resigned his office as commendator of Dryburgh Abbey in favour of his younger brother, John.

014   *'Who'll stay in the west that's worth a docken?'*

A docken is something of no value or importance.

014   *'...to hound down his brother baying like the Wild Jagd...'*

The Wild Jagd is an ancient folk myth prevalent across Northern, Western and Central Europe. The central theme is a phantasmal group of huntsmen raging in mad pursuit across the skies or just above the ground.

014   *'He's in the Low Countries, I believe.'*

Historically, the Low Countries were an area of lands which included the modern countries of Belgium, the Netherlands, Luxembourg, and parts of northern France and western Germany.

015   *'As my lady of Suffolk saith...God is a marvelous man.'*

Catherine Willoughby, Lady of Suffolk (1519-1580), the fourth wife of Charles Brandon, 1ˢᵗ Duke of Suffolk, was an outspoken adherent of the reformed Protestant religion. Catherine Parr, the last of the six wives of Henry VIII, wrote in a letter to Lord Seymour in 1547: *I can say nothing but, as my lady of Suffolk saith, 'God is a marvelous man.'*

015   *Nouvelle amour, nouvelle affections;*
         nouvelles fleurs parmi l'herbe nouvelle.

> *New love, new affections;*
> *new flowers amid new grass.*

From a poem by Maurice Scève (c.1500-c.1564), a French poet at the center of the Lyonnese côterie, which elaborated on the theory of spiritual love, derived partly from Plato and partly from Petrarch.

015   *'...her Sea-Scorpion, beautiful in breeding season.'*

Ancient sea scorpions are an extinct group of bug-like creatures with claws, sharp spines, and tails ending in spikes. They were believed to be terrors of the seas millions of years ago, and to reach more than eight feet in length.

015   *'The city is not full great, but it hath good baths within him.'*

From *The Travels of Sir John Mandeville*, a book detailing the author's supposed travels, first circulated between 1357 and 1371:

*From Safra men go to the sea of Galilee
and to the city of Tiberias, that sits upon
the same sea. And albeit that men clepe
it a sea, yet is it neither sea ne arm of the
sea. For it is but a stank of fresh water
that is in length one hundred furlongs,
and of breadth forty furlongs, and hath
within him great plenty of good fish, and
runneth into from Jordan. The city is not
full great, but it hath good baths within
him.*

**015   '*And tonight the frogs and the mice
fight, eh, Mungo?*'**

A reference to 'The Battle of Frogs and Mice'
(*Bat'rachomyomach'ia*), a mock-heroic poem
originally ascribed to Homer, now thought to be

Woodcut, MS, c.1459

the work of Pigres of Caria. A delightful parody on the *Iliad*, it describes with
brilliant humour military preparations, contests, single combats, speeches and
posturing, and the intervention of the gods to stop impending war. The term
batrachomyomachia is now used to indicate a silly altercation.

016   '*His mind is on fleshly lusts and his treasure.*'

From *The Summoning of Everyman*, a late 15th
century English morality play. Called by Death,
Everyman can persuade none of his friends –
Beauty, Kindred, Worldly Goods – to go with
him, except Good Deeds.

DEATH:

*Lord, I will in the world go
     run overall.
Lo, yonder I see Everyman walking.
Full little he thinketh on my coming;
His mind is on fleshly lusts
     and his treasure.
And great pain it shall
     cause him to endure
Before the Lord, Heaven King.*

Woodcut from Everyman, MS, c.1500

016 *'O mea cella, vale, you know...'*

O mea cella, mihi habitation dulcis amata
Semper in æternum, O mea cella, vale![19]

O my loved cell, sweet dwelling of my soul,
Must I forever say, 'Dear spot, farewell!'

From a poem by Alcuin of York (c.730-804), considered the most distinguished scholar of the 8th century, and a confidant and adviser of Charlemagne, who persuaded him to come to his court to create schools and to revive learning in France. He founded a school at the abbey of St. Martin at Tourse which was a model for excellence, and where he had numerous manuscripts copied with calligraphy of extraordinary beauty. Alcuin is more famous for the influence he exerted than for his own writings, although his letters are a source of information on the literary and social conditions of the time, and the history of humanism of the Carolingian age. A powerful stimulus to Western learning, Alcuin 'occupies a conspicuous place in the history of letters as the apostle of culture and urbanity in a rude and indeed barbarous age'[21]. Here, the poem is used by Lymond as a threat to expose Mungo Tennant as a smuggler.

016 *...jamming the stair foot like stooks at a threshing.*

A stook is a circular arrangement of swathes of cut grain placed on the ground in a field. Threshing is the process of loosening the edible part of cereal grain from the scaly, inedible chaff which surrounds it.

017 *'There was a lady lov'd a hogge – Honey, quoth she*
Won't thou lie with me tonight? – Hoogh, quoth he.'

From a popular nursery rhyme of the time.

018 *'And how's Will?' she said rashly...*

William Scott of Kinkurd, Younger of Buccleuch (born c.1525), was the oldest surviving son of Wat Scott and his first wife, Elizabeth Charmicael.

018 *...Janet, third and most formidable wife of Wat Scott of Buccleuch...*

Janet Beaton
Lady of Branxholme and Buccleuch
1519 - 1569

Janet Beaton, Lady of Branxholme and Buccleuch, was the daughter of Sir John Beaton, 2nd Lord of Creic, and a cousin of Cardinal Beaton. Her sister Elizabeth was a mistress of King James V, by whom she had an illegitimate daughter. Another niece, Mary Beaton, was a lady-in-waiting to Mary, Queen of Scots.

At the age of nineteen, Janet married her first husband, Sir James Crichton of Cranston Riddell. Following his death, she married Sir Simon Preston of Craigmillar Castle; they divorced in 1543 after her admitted adultery with Sir Walter Scott of Branxholme and Buccleuch. They married in 1543 and had five children: Walter, David, Grizel, Janet, and Margaret.

In 1558, after the death of Wat Scott, the 40-year-old Janet had a love affair with 24-year-old James Hepburn, Earl of Bothwell, who would later become the third husband of Queen Mary. Janet had an 'unfading beauty'[22] combined with 'audacity, determination, and sexuality'[23]. She was accused of witchcraft, and immortalised as the *Wizard Lady of Branxholm* in the narrative poem *Lay of the Last Minstrel* by the Scottish poet, Sir Walter Scott:

> *Of noble race the Ladye came,*
> *Her father was a clerk of fame,*
> *Of Bethune's line of Picardie.*
> *He learned the art that none may name,*
> *In Padua, far beyond the sea.*
> *Men said, he changed his mortal frame*
> *By feat of magic mystery...*
> *And of his skill, as bards avow*
> *He taught that Ladye fair*
> *Till her bidding she could bow*
> *The viewless forms of air.*

Signature of Janet Beaton of Buccleuch, c.1553

A mediæval university was an institution of higher learning, the first of which were established in Italy, France, and England in the 11th and 12th centuries. 'At every period of their existence it may be said that universities have fulfilled a double function in the social order. They have been the great training-schools for the different learned professions, and they have been the custodians and exponents of the ideal elements on which society ultimately rests. As the condition of their being, therefore, is to respond to the needs and aspirations of society, the history of universities has of necessity been determined by the revolutions of the human spirit and the changing ideals which men have set themselves to follow.'[24]

Meeting of Doctors at the University of Paris, Mediæval MS.

018 *'They've taught poor Will moral philosophy and his father's fit to boil.'*

Moral Philosophy, also known as ethics, is a branch of philosophy which addresses questions about morality: concepts such as good and evil, right and wrong, virtue and vice, justice and crime, etc.

018   '...if he sticks like Lindsay to the vulgarities of iambics...'

Sir David Lindsay of the Mount (c.1490-c.1555) was a Scottish poet. A Lyon King-at-Arms, he was knighted, served on several diplomatic embassies abroad, and was a sort of Master of Ceremonies upon the arrival of Mary de Guise in Scotland.

Sir David Lindsay

Extremely popular as a poet, Lindsay's humour was 'equally appreciated in the cottage as in the castle'[25]. He chastised all classes, from the king to the peasantry. He exposed the errors and abuses of Catholicism, and 'gave no quarter to the oppression of the nobles, the abuses of the law, or the vices of the court'[26]. It is said the 'verses of Lindsay did more for the Reformation in Scotland than all the sermons of Knox'[27]. 'He was a reformer before the Reformation, and an advocate for the "Common Weil" before the word "Commonwealth" had a place in English speech.'[28] Lindsay's verse was full of fancy, genial humour, good sense, varied learning, and knowledge of the world, with a good bit of licentiousness and vulgarity thrown into the mix.

'Iambics' refers to classical poetry and verse. An iamb is a metrical foot used in various types of poetry, consisting of an unstressed syllable followed by a stressed syllable, or a short syllable followed by a long syllable.

018   '...but if he's developing into a Calvinist or a Lutheran or an Erasmian or an Anabaptist it isn't very healthy...'

John Calvin (1509-1564) was an influential French theologian of the Protestant Reformation. Calvin moved to Paris in 1533, the centre of the new learning and a growing religious excitement within the Sorbonne and the court. Tensions, however, provoked a violent uprising against Protestants and Calvin fled to Switzerland. In 1547, he issued his *Christianæ Institutio,* a 'masterpiece of luminous argument'[29] which presented a complete system of Christian faith based on the principal that the Scriptures are the source of Christian truth. Calvin systemised Protestant doctrine and organised its ecclesiastical discipline. 'He was at once the great theologian of the Reformation, and the founder of a new church polity, which did more than all other influences together to consolidate the scattered forces of the Reformation, and give them an enduring strength.'[30]

Portrait of Jean Calvin by Titian, 16ᵗʰ century

Martin Luther (1483-1546), a German theologian considered the leader of the Protestant Reformation, was ordained a priest in 1507. At the time, the organised papal system of 'indulgences' – the sale of pardons by the pope exonerating one from the consequences of sin – had reached a scandalous height. Money was needed to feed the extravagances of the papal court, and emissaries sought to raise funds by the sale of these indulgences, the principal of which was John Tetzel, a Dominican friar at Jüterbog. Luther was incensed by the shameless traffic, and wrote his 95 theses on the doctrine of indulgences – denying the pope all right to forgive sin – which he posted on the door of the church at Wittenberg in 1517. In the ensuing fray, Luther expanded his argument to include the general power of the pope and the papal system as a whole. In his works is contained 'the kernel of the whole Reformation'[31]. His refusal to retract his writings at the demand of Pope Leo X and the Holy Roman Emperor Charles V resulted in his excommunication by the pope and condemnation as an outlaw by the Emperor. 'To initiate the religious movement which was destined to renew the face of Europe, and give a nobler and more enduring life to the Teutonic nations, require a gigantic will, which, instead of being crushed by opposition, or frightened by hatred, should only gather strength from the fierceness of the conflict before it. To clear the air thoroughly, as he himself said, thunder and lightning are necessary.'[32]

Martin Luther by Lucas Cranach, 1529

Desiderius Erasmus (c.1466-1536) was a Dutch humanist and theologian, considered the leading northern European Renaissance scholar. Highly esteemed by men of the period, Erasmus 'rescued theology from the pedantries of schoolmen, and referred it to its original sources; he did more than any other single person to advance the cause of the new studies of the Revival of Learning; he exposed the abuses of the church, and he protested in the interests of the people against the thoughtless tyranny of its rulers'[33].

Desiderius Erasmus by Hans Holbein the Younger, 1523

The term Anabaptists (from Greek, 'to baptise again') is now generally applied to Christians who reject infant baptism, but the name historically designated a sect of fanatical enthusiasts during the Reformation, specifically the followers of Thomas Münzer, who was killed in the Peasants' War in 1525. Despite severe persecutions, the

Anabaptist movement spread. Two of the sect's adherents, Melchior Hoffmann and John Mattheiesen, attempted to establish a socialistic kingdom of New Zion in Münster. The city became the scene of wild licentiousness until the leaders, after being cruelly tortured, were hung up in iron cages and executed in 1535. Many of the scattered adherents of the sect gathered around Menno Simons, and founded Mennonite congregations in the Netherlands and Germany, expressly repudiating the doctrines of the Münster fanatics and adopting a sober and moderate life.

The burning of Anabaptist Annekin Hendriks in 1571 by Jan Luyken, c.1685

018 *'...look at George Wishart and the Castillians.'*

George Wishart (c.1513-1546) was a Scottish religious reformer. Accused of heresy in 1538, he fled to England but returned to Scotland in 1543, under the protection of pro-Reformation nobles. Despite almost constant threat to his life, Wishart denounced the errors of Rome and the abuses of the church. He was seized in December 1543, and delivered to Cardinal Beaton, one of the most powerful opponents of Reformation in Scotland. He was tried in an ecclesiastical court, and sentenced to death. He was first strangled by rope and then burned to ashes outside the castle of St. Andrews. Wishart's boldness of preaching made him immensely popular, and his cruel execution in

George Wishart

the absence of any civil authority was considered by many to be unjust and unfair. Cardinal Beaton was assassinated just three month after the execution, partly in revenge for Wishart's death.

The Spanish Inquisition was a tribunal established in 1480 by Ferdinand II of Aragon and Isabella I of Castile. It was intended to maintain Catholic orthodoxy and convert members from Judaism and Islam. At the first *auto-da-fé* (ritual of public penance of condemned heretics) held in 1481, six people were burned alive. The Inquisition grew rapidly in the Kingdom of Castile. Those who refused to convert were expelled; approximately 80,000 Jews emigrated to Portugal to evade the Inquisition.

018 *'He's quoting Aristotle and Boethius and the laws of chivalry and the dreichter speils of the Chevalier de Bayard on loyalty and the ethics of warfare. He's so damned moral that he ought to be standing rear up under a Bo Tree.'*

Aristotle (384-322 BC) was a Greek philosopher, a student of Plato, and teacher of Alexander the Great. His writings cover physics, metaphysics, poetry, theater, music, logic, linguistics, rhetoric, politics, government, ethics, biology, and zoology. His writings were the first to create a comprehensive system of Western philosophy, encompassing morality and aesthetics, logic and science, politics and metaphysics.

Nuremberg Chronicle, MS, 1493

Boethius (c.480-524) was a philosopher of the 6th century. While jailed, Boethius composed his *Consolation of Philosophy*, a philosophical treatise on fortune, death, and other issues. *Consolation* became one of the most popular and influential works of the Middle Ages.

Nuremberg Chronicle, MS, 1493

Pierre Terrail, seigneur de Bayard (1473-1524) was a French soldier known as 'the good knight without fear and without reproach'[34]. Considered the epitome of chivalry, he was highly esteemed for his romantic heroism, loyalty, and scrupulous honour. Bayard, a chevalier of the Order of St. Michael, was 'simple, honest, a sterling friend and tender lover, pious, humane, and magnanimous'[35].

The Bo Tree is the Bodhi Tree under which the Buddha achieved enlightenment.

019 *'...Buccleuch isn't a plaster saint...'*

A plaster saint is a person without human failings; *or,* a person who makes a show of being without moral faults or human weakness, especially in a hypocritical way.

Le Chavelier Bayard, c.16th century

019 *'...Will would drive the Archangel Gabriel to lunacy and drink.'*

Gabriel is one of three archangels mentioned in the Bible. In Christian tradition, he is the angel of mercy. In Islam, he is believed to have revealed the Qu'ran to the prophet Muhammad, and is the chief of the four favoured angels and the spirit of truth.

The Annunciation by Sandro Botticelli, c.1489

019 *'...like the Ghibellines and the Guelphs.'*

Different factions were at odds in central and northern Italy during the 12th and 13th centuries: the Guelphs, wealthy mercantile families who supported the Pope; and the Ghibellines, the imperial, landed party who supported the Holy Roman Emperor. The split between the two parties was an important aspect of the internal policy of the Italian city-states and persisted into the 15th century.

019 *'Damn them both,' she said thoughtfully, 'for a couple of sumphs.'*

A sumph is a stupid person; a simpleton; a blockhead.

020 *'Criminals at the horn...'*

'At the horn' or *'put to the horn'* is a Scots term meaning one is proclaimed as an outlaw or bankrupt.

020 *'Did you try some brazil on your curtains?'*

Brazil refers to a red dye made from the wood of Brazilian trees.

019 *...by the wheel stair...*

Wheel stairs were a common architectural feature of mediæval castles, connecting the lower service areas and the upper floors, which housed common rooms and apartments.

019 *...a nautilus from the shell.*

A nautilus is a mollusc which grows spirally within its shell. As the animal draws itself onward it closes a door behind it[36/D]; the result is a chambered spiral with the original shell in the very centre.

020 *...howled like a cluricane.*

Wheel Stair, Linlithgow Palace

A cluricane (Irish, *Clobhair-cean*) is an Irish mythological being, kin to the leprechaun. Solitary and sottish, he prefers to lounge about and primp his handsome clothing. He is quick-witted, cunning, and possesses the knowledge of hidden treasures. With a propensity for mischief and roguery, the cluricane can become extremely angry if forgotten. Detested on account of his disposition, his name is used as an expression of contempt.

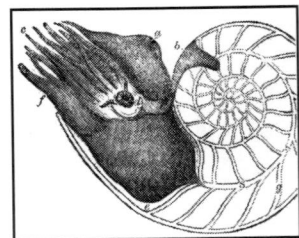

Diagram of a nautilus

020 *'This place was built by mouldiewarps for mouldiewarps...'*

Mouldiewarp is an archaic term for a mole.

020 *'Come dance with me in Ireland.'*

From the 14ᵗʰ century poem, *I Am of Ireland*:

> Icham of Irlaunde
> Ant of the holy londe of irlande
> Gode sir pray ich ye
> for of saynte charite,
> come ant daunce wyt me,
> in irlaunde.

020 *'You don't believe in polyandry by any chance?'*

Polyandry is the state of having more than one husband at the same time; thus a plurality of husbands. Its custom was sometimes limited to the marriage of a woman to two or more brothers, termed fraternal polyandry.

021 *'...let us mount like Jacob to the matriarchal cherubim above.'*

In Judaism, Jacob was the third patriarch of the Hebrew people with whom God made a covenant, and ancestor of the tribes of Israel. Jacob experienced a vision of a ladder or staircase reaching into heaven with angels going up and down it, commonly referred to as Jacob's Ladder. From the top of the ladder he heard the voice of God, who repeated many blessings upon him.

Jacob's Ladder
by Gerard Hoet, c.1728

021 *Every line of him spoke, palimpsest wise, with two voices.*

A palimpsest is a manuscript page from which text has been scraped off and then used again; thus, something with diverse layers apparent beneath the surface.

021 *'...Milo with the ox on his shoulders...'*

Milo of Croton was an athlete and soldier of ancient Greece famous for his great strength. He was a six-time victor in wrestling at the Olympic Games. One legend says he carried a live ox on his shoulders through the stadium of Olympia before eating it whole in one day. Another legend says he upheld the pillars of a house so as to give an assembly of scholars time to escape before the house collapsed. When enfeebled by old age, he attempted to tear apart a partially split tree, but he was caught by the closing of the fissure, and was devoured by wolves.

021 *'...Angra-Mainyo prepared to do battle with Zoroaster...'*

Angra Mainyu is the name given in Zoroastrianism to the 'destructive spirit' or the 'angry mind'. In Zoroastrianism, once amongst the world's largest religions, good and evil have distinct sources, with evil trying to destroy the creation of Ahura-Mazda, the Supreme God, and good trying to sustain it.[37]

021 *'...or the Golden Ass?'*

The *Golden Ass* or *Metamorphoses* was written in the 2nd century by the Latin satirist, Lucius Apuleius (c.125). Educated at Carthage and Athens, Apuleius devoted his life to literature and philosophy. The *Golden Ass* is an elaborate romance, interspersed with numerous episodes which follow the adventures of the youthful hero in the form of an ass who is restored to human form only with the aid of the goddess Isis. The most poetically exquisite episode is the famous tale of Cupid and Psyche. The *Golden Ass* is 'full of entertainment from beginning to end'[38] and 'wit, humour, satire, learning, and even poetic eloquence abound'[39]. In his works 'the dignified, the ludicrous, the voluptuous, the horrible, succeed each other with bewildering rapidity; fancy and feeling are everywhere apparent, but not less so affectation, meretricious ornament, and that effort to say everything finely which prevents anything being said well'[40].

021   'Red wise; Brown trusty; Pale envious – '

> *The red is wise, the brown trusty*
> *The pale envious, and the black lusty...*
> *To a red man rede thy rede*
> *With a brown man break thy bread*
> *At a pale man draw thy knife*
> *From a black man, keep thy wife.*

022   '...May dew or none...'

May dew is the morning dew of the first day of May, to which magical properties are attributed.

022   'Here I am, weeping soft tears of myrrh, to prove it.'

> *Who is this coming up from the wilderness*
> *Like palm-trees of smoke,*
> *Perfumed with myrrh and frankincense,*
> *From every powder of the merchant?*   -Song of Solomon 3:6

In Greek mythology, the goddess Myrrha fell in love with her father, Cinyras, and tricked him into sex. After discovering the deception, Cinyras sought to punish her. She fled and turned to the gods for help, and they turned her into a myrrh-tree. While in plant form, she gave birth to Adonis. According to legend, the aromatic exudings of the myrhh-tree are Myrrha's tears. The deep, rich, penetrating bitterness of myrrh was once a luxurious attractant available to the wealthiest only. The offering of frankincense and myrrh burned upon hot coals carried prayers to heaven.

022   '...we are about to create a climacteric of emotion.'

Climacteric is a critical period; a crisis in life[41/D] or climax.

022   '...spread with uncials...'

Uncial is a script written entirely in rounded, capital letters, used in ancient Greek and Latin manuscripts from the 1st century BC to the 8th century AD. The Book of Kells (c.58 AD) is lettered in a variety of uncial scripts which originated in Ireland.

022   '...and full, as the poet said, of fruit and seriosity.'

From *Orpheus and Eurydice* by Robert Henryson (c.1460-c.1500), considered 'a significant poetic voice of the Middle Ages and the most important writer of fifteenth-century Scotland'[42]. The first pure lyrist among the Scottish poets, his poems show him to be a didactic philosopher and Christian optimist. His major works include *The Morall Fabillis of Esope the Phyrgian*, *The Tale of Orpheus and Erudice his Queen*, and *The Testament of Cressied*.

The Book of Kells, c.58 AD

> And hid under the cloak of poetry,
> Yet Master Trivat, doctor Nicholas,
> Which in his time a
>   noble theologian was,
> Applies it to good morality,
> Right full of fruit and seriousness.[43]

(Tr.L.R.)

023   ...but old Harry of England...

'Old Harry', a slang term for the devil, refers to King Henry VIII of England (1491-1547). It was a sly dig which could be innocently explained away, as Harry is also a traditional English nickname for Henry. He is known for his six marriages and his role in the separation of the Church of England from the Roman Catholic Church.[44]

Henry VIII by Hans Holbein the Younger, c.1537.

Branxholm, c.1878

Branxholm was once the feudal castle of the Scotts of Buccleuch, located three miles southwest of Hawick in the valley of the Teviot. One half of the barony came into the possession of the Scotts during the reign of James I, the other half during the reign of James II. The castle originally consisted of a central quadrangle with a turret at each corner.

> *It was long the residence of the Scotts, the master-fort of a great surrounding district, the keep of Upper Teviotdale, the key of the pass between the Tweed basin and Cumberland, the centre of princely Border power, the scene of high baronial festivity, and the focus of fierce, hereditary, feudal warfare.*[45]

Because of its location so near the Border, Branxholm frequently suffered attack. The ancient castle was burned in 1532 by the Earl of Northumberland, was attacked again by the English in 1547, and in 1552, in an extensive raid the barmekyn was burnt and some 600 oxen and 600 sheep were carried away. In 1570, it was totally demolished and its lands laid waste after Sir Walter Scott (grandson of Wat Scott, son of William Scott of Kirkud) incurred the wrath of Elizabeth I for his attachment to the cause of Queen Mary. It was rebuilt from 1571-1574. In the late 1800s, only an old square tower of five stories remained, popularly called 'Nebsy', with additional buildings encompassing the manor.

Boghall Castle by John Clerk, c.1867

The Castle of Boghall, stood, as its name suggests, in the middle of a bog. When the castle was built is uncertain, but it was probably rebuilt during the reign of James IV or James V. One of the largest and most imposing edifices in the south of Scotland, its spaciousness and elegance led to the opinion it was constructed in the style of the large châteaux of France. Only the ruins of three of the castle towers now remain on the site.

023 *...a family uniquely loyal to the Queen, whose head Lord Fleming...*

The Flemings of Biggar settled in Lanarkshire in about 1150, and were long associated in service to the royalty of Scotland: Waldeve Fleming was taken prisoner with William the Lion (1174); Sir Robert Fleming was amongst the first to join Robert the Bruce in his attempt to recover Scotland's independence (1305); Sir Malcolm Fleming fought at the Battle of Halidonhill (1333); Sir David Fleming distinguished himself at the Battle of Otterbourn (1388); Sir Malcom Fleming was knighted by King Robert III (1421); and John Fleming, 2nd Lord Fleming, was appointed guardian of King James V in 1515.

Malcolm Fleming, 3rd Lord Fleming (c.1494-1547), was Lord Chamberlain of Scotland to King James V. He married Janet Stewart, natural daughter of King James IV of Scotland. In November 1542, he was taken prisoner by the English at the Battle of Solway Moss, but released after a ransom was paid. Initially a supporter of the marriage of Queen Mary to Prince Edward, he was accused of treason, but was later declared innocent by Parliament, and proclaimed to be 'a true baron and liege of the queen'[46]. He founded the collegiate church of St. Mary's in 1545, one of the last of Scotland's pre-Reformation churches.

023   *Lady Fleming, who was governess as well as aunt to the baby Queen...*

Janet ('Jenny') Stewart, Lady Fleming (1502-1562), a natural daughter of James IV of Scotland, served as governess to her niece, Queen Mary. Lady Jenny married Malcolm Fleming, 3rd Lord Fleming. They had eight children: Johanna, Janet, John (later, 4th Lord Fleming), Bridget, James (later, 5th Lord Fleming), Agnes, Margaret, and Mary (one of the little Queen's 'Four Marys').

026   *Lucent and delicate, Drama entered, mincing like a cat.*

Drama, (literally 'action' from the Greek) is a performance before spectators of a story presented by action, depicting a sequence of events, grave or humorous, leading to a catastrophe or crowning issue. The two masks associated with drama represent the division between comedy and tragedy.

2nd-century Roman Theatre Masks

027   *'I've decided on pantomime.'*

Pantomime was a musical-comedy theatrical production, a popular form of entertainment in ancient Greece and later, Rome. In Lymond's time, it would have included improvisation and audience participation.

027   *'I was all ready for buskins, and it's nothing but socks.'*

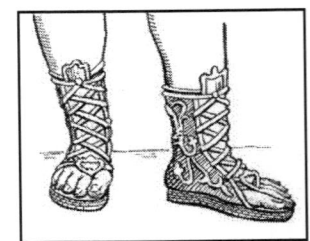

A buskin is a knee- or calf-length boot made of leather or cloth which laces closed but is open across the toes, traditionally worn by Athenian tragic actors. Figuratively, the buskin refers to tragedy, contrasted with the sock, the low shoe worn by comedians. The masks of comedy and tragedy are often referred to as 'Socks and Buskin'.

027   *'Oimè el cor, Oimè la testa...'*

Alas, my heart, Alas, my head...

From a song by Marchetto Cara (c.1465-1525), an Italian Renaissance composer recognized as one of the most important composers of the vocal form called *frottola*. Cara was a musician at the court of Francesco II Gonzaga and Isabelle d'Este, and travelled to sing and play the lute for Italian royalty, including the Medici family and Elsabetta of Urbino.

027 '...I have the refinement of a cow-cabbage.'

The common cow-cabbage (*Brassica oleracea palmifolia*), also known as Jersey Kale, can grow to 10-12' in height. 'Five of these stupendous cabbages have been found to provide an ample allowance of food for one hundred sheep or ten cows, and the nutrition thence supplied by this delicious vegetable will speedily produce the most surprising improvement in the growth and utility of every description of cattle.'[47] The stalks, when dried, make excellent walking sticks.

Cow Cabbage

027 '... choose the trussell or the pile.'

In the 16th century, the die for the top of a coin was called the *taselli*, the lower die the *pila*. In English, 'trussell' and 'pile'.

027 'De los álamos vengo, madre.'

From a song by Miguel de Fuenllana (c.1500-1579), a musician at the court of Phillip II of Spain:

> *I come from the poplar trees, mother,*
> *Where I saw how they swayed in the breeze.*
> *From the poplar trees of Sevilla,*
> *Where I saw my beautiful girl.*
> *I come from the poplar trees, mother,*
> *Where I saw how they swayed in the breeze.*[48]   (Tr.V.S.)

'I come from the poplar trees,' is the literal translation of '*de los álamos vengo*', but it is more commonly used to indicate, '*I am coming from a far-out place*'. Here, Lymond is emphasising his return from exile.[49]

028 *Strophe and counterstrophe reached their epode.*

A strophe forms the first part of the ode in Ancient Greek tragedy, followed by the antistrophe and epode.

028   *...the big man, cursing, scraped at blancmange with both hands...*

Blancmange (from Middle English, *blankmanger*, a dish made with almond milk, from Old French, *blanc-manger*, literally, 'white food') is a sweetened milk pudding thickened with gelatin or cornstarch, and usually molded. In the Middle Ages, blancmange was made with capon or chicken, almond milk, rice, and sugar. The *blanc-manger* of Chaucer's *Canterbury Tales* (*General Prologue*, line 387) was apparently a mixture of minced capon, flour, sugar, and cream.

028   *Bruslez, noyes, pendez, ompalles, descouppez, fircassez, crucifez, buillez, carbonnadez ces mechantes femmes.*

> *Burn, drown, hang, stuff, cut up, fricasee,*
> *crucify, boil, incinerate these wicked women.*

From *The Life of Gargantua and Pantagruel* by François Rabelais (c.1494-1533), wherein he lists the potential tortures and forms of execution for heretics, used here as Lymond's threat against 'these wicked women'. Amid its chaos of eccentricities, *Gargantua and Pantagruel* is a ruthless attack on monks, princes, kings, and ecclesiastic and civil authorities.

028   *'Leave your female Telemachus alone for a moment...'*

Telemachus is a figure in Greek mythology and a central character in Homer's *Odyssey*. The first four books in particular focus on the journey of Telemachus, the son of Odysseus and Penelope. After unsuccessfully attempting to eject Penelope's troublesome suitors from the house, he set out in search of news of his father, who has been away at war. He returned home to find Odysseus in the guise of a beggar and aided him in slaying the suitors.

028   *'Qu'es casado, el Rey Ricardo.'*

> *'He is married, the King Richard.'*

029   *'Their eyes lit like corpse candles.'*

Corpse candles were used at wakes, or to hold vigil over a corpse on the night before its interment. The term also describes a luminous appearance resembling the flame of a candle, sometimes seen in churchyards and other places, superstitiously regarded as portending death.

029   *'The Olla Podrida, my sweethearts, will now be set on fire.'*

Olla Podrida (Spanish, 'putrid mess') is a stew made from pork and beans and a wide variety of other meats and vegetables. The dish is kept so long its odor and flavour become highly offensive. The name is used metaphorically, like *pot pourri*, to denote a medley.

029   '*God hath a thousand handēs to chastise and I have two –*'

> *God hath a thousand hands to chastise,*
> *A thousand darts of punishment,*
> *A thousand bows made in diverse ways,*
> *A thousand cross-bows bent in his fortress,*
> *Ordained each one for castigation,*
> *But where he finds meekness and repentance,*
> *Mercy is mistress of his ordinance.*[50]   (Tr.L.R.)

From the poem *God's Providence* in *The Fall of Princes* by John Lydgate of Bury (c.1370-c.1451), an English monk and poet. *The Fall of Princes* is an English translation of *De Casibus Virorum Illustrium* (*On the Fates of Famous Men*) by Giovanni Boccaccio, a series of moral stories on the fortunes of famous men, and their downfall.

Lydgate studied at Oxford and travelled to France and Italy, before returning to England and becoming associated with the Benedictine abbey of Bury St. Edmunds. While a young man he met Chaucer, and became very close with Chaucer's son, Thomas. In several poems, he reverently gives tribute to his master, Chaucer. He was a voluminous writer, penning some 250+ poems, in addition to several lengthy ones on a wide variety of themes. For several hundred years, Lydgate's reputation equaled or even surpassed that of Chaucer. During the 18th and 19th centuries, his reputation suffered, and some critics called his work 'stupid and disgusting,' and 'cart-loads of rubbish'[51]. A more impartial criticism recognizes Lydgate was 'characteristically medieval – medieval in his prolixity, medieval also in his pessimism, his Mariolatry and his horror of death. Lydgate himself, with offensive lightheartedness, admits his poor craftsmanship.'[52]

THE PLAY FOR
JONATHAN CROUCH

Holyrood Palace by H. D. Harding

I: Taking en Passant

Caxton: Tract 3, Chapter 7

*The guards and keepers for the cities having been signified by
the Pawn, they ought to inquire of all things and ought to report
to the governors of the city such things as pertain to it, and if it
be time of war, they ought not to open the gates by night to any man.*[1]

1. The English Opening

Pawns have the privilege of moving one or two squares on their first move. If a
pawn moves two squares from its starting point, and in so doing, passes an enemy
pawn which could have taken it if it moved only one square, the enemy pawn may,
on its next move only, capture it *en passant*, as though it had moved only one
square. If no other move is possible, the pawn must be captured *en passant* ('in
passing'). The *en passant* rule was added in the 15th century. It prevents a pawn
from using the initial two-square advance (also introduced in the 15th century) to
pass an enemy pawn without risk of being captured.

**035 *On Saturday, September 10th, the English Protector Somerset and his
army met the combined Scottish forces on the field of Pinkie, outside of
Edinburgh, and smashed them to pieces in a defeat as dire as any the Scots had
suffered since Flodden.***

The Battle of Pinkie Cleugh, known as Black Saturday, was fought between
14,000 English under Protector Somerset, and approximately 30,000 Scots under
Governor Arran. Although an utter defeat for the Scots, the English failed to
accomplish their main goal of carrying off the young Scottish queen.

Despite having a superior position on the left bank of the River Esk and
superior numbers, the Scots laboured under the disadvantage of no commander to
guide and control its various sections. Somerset, upon seeing the Scots position,
recognized he could not attack with advantage, so gave orders to withdraw. This

movement made the Scots believe the English were retreating to their ships lying in the bay. Against the advice of experienced leaders, the Scots crossed the Esk, giving the English the advantage of the rising ground. The Scots repelled their opponents in some skirmishing, but when executing a manœuvre to change position, the Highlanders, having left ranks to plunder, thought the army was retreating, and immediately followed suit. Panic infused the entire Scottish army; the English cavalry rallied and pursued their foes, cutting them down without mercy.

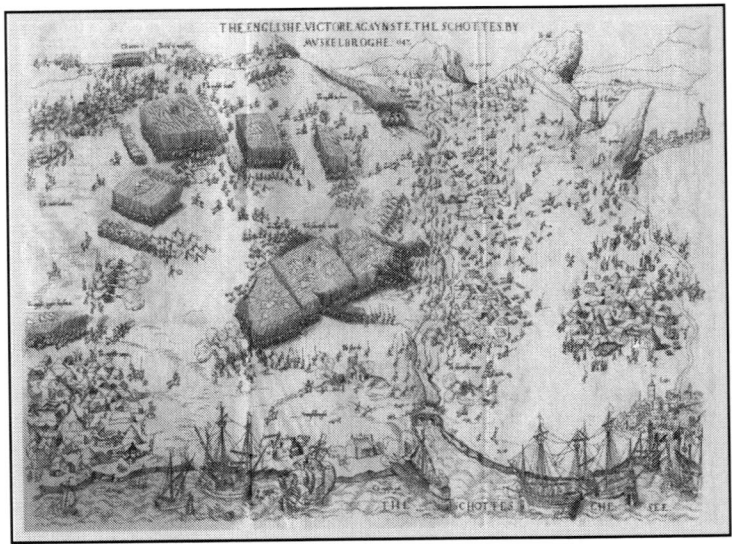

Battle of Pinkie Cleugh 1547, 16ᵗʰ-century lithographic facsimile.

The [Scots] body which had so lately opposed an impenetrable front to the enemy, beginning first to undulate to and fro, like a steely sea agitated by the wind, after a few moments was seen breaking into a thousand fragments, and dispersed in all directions. Everything was now lost, the ground over which the flight lay was as thickly strewed with pikes as a floor with rushes; helmets, bucklers, swords, daggers, and steel caps, lay scattered on every side, cast away by their owners, as impeding their speed, and the chase, beginning at one o'clock, continued until six in the evening with extraordinary slaughter. The English demi-lances and men-at-arms, irritated by their late defeat, hastened after the fugitives with a speed heightened by revenge, and passing across the field of their late action, were doubly exasperated by seeing the bodies of their brave companions stripped by the Highlanders lying all naked and mangled before their eyes. Crying to one another...they spurred at the top of their speed after the fugitives, cutting them down on all sides, and admitting none to quarter but those from whom they hoped for a heavy ransom.[2]

And thus with blood and slaughter...the chase continued for five miles westward from the place of their standing, which was in the fallow-fields of Inveresk, until Edinburgh Park and well nigh to the gates of the town itself, and unto Leith; and in the breadth near four miles, from the shore of the Frith up to Dalkeith southward; in all which space the dead bodies lay as thick as cattle grazing in a full replenished pasture. The river Esk was red with blood, so that in the same chase were counted, as well by some of our men who diligently observed it, as by several of the prisoners, who greatly lamented the result, upwards of fourteen thousand slain.[3]

035   *...in the near-Border town of Annan on its triumphant way north.*

Annan, c.1560, showing the Motte and Tower

Annan (Gaelic, 'quiet river') is a seaport in Dumfriesshire on the east bank of the River Annan, near its entrance into the Solway Firth.

The country round is flat upon the whole, but near the town are two or three heights, one of which, dignified as 'Annan Hill', commands a magnificent view of Annandale, the Solway, and the Cumberland

Mountains. Northward, are seen the little red town, lying amid green trees, the gleaming river, and numberless small dark woods and bare monotonous hills; southward, the sandy shore of the Firth, the Solway Viaduct, the sunlit sea, the grey hills of Kirkcudbrightshire, the long English coast, the picturesque windmill of Bowness, and the great Lake mountains, with Skiddaw, in what Wordsworth calls his 'natural sovereignty' towering over the rest.[4]

Its location close to the Border exposed Annan and its inhabitants to repeated assaults. The motte-and-bailey castle was built in the 12th century by the de Brus family, Lords of Annandale. Burned by the English in 1298, it was restored by Robert Bruce two years later and made his occasional residence. Edward Balliol, in December 1332, summoned the nobles to the castle to pay him homage, and here 'Archibald Douglas, at the head of 1000 horsemen, surprised him by night, slew Henry, his brother, with many lesser adherents, and drove him to flee on a bare-backed steed, half-naked, to Carlisle'[5].

In 1547, after valiant resistance, Annan was captured by the Earl of Lennox and Lord Wharton, at the head of 5000 men. The town was sacked and burned, its church and steeple blown up, and the town razed to the ground. The whole of Annandale submitted to Lennox, who compelled the inhabitants to give pledges of fidelity to the English.[6] The town suffered severely over the next two years from English raids.

036   '...a front seat at the Widdy-Hill the day after the Assizes.'

An Assize is a trial session, civil or criminal, held periodically in specific locations, usually by a judge of a superior court. A widdy is a rope for hanging, or the gallows, derived from the early use of twisted willow *withes*, hence *withy, or widdy.*

037   *He dismounted, emitting a feu de joie of explicit orders...*

A *feu de joie* (French, 'fire of joy') is a musketry salute fired in rapid succession along a line of troops in token of joy, creating a 'rat-tat-tat' effect; thus, a bonfire.

038   'I have peper and piones, and a pound of garlik; a ferthing-worth of fenel-seed for fasting dayes, but dullness have I none...'

From *The Vision of William Concerning Piers the Plowman* by William Langland (c.1332-c.1400), a 14th-century allegorical poem considered one of the great works of English literature. The poem 'narrates the dreams of Piers Ploughman, who, weary with the world, falls asleep beside a stream in a vale among the Malvern hills. While satirizing, in vigorous allegorical descriptions, the corruptions in church and state, and the vices incident to the various professions of life, and painting the obstacles which resist the amelioration of mankind, it presents a simple ploughman as the embodiment of virtue and truth, the representative of the

Saviour.'[7] Not much is known about the author, William Langland. It is thought he was born in Shropshire, and lived many years in London. From evidence from the text itself, prolonged poverty seems to have made him embittered and churlish.

038   *'But yours, like Midas whispering in the hole, are closer to the ground...'*

The legendary king of Phyrgia, Midas was appointed to judge a musical contest between Apollo and Pan. Midas judged in favour of Pan; in retaliation Apollo gave the king a pair of ass's ears. Midas hid them under his cap, but his barber discovered them. Fearful to mention them, but not able to fully resist, the barber dug a hole and whispered into it, 'Midas has ass's ears'. He then covered the hole again. In another version of the legend, Midas kept spies to tell him everything which transpired in the kingdom, giving rise to the proverb, 'Kings have long arms', which evolved to 'Midas has long ears'.

Midas by Andrea Vaccaro, c.1670

038   *'A silken tongue, a heart of cruelty.'*

From *The Taill of the Paddock and the Mous* in *The Morall Fabillis of Esope the Phyrgian* by Robert Henryson (1460-1500). The old themes of the thirteen fables are 'retold with such vivacity, such fresh lights on human character, and with so much local "atmosphere" that they deserve the credit of original productions. They are certainly unrivalled in English fabulistic literature.'[8]

A False intent under a fair pretense,
Has caused many innocent for to die:
Great folly is to give over soon to credence,
To all that speaks fairly unto thee.
A silken tongue, a heart of cruelty,
Smites more than any shot of arrow,
Brother if thou be wise I beg thee flee,
Than match thee with a crooked mate.[9]

(Tr. L.R.)

038   Terror,' said Lymond, 'is our daily bread in the Wuthenheer. We eat it, live by it and disseminate it; and not only between Christmas and Epiphany.'

Wuthenheer, or Wilde Jagd, in German folklore is a fancied noise in the air at night, heard between Christmas and Epiphany. The sound is compared to that of a spirit host rushing along, accompanied by the shouting of huntsmen and the baying of dogs.

039   '...awful   and   stern,   strong   and corpulent– '

Woden's Wild Jagd, c.1882

Another Court there saw I subsequent.
Cupid the King, with bow in hand ybent,
And dreadful arrows grounden sharp
and square.
There, saw I Mars, the God omnipotent,
Awful and stern, strong and corpulent.

From *The Goldyn Targe* by William Dunbar (c.1460-c.1520), considered the greatest of the old Scottish poets. Dunbar graduated from St. Andrews University with a Master of Arts in 1479. He became a Franciscan friar, travelled to England and France, returned to Scotland about 1500, and was retained at the court of James IV, whom 'he delighted with his poetical compositions and with the charms of his conversation'[10]. *The Golden Targe* is a dream allegory of the poet's futile endeavor 'to ward off the arrows of Dame Beautee by Reason's "scheld of gold."' When wounded and made prisoner, he discovers the true beauty of the lady: when she leaves him, he is handed over to Heaviness. The noise of the ship's guns, as the company sails off, wakes the poet to the real pleasures of a May morning.'[11]

039 *'So did Heliogabalus at an early age,' said Lymond. 'And Attila the Hun and Torquemada and Nero and the man who invented the boot.'*

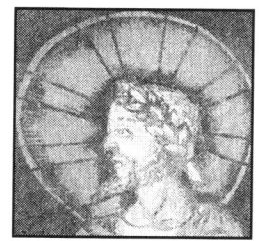

The Roman Emperor Heliogabalus (ruled 218-222 AD) was known for his eccentricity, decadence, and zealotry, abandoning himself 'to the grossest pleasures and ungoverned fury'[12]. He was assassinated at the age of 18.

Attila the Hun (died 453 AD) was one of the most feared enemies of the Western and Eastern Roman Empires.

Tomás de Torquemada (1420-1498) was the first Grand Inquisitor in Spain's movement to restore Christianity in the late 15th century. His name has become synonymous with the horror, religious bigotry, and cruel fanaticism of the Spanish Inquisition.

The Roman Emperor Nero (ruled 37-68 AD) is associated with tyranny and extravagance. He is known for executing, among others, his mother and stepbrother.

The boot was a torture device designed to crush the foot and leg. The first Scottish boot was a leather boot bound with cords, which was soaked in water and then slowly heated, contracting the leather and squeezing the foot until the bones dislocated. More progressive forms used wood and also crushed the bones of the leg.

TORTURE OF THE BOOTS.

039   '...then quicquid libet, licet...'

From *The Anatomy of Melancholy* by Robert Burton:

> *Roman Emperor Antoninus Carcalla (ruled 211-217 AD) observed his mother-in-law with her breasts amorously laid open. He was so much moved, he said, 'Ah, si liceret.' ('O, that I might.') To which she, by chance over-hearing, replied as impudently, 'Quicquid libet licet.' ('Thou maist do what thou wilt.') Upon that temptation, he married her.*

039   'Oh, little Peg-a-Ramsey, we are going to do well together.

Peg-a-Ramsey is a term of contempt, from a character in a folk ballad.

039   'Gif thou should sing well ever in thy life...'

> *If thou should sing well ever in thy life,*
> *Here is, in faith, the time and here is the space:*
> *Would thou then?*
> > *Some bird may come and strive*
> > *In song with thee, the master to purchase.*
> *Should thou then cease, it would alas, be a great shame*
> *And here to win victory happily ever after*
> *Here is the time to sing, or else never.[13]*   (Tr. L.R.)

From *The Kingis Quair* by King James I of Scotland (1394-1437). James was the second son of King Robert III. After the suspicious death of James's older brother, possibly at the hands of his uncle, Robert, Duke of Albany, King Robert sent James to France for safety. His ship was seized by the English and James remained a prisoner in England for the next eighteen years. *The Kingis Quair*, or *The King's Book*, was written during his captivity and celebrates his courtship with Lady Jane Beaufort, the daughter of the Earl of Somerset. He sees her out his window, *'the fairest and the freshest flower that e'er he saw'.*

James was released in 1423, and shortly thereafter married Lady Jane with pomp and circumstance. The royal pair arrived in Scotland in the spring of 1424, and James immediately set out to restore order and legitimacy to the crown by enacting a series of laws, considered

James I, watching Lady Jane Beaufort from his Prison Window

enlightened for the day, addressing agriculture, commerce, foreign and domestic manufacturing, regulation of weights and measures, and the administration of justice. These reforms, along with the imposition of harsh measures to curb the power of the nobles, created strong discontent with his reign. A group of conspirators assassinated the king at the Dominican monastery at Perth on 20 February 1437. His murderers were tortured and executed. By his wife, the heroine of the *The Kingis Quair*, he had two sons and six daughters. His second son, James, succeeded him. His daughter, Margaret, became the queen of Louis XI of France.

039 *'Frae vulgar prose to flowand Latin.'*

From *The Proheme of the History* by John Bellenden (fl.1533-c.1587), a forward to his translation of *The Chronicle of Scotland* by Hector Boece. Born towards the end of the 15th century, Bellenden was educated at St. Andrews and Paris, graduating with a degree from the Sorbonne. He was a favourite of James V, who commissioned him to translate Boece's *Historia gentis Scotorum* and five chapters of the Roman historian Livy, to which he prefixed his own poetical prologues. Considered a remarkable specimen of Scottish prose, the *History of Scotland* was published in 1536. Bellenden was one of the greatest scholars of his time and 'unquestionably a man of great arts and one of the finest poets his country had to boast'[14].

Manuscript Frontispiece, c.1536

039 *Volavit volucer sine plumis...*

There came a bird featherless,
Sat on a tree leafless;
Then came the maid mouthless,
And ate the bird featherless,
High on the tree leafless.

The answer to the riddle is snow.

040 *'What about Pharaoh's chickens appealed to you?'*

A Pharaoh's chicken is a small vulture, *Neophron pernopterus*. Its association with Egyptian royalty led to its name.

Neophron pernopterus

61

041   *'All, all in vain, this flors de biauté?'*

flors de biauté: flowers of beauty

From the 13th century French romance poem, *Guillaume de Palemre*:

> *Dist Guillaumes: 'Suer, douce amie,*
> *Flore de biauté, rose espanie...*

> *Spoke Guillames: 'Sweet, darling friend,*
> *Flower of beauty, rose in full bloom,*
> *To what mischief, to what suffering*
> *Departs us now on this day!'*[15]   (Tr. E.R.)

041   *'Careful, careful! my slave of sin.'*

From *Anatomy of Melancholy* by Robert Burton:

> *The main matter which terrifies and torments most that are troubled*
> *in mind, is the enormity of their offences, the intolerable burden of*
> *their sins, God's heavy wrath and displeasure so deeply*
> *apprehended, that they account themselves reprobates, quite*
> *forsaken by God, already damned, past all hope of grace, incapable*
> *of mercy,* diaboli mancipia, *slaves of sin, and their offences so great*
> *they cannot be forgiven. But these men must know there is no sin so*
> *heinous which is not pardonable in itself, no crime so great but by*
> *God's mercy it may be forgiven.*

041   *'These are Sordidi Dei.'*

Sordidi Dei: Dirty Gods

From *Anatomy of Melancholy:*

> *And what so base as to reveal their*
> *counsels and give oracles* e viscerum
> sterquiliniis, *out of the bowels and*
> *excremental parts of beasts?* Soridios
> deos *[Dirty Gods],Varro truly calls*
> them...

Nuremberg Chronicle, MS, c.1493

Marcus Terentius Varro (116-27 BC) was an ancient Roman scholar. An upright,
honourable man, a 'monument to old-fashioned Roman virtues'[16], Varro wrote
about 620 books on nearly all branches of knowledge and literature. 'Here we
find in singular medley grotesque personifications of ideas, ridicule of the
philosophers, mythology, erudition, proverbs, bitter satire at the social corruptions

of the day, and praise of the homely virtues of the good old times, the whole spirited and rich in humour, if seldom artistic in form.'[17]

041 *'...when it comes to one's own amour propre.'*

Amour propre (From the French, *amour*, love, + *propre*, own) is self-esteem or self-respect, a belief and confidence in one's own ability and value. It is sometimes used in an unfavourable sense to indicate pride, vanity, or egotism.

041 *When a hatter - Will go smatter - In philosophy*
Or a pedlar - Was a medlar - In theology...

From *A Merry Jest – How a Serjeant Would Learn to Play the Friar* (c.1516) by Sir Thomas More (1478-1535), an English lawyer and opponent of the Protestant Reformation. A noted Renaissance humanist, he described his ideal political system in *Utopia*, and was an important councillor and finally Chancellor to Henry VIII. More was executed for treason after refusing to take the Oath of Supremacy transferring Papal authority in England to the Crown, and for not upholding Henry's annulment from Catherine of Aragon.

Sir Thomas More by Hans Holbein

042 *'The warning cock and the Devil's bath,' said Lymond, amused.*

From *Anatomy of Melancholy* by Robert Burton:

> *Galgerandus of Mantua, a famous physician, so cured a demoniacal woman in his time, that spake all languages, by purging black choler, and thereupon belike this humour of melancholy is called* balneum diaboli, *the devil's bath; the devil, spying his opportunity of such humours drives them many times to despair, fury, rage, &c, mingling himself amongst those humours.*

042 *'...Don't be a Churl, Marigold. Full of sloth in his wars, full of boasts in his manhood, full of cowardice to his enemy...'*

A churl is a rude, boorish person; a mediæval English peasant. The remainder of the passage is a quote from *Caxton's The Game and Playe of the Chesse.*

043 *'With Johnnie, it's Paracelsus, Mat here follows Lydgate; and your father and Ascham fit very well together.'*

Paracelsus was a name coined for himself by the Swiss alchemist, Theophrastus Bombastus von Hohenheim (c.1490-1541), arrogantly implying he was greater than Celsus. Paracelsus travelled on foot throughout Europe, and visited Constantinople to learn the secret of the elixir of Trismegistus. He proclaimed to know the art of prolonging life, and to 'hold more learning in the hairs of his beard than was possessed by all the universities and medical writers united'[18].

Paracelsus by Jan van Scorel, c.1517

His own oddity, vanity, aggressiveness, and intemperate habits caused enmity and dispute amongst the learned class, and he was forced to wander for more than a dozen years, seldom staying in one place for more than a few months. According to Paracelsus, man was an image of the Trinity: the intellect representing God, with a connection between the intellect, air and sulphur; the body representing the world, with a connection between the body, earth, and salt; and the body's fluid representing the stars, with a connection between the soul, water, and mercury.

John Lydgate of Bury (1370-1451) was an English monk and poet. His poems are considered by some to be mediocre, dull, and tediously prolonged.

John Lydgate of Bury

Roger Ascham (1515-1568) was an English scholar and writer. He earned several degrees from St. John's College, Oxford, and remained at Cambridge, where he was appointed Greek reader at the college in 1538. He was known for his penmanship and his devotion to the sport of archery. In 1545 he published *Toxophilus*, a treatise on archery, which ranks amongst the English classics due to its pure English style.

043 *'If he thunder, they quake; if he chide they fear; if he complain –'*

Roger Ascham

From *Toxophilus* by Roger Ascham:

> *Beside all these commodities, truly two degrees of men, which have the highest offices under the King in all this realm, shall greatly lack*

the use of singing, preachers and lawyers, because they shall not, without this, be able to rule their breasts for every purpose. For where is no distinction in telling glad things and fearful things, gentleness and cruelness, softness and vehemence, and such-like matters, there can be no great persuasion. For the hearers, as Tully saith, be much affectioned as he is that speaketh. At his words be they drawn; if he stand still in one fashion, their minds stand still with him; if he truly thunder, they quake; if he chide, they fear; if he complain, they sorry with him; and finally, where a matter is spoken with an apt voice for every affection, the hearers, for the most part, are moved as the speaker would. But when a man is always in one tune, like a humble bee, or else now in the top of the church, now down, that no man knoweth where to have him; or piping like a reed, or roaring like a bull, as some lawyers do, which think they do best when they cry loudest, these shall never greatly move, as I have known many well-learned have done, because their voice was not stayed afore with learning to sing. For all voices, great and small, base and shrill, weak or soft, may be holpen and brought to a good point by learning to sing.

044   *'Then we move to the Peel Tower.'*

Peel Towers were small, fortified tower houses, built along the Borders as watch towers in which beacon fires could be lit, repeated from one to the other with 'marvellous rapidity'[19] to warn of approaching danger.   The regular system of beacons, established by an act of Parliament, allowed the force of an invading army to be known almost as it crossed the Border, even at Edinburgh.

Most of these peels were surrounded by an outer wall or barmeykin, which by an Act of Parliament in 1535, was directed to be one ell thick, and six ells in height [one Scottish ell equaled approximately 18"], and enclosing a space of at least 60 feet, into which cattle could be driven. They were sometimes further surrounded by a moat. The lower room was usually vaulted, those above being reached by a turnpike stair, each story being capable of defence. They also had projecting battlements or machicoles, from which the defenders could annoy their assailants with stones, arrows, shot, etc. The usual mode of attack was by setting fire to damp straw in the basement; but it was seldom that the occupants attempted to withstand a siege, preferring to retire to some fastness with their cattle, and either again assemble to resist an attack, or leave the stronghold to its fate...Owing to the want of security and constant risk of destruction, or of having to leave them to their fate, in the event of an attack by a superior force, the Border peels or strongholds on the Scottish side were devoid of all comfort or luxury.[20]

Sandyknowe Tower by William Smith, Jr., c.1903

2. Pins and Counterpins

044 *O wow! quo' he, were I as free / As first when I saw this countrie...*

From *The Gaberlunzie Man* by James V, King of Scotland (1512-1542), one of several ballads written of his amorous exploits while in disguise wandering his kingdom as the *Gudeman of Ballengeich.*

045 *'You shall help me find him and then, Aenobarbus...'*

Aenobarbus ('red beard') was the name of a powerful family of ancient Rome. According to legend, to confirm the truth of the announced victory of the Romans at the battle of Lake Regillus, one of the Aenobarbus ancestors stroked his black hair and beard, which immediately became red, confirming the news.

045 *'...and the Earl of Lennox has a personal price...'*

Matthew Stewart, 4ᵗʰ Earl of Lennox
1516 - 1571

*Detail, family tree of King James I and VI
of Scotland and England, c.1603*

Matthew Stewart, 4ᵗʰ Earl of Lennox (1516-1571), spent most of his early life in service to the king of France in the wars in Italy, and was a naturalized French subject. After the death of James V, he was invited to return to Scotland by Cardinal Beaton and the French faction to oppose Regent Arran. Like Arran, Lennox was descended from the sister of James III and next in line to the Scottish throne after the infant queen Mary and the family of Arran. On the promise of assistance from the king of France, and with the prospect of marriage to the Queen Dowager, Lennox arrived in Scotland in March 1543, with two ships, a small company, and 'much French gold'[21]. He immediately took measures to oust Arran.

Lennox's first act was to march toward Linlithgow to rescue Queen Mary. Arran surrendered the queen and her mother, and Lennox escorted them to Stirling Castle. Later that year, Beaton reconciled with Angus; an enraged Lennox deserted Beaton's party and became a zealous supporter of the proposed match between Queen Mary and Prince Edward, and signed a treaty in 1544 with Henry VIII. Lennox promised to deliver the young queen and the principal Scottish fortresses to Henry, while Henry promised to deliver the government of Scotland and the hand of his niece, Margaret Douglas. Lennox sailed for England and was welcomed with distinction at the English court. (When news of Lennox's desertion reached Francis I of France, he immediately deprived Lennox's brother, Lord d'Aubigny, of his offices and threw him in prison.)

In August 1544, Lennox attacked and plundered the island of Arran, occupied Bute, and took Rothesay Castle. Henry VIII appointed him chief of command of a western expedition into Scotland in 1545, and gave him the grant of the manor of Temple Newsam in Yorkshire. The Scottish parliament declared him and his brother guilty of treason and their lands were forfeited. Lennox remained in exile in England until 1564.

045 *He quoted dryly. 'This officer but doubt is callit Deid.'*

From the anonymous Scots poem, *The Three Priests of Peblis*, thought to be written sometime in the late 15th century or early 16th century. 'The three priests of Peebles, having met on St. Bride's day for the purpose of regaling themselves, agree, that each in his turn shall endeavor to entertain the rest by relating some story. They acquit themselves with sufficient propriety. The tales are of a moral tendency, but, at the same time, are free from the dulness which so frequently infests the perceptive composition of earlier poets.'[22]

045 *'Si mundus vult decipi, decipiatur.'*

> *'Since the world wishes to be gulled, let it be gulled.'*

From *Anatomy of Melancholy* by Robert Burton:

> *...be they of no religion at all, they will make others most devout and superstitious, by promises and threats, compel, enforce from, and lead them by the nose like so many bears in a line; when as their end is not to propagate the church, advance God's kingdom, seek His glory or common good, but to enrich themselves, to enlarge their territories, to domineer and compel them to stand in awe, to live in subjection to the See of Rome. For what otherwise care they?* Si mundus vult decipi, decipiatur, *"Since the world wishes to be gulled, let it be gulled,"* 'tis fit it should be so.*

047 *'I don't suppose Lord Wharton's son Harry is anywhere about? I once knew his sister, and I'd like to meet him.'*

Henry Wharton was the second son of Thomas Wharton, 1st Lord Wharton. In 1547, Henry, 'a dashing leader of horse'[23] along with John Musgrave, overthrew the Scots at Wamphrey, near Lockwood. He was knighted in 1548 for his role in an English expedition to Durisdeer, a small village in the southwest of Scotland which houses Drumlanrig Castle, home to the Douglases. He almost lost his life in the battle, owing to the treachery of the Maxwells. In retaliation, Wharton hanged Maxwell's pledges held at Carlisle, thus initiating a lasting feud between the Whartons and the Maxwells. Lord Wharton's two daughters were Joanna and Agnes; his oldest son, Thomas, was knighted in 1545.

048 *'If wishes were like buttercakes...beggars might bite.'*

English proverb.

049 *At the desk sat Lord Wharton...*

Thomas Wharton, 1st Baron Wharton
1495-1568

Thomas Wharton, 1st Baron Wharton (1495-1568), while young, served on several raiding expeditions into Scotland, for which he was knighted by Henry VIII in 1527. In the fall of 1542, when both the English and Scots were preparing for war, Wharton proposed a scheme for raiding Scotland and seizing King James V. The plan was not approved, so Wharton burnt Dumfries and conducted a day-foray doing as much damage as possible. On the evening of 23rd November, Wharton was being kept apprised of an extensive Scots invasion of the west marches. With a troop of only a few hundred, Wharton watched the Scots – 13,000 strong[24] – cross the River Esk. Towards evening Wharton attacked their left. The Scots, entangled in the Solway Moss, lost enormous numbers – slain, drowned, or taken prisoner – while the English loss was 'trifling'[25]. Wharton was given a barony for his role in the victory.

Border forays and intrigues attempting to force the marriage of Queen Mary to Prince Edward afforded Wharton 'active employment for the rest of Henry VIII's reign'[26], and continued under Protector Somerset. In September 1547, while Somerset invaded Scotland from Berwick, Wharton and the Earl of Lennox entered Scotland on the west, and 'won the church of Annan, took sixty-two prisoners, fired most part of the spoil, and overthrew the fort with powder; took Milk Castle, which they fortified strongly, and planted a garrison therein, after much spoil and waste of the country returned safely to England'[27].

According to family history, Wharton was extremely unpopular, and was so hated by the common people he was forced to leave his Westmoreland estates for his home of Healaugh in Yorkshire[28], and was 'vilified ... for having demolished the town of Wharton because it marred his view of the valley'[29].

Archibald Douglas, 6ᵗʰ Earl of Angus
1489 - 1557

Archibald Douglas, 6ᵗʰ Earl of Angus (1489-1557), was a Scottish nobleman. In 1514, he married Margaret Tudor, widow of James IV and elder sister of Henry VIII of England. The marriage was opposed by the Scottish nobility and those supporting the French alliance. They had one daughter, Margaret Douglas.

Angus began an affair with Lady Jane of Traquair, to whom he had been formerly affianced, and openly lived with her and their illegitimate child in his wife's property. Margaret avenged this outrage by joining with the Duke of Albany against him. Douglas made a close alliance with Henry VIII, and with his support, was able to regain power in Scotland and took custody of the fourteen-year old King James V. After Margaret obtained her divorce in 1528, James escaped the custody of Angus and sought refuge with his mother at Stirling. James denounced Angus and confiscated his lands; Angus escaped to England. The lands of Angus's brother, Sir George Douglas of Pittenrich, Master of Angus, were also declared forfeit and he fled into exile. Angus's sister, Janet, Lady Glamis, was tried and found guilty of conspiring against the king's life. She was burnt on Castle Hill, Edinburgh, in 1537.

After the death of James V in 1542, Angus negotiated a peace treaty and the marriage of Queen Mary to Prince Edward. His lands were restored and he regained some of his power. He switched sides again, joining forces with Regent Arran in support of the marriage of Queen Mary to the Dauphin of France. He resigned his earldom in August 1547, and commanded the foremost division of the advancing military at Pinkie Cleugh. He died several months later.

051 *'Sweet rose of virtue and of gentleness.'*

From *Sweet Rose of Virtue* by William Dunbar (c.1459-c.1525):

> Sweet rose of virtue and of gentleness,
> Delightful lily of youthful vigour,
> Richest in bounty and in beauty clear,
> And every virtue that is held most dear –
> Except, only, that you are merciless.
>
> Into your garden, this day, I did pursue:
> There I saw flowers that fresh were of hue;
> Both white and red most pleasant were to see,
> And wholesome herbs upon stalks green –
> Yet leaf nor flower find could I none of rue.
>
> I fear that March with his cold blasts is keen,
> Has slain this gentle herb that I of complain,
> Whose impetuous death does to my heart such pain,
> That I would make to plant his root again,
> So comforting his leaves unto me have been.[30]

(Tr. L.R).

051 *'I hope to be appreciated for my beaux yeux alone...'*

beaux yeux: beautiful eyes

051 *'Manhood but prudence is a fury blind.'*

From *A Political Homily* by John Bellenden (c.1492-c.1557), the Scottish historian and scholar.

> Manhood without prudence is a fury blind,
>   And brings a man to shame and indigence;
> Prudence without manhood comes often behind,
>   But has no less intelligence
> Of things to come than gone by sapience.
>   Therefore, when wit and manhood doth concur,
> To honour rises magnificence,
>   For glory to nobles is a sharpened spur.[31]

(Tr. L.R.)

051 *'Not all of us have your lordship's gift for trusteeship.'*

A reference to Matthew Stewart absconding with a huge amount of the Queen Dowager's gold. He was to bring it from France to Scotland, but seized it instead.

051 *'Bring a cow to the hall, and she will to the byre again.'*

Scottish proverb meaning you can take the cow out of the barn, but it won't change, it will go right back to the barn and its old ways.

051 *'And foul water slockens fire,' added Lymond.*

'Foul water slockens fire' is a Scottish proverb meaning bad water quenches (*'slockens'*) fire as well as clean water. Lymond alludes to a darker meaning: for slaking one's lust, an evil woman is as useful as a moral woman.[32]

051 *'...I was brought up in bad company. From oar to oar, you might say.'*

From the reaction of Lennox, this is obviously a remark derogatory to his wife, Margaret. 'From oar to oar' may be a reference to Lymond's term of service on the galleys, or the Viking technique of jumping oar-to-oar on a longboat, Vikings being notoriously 'bad company'.[33]

051 *'And how,' pursued the Master suavely, 'is the Pearl of Pearls?'*

Marguerite d'Angoulême (1492-1549) was the sister of François I of France who affectionately called her *'la Marguerite des Marguerites'* – 'the pearl of pearls'. Marguerite was one of the most influential women in France, and her salon was known internationally. As an author and patron of humanists and reformers, she was a prominent figure of the French Renaissance.

Marguerite d'Angoulême by Jean Clouet, c.1530

Margaret Douglas, Countess of Lennox
1515 - 1578

Detail, family tree of King James I and VI of
Scotland and England, c.1603

Margaret Douglas, Countess of Lennox (1515-1578), was the daughter of Archibald Douglas, 6th Earl of Angus, and Margaret Tudor, Queen Dowager of Scotland. Margaret was the granddaughter of Henry VII of England, and half-sister of James V of Scotland, making her, and her children, prominent in the line of succession to the English and Scottish thrones.

Margaret was born in England, her mother having taken refuge from the control of the Duke of Albany, then Regent of Scotland. When her parents separated three years after her birth, the Earl of Angus took her from her mother and sequestered her at Tantallon Castle. When Angus was driven from Scotland, Margaret was placed under the care of her godfather, Cardinal Wolsey. After the fall of Wolsey, she was placed by her uncle, Henry VIII, in the household of Princess Mary, with whom she formed an intimate relationship. Margaret was made first lady-in-honour to the newly born Princess Elizabeth and was a favourite of Ann Boleyn. Henry treated Margaret 'like a queen's daughter'[34] and she was highly esteemed.

After the fall of Anne Boleyn, and the declared illegitimacy of Princesses Mary and Elizabeth, Margaret advanced to the position of the lady with the highest rank in England. Although a favourite of her uncle, King Henry VIII, she fell from his grace for her unauthorised engagement to Lord Thomas Howard, who died in the Tower of London in 1537 because of his méssalliance with her. Margaret was also placed in the Tower, but fell ill and was released.

The birth of Prince Edward demoted Margaret's claim to the throne, but

Henry VIII, conscious of the questionable legitimacy of the new prince, sought to declare the marriage of Margaret's parents unlawful. Convinced her ability to inherit the throne was sufficiently thwarted, Margaret was returned to the king's favour and was made first lady to Anne of Cleves, and then to her successor, Catherine Howard. She again fell from grace in 1540 for an affair with Sir Charles Howard, the nephew of Thomas Howard and the brother of Queen Catherine Howard.

The death of James V and the restoration of Angus's influence in Scotland once again restored Margaret to the favour of Henry VIII. She was a bridesmaid at the wedding of Henry and Catherine Parr. The following year, 1544, Henry arranged her marriage with Matthew Stewart, 4th Earl of Lennox, one of Scotland's leading Catholic noblemen. She had four sons and two daughters, all of whom died young except Henry, Lord Darnley (1545-1567) and Charles, 5th Earl of Lennox (1555-1576).

053 *'Wrap 'em up, my Pyrrha!'*

Pyrrha is a goddess in Greek mythology with red hair. In Latin the word pyrrhus means red, from the Greek term πυρρός (purros), meaning 'flame-coloured', 'the colour of fire' or simply 'red'.

054 *'I bring, lover, I bring the newis glad.'*

From *The Kingis Quair* by King James I of Scotland (1394-1437):

King James I

Awake! Awake! I bring, lover, I bring
The glad news, that blissful been and sure
Of thy comfort; now laugh, and play, and sing,
Thou art beside so glad a chance,
For in the heaven decreed is the cure.[35]   (Tr. L.R.)

054 *'...and now, my frivol Fortune...'*

Oh ladies fair of Troy and Greece attend
My misery, which none may comprehend,
My frivol fortune, my infelicity,
My great mischief, which no man can amend.
Be war in time, approach is near the end,
And in your mind a mirror make of me:
As I am now, perhaps that ye
For all your might may come to that same end,
Or else war, if any war may be.[36]   (Tr. L.R.)

From *The Testament of Cresseid* by Robert Henryson (c.1460-c.1500), a kind of supplement to Chaucer's poem, *Troilus and Criseyde*. Henryson introduces Cresseid's leprosy, realistically detailing the disease. In the Middle Ages, leprosy and sexual excess were associated, thus giving rise to the central conflict in the poem: is Cressieid's fate well-deserved or can she be redeemed through purgation and self-realization of her error?[37]

054 *'I'll trip upon trenchers; I'll dance upon dishes –'*

From an old Scots song:

I'll trip upon trenchers[a]*, I'll dance upon dishes*[b]*;*
My mother sent me for some barm, some barm[c]*:*
And through the kirk-yard I met with the laird,
The silly, poor body could do me no harm.
But down in the park, I met with the clerk,
And he gave me my barm, my barm.

a. Trenchers are clogs or wooden boots.
b. Dishes are high, iron-heeled shoes once worn by countrywomen when working around a farmstead.
c. Barm is the froth formed on top of fermenting malt liquors, used to leaven bread.

3. *Capture of a King's Pawn*

058 *'I wonder if the Protector insists on merchetis...'*

Merchitis, or *Mercheta mulierum*, was a duty paid to a lord by a tenant on the marriage of a daughter. The tenant, being 'annexed to the soil', had to pay a fine for the loss of his daughter as 'property' of the proprietor; no baron or military tenant could marry his sole daughter and heir without purchasing such leave from the king. The term derived from the ancient British, *Merch*, signifying a daughter or young woman; the plural, *Merched*, was latinized to *Mercheta*; hence, *Mercheta Mulierum*.

058 *'...who would be all the better for a fate plus mal que morte.'*

fate plus mal que morte: fate worse than death

058 *'Changeons propos, c'est trop chante d'amours.'*

Let's change the subject: we've sung too much about love.

From a drinking song with lyrics by Clément Marot (1496-1544) set to music by Claudin de Sermisy (1490-1562):

> *Let's change our song, we've sung too much about love:*
> *That is noise, let us sing of the pruning knife.*
> *All vineyard keepers have recourse to it,*
> *It is of help to cut the little vine.*
> *Oh little knife, Oh very little knife,*
> *The little vine is by you made to fall,*
> *Whereby good wines every year are produced.[38]*

058 *'I'll meet you at the Popinjay...'*

'Papingo, by the way, is but the old Scottish word for the Anglicized popinjay, and a popinjay, all the world knows, is a parrot.'[39]

Popinjay, or Papingo, is a shooting sport performed with either rifles or archery equipment. The archery form of popinjay dates back to at least the 15th century. The object of popinjay is to knock birds off their perches; the current form of the sport utilises artificial birds. The perches are cross-pieces on top of a 90-foot mast. The 'cock' (the largest bird) is set on the top cross-piece. Four smaller 'hens' are set on the next cross-piece down. Two dozen or so 'chicks' (the smallest birds) are set on the lower cross-pieces. The archer stands near the base of the mast and shoots arrows upwards at the birds.

A Wapenshaw (from Old English for 'weapon show') was a gathering and review of troops. The object of a Wapenshaw was to satisfy the military chiefs the armaments were in good condition and the troops properly trained.

Playing popinjay in Anjou in the time of the Renaissance, 16ᵗʰ century woodcut

II: Blindfold Play

Caxton: Tract 1, Chapter 1

*And it is not a fitting or appropriate thing for a woman to go
to battle for she is fragile and feeble. And therefore,
she does not hold the way in her as the knights do.*[1]

When playing blindfold chess, the players do not see the pieces on the board, or touch them, but keep mental note of the positions of the pieces.

060   *...and pounced, like divine Calypso, on his prey.*

*Hermes Ordering Calypso to Release Odysseus
by Gerarde de Lairesse, c.1670*

In Greek legend, Calypso was a nymph living on the island of Ogygia, on the coast of which Odysseus was thrown when shipwrecked. Having fallen in love with Odysseus, she offered him eternal youth and immortality if he stayed with her; he remained on the island for seven years until she was obliged by the gods to allow him to continue his homeward journey.

062 *Like the jewelled aiglettes...*

Aiglettes were braided tassels, often set with jewels and pearls. They were used on the ends of lacets as a means of fastening garments, or used as decoration, usually in pairs, on garments and caps. Over the course of fashion during the Tudor era, aiglettes became increasingly rich and ornate, and were worn by both gentleman and ladies of the period.

062 *'There's a bump on your head like the Old Man of Storr.'*

The Old Man of Storr is a elongated pear-shaped pillar of the Storr (derived from *Fiacaill storāch*, buck-tooth, suggestive of the pinnacles), a rocky hill on the Isle of Skye.

> *In front all the way is the Storr, its black face tossed skywards, and facing it, on a high ridge, stand the many pinnacles of which the Old Man is the most prominent. It is a steep climb to the top of this green ridge, but once the summit is gained, you find yourself at what seems a giddy height, and among a series of ghostly pinnacles, broken and weather-worn, standing at various angles, and looking down into a dark ravine below and black precipices which tower grimly high overhead.[2]*

The Old Man of Storr, c.2004

062   *'But I'll try. Like the spider, I'll try.'*

A reference to King Robert I (1274-1329), the famous warrior who lead Scotland during the Wars of Scottish Independence against England. According to legend, Robert the Bruce spent the winter of 1306-07 in a cave where he watched a spider spinning a web. Each time the spider failed to make the connection from one area of the roof of the cave to another, it would try again until it succeeded. Inspired by the spider, Bruce returned to inflict a series of defeats on the English: *If at first you don't succeed, try, try again.*

Robert the Bruce: The First Stroke at Bannochburn

062   *'That lightlie comes will lightlie ga...'*

From *The Three Priests of Peblis*:

> And from that he was dead, and then came his son,
> And inherited all the wealth that he had won.
>   He stepped not his steps into the street,
>   To win this wealth, not for it was he wet.
> When he would sleep, he wanted not for a wink,
> To win this wealth, nay for it did he sweat nor swink [a]
>   Therefore, that lightly comes will lightly go.
>   To win this wealth he had no work, nor woe.

To win this gold he had not one ill hour,
Why should he have the sweet, and not the sour?
* Upon his fingers are rich rings on row,*
* His mother did not suffer the smoke on him to blow.*[b3]   (Tr.L.R.)

a. To swink is to toil.
b. The word used in the poem is 'blaw', which in Scots is to blow up, to boast, or to brag; to exaggerate a story; to inflate with air. A 'Blaw-i'-my-lug' is a flatterer, a cajoler, a wheedler; one who blows fair words into the ear of a ready listener for selfish or sinister purpose.[4]

062   *'The counterpane is not improved by the spilt broth.'*

A counterpane is a cover for a bed, a bedspread or a type of quilt.

063   *'Without pitie, hanged to be, and waver with the wind.'*

From *The Nut-Brown Maid*, an anonymous ancient ballad:

HE: *I counsel you, Remember how*
          It is no maiden's law
      Nothin to doubt, but to run out
          To wood with an outlàw.
      For ye must there in your hand bear
          A bow ready to draw;
      And as a thief thus must you live
          Ever in dread and awe;
      Whereby to you great harm might grow:
          Yet had I liever than
      That I had to the green-wood go,
          Alone, a banished man.
SHE: *I think not nay, but as ye say;*
          It is no maiden's lore;
      But love may make me for your sake,
          As ye have said before,
      To come on foot, to hunt and shoot
          To get us meat and store;
      For so that I your company
          May have, I ask no more;
      From which to part, it maketh my heart
          As cold as any stone:
      For, in my mind, of all mankind
          I love but you alone.
HE: *For an outlàw, this is the law*
          That men him take and bind;
      Without pitie, hangëd to be,

And waver with the wind.
If I had need, (as God forbede!)
What rescues could ye find?
Forsooth, I trow, you and your bow
Should draw for fear behind.
And no mervail; for little avail
Where in your counsel than:
Wherefore I to the wood will go,
Alone, a banished man.

063   *'My beard...is full young yet to make a purfle of it...'*

The Last Sleep of Arthur in Avalon (detail) by Edward Burne-Jones, c.19th-century

A purfle is an ornamental border or edging, but here referring to a beard as related in a story from *Le Morte d'Arthur (The Death of Arthur)*, a compilation of tales about King Arthur, Guinevere, Lancelot, and the Knights of the Round Table by Sir Thomas Malory (1405-1471). First published in 1485 by William Caxton, the book is the best-known work of English-language Arthurian literature.

> *...King Rience had discomfited and overcome eleven kings, and every each of them did him homage, and that was this, they gave him their beards clean flayed off, as much as there was; wherefore the messenger came for King Arthur's beard. For King Rience had purfled a mantle with kings' beards, and there lacked one place on the mantle; wherefore he sent for his beard, or else he would enter into his lands, and burn and slay, and never leave till he have the head and the beard. Well, said Arthur, thou has said thy message,*

*the which is the most villainous and lewdest message that ever man
heard sent unto a king; also thou mayest see my beard is full young
yet to make a purfle of it.*[5]

063   '...*defend me from death and horrible maims?* '

From *Le Morte d'Arthur* by Sir Thomas Malory:

*When King Lot had espied King Bors, he knew him well, then he
said, O Jesu, defend us from death and horrible maims! for I see we
be in great peril of death; for I see yonder a king, one of the most
worshipfullest of men and one of the best knights of the world, is
inclined unto his fellowship.*[6]

063   '*For gold, for gude, for wage or yet for wed.* '

From *The Three Priests of Peblis* (lines 827-830):

*I am so full of lust and fantasy,
with this maiden, on bank that fits me by,
for gold, for good, for wage, or yet for wed
This night I would have her to my bed.*[7]

(Tr. L.R.)

063   '*This officer, but doubt, is callit Deid.* '

From *The Three Priests of Peblis* (lines 1240-1246):

*In one Godhead, and in persons three,
Therefore the King of kings him call we.
This officer but dout is callit Deid;
In none his power again may be replied:
Is none so right, so wise, nor of such wit,
Again his summoned suitly may sit.*[8]

(Tr.L.R.)

063   '*O lady: nor later. Deceit deceiveth and shall be deceived.* '

*Deceit deceiveth and shall be deceived,
For be deceitful who is deceivable,
Though his deceits be not out perceived,
To a deceiver deceit is returnable;
Fraud quit with fraud is a fitting reward,
For who with fraud fraudulent is found,
To a defrauder fraud will always rebound.*[9]

(Tr.L.R.)

From *The Fall of Princes* by John Lydgate of Bury (c.1370-c.1451), an English monk and poet. *The Fall of Princes* was a translation of *De Casibus Virorum Illustrium*, a collection of moral stories about the fall from fortune of famous men. Meaning, *'deceit shall itself be deceived, for to him who is double, his deceit returns: his fraud is quit with fraud.'*[10]

063 *'I shall be as much use to you as the Nibelunglied.'*

The Nibelungenlied, or *Der Nibelunge Nôt*, is a German poem considered one of the world's great epics. The poem embodies the spirit, the sentiment, the life, and the circumstances of the crowning age of chivalry.

The Fall of Princes, MS, c.1450

Sigfried, the son of the king of the Netherlands, has become the possessor of the storied treasure of the Nibelungs, which carries with it the curse of dire evil to its owner. Sigfried marries Kriemhild, sister of Gunther, king of the Worms, and then helps Gunther to win the wife of Brunhild of Iceland, by taking Gunther's place without her knowledge and overcoming her in three trials of bodily skill and strength.

After some years a bitter dispute breaks out between the heroines as to whether Gunther or Sigfried is the greater. Brunhild's jealousy is so great that she induces Hagen, one of Gunther's vassals, to murder Sigfried. Kriemhild, though she mourns long years for her husband, at length marries Etzel (Attila), king of the Huns. After Sigfried's death she had become the possessor of the Nibelung's treasure; but Hagen had wrested it from her and sunk it at the bottom of the Rhine.

At the end of several years Kriemhild, who still mourns for Sigfried, and still nourishes the desire for revenge upon Hagen and Gunther, invites her brother and his court to visit her. They do so, accompanied by a body of 11,000 knights and men-at arms. The conclusion of the epic relates the bloody incidents attendant upon the total annihilation of the Burgundians at the court of Etzel, and the slaughter they made amongst their foes.[11]

064 *'... but as the poet said, words is but wind, but dunts is the devil.'*

John Skelton (c.1460-1529) was an English poet, the author of *Magnificence*, a morality play with the line: *'Thy words be but wind, never they have no weight'*; meaning your words mean nothing. *Fegusson's Collection of Proverbs* (1641) offers a variation of 'Sticks and stanes may brak my banes...' in the form of, *'Words are but wind, but dunts are the devil.'* (A dunt is a stroke; a dull-sounding blow.) Another variation on the proverb is *'Words is but wind; but actions are the frame of man.'*

Magnificence is considered one of the best examples of the morality play. It deals with the evils of ambition, and *'how suddenly worldly wealth doth decay'*.

064   *'...like the gentleman who sat under palm trees feeding fruit to a lion...'*

From *The Paradise of the Desert Fathers*, a collection of sayings and accounts written by and about the Desert Fathers of Egypt:

> *We came near to a tree, led by our kindly host, and there we stumbled upon a lion. At the sight of him my guide and I quaked, but the saintly old man went unfaltering on and we followed him. The wild beast – you would say it was at the command of God – modestly withdrew a little way and sat down, while the old man plucked the fruit from the lower branches. He held out his hand, full of dates; and up the creature ran and took them as frankly as any tame animal about the house; and when it had finished eating, it went away. We stood watching and trembling; reflecting as well we might what valour of faith was in him and what poverty of spirit in us.*[12]

064   *'I am but ane mad man that thou hast here met –'*

From *The Taill of Rauf Coilyear*, a humorous metrical romance highly popular in Scotland in the beginning of the 16th century:

> *I am but one, mad man, that thou hast here met,*
> *I have no master to match with masterful men,*
> *Fair and o'er the fields, fuel to fetch,*
> *And oft feel my feet in many foul fen (marsh).*[13]   (Tr. L.R.)

064   *' I do you pray,' she said gravely, 'cast that name from you away.'*

From *The Pleasant History of Roswall and Lillian*, a mid-16th century Scottish chivalric romance with underlying themes of friendship and spontaneous generosity rewarded. The princely hero Roswall is exiled after he frees three lords imprisoned by his father; the lords, in gratitude, promise perpetual friendship. While Roswall is working as Lillian's chamberlain under the name Dissawar, he and Lillian fall in love. A three-day tournament, however, is called to celebrate Lillian's upcoming marriage to a wicked steward who has been impersonating Prince Roswall. While hunting, Roswall encounters a strange knight who gives him horse and armour so he may participate in the tournament. Each day brings a new knight, and Roswall is able to compete incognito to win each day's tournament. So as not to reveal his identity, as promised to the false steward,

Roswall does not claim his prize. Just before Lillian is to marry the false steward, the three knights reveal their identities to Roswall as the three released prisoners, and they then reveal Roswall's true identity to the king. Roswall is restored to his rightful inheritance, and he and Lillian are united.

> *I do you pray,*
> *Cast that name from you away;*
> *Call you Hector or Oliver,*
> *Ye are so fair without compare:*
> *Call your self Sir Porteous,*
> *Or else the worthy Amadass;*
> *Call you the noble Perdiccas,*
> *Who was fair and comely of face;*
> *Because that I love you so well,*
> *Let your name be Sir Lawnfal,*
> *Or great Florent of Albanie,*
> *My heart, if ye bear love to me.*

065 *'Call you Hector, or Oliver...'*

In Greek mythology, Hector is a Trojan prince and the greatest fighter for Troy in the Trojan War. In the European Middle Ages, Hector was known for his courage and his noble and courtly nature.

Ajax & Hector Exchange Gifts
MS, c.1531

Oliver is a knight in the French epic, *The Song of Roland*. The poem is one of the greatest examples of *chanson de geste*, long narrative poems about the adventures and deeds of a hero popular in the Middle Ages. It tells the story of Charlemagne's nephew, Roland, and his chivalric exploits, daring passion, and exaggerated conception of honour in picturesque and marvellous detail. Oliver, Roland's friend, represents wisdom.

065 *'What else? Sir Porteous – Amadas – Perdiccas – Florent...'*

It is thought the author of *Roswall and Lillian* borrowed the name 'Sir Porteous' from an early Scottish book entitled *The Porteous of Noblenes*, printed at Edinburgh in 1508, as the name Porteous does not otherwise occur in the roll of chivalry. [14] *The Porteous of Noblenes*, an English translation by Andrew Cadiou of *Breviaire des Nobles* by Alain Chartier, was 'standard reading in courtly circles in the 15th century'[15], and enumerates twelve virtues appropriate to the noble man: faith, truth, honour, reason, worthiness, love, courtesy, diligence, cleanliness, largesse, soberness, and perseverance.[16]

Sir Amadas is a mediæval chivalric romance, a story of generosity, and of wealth lost and regained. Sir Amadas gives his property in generosity, even spending the last of his money to pay the debts of a stranger to ensure his burial. He then meets with a white knight and they adventure together, procuring lands and wealth, half of which Sir Amadas promises to the white knight. Sir Amadas marries a princess and they have a child. The white knight demands payment of his promised half, including half of the princess and half of their child. When Amadas prepares to fulfill his promise, the white knight reveals he is the stranger whose debts Amadas paid.

Mediæval Chivalric Romance Illustration, c.1922

Perdiccas (died c.321 BC), one of Alexander the Great's generals, distinguished himself at the conquest of Thebes (335 BC), and was a descendant of the independent princes of the province of Orestis. After Alexander's death, Perdiccas was appointed regent over joint kings, and acting on their behalf sought to hold the empire together. During his attempt to attack Ptolemy, he lost so many of his men in the attempt to cross the Nile his army broke out in mutiny, and he was assassinated by his own officers.

Alexander Before Thebes

Florent of Hainaut (died 1297) was Prince of Achaea, governor of New Zealand, and Constable of Naples under Charles II, King of Naples. He is one of the heroes of *La Tournoi de Chauvency* by Jacques Bretel, a poem detailing the magnificent festivities of the six-day tournament held by Louis V, Comte de Chiny, in 1285 at Chauvency-le-Château, where more than 500 knights competed in games and a melee tournament. Considered a masterpiece of French literature of the Middle Ages, the work offers a picture of the life of late 13th-century aristocracy and the Golden Age of Chivalry.

Seal of Florent de Hainaut, c.1289

The Song of Roland from Les Grandes Chroniques de France, mid-15th-century

065 *'I am as I am, and so will I be, but how that I am, none knoweth truly...'*

From *Disdain Me Not* by Thomas Wyatt (1503-1542), an English poet. Wyatt earned two degrees from St John's College, Cambridge; as a member of the cultivated circle of Henry VIII's court, he distinguished himself as a polite and elegant scholar who held contempt for vice and an exalted love of virtue.

Disdain me not without desert,
Nor leave me not so suddenly;
Since well ye wot that in my heart
I mean ye not but honestly.
Disdain me not.

Refuse me not without cause why,
Nor think me not to be unjust;
Since that by lot of fantasy
This careful knot needs knit I must.
Refuse me not.

Mistrust me not, though some there be
That fain would spot my steadfastness;
Believe them not, since that we see
The proof is not as they express.
Mistrust me not.

Forsake me not till I deserve,
Nor hate me not till I offend;
Destroy me not till that I swerve;
But since ye know that I intend,
Forsake me not.

Disdain me not that I'm your own:
Refuse me not that I'm so true:
Mistrust me not till all be known:
Forsake me not ne for no new.
Disdain me not.

065 *Li rosignox est mon père, qui chante sur le ramée,*
el plus haut boscage.
Le seraine, ele est ma mère, qui chante en la mer salée,
el plus haut rivage...

> *My father is a nightingale,*
> *who trills on tallest tree*
> *From soaring wave my mother sings,*
> *by birth a mermaid she...*

From the anonymous 13th century French song, *'Voulez vous que je vos chant un son d'amours avenant?'*

> *Do you wish me to sing*
> *a charming song of love?*
> *No peasant wrote it,*
> *but a fine chevalier,*
> *In the arms of his beloved*
> *beneath an olive tree's shade.*
>
> *Her chemise was of fine linen,*
> *and silks all heaped with fur*
> *Green leaves of rain her girdle made,*
> *her buttons all were golden*
> *Her flower-hung wallet, shaped for love,*
> *was from her love a token.*
>
> *She rode a palfrey, silver-shod*
> *upon her golden saddle,*
> *Rose trees hung behind her head*
> *to give their lady shadow.*
> *Those knights she met while riding free,*
> *would come to her to wait.*
>
> *'Lady! Say, where were you born?'*
> *'In France, of high estate.*
> *'My father is a nightingale,*
> *who trills on highest tree,*
> *'From soaring wave my mother sings,*
> *by birth a mermaid she.'*
>
> *'High born indeed were you,*
> *and sprung of high degree.*
> *'Pray God that now you may be given,*
> *a wedded wife to me!*[17]

(Tr.L.R.)

066 *'Avoiding your traps, O virtuous lady, O mixt and subtle Christian.'*

From the *Palice of Honour* by Gavin Douglas (c.1474-1522), 'one of the most distinguished luminaries that marked the restoration of letters in Scotland at the commencement of the 16th century'[18]. A dream-allegory dedicated to James IV, *The Palice of Honour* is an apologue for the conduct of the king. The theme is 'the career of the virtuous man, over manifold and sometimes phenomenal difficulties, towards sublime heights which his disciplined and well-ordered faculties should enable him to reach...The poem is a crystallization of the chivalrous spirit, in the enforcement of a strenuous moral law and a lofty but arduous line of conduct.'[19]

066 *'But as you see, I am honest and good, and not ane word could lie.'*

Frontispiece, MS. 1533

From *The Testament of Cresseid* by Robert Henryson (c.1460-c.1500). Considered Henryson's most important work, the poem describes Cresseid's leprosy, the sorrow and charity of Troilus, and Cresseid's death.

066 *'I deduce that you've lived on Hymettus on honey and larks' tongues.'*

Hymettus is a mountain to the southeast of Athens famous for its honey.

066 *'Ho, ho: say you so; Money shall make my mare to go.'*

From a traditional English nursery rhyme:

> *Wilt thou lend me thy mare to ride but a mile?*
> *No, she's lame goinge over a stile.*
> *But if thou wilt her to me spare,*
> *Thou shalt have mony for thy mare.*
> *Ho ho say you soe,*
> *Mony shall make my mare to goe.*

Meaning, if you are prepared to pay enough, most people will be willing to do something which at first they would not do.

067 *'Man, it's not shinty!'*

Shinty (Gaelic, *sinteag*, a skip, bound) is a team game played with sticks and a ball, the precursor to hockey, handball, and bandy, and is older than the recorded history of Scotland. Colloquially, to 'shinny on your own side', is to keep or act within your own lines.

Shinty, c.1845

068 *'You deserve to hop like St. Vitus...'*

It was believed dancing in front of the statue of St. Vitus on the day of his festival (June 15th) would bring good health for a year. This practice gave rise to the name St. Vitus's Dance being given to the neurological disorder Chorea, which causes involuntary muscle spasms.

068 *'Your head– ' '– Would serve a cat in a bowl eight days,' he said...*

Meaning, Lymond's head is filled with mush.

Nuremberg Chronicle, c.1493

068 *En mai au douz tens nouvel*
Que raverdissent prael,
Oi soz un arbroisel...

From an old French song:

> *In May at the sweet Spring time,*
> *When the meadows grow green again.*
> *I heard beneath a tree*
> *The pretty nightingale sing.*
> > *Salera don!*
> > *So good it is*
> > *To sleep beside the little bushes.*

068 *'Sang School! I knew it!'*

Sang Schools were Scottish institutions for teaching singing, dating from the 13th century. A school existed in almost every one of the cathedral cities in Scotland, and in many smaller towns.

068 *Plucking crotchets like raindrops, he responded.*

A crotchet is a quarter note.

069 *...and from there to an estampie she did not recognize.*

Estampie was a dance and musical style popular in the 13th and 14th centuries.

069 *'O Dermyne, O Donnall, O Dochardy droch...'*

From *The Buke of the Howlat* (*The Book of the Owl*) by Richard Holland. The tediously alliterative poem was written during the ascendancy of the house of Douglas, and before its fall in 1452. Written to please Lady Elizabeth Dunbar, who married the son of James Douglas, 7th Earl of Douglas, the poem is an elaborate public laudation of the virtues of the family descended from Sir James 'The Good' Douglas. The poem describes the successful attempt of the owl to relieve the peacock, as pope amongst feathered fowl, of his shameful form.

Frontispiece, c.1823

069 *'...let there be dancing and singing and all manner of joy...'*

From *Le Morte d'Arthur* by Sir Thomas Malory:

> *Presently he saw a hundred ladies and many knights*
> *that welcomed him with fair semblance,*
> *and made him passing good cheer unto his sight,*
> *and led him in to the castle, where there was dancing*
> *and singing and all manner of joy.*[20]

069 *'The Frogge would a wooing ride...'*

Frog Went A-Courtin' is folk song first published in 1548 in the *Complaynt of Scotland*. A version of the ballad 'of a moste straunge weddinge of the frogge and the mouse' was printed in 1580:

> *It was ye frog in ye wall,*
> *Humble doun, humble doun,*
> *And ye mirrie mouse in ye mill...*
> *Ye frog wald a wowing ryd,*
> *Sword and buckler by his syd.*

070 *What lay at the bottom of a well? Cats; and kelpies; and curses; and cures for warts...and Truth, of course.*

A reference to a popular English nursery rhyme first recorded in 1580, and printed in 1609 in *Pammelia Musicks Miscellanie* by Thomas Ravescroft (c.1582-1635). It also appears in the Shakespearean plays, *The Tempest* and *The Merchant of Venice*.[21]

> *Ding, dong, bell,*
> *Pussy's in the well.*
> *Who put her in?*
> *Little Johnny Green.*
> *Who pulled her out?*
> *Little Tommy Stout.*
> *What a naughty boy was that,*
> *To try to drown poor pussy cat,*
> *Who ne'er did him any harm,*
> *But killed all the mice in the farmer's barn.*

'Truth lies at the bottom of a well' is a proverb attributed to Heraclitus (c.535-c.475 BC), a pre-Socratic philosopher known as 'The Obscure' for the riddling nature of his philosophy. A kelpie is a supernatural water horse of Celtic folklore believed to haunt the rivers and lochs of Scotland and Ireland.

070   *Se'l ser un si scrivero 'n rima;*
        Se'l ser un no, amici come prima.

   If it is a yes, a 'yes' I in rhyme shall spin you;
      If it is no, as friends we shall continue.[22]

From *Madonna non so dir* by French Renaissance composer Philippe Verdot (c.1480-c.1540), one of the leading composers and creators of the madrigal musical form, an unaccompanied polyphonic song for three to eight voices, full of counterpoint and imitation, and following ecclesiastical modes. It was often an amorous poem containing delicate and tender, yet simple, thoughts. Many musicians set poems as serenades to a *'madonna'* – frequently a courtesan – for whose favours a noble might sue. Although some of the *'madonna'* madrigal texts are direct and crude, others with more refined text pay homage to a lady of quality.

071   *'I'm unlikely to insist on furca and fossa out of spite or low curiosity.'*

In the Middle Ages, a sentence of death was read with the words *cum fossa et furca,* meaning 'with drowning-pit and gallows'. If the criminal were male, he would get the noose; if female, she would be drowned in a pit.

071   *'...like the wonders of Mandeville, my probity is problematic.'*

Jehan de Mandeville was the assumed name of the compiler of *The Travels of Sir John Mandeville*, first circulated in the second half of the 14th century. In the course of his chimeric travels, Mandeville served the Sultan of Egypt against the Bedouins and the Emperor of China against the king of Manzi, saw the glory of Prester John, and drank from the Fountain of Youth, before returning home, unwillingly, owing to arthritic gout.

Probity is complete and confirmed integrity; uprightness.

072   *'...Culter took a chance I wouldn't have touched with a billhook.'*

A billhook is a mediæval European polearm weapon with a hooked blade used by infantry. It combines the features of a knife and a hatchet in one tool, and although very dangerous, many cottage dwellers kept them for general use.

073   *'Happier than Augustus, better than Trajan.'*

'Felicior Augusto, melior Traiano', Latin for 'more fortunate than Augustus, better than Trajan', was the wish delivered by the Roman Senate at the inauguration of each emperor after Trajan. It refers to the well-being experienced by the Roman Empire during their respective reigns. Augustus (63 BC - 14 AD) is considered the first emperor of the Roman Empire; his reign initiated an era of relative peace. Trajan (ruled 98-117 AD) was a popular Roman emperor who ruled

well and without the bloodshed of the previous reign. His popularity was so great the Roman Senate bestowed upon him the honorific of *Optimus Princeps*, 'The Best Chief'.

073 *'Like the elephants of Mauretania, my friends are foregathering to perform mysterious rites.'*

From *Naturalis Historia* by Pliny the Elder (23-79 AD), one of the largest surviving works from the early Roman Empire. It covers the entire field of ancient knowledge, and is the model for the modern encyclopædia.

> *The elephant...is sensible alike of the pleasures of love and glory, and, to a degree that is rare among men, even possesses notions of honesty, prudence, and equity; it has a religious respect also for the stars, and a veneration for the sun and moon. It is said by some authors, that, at the first appearance of the new moon, herds of these animals come down from the forests of Mauritania to a river, the name of which is Amilo; and that they there purify themselves in solemn form by sprinkling their bodies with water; after which, having thus saluted the heavenly body, they return to the woods, carrying before them the young which are fatigued.*[23]

073 *'Thank you, Shahrazad, but I think not.'*

Scheherazade is the legendary Persian queen and the storyteller of *One Thousand and One Nights*. Each day the king would marry a new virgin and send yesterday's wife to be beheaded in retaliation for his first wife's betrayal. By the time he was introduced to Scheherazade, he had killed one thousand women.

> *She had perused the books, annals and legends of preceding Kings, and the stories, examples and instances of bygone men and things; indeed it was said that she had collected a thousand books of histories relating to antique races and departed rulers. She had perused the works of the poets and knew them by heart; she had studied philosophy and the sciences, arts and accomplishments; and she was pleasant and polite, wise and witty, well read and well bred.*[24]

To break this evil tradition, Scheherazade, the daughter of the Vizier, offered herself to the Sultan but for only one night knowing this was a death sentence but believing in her plan. She asked the Sultan to permit her sister, Dinarzade, to sleep in the chamber with them, to which the Sultan agreed. Scheherazade asked her sister to awaken her one hour before dawn, requesting to be told a story. She began her tale, but when dawn broke, Scheherazade interrupted her story, promising an exciting conclusion, if only the Sultan would allow her to live another day to finish the story.

That night, Scherahazade finished her story and began another, stopping again at dawn before the story was finished. And so the Sultan again allowed her to live another day. This pattern continued for 1001 nights and 1001 stories.

Sheherazade, Illustration, c.1886

Chapter III: More Blindfold Play: The Queen Moves Too Far

Caxton: Tract 4, Chapter 3

In figure should be made in chess a queen
A fair lady gaily clad she should be,
And in a chair she should be set on high,
A stately crown of gold upon her head,
Resolute in moving should your woman be,
and swift, and to no far country.[1]

074 *...to bring Christian Stewart and her women to Stirling.*

View of Stirling, c.1673, from a painting by John Vosterman

Located along the natural road from the Highlands to the Lowlands, Stirling occupies a romantic and beautiful position in the centre of Scotland. Long associated with Scotland's chivalric history, the area surrounding Stirling is a wealth of historic memories: the deaths of Alexander I (1124) and William the Lion (1214); Wallace's victory of Stirling Bridge (1297); the great siege of the castle by Edward I (1304); the Battle of Bannochburn, fought immediately south of Stirling (1314); the murder of William, Earl of Douglas, by the hand of his sovereign, King James II (1452); the birth of James III (1451); and the coronations of James V (1513) and his daughter, Queen Mary (1543).

The ancient town of Stirling was clustered along two or three streets, which followed the backbone of Castle Hill and opened onto the castle esplanade. Just below the castle is the path of Ballengliech, a private access to the fortress from which James V made his gallant and amusing adventures. The tilting ground was below the esplanade in an area called the Valley; ladies viewed the jousts from Lady's Rock. The castle itself was entered after crossing a drawbridge and passing through double gates; it was defended by a portcullis and a double ditch.

Although the date of the founding of Stirling Castle is unknown, there was a fortress on the site as early as 1124. Most of its current buildings date from 1490-1600, when Stirling developed as a royal centre of the Stewart kings. James IV sought to establish a palace of European standing at Stirling and built the grand Parliament Hall. James also kept lions in the Lions' Den and retained an alchemist who maintained a furnace in the castle for the mythical fifth element. James V continued and expanded his father's building program, bringing artisans from France to complete the Royal Palace. A mix of Gothic and Renaissance architecture, the palace is adorned with the earliest Renaissance sculptures in Scotland.

Stirling Castle in the Time of James V

Stirling Castle

075   *...because, like proud flesh, it increased on itself.*

Proud flesh is the swelling which surrounds a healing wound, caused by excessive granulation.

075   *...saw Mene, Mene, Tekel, Upharsin in lapidary capitals before him...*

Mene, Mene, Tekel, Upharsin is an idiom meaning 'the handwriting on the wall', a portent of doom or misfortune. It originates from the Biblical book of Daniel in which the fingers of a supernatural being wrote a mysterious message – the words *mene, mene, tekel,* and *upharsin* – foretelling the demise of the Babylonian Empire. The words translate literally as 'numbered, weighted, and divided'. Lapidary means engraved in stone.

075   *...when the company, sleek and splendid, was George Douglas...*

George Douglas of Pittendreich, Master of Angus (d.1552), brother of Archibald Douglas, 6th Earl of Angus, was a member of the powerful Douglas family who seized custody of young James V in 1526. James escaped in 1529, and laid siege to the Douglas castle at Tantallon; their lands and titles were forfeit, and they went into exile in England.

After the death of James V at the Battle of Solway Moss, George Douglas and his brother returned to Scotland. Douglas lands were then restored by the Earl of Arran, who was Regent for the young Queen Mary. Initially, George favoured the marriage of Queen Mary to Prince Edward, and sought to send her to England. Despite his efforts, Mary remained in Scotland, and the 'Rough Wooing' followed the breach of the Treaty of Greenwich. George then worked on behalf of Mary de Guise, and marshaled Scottish forces at the battle of Pinkie Cleugh.

077   *...past the hamlet of Port, the chapel, the barns, the Law Tree.*

The Law Tree was the trunk of an old hawthorn tree, which stood by the lakeside and opposite the manse of Port. Legal business and sales of farm produce and cattle were transacted there, and an annual fair named for St. Michael was held in September around the tree.

077   *Black and unrippled at his feet spread the Lake of Menteith...*

The Lake of Monteith [sic] is a beautiful sheet of water, near the south-western extremity of Perthshire. Situated in one of Scotland's fairest vales, and adorned with three isolated islands, this charming lake becomes at once an object of placid beauty, surrounded by a touch of grandeur. On the north, tower the heath clad hills of Monteith, the home of the wild cat and the eagle – the abode of the wolf and wild boar of old – the hiding place of the outlaw and war-chief of other days...On the west, are the rugged passes and scattered crags of Aberfoyle, with the heath capped hills of the country of Rob Roy. On the south, are the dark forests of Cardross, where the roc roams free and the ospray rears her young; and on the east, mansions dot its pebbled shores, with the lone country highway winding along the sandy beach, like a native adder in its coils, cooling its poisoned tongue in the silvery waters. Landing on Inchmahome, one hundred feet from the shore, the Priory looms before you in gloomy grandeur...[2]

Lake of Mentieth and Inchmahome (shown in the centre)

077   ...organ notes from the Priory of Inchmahome...

The Priory of Inchmahome was built in 1238 as the first Augustinian monastery in Scotland. Dedicated to Colman, the Irish Pict who founded the monastery of Dramore in Ireland (c.514 AD) it flourished as a religious house for three centuries until the Reformation. Robert Bruce visited the island and Priory at least three times, and his son, David II, was married there.

Queen Mary sought refuge at the Priory in 1547 after the Battle of Pinkie Cleugh, under the care of John Erskine, 4th Lord Erskine. The queen-mother selected four young ladies to join Mary as companions and playmates, who came to be known as the Four Marys: Mary Beaton, niece of Janet Beaton; Mary, daughter of Lord Fleming; Mary Livingston, daughter of the queen's guardian; and Mary, daughter of Lord Seton. Queen Mary's Bower, an enclosed garden thought to be her favourite retreat, remains as a memorial of her temporary sojourn on the island.

View of the West Door of Inchmahome Priory

077   *...where monks sang at Compline and children slept...*

Compline is the seventh and final church service of the day, said after sunset.

077   *...a consort playing a galliard from Inchtalla...*

A galliard is brisk, lively, jaunty music written for a dance of the same name, popular in the 16th and 17th centuries.

Inchtalla ('Island of the Halls', or 'The Castle-Island') lies to the west of Inchmahome, separated by a narrow channel. Almost the entire surface of the island was covered by the old Castle and its buildings.

077   *...placidly stitching before Earl John's big fire.*

John Erskine, 4th Lord Erskine, *de jure* Earl of Mar (d.1552), head of the abbey and a Scottish nobleman; father of Thomas Erskine, Master of Erskine.

077   *'...and every one of them with the instincts of a full-grown lemming.'*

Lemmings are small rodents, which, when overcrowded, will take to the waterway in search of new territory, sometimes drowning in the process.

079 *To the north the hills of Ben Dearg reared empurpled...*

Ben Dearg ('Red Mountain') is one of the principal summits of the Hills of Monteith, the other being Ben Dubh ('Black Mountain').

080 *'Hurble-purple, hurble-purple, hurble-purple!' chanted the child.*

From the Holme Riddle-book, considered the most extensive and valuable collection of English problems and their solutions. The answer is a cherry.

> *Hurble purple hath a red gurdle*
> *A stone in his belly, a stake through his arse*
> *and yet hurble purple is neur the worse.*

080 *'She'd cuddle a milk jug, the jaud!'*

> 'She's so desperate (or loose) she'd sleep with a milk jug!'

In English 'cuddle' means to embrace or fondle; in Lowland Scottish parlance it means to sleep, derived from the Gaelic *caidall*, sleep. 'Jaud' is a term of abuse for a worn-out horse; by the 15th century it was used to insultingly describe a worn-out woman, or an old or useless article.

081 *'...the attractions of Perkin seem to have played ducks and drakes with our safety precautions.'*

Perkin Warbeck (c.1474-1499) was a pretender to the English throne by claiming to be the younger son of King Edward IV who was murdered in the Tower. Hence, the significance is that someone was playing a role to accomplish a secret goal. 'Ducks and Drakes' is skipping stones; to play ducks and drakes is to behave recklessly.

081 *'But all the monks are at Sext.'*

Sext is a fixed time of prayer said at noon, the sixth hour after dawn.

082 *'Comment le saluroye, quant point ne le congnois?'*

> *'How shall I give him cheer who is to me unknown?'*

From the anonymous French poem, *Le Soldat Mort (The Dead Soldier)*:

> *'Kind gentlemen of France, a-marching out to war,*
> *I pray you, an you please, give cheer to my suitor.'*
> *'How shall I give him cheer who is to me unknown?'*
> *'To know him is not hard, he hath white armour on;*
> *'The cross he bears is white, his spurs are made of gold,*

> A lance, with silver head, well gilded, he doth hold.'
> 'Weep no more, lady fair, for he is dead and gone;
>   In Brittany he died, to death he hath been done.
> 'I saw men dig his grave beside a meadow green,
>   By four St. Francis' Friars, his mass hath chanted been.'

082 'Crying the coronoch on high.'

'Crying lamentations on high.'

From *The Battle of Harlaw*, a Scots ballad about the ferocious clan battle fought in 1411. A coronach is an Irish or Scottish dirge for the dead.

> *From Dunidier as I came through*
> *Down by the hill of Banochie*
> *Against the lands of Garioch.*
> *Great pity was to hear and see*
> *The noise and doleful harmony,*
> *That ever that dreary day did dawn!*
> *Cry and lamentations on high,*
> *Alas! Alas! for the Harlaw.[3]*   (Tr.L.R.)

082 'I fell asleep. Considerably more than doth the nightingale.'

From *The Canterbury Tales* by Geoffrey Chaucer:

> *So hot he loved that, while night told her tale,*
> *He slept no more than does the nightingale.*

082 ' –"M. l'abbé, you 'ave greatly insufficient of tonsure."'

abbé: abbot

Tonsure is a practice in various faiths of cutting or shaving hair from the scalp as a rite of sacrament, often as a renunciation of worldliness.

083 '...crowing like the cocks of Cramond.'

From the ancient Scots poem, *The Gyre-Carling*:

> *Sensing the cocks of Cramond crow never a day*
> *For grief of that devilish dame was with Mahoon married.[4]*   (Tr.L.R.)

The Gyre-Carling, also known as Hecate or the Mother Witch of Scottish peasantry, was said to consort with Jews and Mohammed (Mahoon), which was meant to imply she was an enemy to Christians.[5]

083 *'By all means let's play guessing games. "Will you hide me, Yes, par foi! Shall I be found out? Not through me!"'*

From *Le mystère d'Adam (The Mystery of Adam)*, an Anglo-Norman mystery play of the 12ᵗʰ century. Mystery plays were presented in churches, depicting Bible stories with accompanying song.

Diabolus:	*Will you hide me?*
Eva:	*Yes, by faith!*
Diabolus:	*Shall I be found out?*
Eva:	*Not by me!*
Diabolus:	*Or put in your debt. Nor in your confidence.*
Eva:	*Although you will have to believe my word.*

083 *'Look to me as Wat did to the worm, and relieve my conscience.'*

There is a Scottish proverb which states, *'Tramp on a worm, and she'll turn her head'*; meaning, the meanest, when injured, will show their resentment.

084 *'The God of the Flies, the Lord of the Dunghill.'*

Beelzebub, the demon who first appears in the Bible in 2 Kings, is interpreted in Rabbinical texts as Lord of the Dunghill, and hence, Lord of the Flies.

085 *'I can say naught but Hoy gee ho! – words that belong to the cart and the plough.'*

From *The Clown's Courtship*, a ballad from the reign of Henry VIII:

> *To marry I would have thy consent,*
> *But faith, I never could compliment,*
> *I can say nought but 'hoy, gee ho!'*
> *Words that belong to the cart and the plough.*

085 *'Which describes your case as fortunae telum, non culpae.'*

> *Fortunae telum, non culpae:* Fortune's fault, not mine.

From *The Anatomy of Melancholy* by Robert Burton:

> *One of the greatest miseries that can befall a man, in the world's esteem, is poverty or want, which makes men steal, bear false witness, swear, forswear, contend, murder and rebel, which breaketh sleep, and causeth death itself...*

If fortune hath envied me wealth,
  thieves have robbed me,
  my father have not left me
  such revenues as others have
That I am a younger brother, basely born
  — cui sine luce genus, surdumque parentum —
  nomen, of mean parentage,
  a dirt dauber's son,
  Am I therefore to be blamed?
An eagle, a bull, a lion
  is not rejected for his poverty,
  and why should a man?
Tis fortunae telum, non culpae
  Fortune's fault, not mine.

085   'Heu! The darts which make me suffer are my own.'

From *The Heroines (Heriodes)* by Publius Ovidius Naso (43 BC - 17/18 AD), the Roman poet known as Ovid. *The Heroines,* imaginary love-letters from the heroines of mythology to their lords, show Ovid's dramatic creativeness. The last true poet of the great age of Roman literature, he wrote with lighthearted gaiety and imaginative vision. 'Ovid's chief personal endowment was his vivacity and his keen interest in the enjoyment of life...The great object of his art was to amuse and delight by the vivid picture he represented of its fashions and pleasures, and by creating a literature of romance which reflected them, and which could stimulate the curiosity and fascinate the fancy of a society too idle and luxurious for serious intellectual effort.'[6]

*Nuremberg Chronicle
MS, 1493*

In 8 AD, Ovid was banished for an unknown offense; it is thought because of his alleged affair with the Julia, the daughter of Emperor Augustus, who was also banished. After nearly a year of travel, he reached Getæ, the land of his exile. Severed from his wife, daughter, relatives, and friends, he wrote several works, including *Tristia,* a record of his sufferings and an appeal for pardon.

085   'God clip you close,' he said, and was gone.

To clip (Middle English, *clippen,* to embrace) is to encompass; hug; clasp.

Chapter IV: Several Moves by a Knight

Caxton: Tract 2, Chapter 4

A knight should be wise, liberal, true, strong, and full of mercy and pity and keeper of the people and of the law...And therefore it behooves him to be wise and well advised, for often times art, craft, and ingenuity is of more worth than strength or hardiness...for otherwise it happens that when the prince of battle pledges and trusts in his hardiness and strength, and will not use wisdom and ingenuity for to ride upon his enemies, he is vanquished and his people slain.[1]

1. Mishap to a Queening Pawn

086   *...which all but turned his epithalamics into elegies.*

An epithalamium is a nuptial song or poem in honor of a newly married couple. Among the Greeks, it was a song of praise sung at the door of the bridal chamber, consisting of invocations of blessings and predictions of happiness. Amongst the Romans, the song contained somewhat obscene lyrics. In the hands of the poets, the epithalamium was developed into a specific literary form. The finest preserved in Greek literature is the 18th Idyll of Theocritus, in Latin literature the *Marriage of Thetis and Peleus* by Catullus, and in English literature *Epithalamium* by Edmund Spenser. An elegy is a funeral song or lament for the dead.

087   *With him rode the Baroness Herries...*

The family of Herries came into Scotland during the reign of David I; they were powerful, and possessed a very extensive tract of land in Scotland. Andrew, the 2nd Lord Herries, was slain at Flodden along with four of his brothers. His son, William, the 3rd Lord Herries, died in September 1543, leaving three daughters: Agnes, Katherine, and Janet.

087   *...and a passion for* romans idylliques.

The mediæval French *roman idyllique* was a specific form of romance and adventure story, describing the poignancy of young love of a hero and heroine, whose union is threatened by differences in social or religious background. They each progress to maturity through experiences of loss and separation, often with the hero fighting on foreign land to prove his worth. The couple overcome all obstacles to be reunited and marry. Well-known examples include *Floire et Blancheflor* (c.1160), *Aucassin et Nicolette* (12th or 13th century), *Amadas et Ydoine* (c.1200), and *Guillaume de Palerne* (13th century).

088   *'Daphne! Vision! Shining she-lamb!'*

> *'O nymph, O Peneus' daughter, stay!*
> *I who pursue thee am no enemy. Oh stay!*
> *So does the lamb flee from the wolf;*
> *   the deer from the lion;*
> *So do doves on fluttering wings*
> *   flee from the eagle;*
> *So every creature its foes.*
> *But love is the cause of my pursuit.'[2]*

Daphne Changed into a Laurel, c.1767

Agnes's pinings are a reference to the mythical story of Apollo and Daphne as told by Ovid in *Metamorphoses*, quoted above. Apollo, proud over a victory, mocked Cupid's archery skills. In revenge, Cupid shot two arrows, one of which made Apollo fall in the love with the beautiful nymph Daphne, while the other filled her with aversion to him. Apollo tirelessly pursued her, possessed with love and lust. Daphne fled, begging the gods to free her from her body. At the moment Apollo seized her, she is metamorphosed into a laurel-tree. As a symbol of his everlasting love for her, Apollo pronounced the laurel-tree as sacred to him and used the laurel to adorn his hair, lyre, and quiver.

088   *The Nith, which lay between themselves and Ballaggan...*

Scene on the Nith at Blackwood by D.O. Hill, c.1840

090   *...wearing a loose gown borrowed from Sir James Douglas, their host.*

Sir James Douglas, 7th Baron Drumlanrig (d.1578), along with Sir Walter Scott of Buccleuch, attempted to rescue King James V from the Earl of Angus in June 1526. He later sided with Angus against Lennox and Wharton, the result of which was the plundering of his lands in 1549 by the English. He was knighted in 1553 for his service to the Scottish crown. He was married to Margaret Douglas, sister of the Earl of Angus and Sir George Douglas; they later divorced.

The Douglases of Drumlanrig were 'a strong-boned, hot-blooded race, born leaders of men, and the heads of family never failed to hold their ground against all comers. It is a most remarkable circumstance that from 1388 down to 1778 son succeeded father without a break in the male succession – a unique occurrence, I believe, in the noble families of any country. Every head of the family was a bold, energetic man in the troublous times of these four hundred years.'[3]

The barony of Drumlanrig was bestowed upon the Douglases as early as 1356, and for four hundred years passed from father to son with only a single break (1578) and then from grandfather to grandson. A castle was built as early as 1492 on the last spur of a 'drum' or long ridge of hill on the right bank of the rich valley of the Nith. The current castle, finished in 1689, includes remnants of the ancient building. The property passed to the family of Buccleuch in 1810 and was restored in 1827. Its grounds, woods, and gardens were considered the glory of Upper Nithsdale.

> *The beauties of Drumlanrig are not confined to the highest part of the grounds; the walks for a very considerable way by the sides of the Nith, abound with most picturesque and various scenery. Below the bridge the sides are prettily wooded, but not remarkably lofty; above, the views become wildly magnificent. The river runs through a deep and rocky channel, bounded by vast wooded cliffs that rise suddenly from its margin; and the prospect down from the summit is a terrific depth, increased by the rolling of the black waters beneath.[4]*

Drumlanrig by W.H. Bartlett, c.1838

093 *'...in the midst of his uxorial fluctuations.'*

Uxorial is of, or relating to, a wife.

093 *'...she had a cracking row with him the week before he died...'*

Henry VIII died 28 January 1547, eight months prior to the beginning of *The Game of Kings*. After Margaret's marriage to Matthew Stewart, she began to outwardly express her Catholic leanings, to which Henry took offense; it is suggested this was the root of the 'violent argument'[5] they had, which caused Henry to exclude her from the succession in his will.

094 '... is graithing himself a nice sharp axe for Tower Green.'

King Henry VIII
by Hans Holbein, c.1547

To graith is to prepare; equip; make ready.

Tower Green is a grassy area within the Tower of London where executions by beheading could be conducted in private, as opposed to public executions on Tower Hill or at Tyburn. The following nobles were executed on Tower Green:

1. William Hastings, 1st Baron Hastings – 1483
2. Queen Anne Boleyn, second wife of King Henry VIII – 1536
3. Margaret Pole, Countess of Salisbury – 1541
4. Queen Catherine Howard, fifth wife of Henry VIII – 1542
5. Jane Boleyn, Viscountess Rochford – 1542
6. Lady Jane Grey, the Nine Days Queen – 1554
7. Robert Devereux, 2nd Earl of Essex – 1601

King's House from Tower Green by John Fulleylove, c.1908

Chapter V: Castling

Caxton: Tract 3, Chapter 8

*The ribald players of dice and the messengers and couriers ought
to be set before the rook. For it is important to the rook to have men
suitable for a run here and there for tenure and spying on the place
and cities that might be contrary to the king.*[1]

Each player, once each game, is permitted a compound move called 'Castling',
wherein he moves his King and a Rook simultaneously. The Rook is moved to the
square next to the King, and the King is moved to the other side of the Rook. This
move is only allowed if the King and Rook have not been moved, the King is not
in check, and there are no enemy pieces between the King and the Rook.

1. Capture of Some Advancing Pieces

096   '*Le douxiem' mois de l'an...*'

From the French song, *Les Dans de L'An* (*The Gifts of the Year*), which is similar
to the Twelve Days of Christmas:

At the end of the year
What shall I give my sweet?
Twelve good hogletts
Eleven good hams
Ten good turkeys
Nine horned bullocks
Eight sheared sheep
Seven running hounds

Six country hares
Five rabbits running
Four mallards flying
Three pigeons cooing
Two turtle doves
One partridge wise
That flies and flies and flies
One partridge flying
From the wood field.

098 *'I can thole him, I can thole him.'*

To thole is to suffer pain or grief; to bear; to endure.

098 *'You should see him at work in a fair: it's a scholastic education.'*

Based on the teachings of Aristotle and Arabian commentators such as Avicenna and Averrhoes, scholasticism was the dominant system of philosophy taught in mediæval European schools and universities.

Depiction of a University Class by Laurentius de Voltolina, c.1530

100 *'Of wyne and wax, of gamyn and gle.'*

The earliest poem in the Scots language surviving in written form is a short lyric on the death of Alexander III (ruled 1249-1286), which appears in *The Original Chronicle* of Andrew of Wyntoun, finished in about 1420. The poem itself may date to around 1300.

> *When Alexander our king was dead,*
> *Who ruled Scotland in law and tranquility,*
> *Gone was our fortune of ale and bread,*
> *Of wine and wax and gamine and glee;*
> *Our gold was changed into lead.*
> *Christ, born of virginity,*
> *Succour Scotland and remedy*
> *That which is fixed in perplexity.²*   (Tr.L.R.)

100   'Sic peril lies in paramours.'

From *The Perils of Paramours* by the Scottish poet, Mersar:

> *Wherefore I pray, in terms short,*
> *Christ keeps these brides,*
> *From false lovers and their disport,*
> *Such peril lies in paramours![3]*   (Tr.L.R.)

100   'And that, my Wally Gowdy, was only half the night's work.'

Wally Gowdy is a Scots term of endearment meaning lovely jewel.

100   'This was Maxwell of Threave and Caerlaverock?'

Threave Castle was built on an island in the River Dee by Archibald 'The Grim' Douglas at the end of the 14th century, and was the stronghold of the 'Black Douglases' until their fall in 1455. Threave was the last of the Douglas fortresses to surrender to James II, who employed the cannon 'Mons Meg' against it; custody of the castle was later transferred to the Maxwells.

Threave Castle

Caerlaverock Castle is a moated triangular castle near the mouth of the Nith, seven miles southeast of Dumfries. It was the seat of the Maxwells, earls of Nithsdale, for more than four generations, first acquired by Sir John Macuswell about 1220. From a description of Edward I's Siege of Caerlaverock in 1300:

Caerlaverock was so strong a castle that it did not fear a siege, therefore the king came himself because it would not consent to surrender. But it was always furnished for defence whenever it was required, with men, with engines, with provisions. Its shape was like that of a shield, for it had only three sides all round, with a tower at each angle; but one of them was a double one, so high, so long, and so large, that under it was the gate, with a drawbridge, well made and strong...It had good walls and ditches, filled to the edge with water; and I believe there was never seen a castle so beautifully situated, for at once could be seen the Irish Sea towards the west, and to the north a fine country surrounded by an arm of the sea, so that no creature born could approach it on two sides without putting himself in the danger of the sea.[4]

Caerlaverock Castle, c.1873

100 *'Fie on their labour! Fie on their delight!'*

Fie is an expletive expressing disgust or contempt, or it can be used to express the humorous pretence of being shocked.

101 *'Poor Mat. Sic strange, intestine, cruel strife.'*

'Sic' is a Middle English word for such. Intestine is domestic or civil war within a country. From the ballad *The Brim Battle of Harlaw*, fought on 24 July 1411:

> *There was not since King Kenneth's days*
> *Such strange intestine cruel strife*
> *In Scotland seen, as ilk man says*
> *Where many likely lost their life*
> *While made divorce between man and wife*
> *And many children fatherless*
> *While in this realm full of rife*
> *Lord help these lands! Our wrongs redressed.[5]*
>
> (Tr.L.R.)

101 *'Alas, father, my mirth is gone.'*

From *The Testament of Cresseid* by Robert Henryson (c.1425-c.1500), a poem known for its vigorous descriptive writing, and its passages of strenuously impassioned verse. 'The picture presented in these striking lines possesses the distinctness of outline and conception, and the rich poetic coloring, which marks the hand of genius.'[6]

101 *'Or Cothally Castle –'*

Cothally Castle in Lanarkshire was the seat of the powerful Somerville family from the reign of David I (1124-1153) until 1603. The castle was surrounded by a moat and a rampart, and accessible only by drawbridge. King James V was entertained there 'with great magnificence'[7].

101 *'– Seton's away?'*

George Seton, 4th Lord Seton (d.1549), was a member of one of Scotland's richest and most influential families, known for being intensely loyal to the Stewart dynasty. They received a charter for the extensive lands of Seton, Winton, and Winchburgh in the 12th century by King David I, and built the palaces of Seton and Winton. George, 3rd Lord Seton, was a favourite of King James IV and fell with him at the Battle of Flodden in 1513.

Lord Seaton was a member of the parliamentary committee and an Extraordinary Lord of Session. 'He was one wise and virtuous nobleman; a man well experienced in all games, and took pleasure in hawking, and was held to be the best falconer in his days.'[8] His daughter Mary was one of the celebrated Four Marys who attended Queen Mary.

The Palace of Seton was a place of royal entertainment and splendid hospitality, located nine miles east of Edinburgh. It was considered one of the most elegant, grand and extensive mansions in Scotland. In 1544, the English army 'came and lay at Seton, burnt and destroyed the castle thereon, spoiled the kirk, took away the bells and organs and other portable things, and put them in their ships, and burnt the timber work within the kirk'[9]. The palace was restored and later became a place of refuge for Queen Mary.

Seton Palace in 1745

101   'Or a nice puckle sows from the Malinshaw – '

After Lord Wharton and his 5000 men ravaged Annandale and other areas in the west of Scotland in September 1547, many barons and clans pledged to Lord Wharton to serve the king of England. One such was Johnstone of Malinshaw, along with sixty-five of his followers.

101   'Fond Folie, sall I be thy Clark? And answer thee ay, with Amen?"

From *A Satire of the Three Estates* by Sir David Lindsay (c.1490-c.1555), in which the poet denounces the abuses of both church and state with an amazing degree of frankness. *The Satire* is an attack on the Three Estates represented in the Parliament of Scotland – the clergy, lords, and burgh representatives – symbolised by the characters Spiritualitie, Temporalitie and Merchant. The poem is one of the best illustrations of the transition from the mediæval morality play to the Elizabethan tragedy and comedy, and is regarded as the first open declaration against Catholicism in Scotland.

101 *'And he took out his little knife*
Loot a' his duddies fa'
And he was the brawest gentleman
That was among them a'...'

From *The Jolly Beggar*, a ballad by King James V (1512-1542).

101 *'Not yet, my Hinnysopps.'*

From *A Brash of Wowing* by William Dunbar (c.1460-c.1520), a comic depiction of a courtship. The indecencies lurking behind some of the strange words are part of the joke, and the peasant manners wink at frisky bawdiness. Much of the humour turns on the language and use of exaggerated terms of endearment which border on nonsense. Dunbar was known for his experimental zeal, sheer whimsicality, and topsy-turvy humour, which could reach 'a height of scurrility...without parallel in English literature'[10].

> *Quote he, 'My claver, my Curledoddy,*
> *My Hinnysops, my sweet Possody,*
> *Be not too rough with your Billy,*
> *Be warm hearted, and not nilly-willy;*
>
> *Your neck as white as whale-bone,*
> *Gives rise and loft to my willy-illy*
> *You break my heart, my bonny one.'[11]*

(Tr.L.R.)

Claver:	clover, which is sweet
Curledoddy:	a sweetmeat or sugar-plum, probably in an obscene sense
Hinnysops:	bread soaked in honey
Possody:	a sheep's head broth, considered a delicacy in Scotland
Billy:	lover or companion

101 *'...before you set up as their Rex Nemorensis.'*

The sanctuary and temple of the goddess Diana was on the shores of Lake Nemorensis, twenty miles south of Rome in the Albian Mountains. The priest of the temple bore the title of *rex*, meaning king, and thus Rex Nemorensis. The worship of Diana was once celebrated with human sacrifices, and the Rex Nemorensis won his position by killing his predecessor in a trial by combat, and thus inheriting like risks.[12/D]

102 *'...a supply train of wagons is due to leave Roxburgh Castle for Hume.'*

Roxburgh Castle was founded by King David I. It was captured by the English in 1174, and changed hands several times over the next several hundred years. In 1460, James II captured the town of Roxburgh and then laid siege to the castle.

While James was watching the discharge of a cannon named 'The Lion', it burst and a piece of shrapnel struck and killed him.

The Queen, Mary of Gueldres, upon hearing the news rushed to camp with her eight-year-old son, and inspired the troops to continue the fight, but they were forced to surrender. Before doing so, however, they dismantled the fortress. 'That the place, which the English held for more than a hundred years, might thenceforth cease to be a centre of rapine and violence, or a cause of future strife between the nations, the victors reduced it to a heap of ruins.'[13]

In 1547, the English army under Protector Somerset built a rectangular fortress near the site of the castle, and left a garrison of 300 soldiers and 200 others under the command of Sir Ralph Bullmer.

Ruins of Roxburgh Castle

103 *'Cry boot and saddle, my dears, and we're off.'*

'Boot and saddle' is a perversion of the French *boute-selle* ('place saddle'), a cavalry signal to mount.

105 *'Sawest not you my oxen, you little, pretty boy? With hemp, with howe, with hemp...'*

From *My Twelve Oxen*, a nursery rhyme of the early 16th century.

105 *'All right, Barbarossa.'*

Frederick Barbarossa (1122-1190) whose name in Italian means 'Red Beard', was a German Holy Roman Emperor and considered one of the greatest and most charismatic leaders of his age.

105 *'Allez-vous-en, allez, allez.'*

Go, you, go go.

105 *...leather powder bags with serpentine and corn powder...*

Serpentine and corn powder are both forms of gunpowder.

Frederick Barbarossa
Chronic of Guelph, c.1179-1191

105 *The English lookout at Hume Castle...*

Hume Castle, founded in the 13th century, crowns a rocky eminence and 'figures like a beacon-tower over all the Merse, forming a picturesque feature in a wide and luxuriant landscape'[14]. A lofty and imposing structure, it defended the surrounding country and was thought to be impregnable. In 1547, however, it was captured by Protector Somerset after stout resistance by Lady Home, whose husband, the 4th Lord Home, died the day before the battle of Pinkie Cleugh.

Hume Castle by William Purser, c.1834

A portcullis (from the French *porte coulissante,* or gliding door) is a latticed grille or gate made of wood, metal or a combination of the two. Portcullises fortified the entrances to many mediæval castles, acting as a last line of defence during time of attack or siege.

Inner Gateway of Edinburgh Castle

106 *...where sat Sir William Grey...*

William Grey, 13th Baron Grey de Wilton (d.1562), was a military commander in the reigns of Henry VIII, Edward VI, and Mary I. Grey distinguished himself in the French campaign of 1544, and was lieutenant of Boulogne in 1546. In 1547, Grey, a field-marshal and captain-general of horse, was at the head of the army and made first charge against the Scots at the Battle of Pinkie Cleugh, where he was injured. His son described Grey's injuries in the battle:s

> *In this battle [Grey] receaved a greate wounde in the mouthe with a pyke, sutche as clave one of his teethe, strake hym thowroghe the tongue, and three fyngers deepe into the rouff of his mouthe: yet notwithstondyng hee poursued owte the chase, wheryn, whot with the aboundance of blood, heate of the weather, and dust of the press, hee had surely been suffocated had not the Duke of Northehumberland, then earle of Warwyck, lyghted and lyfted a fyrcken of ale too hys head, as they passed thowroughe the Scottische camp.[15]*

Grey was charged with the delivery of Hume Castle, and was knighted by Protector Somerset at Berwick, where he remained as governor, Warden of the East Marches, and General of the Northern Parts.

106 *'I with to God I wath thtuck with the Crewth again. Even Boulogne and that damn rhymthter Thurrey wath plain thailing to thith.'*

Henry Howard, Earl of Surrey (c.1517-1547) was an English poet and nobleman. A companion to Henry VIII's natural son, Henry Fitzroy, Surrey spent his youth at Windsor 'with a king's son'[16]. He studied classical and modern literature and begin writing verse at an early age.

In August 1545, Surrey was appointed commander of Guisnes. At the time, Lord Grey was captain of an army called The Crews; but the command was to be transferred to Surrey, while Grey took over command of Boulogne. Surrey, however, after sending letters to King Henry VIII, was appointed commander of Boulogne. It appears there was jealousy between the two men, and 'sinister means'[17] were employed to set the two noblemen at odds. Grey finally superseded Surrey as lieutenant of Boulogne in April 1546.

Henry Howard, Earl of Surrey
by Hans Holbein

In the autumn of 1546, King Henry was known to be dying; nobles close to the throne began a struggle to take control after Henry's death. Surrey asserted his father was entitled to the role of protector during the minority of King Edward, and took steps to prove the superiority of his ancestry over that of the Seymours. Henry, however, became convinced Surrey planned to remove Edward and seize the crown. He was tried, convicted of treason, and beheaded on 19 Jan. 1547.

107 *...to keep no secrets from a cousin of the Earl of Warwick.*

John Dudley, Earl of Warwick, 1st Viscount Lisle, 1st Duke of Northumberland (1504-1553), was an English general, admiral, and politician. In 1542 he was made warden of the Scottish marches, and served as Vice-Admiral and Lord Admiral from 1537 until 1547, during which time he set novel standards of navy organisation and was an innovative commander at sea. Dudley's fleet brought the Earl of Hertford into Scotland in 1544, on his 'horrible expedition of fire and sword'[18], during which many of the southern Scottish monasteries were pillaged and destroyed, and Edinburgh burned. An intimate of Henry VIII during the last years of his reign, he was appointed executor of Henry's will and

John Dudley, Earl of Warwick

a joint regent, along with fifteen others, of young King Edward VI. Dudley was appointed lord-lieutenant of the army going into Scotland in 1547, and the victory at the battle of Pinkie Cleugh is attributed to him.

107 *....a crack like the Eildons parting fell on their ears...*

The Eildon Hills are a triple-crested eminence near Melrose, overlooking Teviotdale. A popular tradition holds the hills, once one mass, were cleft in three by the wizard Michael Scott. 'I can stand on the Eildon Hill,' said Sir Walter Scott, 'and point out forty-three places famous in war and verse.'[19] 'To the east lie the rich lands of the Abbeys of Melrose, Dryburgh, Kelso, and Jedburgh, and on the horizon the classic battlefields of Chevy Chase and Flodden, while, over all breathes the magic genius of Sir Walter, whose honoured ashes rest down there among those of the Dryburgh monks.'[20]

Eildon Hills, seen from 'Scott's View', 2006

111 *'Madre Dios! Caballeros, su ayuda...su venganza! Ladrónes!'*

'Mother God! Gentlemen, your help...revenge! Thieves!'

111 *'He sido mortificado, insultado – hombre – me hecho hazmerreir! – Mirame!'*

'I was mortified and insulted – man – made me a laughing stock! – Look at me!'

112 *'Un hidalgo no debe a otro que a Dios, y al Rei nada.'*

*'A nobleman owes nothing to anyone other than God,
and he owes the King nothing.'*

112 *'Mas veen quatro ojos que no dos.'*

'Four eyes see more than two.'

112 *'Ay, ay, dios. Y cuando...'*

' Oh, oh god. And when...'

112 *'Pero – como asi?'*

'But – how so?'

113 **Phrases floated to his lordship: 'defecto de boca...quiere decir 'ideal'...**

'...defect of the mouth...he means 'ideal'...

113 **...only ceased when entangled with the unfortunate word 'embarazar.'**

The word 'embarazar' has three meanings: to embarrass, to make pregnant, and to hamper or restrict, as in one is hampered while pregnant. Myles is attempting to explain Grey's outburst, while also smoothing over any perceived insult to Don Louis: *'Grey has a mouth injury. He meant to say, 'ideal' [not 'idiot']. His defect is impairing his speech.'* [21]

115 *'Aunque manso tu sabuesso, no le muerdas en el beco.'*

*'Even though your hound dog is tame,
do not bite him in the nose.'*
~ Spanish proverb

115 *'Hay un otro, Señor Luis. Ruin señor cria ruin servidor.'*

*'There is another, Lord Luis:
A bad master creates a bad servant.'*
~ Spanish proverb

118 **...passementerie glittering.**

Passementerie are elaborate trimmings and edgings of applied braid, gold or silver cord, embroidery, colored silk, or beads for clothing or furnishings.

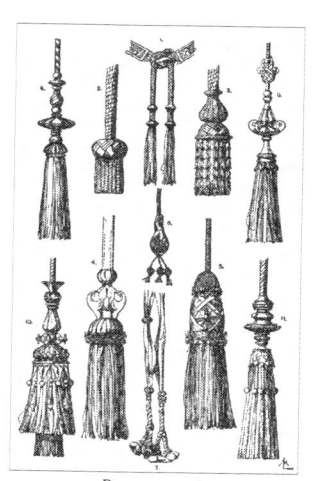

Passementerie

Chapter VI: Forced Move for a Minor Piece

Buke of Chess: Tract 3, Chapter 7

*After your pawn's first move, from point to point your course
shall be forward and never pass diagonally except to slay his adversary
which is like to be passing yon, angle-wise, to despoil another poor man.[1]*

120   ...the entire English troop bound and frozen outside Melrose Abbey...

Melrose Abbey by William Smith, c.1905

David I founded Melrose as a Cistercian abbey in 1136. It was slowly built on a
scale of increasing magnificence, but because of its location lying on the direct
road to England it was frequently assaulted. In 1544, English forces destroyed a
great part of the abbey and defaced the tombs of the Douglases buried there. In
1545, the English again pillaged Melrose Abbey; on their retreat the 6th Earl of

Angus and Scott of Buccleuch avenged the ravaged country and defaced tombs at the Battle of Ancrum Moor. Though donations were given to rebuild, the Abbey never recovered from the damage suffered. Melrose Abbey is considered amongst the most beautiful religious houses in the United Kingdom, and is known for many carved decorative details. It was 'beyond doubt the most beautiful structure of which Scotland could boast in the middle ages'[2].

120   *Sir George Douglas, breakfasting in his castle at Dalkeith...*

William de Graham, an Anglo-Norman knight, was given the manor of Dalkeith by David I; it was held by the Grahams until the death of John de Graham in the 14th century. His sister, Marjory, inherited the estate which was then conveyed to the Douglases upon her marriage into their family. Froissart, in his *Chronicles*, relays an account of 'one of the most chivalrous episodes of the wars of this turbulent age'[3]: James, 2nd Earl of Douglas, by his gallantry captured the pennon of Sir Henry Percy, to Percy's mortification. Douglas threatened to place the pennon on the tower of Dalkeith. This taunt led to the battle of Otterburn (1388) where Douglas was killed.

In 1503, Dalkeith was the site of the first meeting between James IV and his fourteen-year old English bride, Margaret Tudor. The king, with 'all the ardour of a youthful lover, eager to honour the lady of his heart'[4], greeted her 'with knightly courtesy, and passed the day in her company'[5].

In 1642, the castle was sold by William Douglas, 9th Earl of Morton, to Francis Scott, 2nd Earl of Buccleuch, for the purposes of raising money to assist Charles I in the Civil War. The current Dalkeith Palace was significantly rebuilt in the 18th century, and thus bears little resemblance to its predecessor.

Dalkeith

121 *'Today the palace, tomorrow the oubliette and the elegiac distich.'*

An oubliette (from *oublier*, to forget) is an architectural term used to describe a secret dungeon or cell in a castle only accessible through a trap door of another dungeon, or a concealed passage leading from a dungeon to a river or a moat, into which the bodies of prisoners could be secretly conveyed.

An elegiac distich is a short, mournful, meditative poem expressing sorrow or lamentation in alternating verse of hexameter with pentameter, giving this style of poem a particular character. From the beginning of the 16th century in England, the word 'elegy' has been used to describe a funeral song or lament.

121 *'Je suis oiseau: voyez mes ailes...Je suis souris; vivent les rats.'*

> *'Je suis oiseau: voyez mes ailes.'*
> 'I am a bird, see my wings.'
> ' *Je suis souris: vivent les rats.'*
> 'I am a mouse: long live the rats.'

From the fable, *The Bat and the Two Weasels:*

> *A Bat fell to the ground and was caught by a Weasel, and was just going to be killed and eaten when it begged to be let go. The Weasel said he couldn't do that because he was an enemy of all birds on principle.*
> *'Oh, but,' said the Bat, 'I'm not a bird at all: I'm a mouse.'*
> *'So you are,' said the Weasel, 'now I come to look at you'; and he let it go.*
> *Some time after this the Bat was caught in just the same way by another Weasel, and, as before, begged for its life. 'No,' said the Weasel, 'I never let a mouse go by any chance.'*
> *'But I'm not a mouse,' said the Bat; 'I'm a bird.'*
> *'Why, so you are,' said the Weasel; and he too let the Bat go.*
> *The moral: Look and see which way the wind blows before you commit yourself.*[6]

121 *'Rather long, but I'll spare you the clay and disinter the lotus.'*

To disinter is to take out, as from a grave, or to bring from obscurity into view. In this context, meaning to get directly to the matter at hand.

Usually referred to as a lotus though it is actually a water lily, *Nelumbium speciosum*, the Sacred Bean, was a favoured flower of the ancient world. Styled 'Lily Rose of the Nile' by Herodotus, it was made into wreaths by women as an emblem of fertility, and decorated the heads of Isis and Osiris. It was sacred in Egypt, Africa, India, China, Japan, Persia, and Asiatic Russia. Lotus seeds are about the size of an acorn with a taste more delicate than an almond. The ancient

Egyptian mode of sowing the plant was by enclosing each seed in a ball of clay and throwing it into the water.[7/D]

The Sacred Bean
(Nelumbium speciosum)

122 'I'm King of the Fidlers and swear 'tis a truth.'

From *Robin Hood's Birth, Breeding, Valour, and Marriage*, a 12th- or 13th-century ballad about the celebrated outlaw, 'the prince of all robbers, the gentlest of thieves'[8].

> *This battle was fought*
> *near Tutbury town,*
> *When the bagpipes baited the bull,*
> *I'm King of the Fidlers,*
> *and swear 'tis a truth,*
> *And call him that doubts it a gull.*

The quoted stanza from the ballad refers to the ancient, barbaric practice of bull-baiting. A bull, with his 'horns and ears cropped, his tail docked, and his nose filled with pepper'[9], was turned loose for the minstrels to pursue after their day performing at court. After further cruelties the carcass was handed over to the minstrels, for their pleasure or profit.

123 'Oh Douglas, oh Douglas, Tender and true...'

From *The Buke of Howlat* by Richard Holland (stanza 31):

> *Off the warrior Douglas went to write an address,*
> *The arms of ancestry honourable, aye,*
> *Which often gladly assisted the Bruce in his distress,*
> *Therefore he blessed that blood bold in action.*
> *Read the writ of their work to your witness,*
> *The said Pursuivant's guide was harnessed, I guess.*
> *Embroidered with one green tree, goodly and gay,*
> *That bore branches on breadth cheerful of hue,*
> *On ilk bough till embrace written in a bill was,*
> *O Douglas, O Douglas, tender and true!*[10]

(Tr.L.R.)

124 The spirit of Ballaggan Keep...

Ballaggan Castle was approximately one mile northwest of Drumlanrig; there are now no remains.

> *When King Robert Bruce was lying with the Scottish army near Glenwharg, and the English army at the moat in Balagan Holm, a*

man named Hunter, carrying a trumpet, and another named M'Gachen, bearing a pair of colours, came from the Scotch army to the head of the glen called Balagan; the one blew the trumpet and the other flourished the colours in sight of the English army, who, apprehending that the Scottish forces were immediately upon them, were so much affrighted that they fled out of the country. For which achievement King Robert gave Hunter the lands of Balagan, and to M'Gachen the lands of Derwhat.[11]

124   ...this wild cormorant, this acidulous osprey of ours?

A cormorant (*Palacrocorax,* 'bald-headed raven') is a medium-sized seabird. The cormorant was a significant symbol of true and regal life. In Milton's *Paradise Lost,* Satan disguised himself as a cormorant at the top of the Tree of Life in his first attempt to deceive Eve.

Phalacrocora aristolis

An osprey (*Pandion haliaetus*), also known as a sea hawk or fish eagle, is a fish-eating bird of prey. It is a large raptor, reaching 60 cm (2') in length with a 2m (6.5') wingspan. The osprey is depicted as a white eagle in heraldry. There was a mediæval belief fish were so mesmerised by the osprey they turned belly-up in surrender.

124   ...these were set with Spanish azulejos and covered with rugs from Turkey and the Levant...the chests and tables...carried a pellicle of Aldine folios.

Azulejos are Spanish blue glazed tiles[12/D], or more broadly, an earthenware Spanish tile, painted and enamelled in rich colors and having a metallic lustre. In the 16th century, azulejos were used in large quantities to cover walls and floors.

Pandion haleaetus

The Levant (from French, *levant*, a rising) was a term used to describe the Mediterranean regions eastward from Italy, the direction from which the sun rises.

'Aldine folios' were works issued by the celebrated Aldine Press of Venice. The era between 1490-1597 is considered an epoch in the annals of printing whereby the Aldine Press elevated publication practices and introduced the use of italics. The firm published first editions of the Greek and Roman classics, and corrected texts of the modern classic works of Petrarch, Boccaccio, and Dante. Because Aldine editions were prized for their intrinsic value, handsome exteriors, correctness of typography, and innate beauty, demand for them induced printers to begin issuing counterfeits.

124   *...even if gold mines sprang beneath his feet, like Olwen's trefoils...*

Olwen is the heroine of the Welsh tale *Culhwch and Olwen,* believed to be the earliest Arthurian romance. Found in the Red Book of Hergest, the chief repository of Welsh literature (1375-1425), the story was translated by Lady Charlotte Guest in the mid-19th century and published under the title *Mabinogion* (Welsh, *mabinog,* a bard's apprentice).

> *The maiden was clothed in a robe of flame-coloured silk, and about her neck was a collar of ruddy gold, on which were precious emeralds and rubies. More yellow was her hair than the flower of the broom, and her skin was whiter than the foam of the wave, and fairer were her hands and her fingers than the blossoms of the wood-anemone amidst the spray of the meadow fountain. The eye of a trained hawk, the glance of the three-mewed falcon was not brighter than hers. Her bosom was more snowy white than the breast of the white swan, her cheek was redder than the reddest roses. Whoso beheld her were filled with her love. Four white trefoils sprang up wherever she trod. And therefore was she called Olwen.*[13]

Culhwch Riding into King Arthur's Hall

125   *...all the apparatus which enable him, ne plus ultra, to talk.*

Ne plus ultra is the highest point, as of excellence or achievement.

125 *Like the enchanted garden of Jannes, tenanted by daemons...*

Jannes and Jambres were the Pharaoh's magicians who contended with Moses and Aaron in the Book of Exodus, and are also of legend in the Qur'an. They infected their funerary garden with cruel demons.

125 *Episodes from his career in the Princess Mary's household...*

Queen Mary I by Master John, 1554

Princess Mary (later, Queen Mary I; 1516-1558) was the only surviving child of Henry VIII by his first wife, Catherine of Aragon. She was a favourite of her father during her youth, yet when Henry sought to divorce Catherine, he treated Mary harshly and she was separated from her mother for nine years. She was removed from court and treated as a bastard, and on the birth of Anne Boleyn's daughter she was sent to Hatfield to act as lady-in-waiting to her half-sister.

After Anne Boleyn's execution, Mary sought to reconcile with her father, and signed an act of submission acknowledging Henry as 'Supreme Head of the Church of England under Christ'[14], repudiating the Pope's authority, and acknowledging the marriage between her father and mother 'was by God's law and man's law incestuous and unlawful'[15]. After this period she spent most of her time at the royal palaces of Hatfield, Beaulieu, Newhall, Richmond, and Hunsdon. She was on good terms with her stepmother, Catherine Parr, her father's sixth and final wife. Three years before Henry's death he restored her to her place in succession, but under conditions of his will.

Under the reign of her younger brother Edward VI, Mary lived in retirement. She ascended to the throne upon his death in 1553.

127 'H for Henri, D for Diane de Poitiers!'

Henri II (1519-1559) became king of France in March 1547. Prior to ascending to the throne, he married Catherine de' Medici at the age of fourteen. The following year he became romantically involved with Diane de Poitiers (1499-1566), the thirty-five year old widow of Louis de Brézé, count de Maulevrier. Henri's accession to the throne gave rise to a veritable revolution at court, increasing the power of the constable, Anne Montmorency, the brothers de Guise, and, especially, of Diane de Poitiers, who wielded considerable power behind the scenes, even signing royal documents.

Henri II by François Clouet, c.1547   *Diane de Poiters by unknown artist*

128 Belowstairs, even among the crowded majolica ware...

In the 15th century, the term majolica referred to lustreware, a type of pottery or porcelain with a metallic glaze.

129 'How can thou float...without feather or fin.'

From *The Tale of the Paddock and the Mouse* by Robert Henryson (c.1425-c.1500):

> *'I have great wonder' quoth the silly Mouse,*
> *'How can thou float without feather or fin?*
> *This river is so deep and dangerous,*
> *Methink that thou should drowned be therein*
> *Tell me, therefore, what faculty or gin*
> *Thou has to bring thee oure this water?'*

Chapter VII: A Variety of Mating Replies

The Buke of Ye Chess: Tract 2, Chapter 5

*For truth, the Rook into his first move...he may not pass nor bestir from
his site, while knight or pawn is standing too near, and in midfield, if he
be placed still, to four points he passes at his will...Two rooks may a
king alone put down, And deprive him of his life and his crown.*[1]

Meaning a powerful Rook should not be wasted until the lesser pieces are moved.

1. Play with a Rook Proves Dangerous

131   Mr. Liddell was lively as a frog, his small face niellated with gold dust...

Niello-work (Italian, *niello*, from Low Latin,
nigellum, 'black enamel') was a method of
producing delicate ornamentation on silver or
gold plates by engraving the surface and filling
in the lines with a black metallic amalgam. The
art of niello-work was practiced by all of the
great goldsmiths of the mediæval period. The
art, aside from the beauty of the works
produced, led the way to the   invention of
printing from engravings on metal plates.

*Morovingian Brooch, 7th century
Gilded Silver and Niello*

134   '...I shouldn't ask Medusa to share...'

In Greek mythology, Medusa (the Queen) was one of the three Gorgons, along
with her sisters Stheno (the Mighty) and Euryale (the Far-springer), monsters of
the underworld with hissing serpents for hair, brazen claws, short wings, and the
tusks of a boar. Medusa's serpent-entwined head was so awful its appearance
turned all beholders to stone.

135 'Malmsey or Canary?'

Malmsey is a strong, sweet wine, originally made at Napoli di Malvasia, Greece. The name was corrupted into *malmasia*, and then the English form, *malmsey*. Originally made from grapes grown in the islands of the Ægean and the Levant, it was later produced in Spain, Madeira, and the Azores. Canary is a dry white wine produced in the Canary Islands, primarily on the island of Tenerife. The name Canary was, at one time, applied generally to dry white wines, which were often seasoned with sugar, cinnamon, nutmeg, roasted apples, and eggs.

137 ...Mariotta found that, like tesserae in a mosaic...

Tesserae are individual tiles in a mosaic, made from materials such as marble, precious stones, ivory, glass, or wood.

138 The St. Andrew's Cross; the crest (argent, a phoenix azure)...

The St. Andrew's cross, or saltire (from the French, *sautoir,* and Latin, *saltare,* to leap) is one of the eight great ordinaries in heraldry, a figure of simple outline and geometrical form. The St. Andrew's cross is in the form of an X, and appears in the flag of Scotland.

In heraldry, argent is tincture of silver; azure is tincture with the color blue.

The most familiar story of the phœnix as an emblem of immortality is found in the *Physiologus*, a collection of some fifty Christian allegories dating from the 2nd century and much read in the Middle Ages. In the legend, the phœnix subsists on air for 500 years, after which, lading his wings with spices, he flies to the temple at Heliopolis and is burned upon the altar, from which a new, young phœnix arises, reborn to live again. Herodotus tells the legend of an Arabian bird, resembling an eagle with golden and red plumage, who, bearing his father embalmed in a ball of myrrh, buried him in the temple of the sun. According to Pliny in his *Natural Histories*, the phœnix , at the close of his long life, builds a nest of twigs and cassia and frankincense on which he dies; from his corpse a worm generates into a young phœnix.

A direct translation of CONTRA VITAM RECTI MORIEMUR is, *'We will die against a virtuous life'*. A more liberal translation is, *'In spite of life's efforts to thwart us, we will die honourably'*. Or, *'We will prevail and remain virtuous'.*[2]

139 *Having buried her husband at Biggar, Lady Jenny...*

Founded in 1545 by Malcolm Fleming, 3rd Lord Fleming, the collegiate parish church at Biggar (Gaelic, *Bigthir*, 'soft land') is one of the last of Scotland's pre-Reformation churches. Erected near Boghall Castle on the site of an old building dedicated to St. Nicholas, the church was unfinished at the time of Lord Fleming's death at the Battle of Pinkie Cleugh.

Bigger Collegiate Church by Francis Grose, 1789

139 *Of the older children, Margaret had moved...*

Margaret Fleming (b.1536) was the daughter of Malcolm Fleming, 3rd Lord Fleming (c.1494-1547), and Janet Stewart, a natural daughter of King James IV. Both her father and her husband, Robert Graham, Master of Graham, died at the Battle of Pinkie Cleugh. Margaret was pregnant at the time of her husband's death, giving birth posthumously to John Graham, who would succeed to the earldom upon the death of his grandfather in 1571. A great-grandson of King James IV, he became an important member of Scottish nobility in support of Queen Mary.

139 ...between her late husband's home at Mugdock...

Mugdock, a barony in Stirlingshire, was acquired in the early 13th century by David de Graham, ancestor of the noble family of Montrose. William, 3rd Lord of Graham, sat in the first parliament of King James IV in 1488 and fell at the Battle of Flodden (1513). His son, William Graham, 2nd Earl of Montrose (d.1571), was an ambassador to France in 1535, and a member of the commission of regency during James V's absence in France for his first marriage. After James V died in 1542, Montrose voted for the election of Arran as regent and was a leading member of the Regent's Council.

Mugdock Castle is located six miles from Glasgow, on the southwest corner of Mugdock Loch. Originally built in the 14th century and expanded in the 15th century, the castle had four towers connected by a high curtain wall, enclosing an inner courtyard which contained various stone buildings dating from the 16th century, including a Great Hall and accommodations for visiting nobility.

140 'Well, she's not exactly tolling the passing bell yet...'

A passing bell, also known a dead bell, was a handbell rung on behalf of the recently deceased. Its customary use in Scotland is recorded as early as 1454. It was rung to announce a death and funeral arrangements, to seek prayers for the deceased's soul, and to drive away evil spirits.

141 From the spicebooth...some brazil for dyeing her new wool.

A clue as to what Sybilla meant when she said to Janet Buccleuch on page 20: *'Did you try some brazil on your curtains?'* Brazilwood is a dense, orange-red heartwood tree; its wood yields a deep red dye called brazilin. The country of Brazil was so named because of its abundance of the wood.

141 ...paid him for all the verses of 'When Tay's Bank'...

The Ballad of Tay's Bank is one of the oldest known Scots ballads, written in the late 15th century or early 16th century and attributed to King James IV.

> When Tay's Bank was blooming bright
> With blossoms young and broad,
> Be that river that run down right,
> Under the branches, I waited.
> The merle spoke with all her might
> And mirth in the morning made,
> Throw solace, sound, and seemly sight,
> Forthwith a song, I said.[3]   (Tr.L.R.)

The heroine of the verse is Margaret Drummond, the favourite mistress of King James IV. In the poem, her royal wooer steals away from Stobhall Castle to keep a tryst with his fair damsel in the sweetly inviting seclusion of the beautiful, wooded banks of the river Tay. Impatient to enjoy his 'diamond of delight', he arrives early and wiles away his waiting moments by singing verses to her beauty and to the scenery: the flowers and foliage in full colour, and the lark, merle, and nightingale in full song.

Margaret Drummond (c.1472-1501), the youngest of the five daughters of John, 1st Lord Drummond, was 'a lady of rare perfections and singular beauty'[4]. According to some historians, King James was so deeply enamoured of Margaret they were secretly married without the knowledge of the Scottish nobles or his council. Margaret gave birth to their daughter, Lady Margaret Stewart, in 1497. Despite James's passionate affections for Margaret, the nobility urged the King to make an alliance with England and procure peace by way of marriage to Margaret Tudor, which James resisted.

In 1501, while residing at Drummond Castle, Margaret and two of her sisters, Sybilla and Euphemia, Lady Fleming, were served a poisoned dish at breakfast and 'died in great torture'[5] soon afterwards. It is thought Margaret was murdered by those nobles who saw her as an obstacle to the King's marriage to Margaret Tudor, whom he did marry in 1503, more than a year after the death of Margaret Drummond.

141 *'Because it spouts sweet venom in their ears and makes their minds all effeminate, you know.'*

From *A Political Homily* by John Bellenden (c.1492-c.1557):

> *Show now what kind of sound is musical*
> *And most seemly to valiant chevaliers;*
> *As a thunderous blast of trumpet warlike,*
> *The spirits of men to hardy courage steers.*
> *So singing, fiddling, and piping is unbecoming,*
> *For men of honour, and of high estate;*
> *Because it spouts sweet venom in their ears,*
> *And makes their minds all effeminate.*[6]

(Tr.L.R.)

141 *She was dissuaded from buying a channel stone, which Tom, no curling enthusiast, refused utterly to carry...*

Curling is a sport in which players slide large stones across a rink or channel of ice towards a mark called the tee. The game is similar to bowls or shuffleboard. Possibly originating in the Netherlands, the game has been extremely popular in Scotland since at least the 16th century. The first known reference to the game in Scotland is from 1541. A modern curling stone weighs between 17-20 kg (38-44 pounds) and is made of highly polished granite. An early channel stone would have been a boulder taken from a river, fashioned by nature alone.

The Curlers by Roger Griffith, 1860

141 ...and got a toothpick in its case instead.

The most usual means of dental hygiene of the period was with toothpick and rinse. The wealthy in the 16th century kept gold and silver toothpicks, some with precious stones, as luxury accessories. Small toothpick cases ensured the security of one's toothpick and allowed them to be carried on the body. Giovanni Della Casa, in his 1558 book on etiquette, *Galateo of Manners and Behaviours,* states it was considered impolite to pick your teeth prior to the dishes being removed from the table, to carry the toothpick in your mouth ('like a bird going to build his nest'), to stick it behind your ear, or carry a tooth-pick case 'hanging down from their necks: for besides it is an odd sight for a gentleman to produce anything of that kind from his bosom like some strolling pedlar...and I can see no reason why the same persons might not as well display a silver spoon hanging about their necks'.

141 ...among the mute sea of her parcels, like Arion among his fishes.

Arion (c.600 BC) was a Greek poet credited with inventing the dithyramb, a form of chorale honouring Dionysus. A celebrated musician, he travelled to Sicily and Italy to exhibit his skill, where he gained fame and amassed a fortune. While traveling home, the sailors aboard his ship decided to take his treasure for themselves and insisted he should die, either by his own hand or by casting himself into the sea. Arion chose the latter, but was permitted to sing a dirge accompanied by his lyre prior to throwing himself overboard. Instead of perishing, he was miraculously carried safely to shore by a dolphin charmed by his music. His lyre and the dolphin were then placed among the constellations.

142 *'Well. Ce n'est pas tout de boire; it faut sortir d'ici,' said the Dowager.*

"Tis time we were thinking of something else than drinking.'

From the fable *The Fox and the Goat*:

> *A fox once journeyed, and for company*
> *A certain bearded, horned goat had he;*
> *Which goat no further than his nose could see*
> *The fox was deeply versed in trickery.*
> *These travellers did thirst compel*
> *To seek the bottom of a well.*
> *There, having drunk enough for two,*
> *Says fox, My friend, what shall we do?*
> *Tis time that we were thinking*
> *Of something else than drinking.*

142 *There's a cloud over the sun, and if the saffron gets wet, Tom, you'll be* or *as well as* gules, *and very likely rampant as well.'*

In heraldry, 'or' is gold, 'gules' is red, and 'rampant' is upright or rearing on hind legs, as the lion on the Royal Arms of the Kingdom of Scotland.

143 *'That's twice he's breenged through his betters today.'*

Breenged is to barge in without thinking.

144 *...the archer raised his longbow smoothly to the sky, nocked his arrow...*

A longbow is tall, roughly equal to the height of the person who uses it. The longbow originated among the Welsh, predating the Norman Conquest of 1066. The English copied it in the 12th to 16th centuries.[6]

146 *'Terregles, Kirkgunzeon, Moffatdale, Lockerbie, Ecclefechan...'*

A branch of the Anglo-Norman family of Heriz first arrived in Scotland during the reign of David I (1124-1153), and Sir John Herice received a charter for the lands of Travereglis (Terregles) in 1359. The family continued to acquire lands in the Border region of Annandale. The title was conferred on Sir Herbert Herries of Terregles in 1489; he was a member of Parliament. His son, Andrew Herries, 2nd Lord Herries, was slain at Flodden, along with four of his brothers. His only son, William Herries, 3rd Lord Herries, died in 1543 and was succeeded by his three daughters, Agnes, Katherine, and Janet.

146   *'I knew you were going to sound like Grandfather Blairquhan.'*

James Kennedy of Blairquhan (born c.1501; pronounced blair-whahn, with a silent Q) was the maternal grandfather of Agnes. He married Agnes Murray in approximately 1525. They had one daughter, Katherine, Agnes's mother.

The Gardens at Terregles, c.1873

2. Check and Cross Check

149 *'...to match against him, perch or clout.'*

Perch and clout are different forms of archery competition. Perch is a pole used in papingo shooting where the target is affixed on a perch and shot at almost vertically. Clout is a contest of calculated trajectory in which arrows are shot upward and fall downward into targets on the ground.[8]

151 *'That's what makes it unco knotty...'*

Unco is so unusual as to be surprising; uncanny. Knotty is difficult to understand or solve.

151 *'Dod, Sybilla: if you want to know, I'm in the hell of a jawboxy mess.'*

'Dod' is a euphemistic interjection for God. Jawbox is a kitchen sink.

151 *'Seymour's Lord High Suleyman the Magnificent...'*

Suleiman I (1594-1566), 'The Magnificent', was the longest-reigning Sultan of the Ottoman Empire. He was renowned for his organisation of the clerical class, improvement of the empire's civil and military administration, and improvement of the feudal system. He was also famed as a poet, writing under the pseudonym 'Muhbbr'.

152 *'Make the Philosopher's Stone, dear.'*

Suleiman I by Hans Emsworth, 1549

Alchemists of the Middle Ages toiled in vain to discover the secret of transmuting base metals into gold or silver, and the means of prolonging human life. The science of alchemy began in Egypt, and it was the Arabs who brought alchemy to Europe, where it became entangled with the subtleties of scholastic philosophy. Roger Bacon (1214-1294) believed in the convertibility of inferior metals into the perfect metal, gold, by the introduction of the Philosopher's Stone, a substance a thousand-thousand times more perfect than gold. Paracelsus (1493-1541) held the elements were representations of earth, air, water, and fire, along with a 5th element common to the four, the quintessence of creation. He cultivated the dogma there is only one prime element of things, considered to be the universal solvent. Once discovered, it would be at once the Philosopher's Stone, the universal medicine, and the irresistible solvent. This grand elixir could confer immortal youth on the one who quaffed the golden draught.

152   '...and makes frisky old gentlemen senex bis puer...'

Senex bis puer: 'an old man is a boy again'[9], or 'an old man is twice a child' (Latin, *senex*, old man, and *puer*, child). Depending on the context, the saying can indicate man's reversion to a second childhood through dementia (*senility*) or an old man becoming boyish, as old age is considered a man's second childhood. Here, meaning an old man will become frisky again, as when a young man.[10]

153   '...and the Lee penny never out of the house.'

The Lee Penny is a Scottish amulet used to cure fevers, and for other healing purposes. According to tradition, the stone was brought from the Holy Land by Sir Simon Lockhart, 2nd of Lee (1300–1371), a Scottish knight who accompanied Sir James 'The Good' Douglas in his attempt to carry the heart of Robert the Bruce to the Holy Land.

154   ...a bloated Saturnalia, sodden, sottish and leering of voice.

Saturnalia was a seven-day Roman festival beginning on December 17th, and renowned for its unrestrained licence and revelry. Sottish is stupefied from drink; senseless and very foolish.

154   'Buy a rare pippin!' said a voice in her ear.

A pippin is a red and yellow dessert apple.

156   ...and the Durham and York and Newcastle boys, and the landknechts...

Landsknechte by Daniel Hopfer, 1530

Landsknechte were troops of German foot-soldiers formed by Emperor Maximilian I in 1487, and considered to be the finest fighting troops in Europe. They served as well-organized mercenaries and played a distinguished part in the wars of the 15th and 16th centuries. The term *Landsknecthe* was used by

Maximilian to distinguish his troop, the 'men of the land', from the Swiss 'men of the mountain'.

156 '...end up like St. James with their knees hard as camels...'

James the Just, first Bishop of Jerusalem (d.62), was an important figure in Early Christianity. An account of James's ascetic lifestyle:

After the apostles, James the brother of the Lord surnamed the Just was made head of the Church at Jerusalem. Many indeed are called James. This one was holy from his mother's womb. He drank neither wine nor strong drink, ate no flesh, never shaved or anointed himself with ointment or bathed. He alone had the privilege of entering the Holy of Holies, since indeed he did not use woolen vestments but linen and went alone into the temple and prayed in behalf of the people, insomuch that his knees were reputed to have acquired the hardness of camels' knees.[11]

James the Just

156 '...by the Old Man of the Mountains himself, obviously, the Sheikh-al-jebal, twanging his hemp instead of eating it.'

The Old Man of the Mountain is Hassan-i Sabbah, the leader of the Assassins, an order of Nizari Ismailis existing from around 1092 to 1265. Posing a strong military threat to authority in the Persian territories, the Nizari Ismailis, also called Hashishin, captured and inhabited many mountain fortresses under the leadership of Hassan-i Sabbah. In pursuit of their religious and political goals, the Hashishin adopted various military strategies popular in the Middle Ages. One such method was assassination, the selective elimination of prominent rival figures. The murders of political adversaries were usually carried out in public spaces, creating intimidation for other possible enemies.

It is unknown how Hassan-i-Sabbah was able to get his 'Fida'i' to perform with such fervent loyalty. One theory, possibly the most well known but also the most criticised, comes from the observations of Marco Polo during his travels to the Orient. He describes how the 'Old Man of the Mountain' (Sabbah) would drug his young followers with hashish, lead them to a 'Paradise', and then claim only he had the means to allow for their return. Perceiving Sabbah was either a prophet or some kind of magic man, his disciples were fully committed to his cause and willing to carry out his every request. The word 'assassin' comes from 'hashishin' (literally, 'users of hashish') as a result of the group's connection to political murders.

156 *'...except that Culter, Jerome bless his childlike head...'*

St. Jerome (Eusebius Sophronius Hieronymus, c.347 420 AD), is regarded as the most learned and eloquent of the Latin Fathers. While at the monastery he ran in Bethlehem, he translated the Old Testament directly from the Hebrew, with the aid of Jewish scholars. This Latin translation became the Vulgate, or authorised version. He is considered the greatest Christian scholar of his age. In addition to his translation, his commentaries are particularly valuable, and he was a pioneer in the field of biblical archaeology.

156 *'For a humanist,' she said, 'you're very scathing on the subject of virtue.'*

St. Jerome in His Study
by Antonio de Fabriano II, 1451

Humanism was a specific movement of thought in Western Europe in the late 15th century, which assigned a predominant interest in the affairs of men, an insistence on the dignity of humanity, and the secular value of independence. The movement, essentially a revolt against intellectual and ecclesiastical authority, broke through the mediæval tradition of scholastic theology and devoted itself to the study of the ancient classics, emphasising individual expression and the use of reason.

156 *'For one thing, you shouldn't confuse stolidity and self-control.'*

Stolidity is dullness or the state of being phlegmatic, dependable, impassive, or revealing little emotion.

157 *'...I wonder how many that classic bêtise has driven to the river...'*

Bêtise is foolishness.

157 *'Pax! Leave me some pride'*

Pax (Latin, 'peace') is a common expression used by children during games to ask for a truce, like saying, 'Uncle!'[12]

157 *'Pretend at least that you wouldn't collapse in a delirium of joy as I dance a vuelta on the widdy.'*

In Spanish, *vuelta* is a turn. *La vuelta quebrada* is a dance movement where everything is done is such a way as to give the impression of a smooth, oily roll. Widdy is a Scottish and English dialect term for a hangman's noose.

157 *'Si vis pingere, pinge sonum, as Echo rudely remarked.'*

'If you would paint my likeness, paint sound.'

From a poem by Decimus Magnus Ausonius (c.310-394), a Latin poet and teacher. In Greek mythology, Echo was a mountain nymph who loved her own voice.

To a Painting of Echo (In Echo Pictum)

Fond painter, why dost thou essay to limn my face and vex a goddess whom eyes never saw? I am the daughter of Air and Speech, mother of empty utterance, in that I have a voice without a mind. From their dying close I bring back failing strains and in mimicry repeat the words of strangers with my own. I am Echo, dwelling in the recesses of your ears: and if thou wouldst paint my likeness, paint sound.

Echo
by Helen Stratton, 1915

158 *'Well, you'd qualify for M. Rabelais's next Almanac...'*

François Rabelais (c.1490-1553), was a French humourist, called 'the great jester of France'[13], and the 'comic Homer'[14]. He became a monk at age nine, and was educated at the convent of Seuillé and the monastery of La Baumette. He abandoned monastic life in 1530 to study medicine. In 1532, he moved to Lyons to publish his work and became involved with the *Société Angélique*, a company of broad thought and advanced opinions. He is considered one of the great humourists, reveling in 'foulness and filth'[15], and a 'riotous license of mirth, which is restrained neither by decency nor by reverence'[16]. Calvin, in a letter dated 1533, condemns Rabelais's *Pantagruel* as obscene.

François Rabelais

In addition to writing the five-book series *Gargantua and Pantagruel*, Rabelais began publishing an almanac in 1533. The almanac was a long series of publications spanning eighteen years.

158 *'Your loof, lady.'*

The loof is the palm of the hand.

159 *'Well it's a poor apologue, I agree,' he said...*

An apologue (from Greek *apologos*, 'long speech') is a fable or allegorical story intended as a pleasant vehicle meant to convey a moral doctrine or useful lesson, and more particularly a story where the actors are animals or inanimate objects. Æsop's fables are examples of apologues.

159

Li jalous	*The jealous*
Envious	*envious*
de cor rous	*of black heart*
morra	*will die*
et li dous	*and a sweet*
savourous	*savorous love*
amourous	*will be*
m'aura...	*there for me...[17]*

From one or more *chansons de mal-mariée*, traditional French songs reflecting the domestic reality of male dominance, in which a discontented wife or fiancée imagines her unsatisfactory spouse dying and being replaced by a more romantic love. These songs date from the late 12th or early 13th century and are mostly anonymous.

159 *'My measures are mad. They prick, they prance, as princes that were woud...'*

> *Then out they raid to all in a forceful rush,*
> *This courtly King, and all his comely host,*
> *His stalwart banner breathed upon high,*
> *And out they blew with threatening and clamorous boast,*
> *That lady and her lineage should be lost.*
> *They cry on high their war-cry wonder loud:*
> *Thus come they keenly carping on the cost;*
> *They prick, they prance, as princes that were mad.[18]*   (Tr.L.R.)

From the poem *King Hart* by Gavin Douglas (c.1474-1522), Bishop of Dunkeld and uncle of Archibald Douglas, 6th Earl of Angus. *King Hart* was his last poem, written prior to the age of forty, before the loss of two of his brothers at the battle of Flodden, and the political intrigue which would dominate his later life. *King Hart*, a 900+ line poem in eight-line stanzas, is a dream-allegory of the human heart in its struggle with the temptations of the flesh. A synopsis from Pinkerton's *Ancient Scottish [sic] Poems:*

The mystical king is first represented in the bloom of youthhood, with his lusty attendants, the attributes or qualities of youth; next is pictured forth the Palace of Pleasure, nearby the castle of King Hart, with its lovely inhabitants. Queen Pleasance, with the help of her ladies, assails King Hart's castle and takes him and most of his servitors prisoners. Pity at last releases them, and they assail Queen Pleasance, and vanquish her and her ladies in turn. King Hart then weds Queen Pleasance, and solaces himself long in her delicious castle. So far is man's dealings with pleasure; but now, when King Hart is past mid-age, comes another scene. For Age, arriving at the castle of Queen Pleasance, insists for admittance, which he gains. So King Hart takes leave of Youthhead with much sorrow. Age is no sooner admitted, than Conscience also comes to the castle and forces entrance, beginning to chide the King, whilst Wit and Reason take part in the conference. After this and other adventures, Queen Pleasance suddenly leaves the king, and Reason and Wisdom persuade him to return to his own palace: – that is, when pleasure and passions leave a man, reason and wisdom render him his own master. After this Decrepitude attacks and mortally wounds King Hart, who dies after making his testament.[19]

159 *And evermore the Cukkow, as he fley*
      He seyde Farewell, Farewell, papinjay!

From *The Cuckoo and the Nightingale* by Sir Thomas Clanvowe (d.1410), an English courtier and poet. The poem was previously attributed to Geoffrey Chaucer.

> *And as he flew away, the Cuckoo, ever and aye,*
> *Kept crying, 'Farewell! farewell, Popinjay!'*
> *As if in scornful mockery of me;*
> *And on I hunted him from tree to tree,*
> *Till he was far, all out of sight, away.*
>
> *Then straightway came the Nightingale to me,*
> *And said, 'Forsooth, my friend, do I thank thee,*
> *That thou wert near to rescue me; and now,*
> *Unto the God of Love I make a vow,*
> *That all this May I will thy songstress be.*

160 *'I've had a damned carking afternoon. A Moslem would blame my Ifrit...'*

Carking is burdensome or annoying. An Ifrit (or, *Afrit*), is an evil genie or demon in Mohammedan mythology.

Stirling – Castle Wynde by T. Allom

PART TWO

THE PLAY FOR
GIDEON SOMERVILLE

CHAPTER I: SMOTHERED MATE
CHAPTER II: DISCOVERED CHECK
CHAPTER III: FRENCH DEFENCE

Stirling Castle by G.F. Robson

Chapter I: Smothered Mate

Caxton: Tract 3, Chapter 3

The sixth pawn resembles the tavern owners and innkeepers and sellers of vittles. Many perils and adventures may happen on the ways and passages to those who are harbored within their rooms.[1]

1. Removal of a Blocking Knight

A smothered mate is a checkmate delivered by a knight in which the mated king is unable to move because he is surrounded, or smothered, by his own pieces.

163 *Branxholm, great throne of the Buccleuchs...*

Branxholm Tower

Branxholm Castle in the 16th century is the scene of *The Lay of the Last Minstrel* by Sir Walter Scott, a lively depiction of border life in feudal and knightly times:

Knight and page and household squire,
Loiter'd through the lofty hall,
Or crowded round the ample fire:
The stag-hounds, weary with the chase,
Lay stretch'd upon the rushy floor,
And urged, in dreams, the forest race,
From Teviot-stone to Esk-dale moor.

Nine-and-twenty knights of fame,
Hung their shields in Branksome-Hall;
Nine-and-twenty squires of name,
Brought them their steeds
to bower from stall.
Nine-and-twenty yeomen tall
Waited, duteous on them all;
They were all knights of mettle true,
Kinsmen to the bold Buccleuch.

Artist depiction of Branxholm Hall

Ten of them were sheathed in steel,
With belted sword and spur on heel;
They quitted not their harness bright
Neither by day nor yet by night.
They lay down to rest, with corslet laced,
Pillow'd on buckler cold and hard;
They carved at the meal with gloves of steel
And they drank the red wine through the helmet barr'd.

Ten squires, ten yeomen, mail-clad men.
Waited the beck of the warders ten.
Thirty steeds both fleet and wight,
Stood saddled in stable day and night,
Barbed with frontlet of steel, I trow,
And with the Jedwood axe at saddle bow;
A hundred more fed free in stall:
Such was the custom of Branxholm Hall.

163   ...*babies with mouths round and adhesive like lampreys; babies like Pandean pipes, of diminishing size and resonant voice...*

Lampreys are jawless fish, characterised by a toothed, funnel-like sucking mouth. Pandean pipes, or the pan flute, is an ancient musical instrument based on the principle of the closed tube, consisting usually of five or more pipes of gradually increasing length, and at times, girth.

164   *...which confidingly and automatically replaced itself, chumbling.*

Chumbling is to peck at or nibble.

164   *'...in case Grey of Wilton's sitting up the kitchen lum?'*

A lum is a chimney.

165   *'...to put a bit rope round that yellow-headed cacodemon's neck?'*

A cacodemon is an evil spirit[2/D] or a demon. The first known occurrence of the word cacodemon dates to 1398.

166   *'You'll make a bonny figure in a surplice, my lady...'*

A surplice is a white linen liturgical vestment; thus Janet in nun's garb.

166   *The argument became corybantic and public; it blared; it stopped.*

Corybantic is wild, frenzied.

166   *'We have had a visit...from the prospective bridegroom. Arran's son.'*

James Hamilton, (c.1532-1609, later 3rd Earl of Arran), was the eldest son of James Hamilton, 2nd Earl of Arran, by his wife, Lady Margaret Douglas. A descendant of James IV, he was third in the line of succession to the Scottish crown after his father. Originally proposed as a husband to the infant Queen Mary, his father chose instead to negotiate the marriage of Queen Mary to Prince Edward, while entertaining Henry VIII's supplemental proposal of a marriage between James and Princess Elizabeth of England.

After the assassination of Cardinal Beaton in 1546, James was held hostage in the castle of St. Andrews. Fearful he would fall into English hands, the Scots Parliament debarred him from succession to the crown while he remained in custody. He was released in 1547, when the castle was surrendered to French troops. After the repeal of the Treaty of Greenwich, his father and a group of noblemen again pushed for the marriage of James to Queen Mary, but were unsuccessful.

166   *...she launched into a technical description of the cure for tertiary.*

Tertiary is a lesion of tertiary syphilis.

2. *Irregular Partie Between Two Masters*

168 *In the two estuary forts the militia were hagridden...*

Hagridden is to be overburdened by fear or dread.

168 *'And the cooing voice on them like bishop piping for his red bunnet.'*

Meaning, a bishop singing to attain the red cap of a cardinal.

168 *'...and now you've a nose for pips like a peccary hog.'*

Pips are the dots on playing cards, dice, and dominoes. A peccary hog is a fierce swine[3/D], a wild pig with a well-developed snout for rooting up food.

168 *'The best man I ever saw at the tables was Buskin Palmer – '*

Sir John 'Buskin' Palmer, was known for constantly winning money from Henry VIII at cards. He was hanged, though why or when is uncertain.

169 *'...would have done Jimmie of Fynnart...'*

Sir James Hamilton of Finnart (1495-1540) was the illegitimate son of James Hamilton, 1st Earl of Arran, and a second cousin to King James V. He spent his early years abroad and developed a natural gift for architecture at the court of Francis I. He became embroiled in the rivalry between his family and the Douglases, featuring prominently as the 'Bastard of Arran'; many of the most reprehensible acts committed by the Hamiltons are laid at his feet. In the bloody skirmish known as 'Cleanse the Causeway', it was asserted Finnart frustrated attempts at pacification and fueled the fray. After the battle of Linlithgow (1526), Finnart murdered John Stewart, 3rd Earl of Lennox (father of Matthew Stewart, 4th Earl of Lennox) after Lennox had delivered up his sword and declared himself a prisoner.

Despite being described as wild, impetuous, without principles, religiously bigoted, and heavily embroiled in the most turbulent affairs of the era, Finnart was a favourite of King James V. He amassed great wealth and was one of the most powerful Scottish barons. He was retained as the architect in charge of the renovations of both Linlithgow Palace and Falkland Palace, and designed his own Craignethan Castle.

Finnart's downfall, however, came swiftly and at the hands of his own relatives. In retribution of Finnart's role in the martyrdom of Patrick Hamilton, James Hamilton (brother to Patrick and the namesake of Finnart) revealed to King James V an alleged plot for his murder. In 1540, Finnart was convicted of 'art and part in the treachery of shooting arrows and machines without the palace of Linlithgow and its bell tower'[4] at the king and others. Finnart's trial was by combat: Finnart met his accuser in single combat and was slain. The king, seized with remorse over the death of his favourite, was supposedly haunted by the spectre of his companion until his own death in 1542.

169 '...and pointed up the whole of Linlithgow if you laid it on with a trowel.'

The spectacle of an ancient palace...where Princes feasted and heroes fought, resounding alternately with the clang of arms and the dulcet notes of peace, now surrendered to ruin and desolation, cannot fail to inspire feelings of melancholy and regret in the bosom of the lover of the departed glories of his country.

The palace of Linlithgow is venerable for its antiquity, and must be forever hallowed by the mournful associations connected with its time-honoured ruins. No more do those princely halls contain the beauty and chivalry of Scotland, nor those battlements the formidable array of warlike hosts. The owl nightly hoots its dirge from the broken towers, and the note of the wild bird, exchanged for the music of the harp, screams its harsh requiem over departed greatness. The steed of the warrior has long ceased to tread the once crowded court, and the stately damsel to amble it on her palfrey; the weeds are now suffered to grow in unmolested luxuriance, and all is silent as the grave![5]

Linlithgow Palace by G.F. Robson

Linlithgow Palace, one of Scotland's most magnificent monuments, stands on a promontory jutting into Linlithgow Loch. Amongst the principal residences of the monarchs of Scotland in the 15th and 16th centuries, Linlithgow was named either from the Celtic derivation of *Lin-liath-cu*, The Lake of the Greyhound, or the Gothic derivation of *Lin-lyth-gow*, the Lake of the Great Vale.

After the town of Linlithgow was partially destroyed by fire in 1424, King James I began rebuilding the palace into a grand residence. Over the following century, the palace developed under James III, James IV, and James V. Splendour, festivity, beauty, and luxury reigned within its grand walls.

The queen-consort of James IV, Margaret Tudor, spent almost the entire years of James's reign in the palace. Tradition holds Margaret viewed the departure of the king for the field of Flodden and awaited news of the army from an octagonal chamber high atop a turret in the northwest corner called Queen Margaret's Bower.

In preparation for the arrival of Princess Magdalene of France, James V added the chapel and Parliament Hall, and remodeled the east and south sides of the structure. The Palace, now resplendent with painting and gold, prepared for the reception of the Queen, but her death delayed the event until James brought Mary de Guise to the palace in 1539. The elaborate and finely sculpted fountain in the courtyard was erected for her. Of all of the royal houses, the King's great Palace at Linlithgow was the favourite residence of Mary de Guise, who declared it 'the most princely palace she had ever beheld'[6].

Mary, Queen of Scots, was born at the palace in 1542, while her father lay dying at Falkland. The room in which Mary was born was later found to be dangerously insecure, and it collapsed in 1607. It was repaired by James VI in 1617-1619. After James moved his court to London, the glory days of the Palace were over; it was kept in good repair until 1746 when, being used as barracks, it was accidentally set on fire by the king's troops.

169   *'...not the Toll Brig o' Dumfries.'*

Dumfries by A.S. Masson, 1823

The Toll Brig o' Dumfries, also known as the Devorguilla Bridge, was built in 1432, and was the first bridge over the River Nith. It was named for Devorguilla of Galloway (c.1210-1290), mother of John Balliol, King of Scots from 1292-1296.

170 *A shadow, beaded and plateresque, spoke.*

Plateresque (Spanish, *platerisco*, from *plata,* silver), meaning 'silverwork' or 'silver plate'. The word also designates a specific artistic and architectural movement dating from the late Gothic period to the early Renaissance, characterized by ornamentation in a style resembling silver tracing.

170 *'Ring the bells backwards: on his cue, he is here.'*

To 'ring the bells backwards' is to sound the chimes, reversing the common order. It was done as a signal of alarm or danger.

170 *Mr. Crouch peered and was rewarded with a study, sfumato...*

Sfumato is the Renaissance painting technique of allowing tones and colors to shade gradually into one another, producing softened outlines or hazy forms. Sfumato literally means 'gone up in smoke'.

171 *'Here you are in our Paestum...'*

Pæstum was an ancient Greek city founded by the Sybarites in the 7th century BC in Southern Italy. A highly cultivated city, Pæstum was celebrated for its flowers and the Latin poets sang the praises of its roses, which bloomed twice each year.[7/D] Pæstum was destroyed by the Saracens in the 9th century and ravaged again in the 11th century; the site is now deserted yet its magnificent ruins are considered amongst the most interesting in the Hellenic world.

Paestum

171 *'The ass with the voice of Stentor.'*

In Greek legend, Stentor was a Greek herald before Troy, whose voice, according to Homer, was as loud as fifty men together.

172 *'Here we are, our beards smugly shaven, prolixt, corrupt and perpetuall.'*

From *A Satire of the Three Estates* by Sir David Lindsay (c.1490-c.1555):

> *And, through laws Consistoriall,*
> *Prolix, corrupt, and perpetual,*
> *The common people are put asunder,*
> *Though they be pure, it is no wonder.*[8]   (Tr.L.R.)

A Consistory is a Roman Catholic assembly of cardinals presided over by the Pope for promulgation of papal acts. Prolix is tediously prolonged; wordy.

172 *'You have come until the grisly land of mirknes...'*

From *The Pricke of Conscience*, originally attributed to Richard Rolle de Hampole (1290-1349), an English religious writer, now ascribed to an anonymous 14th-century author. The poem is a summary of mediæval theology, strong in its sense of awe and terror of sin; the abuses most strongly condemned are those of individual license and social life.

> *And say thus to it: 'I am thy hell,*
> *for thou art my pilgrim loyal.'*
> *This world is the way and passage,*
> *Through which lies our pilgrimage;*
> *But this way behooves us all to go,*
> *But beware we go naught wrong;*
> *For in this world lies two ways,*
> *Else men may find that them assays;*
> *The one is way of dead called,*
> *The other is way of life to hold,*
> *The way of dead seems large and easy,*
> *And that may lead us over-lightly,*
> *Until the grisly land of mirkness,*
> *There sorrow and pain ever-more is.*
> *The way of life seems narrow and hard*
> *That leads us to our country-ward*
> *That is the kingdom of heaven bright,*
> *Where we shall win, aye, in God's sight*
> *And God's own sons shall be called,*
> *If we the way of life here hold.*[9]   (Tr.L.R.)

172 *'You spend your speech and waste your brain.'*

From the late 15th-century morality play, *Everyman*, considered a masterpiece of the genre. John Gassner, *Mediæval and Tudor Drama*:

> *Everyman in his loneliness and fear cries out for company, but only Good-Deeds is willing to accompany him to the grave. For a time, Five Wits, Strength, Discretion, and Beauty follow him, but they all abandon him before the journey takes its final turn. Finally, as Everyman and Good-Deeds descend together into the grave, Knowledge, which has been man's guide up to this point, also departs (as knowledge must), but not before expressing confidence that Good-Deeds will save the man from perdition. It is noteworthy that, whereas other religious morality plays stress the importance of Mercy or Divine Grace, Everyman relies on the efficacy of 'Good-Deeds' or 'good works'.*[10]

172 *'Quoi! Ce n'est pas encore beaucoup d'avoir de mon gosier retiré votre cou?'*

> *'What! Has not your head safe from these jaws retreated?'*

From the fable of *The Wolf and the Stork*:

> *Into his gaping mouth she thrust her bill,*
> *And pincer'd out the offending bone with ease.*
> *'Now, signor Isgrim, for my potent skill,*
> *'I know,' said she, 'you'll pay me liberal fees.'*
> *'Pay liberal fees!' the surly brute repeated,*
> *'Why Gammar, surely now you must be joking!*
> *'Has not your head safe from these jaws retreated?*
> *'Stork! this ingratitude is most provoking!'*

172 *Mr. Crouch, succumbing to force majeure, drank his wine.*

Force majeure is superior force.

172 *'Blind Fortune, stumbling chance, spittle luck, false dealing...'*

From *Taxophilus* by the English scholar Roger Ascham (1515-1568):

> *Companions of shooting, be providence, good heed-giving, true meting, honest comparison, which things agree with virtue as well. Carding and dicing have a sort of good fellows also going commonly in their company, as blind fortune, stumbling chance, spittle luck, false dealing, crafty conveyance, brainless brawling, false*

*foreswearing; which good fellows will soon take a man by the sleeve
and cause him take his inn, some with beggary, some with gout and
dropsy, some with theft and robbery, and seldom will they leave a
man before he come either to hanging or else some other extreme
misery. To make an end, how shooting by all men's laws hath been
allowed, carding and dicing by all men's judgments condemned, I
need not show, the matter so plain.*

172   *'Away thou dully night.'*

From *The Thistle and the Rose* by William Dunbar (c.1460-c.1520), a nuptial song
composed to celebrate the marriage of King James IV to Princess Margaret Tudor,
in 1503. It is Dunbar's most famous poem, and perhaps 'the happiest allegory in
English literature'[11].

> *And as the glorious orb drove up the sky,*
> *Sang every bird through comfort of light,*
> *And with their sweet melodious throats 'gan cry,*
> *Lovers awake, away thou dully Night;*
> *Welcome, sweet Day, that comforts every wight;*
> *Hail May, hail Flora, hail Aurora, sheen*
> *Hail princess Nature, hail Love's loveliest Queen.*

173   *The familiar, chatoyant glint was in Lymond's eyes.*

Chatoyant is changing in color or lustre; coined from the French *œil de chat*,
meaning 'cat's eye'.

173   *'...a common woman, that dwells there to receive men to folly.'*

From *The Travels of Sir John Mandeville*:

> *And also a young man, that wist not of the dragon, went out of a
> ship, and went through the isle till that he came to the castle, and
> came into the cave, and went so long, till that he found a chamber;
> and there he saw a damosel that combed her head and looked in
> a mirror; and she had much treasure about her. And he trowed
> that she had been a common woman, that dwelled there to receive
> men to folly. And he abode, till the damosel saw the shadow of
> him in the mirror. And she turned toward him, and asked him
> what he would? And he said, he would be her leman or paramour.
> And she asked him, if that he were a knight? And he said, nay.
> And then she said, that he might not be her leman; but she bade
> him go again unto his fellows, and make him a knight, and come
> again upon the morrow, and she should come out of the cave
> before him, and then come and kiss her on the mouth and have no*

dread, – for I shall do thee no manner of harm, albeit that thou see
me in likeness of a dragon; for though thou see me hideous and
horrible to look on, I do thee to wit that it is made by
enchantment; for without doubt, I am none other than thou seest
now, a woman, and therefore dread thee nought. And if thou kiss
me, thou shalt have all this treasure, and be my lord, and lord also
of all the isle.

173   'Let us go to Paradise, where every man shall have fourscore wives, all maidens.'

From *The Travels of Sir John Mandeville:*

And if a man ask them what paradise they mean, they say, to
paradise that is a place of delights where men shall find all manner
of fruits in all seasons, and rivers running milk and honey, and of
wine and of sweet water; and that they shall have fair houses and
noble, every man after his desert, made of precious stones and of
gold and silver; and that every man shall have four score wives all
maidens, and he shall have ado every day with them, and yet he shall
find them always maidens.

173   '...and speir at the Monks of Bamirrinoch gif lecherie be sin...'

From *The Satire of the Three Estates* by David Lindsay (c.1490-c.1555).

173   'These serpents slay men, and they eat them weeping.'

From *The Travels of Sir John Mandeville:*

In that country and by all Inde be great plenty of cockodrills, that is
a manner of a long serpent, as I have said before. And in the night
they dwell in the water, and on the day upon the land, in rocks and
in caves. And they eat no meat in all the winter, but they lie as in a
dream, as do the serpents. These serpents slay men, and they eat
them weeping; and when they eat they move the over jaw, and not the
nether jaw, and they have no tongue.

Crocodile tears, or superficial sympathy, are a false or insincere display of emotion such as a hypocrite crying fake tears of grief. The expression comes from an ancient anecdote that crocodiles weep in order to lure their prey, or that they cry for the victims they are eating.

173 *'But the ravens, the popinjays, the starlings, they make into poets.'*

Even the brute Beasts he instructs in Arts that are denied them by Nature. Ravens, Jays, Parrots, Starlings he makes Poets: he makes Poetesses of Magpies, and teaches them to pronounce human Language, to speak it and sing it. And all for the Belly.

From *The Heroic Deeds and Sayings of the Good Pantagruel* (Book 4, Chapter 57) by François Rabelais (c.1494-1553), a French writer noted for fantasy, satire, the grotesque, and bawdy jokes and songs. John Calvin (1509-1564) condemned *Pantagruel* as obscene.

173 *...or the artifice of the Louvre...*

The present-day Louvre Palace owes its origin to King Philip Augustus, who erected a huge keep and fortress on the site in the 12th century. It was the centre of feudalism and the citadel of Paris. In the 14th century, it became a royal residence under Charles V and an important center of luxury. The fortress was demolished by Francis I, and a new palace was built on the site of the old palace beginning in 1541; it is considered one of the finest examples of Renaissance architecture.

Palais du Louvre, Très Riches Heures de Duc de Berry, 15th century

174 *'...came about us like bedbugs in an almshouse dorter...'*

A dorter is bedroom or dormitory, especially in a monastery.

174 *'...there was no mention of our passing faiblesse.'*

Faiblesse is feebleness; weakness; frailty.

174 *...with running ostler-wraiths...*

An ostler is a stableman. Wraith is a Scottish dialectical word for 'ghost' or 'spirit'.

174 *...golden parhelions blistered the fog.*

A parhelion (Greek, *para*, beside, and *hēlios*, the sun) is a false sun[12/D] appearing in the form of a bright light near the sun and tinged with colors of the rainbow.

175 *'So hop Willieken, hop Willieken: England is thine and mine...'*

The Flemings who invaded England in the days of Henry I sang to each other: *'Hop, hop, Willeken, hop! England is mine and thine.'*

17th-c. depiction of a halo display in Stockholm, 1535

177 *'Multa bibens...'*

From *Anatomy of Melancholy* by Robert Burton:

> But the mischief is, that many men, knowing that merry company is the only medicine against melancholy, spend all their days among good fellows in a tavern or alehouse, drinking venenum pro vino [poison for wine], like so many malt-worms, men-fishes, water-snakes, or frogs in a puddle, and become mere funguses and casks ... Like Timocrean of Rhodes, Multa bibens, et multa vorans [Having drunk much, eaten much], they drown their wits in wine, consume their fortunes, lose their time, and completely ruin their constitutions. In their endeavours to avoid the Scylla of dejections, they plunge into the Charybdis of drunkenness, and use that mirth which was intended for their help to their undoing.

Timocrean of Rhodes (c.476 AD) was a Greek comic and lyric poet, and an athlete of great prowess. He wrote drinking songs and was notorious for his gluttony and drunkenness: 'for his power of pouring out wit and pouring in wine'.[13] His epitaph read:

> *Multa bibens, et multa vorans, mala dinique dicens Multis,*
> *hic jaceo Timocreon Rhodius.*

> *Having drunk much, eaten much, and spoken much evil,*
> *here I lie, Timocreon of Rhodes.*

An alternative translation is, 'Many who drink to excess, and eat to excess, and speak ill of others, will, in the end, end badly'.[14]

178 *'Will – the Master of Maxwell.'*

John Maxwell, Master of Maxwell, was the second son of Robert Maxwell, 5th Lord Maxwell (1493–1546), a member of the Council of Regency. He was a distinguished politician, soldier, Lord High Admiral, a member of James V's royal council, and was one of the ambassadors sent to negotiate the marriage of James to Mary de Guise.

178 *Yellow tiercel eyes notched with black stared at the Master...*

Tiercel is a traditional term for a male falcon.

179 *'...there is no need to show me the hood. I respond quite well to the lure.'*

The hood and the lure are used in the training of falcons. A hood is used to keep the raptor in a calm state. The lure is a pair of bird wings attached to an object which is swung round and round on a cord, for the falcon to chase.

180 *'Of Cat, nor Fall, nor Trap, I haif nae Dreid.'*

Meaning, 'I have no fear'. From *The Tale of the Upland Mouse and the Burgess Mouse* by Robert Henryson (c.1425-1500):

> *The well-known apologue, of which this is the 'moralite' – that of the*
> *Town and Country Mouse – has been delightfully translated, or*
> *rather paraphrased, both by Pope and La Fontaine; yet our ancient*
> *Scottish bard need not dread a comparison with either. There is not,*
> *indeed, in his production (what it would be unreasonable to look for)*
> *the polished elegance, the graceful court-like expressions, and the*
> *pointed allusions to modern manners which mark the versification of*
> *these great masters; but there is 'a quiet vein of humour, a*
> *succession of natural pictures, both burgh and landward, city and*
> *rural; and a felicity in adapting the sentiments of the little four-*
> *footed actors in the drama, which is peculiarly its own. Henryson's*

mice speak and reason exactly as one of these long-whiskered, tiny individuals might be expected to do, were they suddenly to be permitted to express their feelings...The story and the catastrophe are well known: the invitation of the city mouse, its acceptance, their perilous journey to town, their delicious meal, and its fearful interruption by Hunter Gib (the jolly cat), the pangs of the rural mouse, whose heart is almost frightened out of its velvet tenement, her marvelous escape, and the delight with which she finds herself in her warm nest in the country, are described with great facility of humour. No one who has witnessed the ingenuity of the torment inflicted by a cast on its victim will fail to recognize the perfect nature of "Hunter Gib's" conduct, when the unfortunate rural citizen is under his clutches.'[15]

180   'My brother, Lord Maxwell, is still a prisoner in London.'

Robert Maxwell, 6th Lord Maxwell (d.1552), was the oldest son of Robert Maxwell, 5th Lord Maxwell (d.1546). The 5th Lord Maxwell was one of the nobles who attempted to restore order amongst the troops at the Battle of Solway Moss. He was taken as a prisoner to London, but was permitted to return to Scotland after signing an oath to Henry VIII and paying a 1,000-mark ransom. He was a supporter of the Reformation and, in 1543, proposed an act in Parliament to allow all to read the Bible in both Scottish and English; the bill passed.

181   'There are nine devilish notes...'

Border pipes are a nine-note bellows-blown bagpipe whose chanter is similar to the modern Great Highland Bagpipe. The instrument was once common enough in the Scottish border country for most towns to maintain a piper.

182   ...and gave them Baile Ioneraora....

Baile Ioneraora: The Campbells are Coming

> *The Campbells they are a' in arms,*
> *Their loyal faith and truth to show,*
> *With banners rattling in the wind,*
> *The Campbells are coming,*
> *   Ho-Ro, Ho-Ro!*

182   ...which had switched to Gillie Calum.

The ballad *Gillie Calum* was named for the man about whom the song was written, but is now known as the Sword Dance, a traditional Scottish military dance.

182   *'Listen, my friend: put your walking mandrake on Ben Nevis and myself on the Cheviot, and it's still too close for my liking.'*

The mandrake is a plant whose roots were used in magic rituals. According to legend, when the root is dug up it screams and kills all who hear it.

Ben Nevis (Gaelic, *Beinn Nibheis*), the highest mountain in the British Isles, is located near Fort William in the Scottish Highlands. The Cheviot, the highest peak in the Cheviot Hills, is located in Northumberland, near the border between Scotland and England.

Ben Nevis by Thomas Allom, 1836

Storm in the Cheviots by Frank Southgate, c.1909

183 *'You should skip like Alexander.'*

Alexander the Great (356-323 BC), king of Macedonia, created one of the largest empires of the ancient world, was undefeated in battle, and is considered one of history's most successful commanders.

Aristotle Teaching Alexander the Great by Charles Leplant, 1866

183 *...above the variations to* **Spaidsearachd Cloinn Mhic Rath...**

Spaidsearachd Cloinn Mhic Rath: The MacRae's March

184 *...and started, with a nice appreciation, on* **Cath fuathasach, Pheairt.**

Cath fuathasach, Pheairt: Desperate Battle, Perth

184 *Mat took on a stout blacksmith with thews like tubers...*

Thews are muscles.

184 *There was a brief caesura.*

A caesura (from Latin *caedere*, to cut) is a complete pause in a musical composition or line of poetry.

185 *'Dronken, dronken, y-dronken.'*

From an anonymous English poem and drinking song:

> Dronken, dronken, y-dronken,
> (name) is tabart atte wyne.
> hay (name) sister, Walter, Peter!
> Ye drank all deep,
> And so shall I.

185 *'A wilted and forfoughten Marigold,' he said caustically.*

Forfoughten is to be exhausted from fighting.

186 *'Th'erratic starres heark'ning harmony.'*

From *Troilus and Criseyde* by Geoffrey Chaucer. At the end of the epic poem, Chaucer records how Troilus is slain by the fierce Achilles:

> And when he was slain in this manner,
> His light ghost blissfully went
> Up to the holynes of the seventh sphere,
> In converse, letting every element,
> And there he saw, with full clarity,
> The erratic stars, hearkening harmony
> with sounds full of heavenly melody.

3. *Cross Moves by a King's Knight*

186   ...*the River Tweed with Berwick at its mouth...*

For sixteen miles the River Tweed forms the boundary between England and Scotland. Along the Tweed valley there are a number of old castles, keeps, and peel towers along the river marking the 'barbarous times when the Border raids were in continual activity, and when no one on either side of the marches, or debatable land, could lay down his head to sleep at night without the chance of having to stand to his defence, or perhaps to mount and ride ere morning'[16].

Eildon Hills and River Tweed by William Smith, 1905

186   *Like the ancient pike Sir George Douglas had once called him...*

The pike is an abundant freshwater fish. The most characteristic quality of the common pike is voracity. Thoreau described the pike as the 'swiftest, coarsest, and most ravenous of fishes, which Josselyn calls the river-wolf. It is a solemn, stately, ruminant fish, lurking under the shadow of a lily-pad at noon, with still, circumspect, voracious eyes; motionless as a jewel set in water, or moving slowly along to take up its position; darting from time to time at such unlucky fish or frog or insect as comes within its range, and swallowing at a gulp.'[17]

186   ...*pursuing him like hagfish.*

A hagfish, or slime-eel, is a foot or more long with a cirrous sucking mouth and is related to the lamprey. It feeds on dead or trapped fishes by boring into their bodies, thus parasitic, 'like hagfish on a cod'.[18/D]

186 *To the keep at Norham Castle...*

Norham Castle

Norham Castle, a grim looking border fortress, stands on a rocky elevation on the south side of the Tweed, on the border between Scotland and England. Founded in 1121 by Ralph Flambard, Bishop of Durham, to prevent Scottish invasions and border raids, Norham was considered the stoutest stronghold between Berwick and Carlisle; it changed hands between the Scots and the English several times over the centuries.

187 *'And who is this spadassin...?'*

A spadassin (Italian, *spadaccino*, swordsman) is one devoted to fencing and presumed to be expert with the sword; hence, a bravo or a bully.

Chapter II: Discovered Check

Caxton: Tract 3, Chapter 6

The third pawn ought to be figured as a clerk; if they write other than they ought, much harm may ensue and damage to the common good. Therefore, they ought to take heed that they not change nor corrupt in any way the contents of the sentence. For that they are first foresworn. And then they are bound to make amends to those they have damaged by their trickery.[1]

1. Diagonal Mating Begins

A discovered check is an attack opening upon the King when the piece moved does not itself give check, but unmasks another which does.

189 *'...tied to the man's collar like Agrippa's dog with the devil.'*

Henry Cornelius Agrippa von Nettesheim (1486-1535) was a 'wonderful and varied genius'[2] who lived an erratic life. A soldier, diplomat, and writer, Agrippa served the Emperor Maximilian I, was knighted in the field, was physician to the queen-mother of France, taught theology at Dôle, lectured at Pavia, was invited to take part in the dispute over the legality of the divorce of Henry VIII from Catherine of Aragon, and became archivist and historiographer to the Emperor Charles V.

His defence of a witch roused the hostility of the Inquisition, and his later publications secured his title of magician. The first, *De occulta philosophis*, written about

1510, is a defence of magic as a means for men to understand nature and God, and contains his view of the universe as having three worlds or spheres. In the second, *De Incertitudine et Vanitate Scientiarum et Arlium atqua Excellentia Verbi Dei Declamatio*, a sarcastic attack on current science and the pretenses of learned men published in 1531, Agrippa denounces what he sees as extraneous additions to the simple doctrines of Christianity, and a desire for a return to the primitive beliefs of the early church. Fables of Agrippa's life include tales of his black poodle, his magic mirror, and a pupil who was rent into pieces by demons. These tales overshadowed his reputation as an ardent student of alchemy and the occult, and an earnest searcher of truth, who 'would have unlocked Nature's mysteries had he only held the right key'[3].

190 *Nostre et toutdits a vostre desir.*

Your wish is my command.

191 *Cauda Pavonis, Ferrum Philosophorus, Dragon's Blood.*

Cauda Pavonis (Latin for 'peacock's tail'), *Ferrum Philosophorus* (a white calyx), and *Dragon's Blood* are stages in the alchemical process to create *Lapis Philosophorus*, the Philosopher's Stone:

Alchemical Design from Mutus Liber, 1677

> *When the putrefaction of our seed has been thus completed, the fire may be increased until glorious colours appear, which the Sons of Art have called Cauda Pavonis, or Peacock's Tail. These colors come and go, as heat is administered approaching to the third degree, till all is of a beautiful green, and as it ripens assumes a perfect whiteness, which is the White Tincture, transmuting the inferior metals into silver, and very powerful as a medicine. But as the artist well knows it is capable of a higher concoction, he goes on increasing his fire till it assumes a yellow, then an orange or citron colour; and then boldly gives a heat of the fourth degree, till it acquires a redness like blood taken from a sound person, which is a manifest sign of its thorough concoction and fitness for the uses intended.*[4]

192 'Remember Midas, dear.

King Midas is known in mythology for his ability to turn everything he touched into gold. 'So Midas, king of Lydia, swelled at first with pride when he found he could transform everything he touched to gold; but when he beheld his food grow rigid and his drink harden into golden ice then he understood that this gift was a bane and in his loathing for gold, cursed his prayer.'[5]

Midas by H. Stratton, c.1893

192 '...or you can call me Ananias.'

According to the Acts of the Apostles, Ananias and his wife Sapphira were members of the first Christian community. They held back a part of a gift to the church and lied about it, for which they were struck dead by Peter. The name Ananias has become a term for a liar.

193 The great Pan is dead...

In Greek mythology, Pan was the god of shepherds, forests, and flocks. According to the Greek historian Plutarch, during the reign of Tiberius, the pilot Thamus, when steering near the island of Paxæ, was commanded by a loud voice to proclaim, *'The great Pan is dead.'* The news was met with a great cry of lamentation, as if nature itself were expressing its grief. As the story coincides with the life of Christ, it is thought to herald the end of the old world and the beginning of the new.

Pan by H. Stratton, 1915

193 ...will show you only a camelopard...

A camelopard is an archaic term for a giraffe, recalling the old notion animals originated simply by crossing. The giraffe was thought to spring from the camel and the leopard.

193 But birds of paradise feed on dew and rare vapours...

According to fable, Birds of Paradise spent their

Paradisaæ decora

lives floating in the air, never descending to earth, and fed upon the dews of heaven, vapour, and the nectar of flowers. A sacred character was ascribed to them, and the feathers were used as a charm to protect the life of the wearer against danger in battle. It is suspected these attributes were assigned to the birds by imaginative traders to increase their value.

193 ...*and men on Pytan live by the smell of wild apples...*

From *The Travels of Sir John Mandeville*, describing the inhabitants of Pytan:

> *The folk of that country ne till not, ne labour not the earth, for they eat no manner of thing. And they be of good colour and fair shape, after their greatness...These men live by the smell of wild apples. And when they go far way, they bear the apples with them; for if they had lost the savour of the apples, they should die anon.*

193 *From here where all is night, I see a foolish-fire...*

A foolish fire (Latin, *ignus fatuus*) is a flickering light seen at night over marshy ground, churchyards, and graveyards. Also popularly known as will-o'-the-wisp and corpse candle, the foolish fire, a light which misleads by its illusive and evanescent appearance, is regarded with superstitious awe as a portent of evil, the treacherous signal of spirits seeking to lure benighted travelers to their doom.

193 ...*and say, Have pity now, O bright, blissful goddess.*

From *The Kingis Quair* by King James I of Scotland (1394-1437):

> You know the cause of my pain and suffering
> Better than myself, and all my adventures,
> You may convey, and as you list convert
> The hardest heart formed at birth,
> In your hand lies my cure to be whole and hale,
> Have pity now, O bright blissful goddess,
> Of your poor man, and rue his distress![6]   (Tr.L.R.)

193 *You may see here no more than Mercury's finger...*

In Roman mythology, Mercury was the god of trade and merchandise (Latin, *merx*). He was appointed by Jupiter as herald general of the gods, and as such was frequently the medium of communication between the immortal and the mortal. In palmistry, the 'finger of Mercury' is the little finger and connotes powers of communication. In particular, it often refers to someone with persuasive speech or a talent for self-expression.

193 *Rosa das rosas, et fror das frores*
Dona das donas, sennor das sennores...

> *Rose of roses and flower of flowers,*
> *Lady of ladies, Lord of lords.*

Cantigas de Santa Maria
MS 1121-1128

From *Cantiga de loor*, one of the *Cantigas de Santa Maria (Canticles of Holy Mary)*. The *Cantigas*, 420 poems with musical notations, is one of the largest collections of solo songs from the Middle Ages. It is often attributed to Alfonso X of Castille (122-1284), 'The Wise', who is known not only for his poetry, but as a celebrated man of science and the law.

> *Rose of beauty and fine appearance*
> *And flower of happiness and pleasure,*
> *Lady of most merciful bearing,*
> *And Lord for relieving all woes and cares;*
> > *Rose of roses and flower of flowers,*
> > *Lady of ladies, Lord of lords.*
> *Such a Mistress everybody should love,*
> *For she can ward away any evil*
> *And she can pardon any sinner*
> *To create a better savor in this world.*
> > *Rose of roses and flower of flowers,*
> > *Lady of ladies, Lord of lords.*
> *We should love and serve her loyally,*
> *For she can guard us from falling;*
> *She makes us repent the errors*
> *That we have committed as sinners:*
> > *Rose of roses and flower of flowers*
> > *Lady of ladies, Lord of lords.*
> *This lady whom I acknowledge as my Master*
> *And whose troubadour I'd gladly be,*
> *If I could in any way possess her love,*
> *I'd give up all my other lovers.*
> > *Rose of roses and flower of flowers,*
> > *Lady of ladies, Lord of lords.*

195 '...and the Earl of Angus is married to his only sister...'

Margaret Maxwell, Countess of Angus, was the third wife of Archibald Douglas, 6th Earl of Angus. They married in 1543, and had one son, who died in infancy.

2. An Exchange of Pawns is Suggested

196 *'Father is in a tetchy mood.'*

Tetchy is bad-tempered and irritable.

197 *...wrote and read and made music like bells in a campanile...*

A campanile (from *campana*, a bell) is a large, detached bell-tower. One of the most famous is the Leaning Tower of Pisa.

197 *...against the sound of Gideon's voice warbling happily...*

Gideon is singing the 14th century song, *Bon joure à vous*. It is meant to be sung loudly and off-key in a fake French accent.

> *Bonjour, bonjour à vous!*
> *I am come unto this house,*
> *With a par la pompe, I say,*
> *Bonjour, bonjour, bonjour,*
> *Bonjour, bonjour à vous!*
>
> *Is there any good man here*
> *That will make me any cheer?*
> *And if there were, I would come near*
> *To hear what he would say.*
> *   Ay, will ye be wild? by Mary mild*
> *I know ye will sing gay*
> *Bonjour, bonjour à vous!*
>
> *Be glad, masters everyone!*
> *I am come myself alone*
> *To oppose you one by one.*
> *Let see who dare say nay.*
> *   Sir, what say ye?*
> *   Sing on, let us see.*
> *   Now it will be*
> *This or another day?*
> *Bonjour, bonjour à vous!*[6]   (Tr.L.R.)

197 *'Come on, Chanticleer. There is a crisis in the farmyard.'*

A chanticleer (French, *chanter*, sing, + *cler*, clear) is a rooster so called from the clearness or loudness of his voice in crowing. In fables and in Chaucer's *The Nun's Priest's Tale*, Chanticleer was proudly famous for his expert management of the barnyard. Hence, Kate's humorous precision in interrupting Gideon's singing by saying, *'Come on Chanticleer. There is a crisis in the farmyard.'*[8]

199 *...the united four-footed Sabaoth was already ahead of him...*

Sabaoth is plural form of 'host' or 'army' in Hebrew. It is used in conjunction with the Divine as a title of majesty, as in 'Lord of Hosts'. According to some scholars, the 'host' represents the armies of Israel protected by Jehovah; others believe the word refers to the hosts of heaven, the angels, and by metaphor, the entire universe.[9]

199 *...the ice making faint and Aeolian music about their steel helmets.*

In Greek mythology, Æolus was the god and father of the winds. An Æolian Harp is a musical instrument 'played' by wind sweeping over its strings. The sounds produced by the rising and falling wind can range from a barely audible hum to a loud scream.

200 *...and the herd, after much...ponderous caracole...The citizens of Cumberland gambolled after it.*

A caracole is a half turn to the left or right by horse and rider. To gambol is to leap about playfully; to frolic.

201 *...his father's Red Jimmy beak...*

A Red Jimmy is a Scottish puffin (*Fratercula arctica*), a bird characterized by its curious bill: gaily coloured in bright red, blue, and yellow, and extremely high, narrow, and furrowed.

203 *'Do you suppose sheep can play Morales?'*

Cristóbal de Morales (1512-1553) is considered one of Spain's most influential 16th-century composers. He was a member of the papal choir, and wrote numerous compositions for masses, along with several settings of the 'Lamentations' and the 'Magnificat'.

205 *'He came in with the cattle, that also be fair beasts and well smelling.'*

From *The Travels of Sir John Mandeville:*

> *This palace, where his siege is, is both great and passing fair. And within the palace, in the hall, there be twenty-four pillars of fine gold. And all the walls be covered within of red skins of beasts that men clepe panthers, that be fair beasts and well smelling; so that for*

the sweet odour of those skins no evil air may enter into the palace. Those skins be as red as blood, and they shine so bright against the sun, that unnethe no man may behold them. And many folk worship those beasts, when they meet them first at morning, for their great virtue and for the good smell that they have. And those skins they prize more than though they were plate of fine gold.

205 'This child's been a Messalina since birth.'

The Roman empress Valeria Messalina (c.22-48) was a powerful and influential woman, infamous for her avarice, profligacy, and atrocious cruelty. 'Many members of the most illustrious families of Rome were sacrificed to her fears, her jealousy, or her hatred.'[10] She conspired to kill her husband, the Emperor Claudius, and was executed when the plot was discovered. Messalina's name is often used as a synonym for manipulativeness and treachery.

206 'Do you remember when you lived at Hatfield?'

The Royal Palace of Hatfield was built in the late 15th century and acquired by Henry VIII in 1538; his children Edward, Mary, and Elizabeth spent their youth at what is now known as the Old Palace at Hatfield House.

Hatfield House by Joseph Nash

208 'You adhere for three months, and now we are sundered. We are no longer articulated. We are no longer articulate.'

To sunder is to separate; divide; sever. Articulated is having two or more sections connected by a flexible joint. Articulate is to fit together into a coherent whole.

208   *'In that fine, unreasoning, Pharos-like brain...'*

The Pharos was a lighthouse of vast height built on an island at the entrance to the port of Alexandria, Egypt. One of the Seven Wonders of the World, the Pharos, built by Ptolemy I and Ptolemy II, was reported to be 400 feet high. The term pharos has come to mean a lighthouse for the direction of seamen; a watch-tower; a beacon.

208   *'...some minor luminary is sitting intoning disticha...'*

Dionysii Catonis Disticha de Moribus ad Filium, written in the 3rd or 4th century by an unknown author, is a small collection of moral maxims[11/D], each consisting of two hexameters, in four books. The Disticha was popular in mediæval Europe, and is frequently referred to by Chaucer. It was translated into many western languages, and a version was printed by Caxton in 1483.

209   *'And such an offender will never enter the Kingdom of Hawick.'*

Hawick by A. Richardson, c.1850

Situated on the junction of the Teviot and Slitrigg stream, Hawick was once a barony burgh entirely under the dominion of the lairds of Buccleuch. In addition to Branxholm, they sometimes resided at the Black Tower of Hawick, located in the town itself. Hawick was often burned during the border wars. In 1570, when Sussex laid waste to the borders, the townspeople of Hawick stripped the thatch from their homes and set fire to it in the streets, to prevent the English from lodging there.

209   *'...and armed with a moral code like an ogee.'*

An ogee is a curve which changes directions.[12/D] In architecture it is a molding with an s-shaped profile. Here, meaning Will's moral code is pliant and not a rigid line.

209   *'That's what Buridan's Ass kept saying.'*

Buridan's ass is an illustration of a paradox in philosophy. It refers to a hypothetical situation wherein an ass is placed precisely midway between two identically desirable bales of hay, the idea being it cannot possibly determine one as mattering more than the other and thus will starve.[13/D] It illustrates how indecision results because either decision would be acceptable. Here, Lymond is referring to the fact Scott's actions do matter.

The celebrated sophism, while attributed to Jean Buridan, the 14th-century French philosopher, is found nowhere in his writings. It is thought to have been invented by his opponents who wished to ridicule his theories of determinism. In his comments on the Nicomachean Ethics of Aristotle, Buridan makes the will depend entirely on motives with the only liberty being a certain power of suspending judgment and determining the direction of the intellect.

209   *'You'll allow me pogrom and heresy, but not Christian Stewart?'*

A pogrōm (from Russian, 'devastation') is an organized slaughter of helpless people, specifically one with official sanction against an ethnic minority.

Heresy is any doctrine or opinion against established standards, or one which tends to promote division. In theology, heresy is a doctrine or opinion contrary to the fundamental creed of a particular church. More specifically, heresy defines an offense against Christianity, in denying some essential doctrine, which is publicly avowed and obstinately maintained.

209   *'...and the odium will fall on my always inaccessible head.'*

Odium is intense hatred or dislike, especially toward a person regarded as contemptible, despicable, or repugnant. Odium is something one endures, while hatred is a something one exercises.

210   *'...a test case in casuistry or my personal complexity of habits?'*

In ethics, casuistry is the solution of issues of right or duty by the application of general ethical principals or theological dogmas, thus answering questions of conscience. In Jewish and Christian theology, casuistry often degenerated into hair-splitting and sophistical arguments wherein questions of right and wrong were construed to meet selfish aims.[14] Casuistry can also be defined as specious or excessively subtle argumentation intended to be misleading.

210   *'... stumbling about with a candle inside my pia mater.'*

Pia mater (Latin, pious or gentle mother) is the delicate, innermost layer of the membranes surrounding the brain and spinal cord.

211   *'Fide et diffide, in fact: and that is the moral of this little story.'*

Fide et diffide: trust and distrust. Meaning, take heed whom you trust, as caution is necessary before undertaking any enterprise.

211   *'I showed you this, my would-be catharist...'*

A catharist (Greek, *katharos,* pure) is one who pretends to more purity than others, thus a puritan. Specifically, it was a name applied to several heretical sects at various periods. A central tenet of the Catharist faith was Dualism, i.e. the belief in a good and an evil principle, whose creations were, respectively, the invisible and spiritual universe, and the material world.

211   *'My bird Willie, my boy Willie, my dear Willie, he said; How can ye strive against the stream? For I shall be obeyed.'*

From the ancient Scottish ballad, *Gil Morrice.* The ballad, set in Stirlingshire, tells the beautiful and pathetic tale of Gil Morrice, an earl's son who was exceedingly beautiful, and 'especially remarkable for the extreme length and loveliness of his yellow hair, which shrouded him as if it were a golden mist'[15].

> *'O no! O no! my master dear!*
> *I dare nae for my life;*
> *I'll no gae to the bauld barons,*
> *For to triest furth his wife.'*
> *'My bird Willie, my boy Willie,*
> *My dear Willie,' he sayd:*
> *'How can ye strive against the stream?*
> *For I shall be obeyd.'*

Chapter III: French Defence

Caxton: Tract 3, Chapter 2

The second pawn that stands before the Knight has the form and figure of a man...by this is signified all manner of workman, such as goldsmiths.[1]

1. Touching and Moving

The French Defence is an opening move by the second player where he establishes two pawns in the centre of the board, supporting and maintaining them unmoved. Known as a solid and dependable defence, it gives a safe but dull game.

2. A Queen's Knight Fails Signally to Adjust

217 *'You wouldna get finer gin you took an elephant down Spittall Street...'*

'Gin' is Scots for if; whether.

217 *'...or so handy with a knife as yon Italian fellow...'*

Benvenuto Cellini (1500-1571) was a celebrated Italian goldsmith, sculptor, and engraver.[2] His works were sought after by nobles and prelates alike. Equally skilled with sword and dagger, and not loath to use them, he was imprisoned for the murder of a rival goldsmith, and avenged his brother's death by slaying the slayer. In addition to his art, Cellini penned an autobiography, hailed as 'one of the most singular and fascinating books in existence'[3]. With unblushing frankness, animated narrative,

Benvenuto Cellini

187

and racy vigour, Cellini's work gives a vivid picture of Italian Renaissance society.

217   *'...but I've got jewels like peevers and I ken them like weans.'*

A peever (Scots) is a flat stone used in the game of hopscotch; to ken (Scots) is to know; and weans (Scots) are children.

217   *The city of Perth, or St. Johnstone's...*

Perth by Thomas Allom, 1839

Situated on the right bank of the river Tay, the ancient city of Perth was made a royal burgh by William the Lion in 1210. It holds a wealth of historic memories, including the bloody combat in 1396 between Clan Chattan and Clan Quele, described in Sir Walter Scott's *Fair Maid of Perth*, which took place on North Inch in the presence of King Robert III and Queen Annabella Drummond; and the assassination of King James I at Blackfriar's Monastery in 1437. After the assassination, Perth lost its status as capital, and the Parliament Courts were transferred to Edinburgh.

218   *But when he reached Glovers' Yard...*

Perth-made gloves and buckskin breeches were once celebrated all over Scotland. Glovers occupied almost the whole of the shops in the Skinnergate, and Glovers' Yard, the seat of manufacturing for the glove industry, was situated directly opposite the Fair Maid's House (c.1475), featured in Scott's *Fair Maid of Perth*.

218   *As if the words had touched off a hydraulic, Alexandrine weight...*

Hero of Alexandria (c.10-70 AD) was an ancient Greek mathematician, engineer, and inventor. He designed, among other things, a hydraulic hoist for moving weighted objects. His inventions were referred to as Alexandrian designs.[4]

218 *'You'll not see him sober till Twelfth Night...'*

Twelfth Night, the evening of January 5th, is a Christian festival marking the coming of Epiphany and the conclusion of the twelve days of Christmas.

219 *'...you canna bring him back to this Yard by St. Stephen's Day normal...'*

St. Stephen's Day is celebrated on the 26th of December in the Western Church, and commemorates St. Stephen, the first Christian martyr.

219 *'... in the Skinnergate.'*

Skinnergate is one of Perth's oldest streets. During the Middle Ages, it was the center for the tanning of hides and skins, and also of the leather working industry.

220 *...dispensing winkles from a pot...and pins from a wooden box.*

Winkles are tiny edible marine snails, so small they must be coaxed out of the shell with a pin.

221 *'Tohorsh, tohorsh, maroyaleesh...'*

> *To horse, to horse, my royal liege!*
> *Your foes stand on the strand;*
> *Full twenty thousand glittering spears*
> *The King of Norse commands.*
> *Bring me my steed Madge, dapple grey,*
> *(Our good King rose and cried)*
> *A trustier beast, in all the land,*
> *A Scots' King ne'er did stride.*

221 *'Here maun I lie, here maun I die...'*

> *And he has ridden o'er muir and moss,*
> *O'er hills and morry a glen,*
> *When he came to a wounded knight*
> *Making a heavy mane;*
> *'Here maun I lye, here maun I dye,*
> *By treacherie's false guiles;*
> *Witless I was that e'er ga faith*
> *To wicked woman's smiles.'*

Both of the passages above are from *Hardyknute*, a ballad commemorating the

Battle of Largs (1263) between Alexander III of Scotland and Haco III of Norway. Originally offered as a fragment of an old heroic ballad, it was greatly admired by scholars who believed it to be ancient, and published as such in Allan Ramsay's *Evergreen.* Sir Walter Scott wrote, '*Hardyknute* was the first poem I ever learnt – the last I shall forget'[5]. It was later discovered to be the work of Lady Elizabeth Wardlaw (1677-1727). After learning the poem was a forgery, Scott wrote *Hardyknute* is 'a most spirited and beautiful imitation of an ancient ballad'[6].

The Battle of Largs by William Hole
The Attack of the Scots (left) – The Fight at Sea (right)

The Battle of Largs was fought in early October 1263 between King Haco of Norway and Alexander III of Scotland. Haco, seeking to prevent Alexander from annexing the Hebrides, then under Norwegian rule, sailed to the Scottish coast with one of the most formidable fleets ever to sail from Norway. A storm on October 1st destroyed a part of his armada, and the tempestuous weather following made it difficult for the army to land. After a fierce and bloody contest over the next several days, the Norwegians were defeated by the Scots under the command of Alexander III. Haco escaped by leading his decimated fleet through the strait between the Skye and the mainland. He reached the Orkneys, where 'sinking beneath disappointment and mortification of his defeat'[7], he died on 15 December 1263. The victory effectually ended Norwegian rule of the western coasts and islands of Scotland and the Isle of Man.

222 '*...and have some left to spend at Pasche, perhaps.*'

Pasche (from Hebrew *Pas'chà, pesach,* from *pâsach,* to pass over) is the Jewish feast of the Passover; hence, the Christian feast of Easter.

222 '...and I'll spend Lent in a stickleback's front parlour.'

A stickleback (from Old English *stickel*, to prick or sting) is a small, pugnacious, spiny-backed fish; euphemistically, an unpleasant individual.

223 'Ye havena had an encoonter with a sleekit-spoken chiel...'

Sleekit (Scots) is smooth and glossy; flattering, slick, specious. A chiel is a lad, a young man, a fellow.

224 'In aurum coruscante et crispante capillo,' said Richard.

'Into gold, shining, curling hair...'

This specific Latin phrase is associated with Cupid as being yellow-haired. In *The Anatomy of Melancholy*, Richard Burton puts forth several causes of Love-Melancholy: *Sight, Beauty from the Face, Eyes, and other Parts, and how it pierceth.* Discussing beauty as a cause of melancholy:

> *Although for the greater part this beauty be most eminent in the face, yet many times those other members yield a most pleasing grace, and are alone sufficient to enamour.*
>
> *A white and round neck, that...dimple in the chin...sweet breath, white and even teeth...A flaxen hair, golden hair...Apollonius will have Jason's golden hair be the main cause of Medea's dotage on him. Castor and Pollux were both yellow-haired. Paris, Menelaus, and most amorous young men, have been such in all ages...lovely to behold. Homer so comments Helen, makes Patroclus and Achilles both yellow-haired; Pulchricoma Venus, and Cupid himself was yellow-haired, in aurum coruscante et crispante capillo [into gold, shining, curling hair], like that neat picture of Narcissus in Callistratus; for so Psyche spied him asleep...*
>
> *"And Hero the fair,*
> *Whom young Apollo courted for her hair."*
>
> *Leland commends Guithera, King Arthur's wife, for a fair flaxen hair; so Paulus Æmilius sets out Clodeveus, that lovely king of France. Synesius holds every effeminate fellow or adulterer is fair-haired...*

226 'Ruthven, it's become a national pastime.'

Sir William Ruthven, 2nd Lord Ruthven (d.1552), was provost and constable of Perth, an extraordinary lord of session, a member of the privy council, and keeper of the king's house in Perth. After the death of James V in 1543, he was appointed guardian, with seven other nobles, of the young Queen Mary, two of whom were to have charge of her every three months. An early supporter of the Reformation, Knox called him 'a stout and discreet man in the cause of God'[8]. The family of Ruthven traces their descent to Thor, a Saxon or a Dane, who settled in Scotland during the reign of David I.

Sir William Ruthven, 2nd Lord Ruthven

228   '...it's like Abbey Craig speaking to Dumyat.'

Abbey Craig is an abrupt eminence outside of Stirling rising 362 feet above sea level, and was the station of the army of Sir William Wallace in the Battle of Stirling Bridge in 1297. Dumyat is one of the Ochils, rising to 1375 feet. Its towering height offers one of the most magnificent and extensive views in Scotland.

> *The entire landscape, both in itself and in views commanded from it, is exquisitely picturesque; and the southern front of the Ochils in particular, in one continuous chain from east to west, with soaring precipitous acclivity, partly clothed in verdure, partly rugged precipice and naked rock, both offer magnificent features in its own vast façade, and commands most gorgeous and extensive prospects from each of its vantage grounds. Dumyat, standing out boldly in the middle of that grand front, and Abbey Craig, rising isolated in advance of it, and crowned with the conspicuous Wallace Monument, are especially prominent, both for their own picturesqueness and for the views which they command.[9]*

229   ...an account of the raid on Balmerino Abbey...

Balmarino Abbey – Interior of Chapter House

The Cistercian Abbey at Balmerino was founded in 1127 by Ermengarda, the widowed queen of William the Lion. In 1547, when Protector Somerset defeated the Scots at Pinkie Cleugh, the English fleet advanced along the east coast. Admiral Wyndham bombarded Dundee, and, when reporting his movements to Protector Somerset on 18 December 1547, promised 'he will not leave one town, nor village, nor fisher boat unburned from Fifeness to Combe's Inch' and expected 'soon to suppress an Abbey or two'[10]. A week later, he organized an expedition to Balmerino Abbey, and, on the night of Christmas, sailed up the Tay and landed a force of 300 men, including fifty harquebusiers. The monks, aware of the recent burning and sacking of the Border monasteries, opened fire on the English invaders, proving disastrous to the defenders. The Abbey, 'with all things that were in it'[11] was burned, and the English force proceeded to burn the neighbouring villages, and set fire to the season's store of corn.

3. Another Royal Lady Enters the Game

231 *The interview took place in the Castle of Warkworth...*

Warkworth Castle by Thomas Allom, c.1832

Founded in the mid-12th century, Warkworth Castle sits less than one mile from England's coast, and close to the River Coquet. One of Northumberland's strongest and largest fortresses, it was owned by the Percy family until their fall under Henry IV; the property passed to the English Crown in 1537.

232 *'...like the baker of Ferrara, thinks he is made of butter.'*

The story is told of a baker of Ferrara who believed he was made of butter, and thus would not approach the oven lest he should melt.

233 *Her mother, Margaret Tudor of England, had been married to King James of Scotland nearly fifty years before...*

Margaret Tudor (1489-1541) was the eldest daughter of Henry VII of England, and the elder sister of Henry VIII. When James died on the field at Flodden, Margaret was twenty-four years old, the mother of one young son, and pregnant with her second child. Within four months of the birth of her son Alexander (who died in infancy), Margaret determined to choose her own spouse. Rejecting an alliance with either the Emperor Maximilian or Louis XII (advanced by Cardinal Wolsey and Henry VIII, respectively), and smitten by the 'handsome face and figure'[12] of a young Scottish earl, Margaret secretly married Archibald Douglas, 6th Earl of Angus, then only nineteen or twenty himself. By this marriage she forfeited the regency of Scotland, which she held on behalf of her young son, James V, and alienated the Scottish nobles, who feared she and her new husband would support the English cause. According to one historian: 'The real Margaret was an ignorant, deceitful, low-minded, odious woman, whose follies disgraced her gallant husband's memory.'[13]

Queen Margaret Tudor

King James IV

James IV (1473-1513) was King of Scots from the age of sixteen, when his father was killed at the Battle of Sauchieburn (1488) by a rebellious group of barons. James, having been induced to join the rebellion, was so remorseful of his role in the assassination of his father he wore an iron chain around his waist as penance, adding a link each year. 'James's affable manners, frank disposition, and splendid hospitality made him highly popular among his subjects, and his friendship was courted by foreign sovereigns.'[14] After the murder of Margaret Drummond, to whom it is thought James IV was secretly married (see 141 – *The Ballad of Tay's Bank*), he accepted the thrice-offered hand of Princess Margaret to establish a 'sincere, true, sound and firm peace, friendship, league, and confederation to last to all time coming'[15]. James married thirteen-year-old Margaret in August, 1503. In 1513, disregarding the pleas of his counsellors and his queen, James invaded England in the summer, and was killed, along with the 'flower of his nobility and gentry'[16], on the field at Flodden.

235 *'It is another disease that grieveth me.'*

From the late 15th-century morality play, *Everyman*.

237 *'O rubicund blossom and star of humility!*
O famous bud, full of benignity!'

From a poem dedicated to Henry VII in praise of his newborn son, the young Prince Henry (later, Henry VIII) by Stephen Hawes (c.1475-c.1523). Hawes, an English poet, was educated at Oxford and travelled in England, France, and Scotland. Among his various accomplishments and his 'most excellent vein'[17] in poetry procured him a place at the court of Henry VII. His most important poem is *The Passetyme of Pleasure*.

> *O, noble Prince Henry! our second treasure,*
> *Surmounting in virtue and mirror of beauty!*
> *O, gem of gentleness and lantern of pleasure!*
> *O, rubicund blossom and star of humility!*
> *O, famous bud, full of benignity!*
> *I pray to God well for to increase*
> *Your high Estate in rest and peace!*

237 *'Ce n'est rien: c'est une femme qui se noie,' said Lymond, and laughed.*

> *'Tis nothing but a woman drowning.'*

From the fable, *The Woman Drowned:*

> *I hate that saying, old and savage,*
> *"'Tis nothing but a woman drowning.'*
> *That's much, I say.*
> *What grief more keen should have edge*
> *Than loss of her, of all our joys the crowning?*
> *Thus much suggests the fable I am borrowing.*
>
> *A woman perished in the water,*
> *Where, anxiously and sorrowing,*
> *Her husband sought her,*
> *To ease the grief he could not cure,*
> *By honored rites of sepulture.*
> *It chanced that near the fatal spot,*
> *Along the stream which had*
> *Produced a death so sad.*
> *There walked some men that knew it not.*
> *The husband asked if they had seen*
> *His wife, or ought that hers had been.*

One promptly answered, No;
But search the stream below:
It must have borne her in its flow.
No, said another; search above.
In that direction
She would have floated, by the love
Of contradiction.

This joke was truly out of season; —
I don't propose to weigh its reason.
But whether such propensity
The sex's fault may be,
Or not, one thing is very sure.
Its own propensities endure.
Up to the end they'll have their will,
And, if it could be, further still.

PART THREE

THE PLAY FOR SAMUEL HARVEY

Dumbarton Castle by Clarkson Stanfield

Chapter I: Bitter Exchange

The Buke of Ye Chess: Tract 2, Chapter 4

This knight defends his side,
He is courageous, without dread,
And fearing not the enemy,
He both attacks, and strongly keeps his stead.[1]

An exchange is to capture a piece for the loss of one of equal value. To 'win the exchange' is to capture a Rook in return for the loss of a minor piece (the Bishop or a Knight). To 'lose the exchange' is to capture a Knight or Bishop in return for the loss of a Rook.

1. Offer of a Pawn Is Discussed

241 *...so near to the merry ranks of Mahoun...*

Mahoun is a variant form of the name Muhammad, often found in Mediæval and later European literature.

241 *The devyll, they say, is dede; the devyll is dede.*

From *Collyn Clout* by John Skelton (1460-1529), a response to the failure of his courtly audience to appreciate his earlier work, *Speke Parrott*. The opening lines reveal Skelton's frustration at the apparent slow-wittedness of his audience.

> *And if that he hit*
> *The nail on the head*
> *It stands in no stead:*
> *'The devil,' they say, 'is dead,*
> *The devil is dead.'*[2]

(Tr.L.R.)

Collyn Clout is thought to be one of the most scathing pre-Reformation indictments on the clergy. Skelton exposes the greed, ignorance, and ostentation of the church, and corruption through the practice of simony (paying for sacraments and thus purchasing holy offices and positions). Yet he also takes care to write in defence of the church and to not include all of its members in his attack. *'Though my ryme be ragged, tattered and jagged, rudely rain-beaten, rust and moth-eaten, if ye take well therewith, it hath in it some pyth.'*

242   *Here were four rivers, Lymond had told him, and Eldorado between...*

El Dorado (Spanish, 'The Golden' or 'Gilded Land') was a mythical country in which gold and precious stones were found in fabulous abundance. It was thought to lie in the New World. Many attempts were made to discover it, and it was reported to exist after Orellana voyaged down the Amazon in 1540-1541. The name became a metaphor for any place where wealth could be acquired rapidly.

242   *...turning sharp east, began the journey to Tantallon Castle.*

Tantallon Caste by Clarkson Stansfield, c.1840

Considered one of Scotland's great mediæval castles, Tantallon is surrounded on three sides by the sea. The entrance to the castle, protected by two extremely deep ditches and massive towers, was over a drawbridge and through a deep stone gateway. The castle was so strong it was considered impregnable, so much so to 'ding doun Tantallon' was thought as great a feat as to 'make a brig to the Bass'[3].

Originally a stronghold of the 'Black Douglases', the castle was granted to Archibald 'Bell-the-Cat' Douglas, 5th Earl of Angus, by James III in 1470. In 1528, after escaping the compulsory tutelage of Archibald Douglas, 6th Earl of

Angus, the 15-year-old King James V raised a sort of war against Angus and attempted to reduce his strongholds. An act of attainder was passed against the Douglases, with forfeiture of all of their lands and houses, including Tantallon. In December 1528, James V descended upon Tantallon with an army of 12,000 men and attacked the castle. The siege was unsuccessful, but James was eventually able to obtain possession after Angus fled to England.

After the death of James V in 1542, Angus returned to Scotland and his possessions were restored to him, after which he made Tantallon even stronger and more heavily fortified.

243 '...no longer interested in our life, our lust, our Governor, our Queen?'

From *The King's Quair* by James I of Scotland (1394-1437):

> *And ye, fresh May, aye merciful to birdis,*
> *Now welcome be, ye flower of monethis all;*
> *For not only your grace upon us bydis,*
> *But all the world to witness this we call,*
> *That strewed hath so plainly over all,*
> *With new fresh sweet and tender green,*
> *Our life, our lust, our governor, our queen.*

243 ... far out, the Bass Rock stood in a nest of white floss...

Tantallon Castle with Bass Rock in the Distance

Bass Rock is an island near the mouth of the Firth of Forth, about one mile in circumference, nearly round, and 313 feet high. Gannets inhabit the rocky cliffs in vast multitudes, giving the rock a snowy appearance in the distance.

Siècles de foi means, literally, 'centuries of faith', but it is used to describe men who focus not on the end of their life, but on how their lives will live on afterwards. The term is used mainly for religious persons who seek to create objects and buildings which survive them, and is used to describe a piece of religious art or architecture, for example, *'La cathédrale de Reims, huit siècles de foi'*, meaning 'The Cathedral of Reims, eight centuries old'. The opposite of the phrase is *siècles d'incrédulité*, or centuries of disbelief. These men are marked by wanting to fulfil their daily desires, wanting only those things which come easily to them, and planning nothing durable and great.[4]

In this context, Lymond is referring to George's abstract thoughts (i.e. the age of questioning faith and its role in life), as opposed to hard facts (i.e. setting concrete foundations).[5]

244 *'I sometimes feel like a latter-day Hercules.'*

Hercules, the Greek and Roman god of physical strength, courage, and endurance, was the beloved son of Zeus and the mortal Alcmene. His inheritance was the throne of Tiryns, but Zeus's wife Hera, fueled by bitter jealousy, contrived to place her grandson Eurystheus on the throne, and made Hercules serve the inferior Eurystheus. Zeus, upon discovering Hera's treachery, made her promise immortality to Hercules upon his completion of a series of superhuman feats, called the Twelve Labours of Hercules. They were:

1. The wrestling of the monstrous Nemean lion;
2. The destruction of the Lernæn nine-headed hydra;
3. The capture of the bronze-horned and brazen-footed Arcadian stag;
4. The hunt of the Erymanthian boar;
5. The cleansing of the Augean stables;
6. The destruction of the Stymphalian birds, an innumerable swarm of voracious creatures with claws, wings, and beaks of brass which used their feathers as arrows and fed upon human flesh;
7. The capture of the Cretan bull, who was mad and created great havoc;
8. The abduction of the man-eating mares of Diomedes;
9. The seizure of the girdle of Hippolyte, queen of the Amazons;
10. The capture of the oxen of Geryones, a monster guarded by the giant Eurytion and the two-headed dog Orthus;
11. The procuring of the golden apples of Hesperides;
12. The bringing to the upper world the dog Cerberus, guardian of Hades.

2. Brief Return to Home Squares

245 *...gave way to a quincunx of soaring beeches...*

A quincunx is an arrangement of five objects in a square, one at each corner and one in the middle, especially an arrangement of trees in such squares continuously forming a grove or wood presenting parallel rows in different directions.

246 *'...your Englishy friends have burned me out of Newark.'*

Newark Castle by George Cattermole, c.1840

Newark Castle, situated on the south bank of the river Yarrow in Selkirkshire, was a massive border stronghold of the Scotts of Buccleuch. Of the many towers in Etterick Forest, Newark was the most prominent. Thought to have been erected as a hunting-seat for James II, the castle – a square tower with flanking turrets and projecting battlements – was styled the 'New Werk' in contradistinction to the neighbouring 'Auldwark'. It was besieged by Lord Grey in 1548; English forces burned the town and carried off a booty of 3000 sheep and 400 cattle.

247 *'...while bairns starve in Teviotdale...'*

The Scottish border county of Roxburghshire was often referred to as Teviotdale. Some parts of the area, such as Berwick, are now part of England. Teviotdale contained towns once vital to Scotland: Melrose, Selkirk, Jedburgh, and Coldstream. During expeditions by the English in 1544-45, many towns in Teviotdale were burnt and the abbeys of Dryburgh, Jedburgh, Kelso, and Melrose were left in ruins.

249 *...an expression of limpid encouragement on the rosso-antico face...*

Rosso-antico is a deep red Grecian marble used especially by the ancient Romans. It is also the name of a dessert wine made with an infusion of thirty-two herbs macerated in alcohol and then added to wine. The drink is ruby-coloured, with sweet notes of citrus and vanilla.

251 *'Man, you're that bedazzled your thick head's nothing but heliotrope.'*

Heliotrope is any one of various plants which turn toward the sun.

252 *...the plates of his jack flashing...*

A 'jack', or brigandine, was a form of torso armour; a coat made of linen or leather with scales or plates sewn upon it.

Man at Arms in Plate Armour and an Archer in Brigandine
by Francis Grose, 1801

253 'I hear the bosom of your father produced a clatter like the Archbishop's conscience...

In 1520, Dr. James Beaton, Archbishop of Glasgow, gained the name of 'Clattering Conscience' during the Scottish incident known as Cleanse the Causeway. After the disaster at Flodden, the Queen Dowager, Margaret Tudor, married the young and handsome Archibald Douglas, 6th Earl of Angus. The marriage identified the Douglases with the pro-English party in Scotland, in opposition to the pro-French party led by the Duke of Albany and James Hamilton, 1st Earl of Arran. In April 1520, the two opposing parties were both in Edinburgh. It was rumoured the Hamiltons, far greater in number, intended to take advantage of their superior numbers and crush the Douglases. Gavin Douglas, Bishop of Dunkeld, sought to avert the impending conflict by appealing to James Beaton to 'caution them against violence'[6].

Swearing on his conscience, Beaton pledged his oath that no mischief was intended, and struck his breast in emphasis. As he did so, however, the blow returned a rattling sound, betraying Beaton was wearing armour under his bishop's dress. Douglas responded, 'Alas, my Lord, I perceive your conscience clatters!'[7] Meaning, it tells false tales.

The dreadful conflict ensued on the main street of Edinburgh. In each wynd and close, men fought each other with bill and spear, sword and knife, and the sound of harquebus fire resounded throughout the city. At the end of the battle, the panic, and the chaos, the causeways and closes were filled with the dead and dying. The Douglases completely routed the Hamiltons, who fled from the city.

253 'The encounter seems to have had its share of bathos.'

Bathos is an abrupt, unintended transition from the exalted to the commonplace, producing a ludicrous effect; an anticlimax.

254 'Let us bathe in moral philosophy, as in a living river.'

Let us bathe in moral philosophy as in a living stream, these hands...the whole sensual part in which the lusts of the body have their seat and which...holds the soul by the scruff of the neck, let us be flung back from that ladder as profane and polluted intruders.

From *Oration on the Dignity of Man* by Count Giovanni Pico della Mirandola (1463-1494), an Italian Renaissance philosopher, humanist, theologian, and scholar. After two years studying canon law in Bologna, he left at the age of sixteen to wander for the next seven

Pico della Mirandola
by Christofono dell'Altissimo

years through the chief universities of Italy and France collecting a precious library; learning Greek, Latin, Hebrew, Chaldee, and Arabic; and studying the different systems of philosophy. While in Rome in 1486, Pico wrote *Oration* as an introduction to *De omni re scibili*, his list of 900 questions and conclusions addressing all branches of philosophy and theology, which he set forth for public disputation. Declared heretical by the pope, the book was prohibited and the disputations never took place.

Pico defended his theses in an elaborate *Apologia*, which exposed the tall, handsome, fair-complexioned nobleman to ridicule and persecution. His trials induced him to give up the study of profane literature and devote himself to more serious thought, and he published *Heptaplus*, a mystical exposition of the Creation, at age twenty-eight. His plans to publish a seven-fold work against the enemies of the church and give away all he owned to walk barefoot through the world preaching Christ were cut short by a deadly fever in 1494. He was absolved of heresy by Pope Alexander IV just one year before his death.

His writings endeavoured to reconcile Catholic theology with mediæval philosophy, and are a 'bewildering compound of mysticism, scholasticism, and recondite knowledge'[8]. While some scholars consider his writings of little value, others regard *Oration* to be an important treatise of Renaissance Humanism, the concern of which was to define the human place in God's plan and the relation of man to the divine. Regardless of opinion as to the worthiness of his writings, Pico was 'a theologian and an erotic poet, a philanthropist, a scholar, and a traveller...he was one of the most chivalrous, generous and versatile of men, his character as engaging as it is curious and complex'[9] and 'is still interesting...partly from the spectacle of a truly devout mind in the brilliant circle of half-pagan scholars of the Florentine renaissance'[10].

254   'I don't propose to sit here like a pelican in her piety...'

Window Detail
St. Bride's Kirk, Douglas

In mediæval Europe, the Pelican in her Piety became an image of self-sacrifice and an allegorical depiction of the Passion of Jesus and the Eucharist. In heraldry, the mother pelican would pluck at her own breast in order to draw blood to nurture her young.

255   '...they would decorticate you like an onion, and you'd deserve it.'

To decorticate is to remove the bark, husk, or outer covering.

256   ...galloped toward the fire with curses fothering the cleft air at his back.

Fothering is a dialectical variant of foddering, which is itself a dialectical variant of feeding.

Chapter II: The Queen's Progress Becomes Critical

Caxton: Tract 3, Chapter 5

The pawn that is set before the queen
signifies the physician, herbalist and apothecary...
The surgeons ought also be debonnaire,
amiable and to have pity of their patients.[1]

1. A New Pawn is Taken

258   *The sick baby Queen was taken to Dumbarton...*

Dumbarton Castle

Dumbarton Castle (originally Alcluyd, 'the rocky height on the Clyd') sits atop a stupendous mass of basalt, cleft near the center. The rock, almost perpendicular, rises abruptly and is almost completely surrounded by the Clyde and the Leven. Holding an important position as one of the keys to the Western Highlands, the castle has the longest recorded history of any stronghold in Great Britain. After her stay at Inchmahome, Queen Mary was moved to Dumbarton Castle where she remained for several months.

259   *Rowelled by French heels...*

A rowel is a sharp-toothed wheel at the end of a spur. The spur with rowel, shown to the right, was found on the field at Bannockburn.

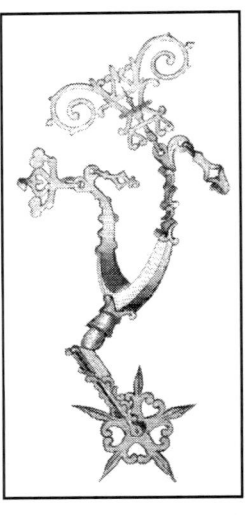

259   *'Build a hedge around the cuckoo?'*

From one of the fairy tales of the *Wise Men of Gotham*:

> *Once upon a time the men of Gotham would have kept the cuckoo so she might sing all the year. In the midst of their town they made a hedge round in compass and put a cuckoo into it and said, 'Sing here all the year through, or thou shalt have neither meat nor water.' The cuckoo, as soon as she perceived herself within the hedge, flew away. 'Vengeance on her!' they said. 'We did not make our hedge high enough.'*

261   *'I gather it would save you from Podagra and the Protector and every evil in Grimoire.'*

Podagra is gout of the big toe. The Protector is Edward Somerset. A Grimoire is a textbook of magic.

263   *She said instead, 'I can go where I please. To the Three Estates?'*

The members of the parliament of Scotland were collectively referred to as the Three Estates (Middle Scots: *Thrie Estaitis*).

2. But Proves to Be Covered

270   *...to supervise an extramural activity on the part of Turkey Mat.*

Extramural (Latin, *extra*, beyond, + *murus*, wall) is beyond the walls, as of a fortified city or university; hence, outside the fixed limits or boundaries of a place.

271   *... rolled like Pluto welcoming one of the damned.*

In mythology, Pluto (Greek, 'to be rich') was the brother of Zeus and Poseidon. When the world was divided amongst the three, he obtained for his share the underworld, the realm of darkness and ghostly shades. Stern and pitiless, Pluto was deaf to prayer and flattery. As a singing role, Pluto is usually written for a bass voice, the low vocal range representing the depths and weight of the underworld.

271   *The silverpoint voice was equally bland.*

Silverpoint is a drawing technique popular in the 15th and 16th centuries, used for precise, indelible images. It was achieved by using an instrument with a silver wire tip on specially prepared paper.

271   *'I think that, like the dolphin, he would be prettier dying.'*

A dying dolphin was thought to display a brilliancy of changing colours. Not to be confused with the sea mammal, a dying dolphinfish (*Coryphaena hippurus)* can display striking colour changes. From Byron's *Childe Harold's Pilgrimage*:

> *Parting day*
> *Dies like the dolphin, whom each pang imbues*
> *With a new colour as it gasps away;*
> *The last still loveliest, till 'tis gone and all is gray.*

272   *At last, the Attic tableau exploded.*

The term Attic is used to define the Athenian characteristic of being pure, classical, refined, and elegant; thus, an Attic tableau is a dramatic form displaying stillness and containment.

272   *'Harry!' She was on her feet. 'Not my baby: no!'*

Henry Stewart, Lord Darnley (1545-1567), was the eldest surviving child of Matthew Stewart, 4th Earl of Lennox, and Margaret Douglas, Countess of Lennox. A descendant of James II of Scotland and Henry VII of England, Darnley was born at Temple Newsam, Yorkshire, in December of 1545, making him three years old at the time of this scene in February 1548.

272 *'Like Petroneus...I take pleasure in committing suicide at leisure.'*

Petronius (c.27-66 AD) was an author, consul, and courtier during the reign of Nero. His collection of satires, *Petronii Arbitri Satyricon*, describes, in verse and prose, the adventures of several young debauchees and depicts the licentious life of the wealthy in Italy. After serving as consul of Bithynia, he returned to the court of Nero and his life of 'vicious indulgence'[2]. He became one of Nero's intimates, and was the *arbiter elegantiæ*, the final authority on taste and luxurious living. The favour he enjoyed at court aroused the jealousy of Tigellinius, another within the emperor's confidence. Banished and disgraced, Petronius chose to take his own life. Tacitus records his elegant suicide in *The Annals*:

> *Yet he did not fling away life with precipitate haste, but having made an incision in his veins and then, according to his humour, bound them up, he again opened them, while he conversed with his friends, not in a serious strain or on topics that might win for him the glory of courage. And he listened to them as they repeated, not thoughts on the immortality of the soul or on the theories of philosophers, but light poetry and playful verses. To some of his slaves he gave liberal presents, a flogging to others. He dined, indulged himself in sleep, that death, though forced on him, might have a natural appearance. Even in his will he did not, as did many in their last moments, flatter Nero or Tigellinus or any other of the men in power. On the contrary, he described fully the prince's shameful excesses, with the names of his male and female companions and their novelties in debauchery, and sent the account under seal to Nero. Then he broke his signet-ring, that it might not be subsequently available for imperiling others.*

273 *'One enjoys being the most debauched chub in the kingdom.'*

A chub is a thick, coarse-fleshed river fish. Its favourite haunts are deep holes or steep embankments, referring back to Margaret's comment about hiding in a hole like a chub.[3]

273 *'I've escaped the grand mal and the petit mal...'*

Epilepsy (*epilepsia*, 'a seizure') is a chronic functional disease of the nervous system. The ancients regarded it as due to demonic possession; the Romans regarded it as an evil omen. Its common English name, 'falling sickness'[4/D] was derived from its most common symptom. In a *grand mal* seizure, the patient falls unconscious in a convulsive fit; in a *petit mal* seizure, the patient suffers momentary confusion of thought or loss of consciousness. It is thought Mohammed and Julius Caesar both suffered from epileptic seizures.

273   *'...and even the Duke of Exeter's daughter...'*

The Duke of Exeter's daughter was a torture rack in the Tower of London, said to be named for John Holland, 2nd Duke of Exeter, the constable of the Tower in 1447. The rack was a device where a person was gradually stretched by means of pulleys and levers until one's joints were dislocated and eventually separated. It caused excruciating pain.

273   *'...by making scapegoats and sin-eaters of half his entourage.'*

A sin-eater was someone, usually very poor, hired to absorb the sins of the deceased so the departed soul might rest in peace. Through a ritual involving bread and drink, sin was transferred from the soul of the departed into the sin-eater, who thus became a pariah. The ritual is thought to have originated from an interpretation of Hosea 4: 8: 'They eat up the sin of my people.'

273   *'...like a shot from Buxted.'*

Buxted is a village in East Sussex. The first cast iron cannon in England was made there in 1543.

273   *'Alas, my sweet nonage.'*

Nonage is a period of youth or lack of maturity; an early stage, or a second childhood.

274   *'My natural habit, like the squirting cucumber.'*

The squirting cucumber (*Ecballium elaterium*), when ripe, squirts a stream of poisonous juice, which is an irritant to the eyes and skin. This juice, called elaterium (Greek, 'driving away'), when collected and dried, produces a drug known to the ancients as a drastic purgative.[5/D]

Ecballium elaterium

275   *'More impressive than Temple Newsam?'*

Temple Newsam was an ancient preceptory belonging to the Knights Templars. After the order was suppressed by Edward II, it was granted by Edward III to Sir John D'Arcy. In 1544, Thomas, Lord D'Arcy was beheaded for his role in the insurrection known as the 'Pilgrimage of Grace'. The mansion, described as the 'Hampton Court of the North', was then given by Henry VIII to Matthew Stewart, Earl of Lennox, and his wife, Margaret Douglas, Countess of Lennox. Their son, Henry, Lord Darnley, was born there. In 1622, the estate was purchased and the mansion rebuilt, incorporating only some of the original structure.

276   *'Poor Thomas Howard. Did you offer him life and liberty too?'*

Lord Thomas Howard (1511-1537), an uncle of Anne Boleyn, met Margaret at court, where they fell in love and became secretly engaged. Henry VIII learned of the engagement after Queen Anne fell from power and Henry had removed both of his daughters from his line of succession, making Margaret the next in line to the throne. Both Margaret and Howard were sent to the Tower. Lady Margaret broke off their relationship; she fell ill with fever and was released. Lord Howard was sentenced to death, but prior to his execution he became ill and died.

276   *'Mine all have whole necks and go to bed with me for joy, not for lions on their quarterings and galloon on their underwear.'*

'Whole necks' is a reference to the affinity of King Henry VIII to behead his wives.

'Lions on their quarterings' is an heraldic reference. Quartering in heraldry is a method of joining several different coats of arms together in one shield by dividing the shield into equal parts and placing different coats of arms in each division. The lion is a common charge in heraldry, traditionally symbolising bravery, valour, strength, and royalty, as it is regarded as the king of beasts.

A galloon is a decorative woven trim sometimes in the form of a braid and commonly made of metallic thread, lace, or embroidery.

277   *'He doesn't suffer from – from satyriasis, if that's what you mean.'*

Satyriasis is excessive or abnormal sexual craving in the male ('sexual insanity'[5/D]), a diseased and unrestrainable venereal appetite, corresponding to nymphomania in women. In classical mythology, the Satyrs were sylvan deities forming part of the retinue of Bacchus. They were fond of music, dancing, wine, lasciviousness and riot, and the deep slumbers following debauchery.

277   *'Chargé d'ans et pleurant son antique prouesse...'*

> *'Mourning, in his age, the wane of might once dreaded...'*

From the fable, *The Lion Grown Old*:

> *A lion, mourning, in his age, the wane*
> *Of might once dreaded through his wild domain,*

Was mocked, at last, on his throne,
By subjects of his own,
Strong through his weakness grown.
The horse his head saluted with a kick;
The wolf snapped at his royal hide;
The ox, too, gored him in the side;
The unhappy lion, sad and sick,
Could hardly growl, he was so weak.
In uncomplaining, stoic pride,
He waited for the hour of fate,
Till the ass approached his gate;
Whereat, 'This is too much,' he says;
'I willingly would yield my breath;
But, ah! your kick is double death!'

277 *'Your antique prouesse was a little better than this.'*

Prouess is bravery, valiance.

277 *'You want to stay here and mend my shirts.'*

In the midst of his affair with Anne Boleyn, King Henry VIII continued contact with Queen Catherine of Aragon, and she would mend his shirts.

279 *'Out, alas! Now goeth away my prisoners and all my prey.'*

From *Piers Plowman* (c.1360-1387) by William Langland. Satan's last appearance shows him bound and condemned to Hades forever, lamenting his fate and cursing the powers of Christ.

Out, alas! now goeth away / my Prisoners and all my pray,
and I might not stirr one Stray / I am so streitly dight.

279 *'Shall I send you each an eye on a thorny stick like St. Triduana to preserve my chastity?'*

St. Triduana was born in the Greek city of Colosse, and travelled from Constantinople with Saint Rule, who brought the bones of Saint Andrew to Scotland in the 4th century. Her illustrious birth, elegant form, and virtuous disposition attracted the attention of Nechtan, a King of the Picts. Hearing the prince was attracted by the transcendent beauty of her eyes, she replied, 'What he asks of me he shall obtain'. She then plucked out her eyes with thorns, and sent them with the messenger, saying, 'Accept what your prince desires.' She retired to Restalrig (Edinburgh) and devoted her life to fasting and prayer. In mediæval times, those with eye disorders and blindness sought relief at St. Triduana's Well.

279 *'... for I should sooner pity Apollyon himself.'*

Apollyon (Greek, 'the destroyer') is personified in the book of Revelation as the angel who has dominion over the bottomless pit, and as king of the locusts.

279 *'Is it possible? Krishna among the milkmaids gored by a cow?'*

Sri Krishna with flute, c.1790-1800

In Vaishnava theology, Krishna is the eighth avatar of the god Vishnu, who played his flute and danced by moonlight with the milkmaids (*gopis*) who had unconditional devotion to him. Their bliss represented union with the Divine. Here, Margaret is rubbing in the irony that a woman could turn on Lymond. Likewise, Krishna among the milkmaids wouldn't be harmed in his own domain, as he was raised by cowherds and had a deep spiritual connection with the gopis. Additionally, Margaret managed to hurt Francis with her words, even though biting words are his domain.[7]

280 *'Always excepting he's raxed himself scaling the window, no.'*

To rax is to stretch; to put oneself to great effort or strain.

283 *'...emerging from your pupa robe a chevalier des dames...'*

A *pupa robe* is a chrysalis. A *chevalier des dames* is a knight of the ladies.

283 *'Strangle your inchoate chivalry and take yourself off.'*

Inchoate is just begun, thus not fully developed; rudimentary.

283 *Already weakened, the seel over Scott's eyes jerked...*

In falconry, seeling is a training technique used to temporarily blind a bird by sewing its eyes shut.

284 *'I am thi master: willt thou fight?'*

From *Mactatio Abel*, one of the Wakefield Mystery Plays, which portrays the Biblical story of the brothers Cain and Abel. This quote, specifically, refers to where Cain lets his ploughboy, Garcio, know a servant can't prevail against his master (which is supremely ironic, considering Cain is about to try to cheat God out of a tithe).[8]

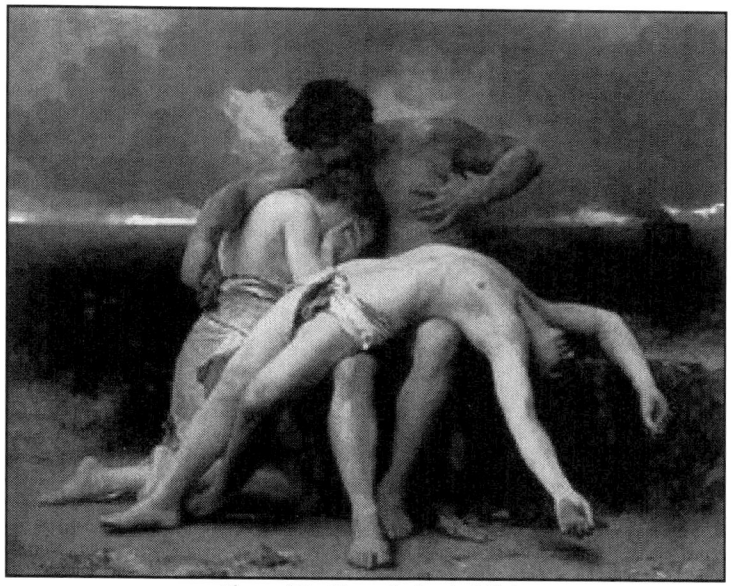

Adam and Eve Mourn the Death of Abel
by William Bouguereau, 1888

284 *'...except perhaps recruiting redheaded predicants...'*

A predicant is one who affirms anything; one who preaches, specifically a preaching friar.[9/D]

285 *'Well, well. And fu' as a puggie...'*

> *'He's as drunk as a monkey.'*

Chapter III: Mate for the Master

The Buke of Chess: Tract 4, Chapter 3

A Queen's moves should keep to the same color.
In her first move may she go a diverse way,
First to the point before her mediciner,
Second to two points very angular,
To the point void (empty) before the other.[1]

1. A Bereft Knight Is Checked by His Own Side

288 *'And go and see Sym's cuddies in a jug.'*

Cuddie is a term for coalfish, *Pollachius virens.*[2/D]

288 *Melting eye and embouchure veered from Sybilla to Lady Fleming...*

Embouchure is the manner in which the lips and tongue are applied to the mouthpiece of a windwood or brass instrument. Meaning, the little Queen is pursing her lips and pouting.

291 *'...he'd have gone about it like Hephaestus with a hatchet.'*

Hephæstus was the Greek god of fire and the metallic arts. Homer depicted him as lame, giving him a grotesque appearance in Greek eyes. His symbols are a smith's hammer and an anvil, although sometimes he is portrayed holding an axe. Hephæstus delivered Athena by opening her father Zeus's head with an ax and she sprang forth. Christian is saying Richard seems to think Lymond is barbaric enough to deliver Mariotta's baby by splitting her open with a hatchet.[3]

292 *'I shall not ask you to outrage your feelings.'*

To outrage is to desecrate or deprive of sacred character; to violate flagrantly.

292 *'You look as if you'd been boiled in a pot with a Pasque flower.'*

Several varieties of the Pasque flower (*Pulsatilla*) are purple. The dye from the flower has long been used to color Easter eggs.

292 *'You'll want to kick my bottom through my merrythought,' he warned.*

The merrythought is the wishbone or breastbone, specifically of a bird; hence, Wat expecting Sybilla to kick his arse up into his chest.

292 *'...you'll have an a priori case for it.'*

Anemone pulsatilla

A priori is a legal term meaning an assumption of truth without further proof.

292 *'I've had that lunatic Culter stotted into a punishment cell...'*

To stot is to bind with a stiff-legged gait.

293 *'...the Governor who's in a stoory panic...'*

A stoor is turmoil or conflict; a cloud of dust; hence, conflicted.

293 *'..and the English to march in again on the hour like the bell for Prime.'*

Prime Bell is the call for the first hour service at 6 a.m. The purpose of Prime service is to meditate on the Creation, the banishment of Adam and Eve from Paradise, and the appearance of Christ before Caiaphas.

293 *'...he's a jelly-footed puddock with his wits in his wame.'*

A puddock is a frog. The wame is the belly.

293 *'...since I taught him all the verses of Sir Guy...'*

Sir Guy of Warwick is the hero of an Anglo-Norman chivalric romance, *Gui de Warewic* written in England in the 13th century. In the early 14th century, approximately one-third of the original story was translated into English as *Guy of Warwick*, and converted into twelve-line tail-rhyme stanzas. The hero, Sir Guy, falls deeply in love with Félice, daughter of the Earl of Warwick. To win her hand in marriage, he demonstrates his knightly prowess in foreign wars and adventures across Europe. He returns and marries Félice, and the celebration lasts for two weeks, during which time Félice conceives a son. Guy, seized with remorse for the violence of his past, repents for having neglected God. He decides to leave his wife and fortune to make a pilgrimage of atonement to the Holy Land. A distressed Félice agrees to let him go, and a disguised Guy sets off wearing her gold ring. Guy reaches the Holy Land, and after years of absence, he returns to England in time to save Winchester from the invading northern kings, and slays their champion giant. He makes his way to Warwick, and, in disguise, visits his wife, who does not recognise him, and then retires to a hermitage in a nearby forest. Before his death, he sends to Félice the gold ring, and she arrives in time to close his eyes. She dies soon after, and is buried alongside Guy.

294 *O row my lady in satin and silk*
  And wash my son in the morning milk.

From a traditional Scottish ballad:

> *Now, or a month was come and gane,*
> *The ladye bare a bonny son;*
> *And 'twas weel written on his breast-bane,*
> *'Cospatrick is my father's name.'*
> *O row my lady in satin and silk,*
> *And wash my son in the morning milk.*

295 *...she looked as if she had been attending decumbitures all her life.*

Decumbiture is confinement to a sick bed.

296 *'There the thorne is thikkest to buylden and brede.'*

From *The Vision of William Concerning Piers the Plowman* by William Langland (c.1332-c.1400). The poem is a series of eleven dream visions and an examination of the lives of the characters of *Do-Well*, one who does a kind act, *Do-Bet*, one who teaches others to act kindly, and *Do-Best*, one who combines both practice and theory, doing well to himself and teaching others to do the same. The poem describe the life and manners of the poor; protests clerical abuses and corruption in the courts of law; represents the miseries caused by hasty marriage; and denounces lazy workmen and sham beggars.

296 *'In any case, it was good of you to come, my orchard of jewels.'*

In one of the tales in *The Book of One Thousand and One Nights*, Aladdin enters the subterranean orchard of jewels, the garden of delights which sends men mad if they are not purified or prepared.

296   *'Come along, my hinny...'*

'Hinny' is Scots term of affection, from honey.

298   *'...I seem to be the disruptive serpent of the Ophites and not Richard?'*

'Ophites' was a term used to describe Gnostic sects which inverted the events of the Fall of Man in Genesis. They held the serpent in the Garden of Eden was a benign emissary of the Supreme Being who wanted Adam and Eve to eat from the Tree of Knowledge so they could know the true deity and their true spiritual natures, and would no longer be subject to the demiurge (lesser god) which created the material world and subsequently brought evil into being. Ophite teachings were heretical to Church orthodoxy and their secret rituals were believed to be lawless and sexually explicit.[4]

298   *'You have an entrancing and hagioscopic view of my character...'*

In Mediæval architecture, a hagioscope was an opening in a wall of a church to enable worshippers in chapels or side aisles to see the main altar; a squint.

298   *'...proposing to join the Portuguese Men of War?'*

Portuguese men-of-war are marine floaters with a numbing sting.[5/D] Portuguese men-of-war were also police officers. Portugal was permitted to retain possession of the islands of Lewis and Arran, an exclusive right to fish part of the coast of Scotland, and the right to land for the purpose of repairing Portuguese boats, drying nets, and curing fish. Affairs along the Scottish coast were subject to the approval of the Portuguese men-of-war.

299   *'The peripetia will be so tidy.'*

The peripetia (From Greek, a turning right about, to change suddenly, reversal) is the turning point in a drama where the plot is unravelled and the whole concludes, the dénouement. The term is derived from the word peripatetic, a follower of Aristotle who taught while walking in the Lyceum of Athens.[6/D]

299   *'Prior exiit, prior intravit.'*

'He came first, and he must go first.'

299   *'Atlas in labour, no less.'*

In Greek mythology, Atlas (the 'Endurer'), leader of the Titans, attempted to storm the heavens. For this supreme treason he was condemned to bear the heavens and earth on his shoulders.

299 *'...like a yaffle on a pear tree?'*

A yaffle (*Picus viridis*) is a green woodpecker.

300 *'One gets a little tired of too much Suivez François and Fan Fan feyne.'*

Suivez François: Follow Francis

Fan Fan Feyne is a string of nonsense syllables from the ballad *La guerre (The Battle)* by Clement Janequin (1485-1558), one of the most famous composers of the Renaissance. *'La guerre's* wonderfully noisy evocation of clanking armor, drum tattoos, rim-shots,

Picus viridis

trumpet fanfares, calls to arms, harquebus fire, and marching troops was strikingly original.'[7] The syllables *'fan frère le le fan fan fan feyne'* are set in a rhythm closely resembling drumming used to issue military commands in the field.

300 *'Mariotta, my Sarmatian poppy!'*

The Sarmatians, referred to as Amazons, were a nation of all-female warriors in Greek mythology and Classical Antiquity. Their name is a term for women warriors in general. Notable queens of the Amazons are Penthesilea, who participated in the Trojan War, and her sister Hippolyta, whose magical girdle was the object of one of the labours of Hercules.

Nuremberg Chronicle, 1493

300 *'Such a violent volte-face! I thought you loved me as the marabou loves its one-legged mother. I thought we should be shikk to shikk, indivisible...'*

A volte-face (from French, from Italian, *volte-faccia*, *volte*, to turn, +*faccia*, face) is a change of position or policy; an about-face. The marabou is a large wading bird in the stork family. In Bengal, the marabou was thought to be possessed by the soul of Brahman. A shikk is a demoniacal creature in Arabian mythology.

301 *'And wha wouldna leer like spring joist,' said the cynics, 'that's just merrit the hale chump-end of Scotland?'*

Chump-end is veal or mutton.[8/D] Here, meaning Agnes Herries's lands cover a huge area of Scotland, so who wouldn't want to marry her?

301 *...seemed to be affected with an uncommon sonority.*

Sonority (Medieval Latin, *sonōritās,* fullness of sound; Late Latin, melodiousness) is using deep and imposing language or sound; resonance; grandiloquent speech.

301 *'I was merely the Baptist, the Bean King: the helical star before the sun.'*

Baptism of Christ by Guido Reni, c.1622

'The Baptist' refers to John the Baptist, who baptized Jesus in the River Jordan. The Bean King refers to a feast on Twelfth Night. In celebration, a bean was buried in a cake. Whoever had the good fortune to have the slice of cake with the bean was crowned the Bean King. This choosing of a king or queen by a bean was formerly a common Christmas diversion at the English and Scottish courts. The helical star before the sun is Sirius, the brightest star in the sky.

All of this is Lymond's way of deferring to John Maxwell for the bride's benefit. The three references all allude to precursors of greater things, or to what owes homage to a greater being: John the Baptist, the miraculously conceived forerunner of Christ; the Bean King on Twelfth Night representing the Magi who brought gifts to Jesus; the helical rising of a star is its first appearance in the Eastern sky at dawn, just before the sun itself rises.[9]

302   *...and worth more than her total parure put together.*

A parure (from Old French, *pareure*, adornment, from *parer*, to embellish, from Latin, *parāre*, to arrange) is a wardrobe of matching pieces of jewellery or ornaments intended to be worn together.

302   *'The Pythia in a lemon fog.'*

The Pythia, known as the oracle of Delphi, was the priestess at the Temple of Apollo. The Pythia, a young maiden, would prepare herself to receive Apollo's revelation by chewing on laurel leaves and sitting upon a tripod perched over a chasm in the centre of the temple, from which arose an intoxicating vapour known as pneuma (Greek, for 'breath' or 'spirit').

Priestess of Delphi by John Collier, 1891

302 *'Unless like the elephant I have two hearts, or like Janus two heads...'*

The ancient Italian god Janus (derived from *janua*, 'a gate' or 'opening'), was the guardian of gates and doors. As the spirit of opening, he was invoked at the beginning of all undertakings; he was the god of the beginning of the day, and the beginning of the year. As the god of the rising and setting sun he had two faces, one looking eastward and the other westward.

302 *'It doesn't help to find oneself bedevilled with persons making Eulenspiegel-like appearances and disappearances.'*

Till Eulenspiegel was an impudent trickster of German folklore. In the stories, he exposed greed and folly, hypocrisy and stupidity among members of every class of late-mediæval society. Eulenspiegel stories are about the misuses and misinterpretations of communication, whether deliberate or accidental. Till Eulenspiegel's adventures revolved around how language both reveals and deceives. He is the complicating factor, by way of word play, punning, and turns of phrase, which at once illustrates the necessity of language and its pitfalls.[9]

302 *'A thief in the night is the phrase.'*

Till Eulenspiegel, MS, 1515

'A thief in the night' is a metaphor used in the New Testament Parable of the Faithful Servant (Matthew 24:42-51, Mark 13:34-37, Luke 12:35-48). The parable implores servants to keep watch, because they do not know the day the Lord is coming so must remain prepared and alert at their posts. The parable also cautions that much is required of a person to whom much is given, emphasizing privilege brings responsibility.

303 *'...with silver trumpets and sarcanet and schorl and satinwood, spring water and roses from Shiraz...would you receive me?'*

Sarcanet (from Latin, *saracenatus*, literally 'Saracen Cloth') was a fine, thin silk valued for its softness. Schorl (French, *schorl*; perhaps from Swedish, *skör* or Danish, *skjör*, brittle, frail) was an early term for a large group of crystallized minerals; it was later limited to black tourmaline. Satinwood is a hard, lemon-coloured wood from India. Its lustrous finish made it popular for use in cabinetry and small luxury items. Shiraz, founded in the 8th century, is a city of Persia which was known in the Middle Ages as a seat of culture. A favourite resort of Persian princes, it was celebrated in Persian poetry for its climate, its wine and roses, and its beautiful gardens.

303   *"'And who is this?   Great Alexander?   Charle le Maigne?'"*

From *Ralph Roister Doister* by Nicholas Udall (1504-1556), the earliest English comedy. 'Ralph Roister Doister, a rich lady-killer with an overweening opinion of his own gallantry (in both senses), has Matthew Merrygreek for companion, sycophant, and go-between. Despite mortifications galore, he falls in love with Dame Christian Custance, betrothed to a merchant, Gawin Goodluck. The attempts of Ralph to "cut out" Gawin, the anger of the lady, the ambiguous letter, the onslaught of the maids with pots and pans, the rout of Ralph's party, the return of Gawin, and the happy dénouement, fully substantiate its claim to an early place in English comedy.'[10]

Alexander the Great of Macedonia (356-323 BC) created one of the largest empires of the ancient world, stretching from the Ionian Sea to the Himalayas.

Charlemagne (742-814), also known as Charles the Great, was King of the Franks; he expanded the Frankish kingdom into an empire covering much of Western and Central Europe.

Charlemagne by Albrect Dürer, 1512

303   *'Royster-Doister, visiting the Castle Perserverence.   Have good day: I goo to helle.'*

> To devylys delle
> I schal thee bere to Helle.
> I wyl not dwelle.
> Have good day! I goo to Helle.

Lymond replies with a line from *The Castle of Perseverance*, the 15th-century morality play, representing the allegorical combat for the soul of man. The play shows the progression of *Humanum Genus*, the representative of mankind, from birth to death. While a youth, he falls into the power of the mortal sin *Luxuria*, but is brought by *Poententia* to trust himself to *Confessio,* who leads him to the Castle of Perseverance, and they foil the assault by the vices. 'But, in his old days, *Humanum* succumbs to the temptation of *Avarice*; after his death, the evil angel claims the right to drag him into hell, but he is set free by God at the prayers of Pity and Peace.'[12]

303 *'I have been gifted with a surfeit of Satanity...'*

Satanity is inherent evilness.

303 *'Oh. At which Court?' she quoted...*

Christian references *Why come ye nat to Courte?* by John Skelton (1460-1529), an English poet who studied at Cambridge and Oxford and was tutor to the young Prince Henry (later, Henry VIII). He was known for his satirical vernacular poetry, rattling verses and quickly-recurring rhymes, 'overflowing with grotesque words and images and unrestrained jocularity'[13], lightened by 'bright gleams of fancy'[14]. An incorrigible practical joker, he was beloved at court, yet fell victim to his sarcastic wit and bitter tongue. *Why come ye nat to Courte?* is a direct attack against Cardinal Wolsey, Skelton's former patron. He assaults, with plain-spoken boldness, Wolsey's ostentation, overbearing manner, and almost-royal authority. Wolsey attempted to arrest him, but Skelton sought sanctuary in Westminster, where he was sheltered until his death.

303 *'Don't you think that if you didn't clutch them to your evil chest like Epaminondas and his javelin, your affairs might be less ruinous?'*

Epaminondas (c.418-362 B.C.) was one of the noblest figures in Greek history. In his final battle, Epaminondas charged at the head of his army of 33,000 men, and was wounded in the breast by a javelin. Knowing he would die as soon as the weapon was extracted, he waited to hear his troops were victorious before drawing out the javelin with his own hands. His last words were, 'I have lived long enough; for I die unconquered'.[15]

Epaminondas

304 *'...the habit of lying on my face even when turned, like George Faustus.'*

Faustus was the name of a magician and charlatan of the early 16th century, now famous in legend and literature. The historical Faust (c.1480-c.1538), also known as Faustus, was described by contemporaries as a fool rather than a philosopher, a vain babbler, and a mountebank. Holding himself out as skilled in necromancy, astrology, and magic, Faustus boasted that if all the works of Aristotle and

Joannes Faustus, c. 17th century

Plato were blotted from the minds of man, he could restore them with even greater eloquence, and if required, could reproduce the miracles of Christ. The Protestant theologian Johan Gast credited Faust with genuine supernatural qualities, yet believed him to be in league with the devil, and described his deplorable end. Faust was strangled by the devil, and his dead body lay constantly on its face on its bier, even though his body was turned upwards five times.

304 *'I should make a wonderful epopee, don't you think?'*

An epopee is an epic poem.

304 *'I should be all on the right side like a halibut...'*

Halibut is a flatfish; its name is derived from *haly* (holy) and *butt* (flat fish), for its popularity on Catholic holy days. Here, Lymond is showing the best in his nature, describing the pleasantness of being right with the world and able to be introduced to Christian formally. He is also acutely perceptive when he says her blindness has been a gift to them both (*'You know that if you hadn't been blind, these meetings would never have been possible?'*); he must guess it is now, more than ever in her life, that she wishes she could see, so she could look on his face.[16]

305 *'...be twelve feet tall like St. Christopher.'*

St. Christopher is a Christian martyr believed to be more than 12 feet tall. He is often depicted as a giant of a man carrying the Christ child on his shoulder.

305 *'A woman,' he said, 'with a familiar spirit.'*

Saul Consults the Witch of Endor by Caspar Luikin, 1712

In I Samuel 28: 7 Saul said unto his servants, 'Seek me a woman that hath a familiar spirit, that I may go to her and inquire of her.' And his servants said to him, 'Behold, there is a woman that hath a familiar spirit at Endor.' The Witch of Endor called up the ghost of the recently deceased prophet Samuel at the demand of Saul, King of Israel.

Lymond is saying several things with one phrase. He is referring to the Book of Samuel where the witch consults with a ghost (Lymond being the one ghosting around the place); he is implying Christian has bewitching qualities; and he is also saying he is her 'familiar' or spirit companion, working together like a magician and his totem, or an enchantress and her supernatural servant; and he is saying they are familiar in spirit, kindred souls, much alike.[17]

306   *'Or could you stomach a rapprochement if I arranged it?'*

A rapprochement is the resumption of harmonious relations.

306   *'Some of you laddies talk as if I were Michael Scott the wizard...'*

Sir Michael Scot (c.1175-c.1234) was a Scottish mathematician, physician, and scholar who studied at Oxford and Paris, received a Doctorate degree in Theology, and was an ordained priest. He was invited to the court of Frederick II, and at his instigation translated many of the works of Aristotle, along with the Arabian commentaries of Averroes. It is thought the connection with both Frederick II and Averroes, both of whom held a reputation of evil in the Middle Ages, led to the formation of the legend of 'Ault Michael' as a wizard and magician. Dante consigned him, in the *Inferno*, to the circle of Hell reserved for sorcerers, astrologers, and false prophets. In Border folklore, the 'wondrous wizard' of Sir Walter Scott's *The Lay of the Last Minstrel*, 'cleft the Eildon Hills in three, and bridled the Tweed with a curb of stone'[18]. It was said, 'In the south of Scotland any work of great labour and antiquity is ascribed either to the agency of Auld Michael, or Sir William Wallace or the devil.'[19]

306   *'...planted there like a couple of bauchly tenors at a glee.'*

One who is bauchly is ungainly or shabby-looking. Wat may be using the affectionately derisive definition of *bauchly* or *bauchlie* here, meaning clownishly worn-looking, or bent out of shape. Bauchly can also mean indifferent, poor, as in a sorry excuse for something.[20]

307   *'...counts as much as two tallow dips in the circles of Hell.'*

Tallow dip was a strip of burning cloth in a saucer of tallow grease, a poor man's substitute for the tallow candle, in itself a cheaper substitute for wax candles.

308   *'I'm Mère-Sotte...'*

The term *Mère-Sotte* (French, Mother Fool) derives from a character name in a *sotie*, a short comic play of 15th- and 16th- century France. In these intellectual dramas, the characters were designated by a number – Premier Sot, Second Sot, etc., and were often controlled by a *meneur du jeu* (a game leader), *Mère-Sotte*. Soties were cruelly sarcastic in tone, and consisted of a series of verbal exchanges full of vicious mockery, and used 'bitter laughter to provoke thought or political action'[21].

Chapter IV: Concerted Attack

Caxton: Tract 1, Chapter 3

There is no time so strong and firm but that sometime a
feeble thing is cast down to overthrow it.
How well that the lion be the strongest beast...
yet sometimes a little bird eats him.[1]

1. The Four Knights' Game

309 *Playing cards with Palmer, Grey's new engineering adviser...*

Sir Thomas Palmer (d.1553) was an English soldier and courtier. A favourite of
Henry VIII, he played dice with him and was gentleman-usher to the king at the
Field of the Cloth of Gold in 1520. He was knighted at Calais in 1532. After
Henry died, Palmer, who had secured a reputation for unbounded courage, was
sent for service on the border under Somerset. In 1548, he distinguished himself
bringing provisions into Haddington, and had command of the lances in an
expedition from Berwick, but his 'self will and glory in that journey did cast away
the whole power for they were all overthrown'[2].

312 *'Orpheus wriggling rump first out of Hades...'*

In Greek mythology, Orpheus, the son of Apollo, possessed the power of charming
all objects – animate and inanimate – with his lyre. He was permitted to descend
into Hades to bring back his wife, Eurydice, on the condition that he walked in
front of her and not look back, until both were safely arrived in the Upperworld.
Overcome by anxiety, Orpheus looked round, consigning Eurydice to the
Underworld. Here, Janet is drawing a parallel between Orpheus trying to lead
Eurydice out of Hades and Will seeking to remove Mariotta from the wicked
Lymond.[3]

Orpheus Leading Eurydice from the Underworld
by Jean-Baptiste-Camille Carot, c.1861

312   '...with his chivalry ashine like a ten-thread twill.'

A ten-thread twill refers to a lustrous satin.

313   ...the commander, Sir Robert Bowes....

Sir Robert Bowes (c.1495-1554) was an English lawyer and military commander in active service on the Borders. In 1541, he advised the privy council on Scottish business, and in 1542 was sent into Scotland to 'harry'[4] Jedburgh with 3000 men. He wrote the authoritative record of the state of the border country in the 16th century, describing the nature of the land, its military organisation, condition of its fortresses, and information about the character of the borderers. A lawyer as well as a soldier, he wrote a legal treatise on the complicated system of international law by which disputes between the borderers of England and Scotland were settled.

313   'Like Glaucus, we have a but, but no honey in it.'

Glaucus was a son of Minos and Pasiphaë. One day, Glaucus was playing, fell into a barrel of honey and died. King Minos entreated a seer to find Glaucus, and then to restore the boy to life. The seer did, but he wasn't rewarded; all he received was Minos forcing him to impart all his wisdom to Glaucus.[5]

314 'Not the honey barrel, but the tilly-seeds of torture...'

Tilly seeds are the seeds of the Purging Croton (*Croton tiglium*), a small tree native to India and other tropical parts of Asia. The seeds are a very powerful drastic purgative.[6/D] While once much employed in Europe, use diminished because of the violence and uncertainty of action. Here, Lymond is saying his fate won't be like Glaucus (drowning in a honey barrel) but being tortured to release his secrets.[7]

Croton tiglium

314 '...from fustic head to silver spurs.

Fustic is a dye of a light-yellow colour made from the wood of a tropical tree, *Maclura tinctura*.

314 '–But even a gib-cat has claws.'

A gib-cat is a tom-cat, usually neutered. It traces back to a time when a male cat was called Gilbert, or in French, Tibert. Chaucer renders *Thibert le Cas* in *Romaunt of the Rose* as *Gibbe, our Cat*. Likewise, Sir Tybert is the cat in the *Tale of Reynard the Fox*. Lymond correctly interprets Sir Robert's assessment of him as an innocuous dandy, and warns him that 'even a neutered cat can scratch'.[8]

Maclura Tinctura

314 'Thumbscrews,' said Bowes picturesquely. 'The iron glove – hot lead – pincers – knives. And the whip.'

Thumbscrews, or pilliwinks, was a torture instrument first used in mediæval Europe: the victim's thumbs or fingers were placed in the vice and slowly crushed. The iron glove was a mesh mitt heated in white-hot coals and strapped onto a prisoner's hand. Hot lead was used to burn an individual's flanks, often employed simultaneously with torture on the rack. Pincers made with specially roughened grips were used to tear out the nails of the fingers and toes.

315 ...and generally sacrificed to the playful god Momus.

In Greek mythology, Momus was the god of satire and mockery, of censure and ridicule.

315   *The patch of ground at Heriot chosen by Lymond for the vigil...*

Heriot is a small village in the Moorfoot Hills, southeast of Edinburgh.

315   *...melting as the tears of the Heliades...*

In Greek mythology, the Heliades ('children of the sun') were the seven nymph daughters of the sun-god Helios, who grieved the loss of their brother; the gods turned them into poplar trees and their tears into amber.

315   *...He and the King of Naverne*
          Were fair feared in the fern
          Their headēs for to hide –

From the song *How Edward the King come in Braband And toke homage of all the land* by Laurence Minot (c.1300-1352), an English writer of a series of poems celebrating English victories on the Scottish border and in Europe.

315   *'Well, yours are the marybones...'*

From *The Cook's Portrait, The Canterbury Tales* by Geoffrey Chaucer. 'Marybones' are marrowbones.

>   *A cook they hadde with hem for the nones,*
>   *To boille the chiknes with the marybones.*

315   *'Let Parrott, I pray you, have lyberte to prate.'*

>   *Let Parrot, I pray you, freely prate [speak on and on],*
>   *For Greece's golden tongue ought to be extolled,*
>   *If it were learned perfectly, and in the same custom,*
>   *As Latin, in school matters employed,*
>   *But our Greeks their Greek so well have applied*
>   *That they cannot say in Greek, riding by the way,*
>   *How, hostler, fetch my horse a bundle of hay!'* [9]   (Tr.J.J.)

From *Speke, Parott*, by John Skelton. The Grammarians' War (1519–1521) was a conflict between rival systems of teaching Latin; many joined in the exchange of pamphlets; the back-and-forth was personal and caustic. In *Speke, Parrott*, Skelton heavily criticised the 'Greek' way of teaching, wherein students were not required to master the basics of grammar before progressing to reading classical writings, and so were unable to compose even basic sentences because they lacked the fundamentals.

316   *'Art thou Heywood, with the mad, merry wit?'*

From an epigram by John Heywood (c.1497-1580), an English dramatist and writer. After studying at Oxford, Heywood was introduced to court by Sir Thomas More, the uncle of Heywood's wife, Eliza Rastell. His 'inexhaustible wit'[10] and skill in music made him a favourite with both Henry VIII and Princess Mary. He gave an oration in Latin at Queen Mary's coronation, wrote several poems in her honour, and was said to be with her at her last moments.

Heywood is important in the history of English drama as the first writer to turn the abstract characters of morality plays (i.e. Youth, Felicity, etc.) into individual persons (i.e. the Pedlar, the Pardoner, etc.), thus linking morality plays to the modern drama.

> *Art thou Heywood, with thy mad, merry wit?*
> *Yea, forsooth, master, that name is even hit.*
> *Art thou Heywood, that appliest mirth more than thrift?*
> *Yes, sir, I take merry mirth a golden gift.*
> *Art thou Heywood, that has made many mad plays?*
> *Yea, many plays, few good works in my days.*
> *Art thou Heywood, that hath made men merry long?*
> *Yea, and will, if I be made merry among.*
> *Art thou Heywood, that wouldst be made merry now?*
> *Yes, sir, help me to it now, I beseech you.*

316 *'Behold,' he quoted sadly, 'my countenance and my colour.'*

From *A Miracle Play of the Nativity*, a mediæval play in which Herod proudly sings his own hymn of praise:

> *Behold my countenance and my colour,*
> *Brighter than the sun in the middle of the day.*
> *Where can you have a more greater succour,*
> *Than to behold my person that is so gay?*
> *My falcon and my fashion, with my gorgeous array –*
> *He that had the grace alway thereon to think,*
> *Live he might alway without either meat or drink.*

316 *'It's only Sweet Cicely awaiting the bees...'*

Sweet Cicely (*Myrrhis odorata*) is a tall perennial plant which is very attractive to bees. Its essence is said to be an aphrodisiac used as a love medicine.

316 *'God save Flamens and keep all the knotless...'*

In ancient Roman religion, a Flamen (Latin, *flāmen*, perhaps originally, *flagmen*, 'he who burns the sacrifices') was one of fifteen priests devoted to the service of a particular deity. They were installed into office by the supreme dignitary of the religion. The Flamen of Jupiter, the *Flamen Dialis,* was a privileged person: he was attended by a lector, his house was an asylum, and he held a seat in the senate. But with these privileges also came restrictions: the Flamen might not have a knot on any part of his attire; touch flour, leaven, or leavened bread; touch or name a dog; mount a horse; or be a night out of the city.[11/D]

316 *'Muy illustrissimo y excellentissimo señor.'*

'Most illustrious and most excellent Sir.'

316 *'Manerly Margery, Mylk, and Ale.'*

From *Mannerly Margery Milk and Ale* by John Skelton (1460-1529), the English poet known for his satires on court and clergy, and for his rattling verse and unrestrained jocularity.

> *Ay, beshrew you! by my fay*
> *These wanton clerks be nice alway!*
> *Avaunt, avaunt, my popinjay!*
> *What, will ye do nothing but play?*
> *Tilly, vally, straw, let be I say!*
> > *Gup, Christian Clout, gup, Jack of the Vale!*
> > *With Mannerly Margery Milk and Ale.*

316 *'Por vos suis en prison mis; Por vos, amie!'*

'For you I am in prison;
for you, friend!'

From *Aucassin et Nicolette*, an anonymous mediæval French chantefable, or 'song-story'. The story is about a love between the son of a count and a Saracen slave girl, who converted to Christianity and was adopted by a viscount. Their marriage opposed by Aucassin's father, the lovers endure imprisonment, flight, and separation in foreign lands before their love and determination bring them together.

Nicolette by Maxwell Armfield, 1910

> *I for love of thee am bound*
> *In this dungeon underground,*
> *All for loving thee must lie*
> *Here where loud on thee I cry,*
> *Here for loving thee must die*
> *For thee, my love!*

Haman, a Persian courtier of the 5th century BC, is the main antagonist in the Old Testament book of Esther. Haman and his wife instigate a plot to kill all the Jews of Persia. The plot is foiled by Queen Esther, herself a Jew, and Haman is hanged from the gallows. The Jewish feast of Purim celebrates their deliverance from the hostile contrivances of Haman.

Hume Castle was a Scottish stronghold in Berwickshire (*see*, 094 and 105). It sits at an impressive height above the castle village, commanding views across to the English border.

316   *'– More successfully than Polycarp.'*

Saint Polycarp (69-155) was one of the Apostolic Fathers, bishop of Smyrna, and author of the epistle to the Philippians. During persecution under Marcus Aurelius he was brought before the Roman proconsul at Smyrna. When urged to revile Christ, he replied: 'Fourscore and six years have I been His servant, and He hath done me no wrong. How then can I blaspheme my King, who hath saved me?'[12] He died a martyr, bound at the stake, but the flames arched about his body, failing to touch him, and he had to be stabbed to death.

316   *'And ripped, salted and stuffed with myrrh and cassia and set up painted...'*

Lymond is referring to the process of embalming, the art of preserving the body after death. The ancient Egyptian method involved cutting a deep line on the left side of the body and removing the entrails and lungs; the belly was rinsed with palm-wine and filled with myrrh and cassia. The mummy was then pickled in salt or natron for seventy days[13/D]; afterwards it was washed, elaborately bandaged and painted, and then set upright in a wooden coffin against the walls of the tomb.

317   *'But where? My joy, cry peip! where ever thou be!'*

From *The Tale of the Uponlandis Mous and the Burgess Mous by* Robert Henryson (c.1425-1500). The moral of the fable is to recommend and praise simple living. When served dinner by a servant, the country mouse falls and swoons. Her sister calls, *'How faire ye, sister? cry peip, quahair ever ye be.'* Gib hunter, our jolly cat, catches the country mouse:

> *From foot to foot he tossed her to and fro*
> *Where is up, where is down, as merry as any kid*
> *Where would he lay her under the straw*
> *Where he would play hide-and-seek with her*
> *Thus he did to the Mouse's innocent distress*
> *Where at last through good fortune and good luck*
> *Betwixt the burn and the wall she crept.*[14]

(Tr.L.R.)

317 *'Nay, not so. I am too brittle; I may not endure....'*

From the late 15th-century morality play, *Everyman.*

317 *...this was no broken Colossus, waiting to be whisked off for old metal...*

The Colossus of Rhodes was a statue of the sun-god Helios. The statue, one of the seven wonders of the world, was between 27m-37m (90-120 feet) tall, and hollow, with a winding staircase which ascended to the head. The statue stood for only 56 years; when an earthquake struck Rhodes in 224 BC, the statue snapped at the knees and fell over. Its remains lay broken for nearly 1000 years, before the pieces were sold for scrap metal.

318 *...a sparkling comber on the horizon...*

Colossus of Rhodes
by G. De Jode, c.1580

A comber is a long curling wave.

319 *'...rolled you like Sisyphus's stone...'*

In Greek mythology, Sisyphus, the craftiest of men, was condemned to the underworld and compelled to roll a boulder up a hill; before it reached the summit, the boulder would roll down, thus the task of Sisyphus would begin anew, to be repeated throughout eternity.

320 *'Nemesis nodded. I know.'*

Sisyphus by Titian, c.1548

In Greek mythology, Nemesis was the goddess who personified divine retribution to every man of his precise share of fortune, good or bad. It was her function to see the proper portion of prosperity was preserved; one who became too prosperous, or was too uplifted by his prosperity, was reduced or punished.

320 *'Now in dry, now in wete,*
Now in snaw, now in slete,
When my shone freys to my fete –'

From *The Second Shepherds' Play,* a famous mediæval mystery play attributed to the Wakefield Master. The Shepherds enter lamenting the harsh conditions of life in a mortal world in desperate need of redemption.

322   '...from leaping like a chamois to unutterable conclusions.'

A chamois is an agile, goat-like antelope inhabiting high, inaccessible mountains in Europe and western Asia; it can clear a 5-6m (16-18 ft.) crevice at a bound.

322   ...with which the dominus quod-libetarius did his job.

In the Middle Ages, universities trained students in the art of reasoning and demanded a high level of proficiency in disputation. A disputation could last several hours, or all day, and the student was expected to examine various aspects of the question presented, and deliver his reply, without hesitation, 'clear cut into fine distinction and bristling with citations'[15], and, of course, in Latin. In order to train students, university professors gave exhibitions of disputations, presided over by a dignitary with the title *dominus quodlibertarius*.

In addition to weekly disputations, German universities held a grand annual debate known as *disputations de quolibet* ('disputations on any given topic'), which highlighted the academic calendar and were held in the main university building in the presence of the rector, deans, faculty, guests, and students. The proceedings were conducted by the *dominus quodlibertarius*, who was elected to the office and set the main debate questions.

325   ...wondering if, like Evagrius, he would receive the receipt for these pious outgoings in his coffin.

Gideon is referring to a legend regarding Evagrius Ponticus (345-399 AD), a Christian mystic and one of the earliest and most important writers on asceticism.

> *The Christian bishop Synesius succeeded in converting a Pagan named Evagrius, who for a long time, however, felt doubts about the passage, 'He who giveth to the poor lendeth to the Lord.' On his conversion, and in obedience to this verse, he gave Synesius three hundred pieces of gold to be distributed among the poor; but he exacted from the bishop, as the representative of Christ, a promissory note, engaging that he should be repaid in the future world. Many years later, Evagrius, being on his death-bed, commanded his sons, when they buried him, to place the note in his hand, and to do so without informing Synesius. His dying injunction was observed, and three days afterwards he appeared to Synesius in a dream, told him that the debt had been paid, and ordered him to go to the tomb, where he would find a written receipt. Synesius did as he was commanded, and, the grave being opened, the promissory note was found in the hand of the dead man, with an endorsement declaring that the debt had been paid by Christ. The note, it was said, was long after preserved as a relic in the church of Cyrene.[16/D]*

In addition to a catalog of ascetic practices for the hermit and mystical theology, Evagrius developed a comprehensive list of eight terrible temptations, from which all sinful behavior springs. The list was intended to help readers identify the process of temptation, their own strengths and weaknesses, and the remedies available for overcoming temptation. The eight patterns of evil thought are gluttony, greed, sloth, sorrow, lust, anger, vainglory, and pride, later revised by Pope Gregory (590 AD) to the more commonly known Seven Deadly Sins. Evagrius spent the last fourteen years of his life in the Egyptian desert as a hermit.

The Seven Deadly Sins
by Boccaccio, c.15ᵗʰ century

325   ...and found a wind egg which had to become a monolithic fortress.

A wind egg is an addled, or imperfect egg, such as one which will produce nothing but wind, or gas.

2. The Pinning Move

326   The bright, mystagogue's eyes appealed for sympathy...

A mystagogue (from Greek, one initiated in mysteries, and a leader) is one who instructs or interprets mysteries; specifically, in the early church the priest who prepared candidates for initiation into the sacred mysteries.

327   His expression altered from the grave to the bonzelike.

A bonze is a Buddhist monk; hence, monk-like.

327   ...the litter and alembics...

An alembic (Arabic, *al-anbīq*, 'the still') was an apparatus used by alchemists for the distillation and sublimation of substances.[17/D]

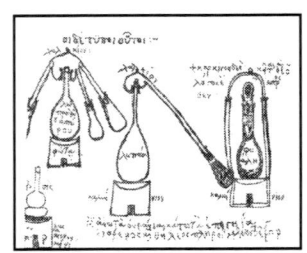

Diagram of Alembic of Zosimus of
Panopolis, c.300

PART FOUR

THE END GAME

Linlithgow Palace by D. Roberts

Chapter I: Twice-Taken

Caxton: Tract 4, Chapter 1

And what is a Knight worth, without horse and arms?
Certainly nothing more than one of the people, or lassie, perchance.[1]

1. Forced Play Against Time

A move is said to be forced when it is the only move which can be made.

331 *'Not while he can act like Cyrus King of the World...'*

Cyrus the Great, the Koresh of the Hebrew Scriptures (from the Persian, *Kurus*, perhaps from *kur*, 'the mountain', or *kohr*, 'the sun'; c.600-c.530 BC) was the founder of the Persian Empire and titled 'King of the World'. Cyrus is known for his policy of religious conciliation: nations carried into captivity in Babylon were restored to their native countries, and permitted to take their gods with them. This policy included the Jews, who resettled and rebuilt Jerusalem, for which Cyrus earned an honoured place in Judaism and was called the Anointed of Jehovah in the Hebrew Bible.

Cyrus the Great

332 *...to the Castle of Wark...*

Located on the English side of the River Tweed, Wark Castle was used as a base to conduct raids into Scotland: 'situate for annoyance and defence in the best place of all the frontiers'[2], it was 'the stay and key'[3] of England. 'The strategic importance of Wark is illustrated as much by the consistent desire of the English kings to have it under their direct control, as by the frequent attempts of the Scots to capture it.'[4]

Franco-Scottish forces attack Wark Castle in 1385
Illustration from Froissart's Chronicles, c.1470

333   ...or the Pischon, Dichon, Chiddikel and Perath of Paradise...

A saying of Zoroaster was that the soul is winged and when the wings drop off, she falls headlong into the body. When her wings have grown again, she flies back to heaven. When asked how one could obtain well-feathered wings, Zoroaster replied: 'Refresh ye your wings in the waters of life.' When asked where to seek these waters, he answered:

> *God's paradise is laved and watered by four rivers, from whose same*
> *source ye may draw the waters of your salvation. The name of that*
> *in the north is Pischon, which meaneth right. The name of that in the*
> *west is Dichon, which signifieth expiation. The name of that in the*
> *east is Chiddikel, which expresses light, and of that in the south,*
> *Perath, which we may interpret as piety.*[5]

334 ...flinging themselves among the toadflax...

Toadflax (*Linaria vulgaris*) is a wildflower found in great abundance on waste ground, adorning hedge-banks, and bordering cornfields. Also known as Snap Dragon because of its fancied resemblance to the face of a dragon which opens and closes its mouth when squeezed, thus the 'snap'; and Butter-and-Eggs because of its showy yellow flowers which bloom August through September. Toadflax was said to avert witchcraft, and possess the power to destroy charms.

Linaria vulgaris

334 ...flickered like St. Elmo's fire...

St. Elmo's fire is a weather phenomenon named from a corruption of St. Erasmus, the patron saint of sailors. During stormy weather, a glowing ball of light would appear at the tip of the mast of a ship at sea, often accompanied by a crackling noise. Its appearance was regarded as a sign of protection.

334 ...like a grey and shining harrow ...

In agriculture, a harrow is a cultivating implement set with spikes, spring teeth, or discs and used primarily for pulverizing and smoothing the soil.

St. Elmo's Fire on Masts of a Ship

334 ...and twisting like a dorcus...

A dorcus is a stag beetle, the largest insect in Europe. From *Pliny's Natural History*:

> ...In one large kind [the stag-beetle] we find horns of a remarkable length, two-pronged at the extremities, and forming pincers, which the animal closes when it is its intention to bite. These beetles are suspended from the neck of infants by way of remedy against certain maladies: Nigidius calls them 'lucani'.

335   '...otherwise they fire stoneshot, and then Greek fire...'

Greek Fire was an incendiary weapon first used by the Byzantine Greeks in defence of Constantinople during the sieges by the Saracens (668-675 AD and 716-718 AD). This particularly deadly liquid was projected, burning, from tubes. It would ignite spontaneously on contact with water, stuck to almost any surface, and was nearly impossible to extinguish except with sand, salt, or urine. The ingredients of this devastating weapon were a closely guarded secret, so much so its precise composition remains unknown. John, Lord of Joinville (b.1225), wrote of its use:

> *...the tail of fire that trailed behind it was as big as a great spear; and it made such a noise as it came, that it sounded like the thunder of heaven. It looked like a dragon flying through the air. Such a bright light did it cast, that one could see all over the camp as though it were day, by reason of the great mass of fire, and the brilliance of the light that it shed.[6]*

Fleet of Romans Setting Ablaze Their Enemies. Illuminated MS, c. 12th century

335   '...and there'll be an explosion like Muspelheim.'

Muspelheim, one of the Nine Worlds in Norse mythology, is the realm of fire and desolation, a glowing region of heat and flame.

336   '...a fairly simple thing to do without the busking.'

Busking is a street performance.

336 'Unless like Hanno you wish to sail by streams of fire.'

Hanno was a Carthaginian navigator who undertook a celebrated voyage of discovery and colonization along the west coast of Africa in the 5th or 6th century BC. Setting sail with sixty penteconters (vessels of fifty oars each) carrying 30,000 men and women, he founded numerous colonies and trading stations. From *The Periplus of Hanno*:

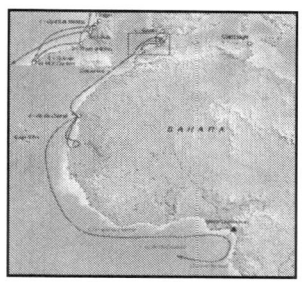

Voyage of Hanno

We sailed forward five days near the land until we came to a large bay, which our interpreters informed us was named the Western Horn. In this was a large island, and in the island a salt-water lake; and in this another island, where, when we had landed, we could discover nothing in the day-time except trees; but in the night we saw many fires burning, and heard the sound of pipes, cymbals, drums, and confused shouts. We were then afraid, and our diviners ordered us to abandon the island. Sailing quickly away thence, we passed a country burning with fires and perfumes, and streams of fire supplied from it fell into the sea.

336 '...I'm not likely to be goaded into triple suttee...'

Satī, or suttee, is the former Hindu practice of a widow immolating herself on her husband's funeral pyre.

336 '...even to enable you to expire in a spray of madder-fed milk.'

Madder (*Rubia tinctorum*) is a perennial herb with small yellow flowers; its roots are an important source of the dye alizarin which gives its red colour to a textile dye known as Rose Madder. The plant has been cultivated as a dyestuff since antiquity; cloth dyed with madder pigment was found in the tomb of Tutankhamen (1325 BC). To make the pigment the roots are dried for at least two years and then ground into powder which produces a bright red color if soaked overnight and briefly steeped.

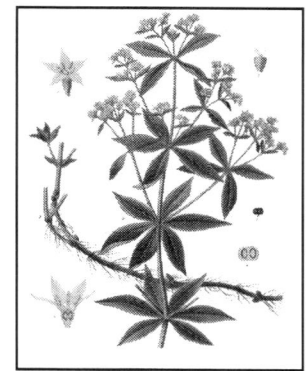

Rubia tinctorum

339 *...the elms passed like weeping seneschals.*

A seneschal (from Latin, *senere*, to be old, and

scalc, scalh, a servant) was an officer in the household of royalty or dignitaries who superintended ceremonies and feasts. In some instances, a seneschal was an officer serving as a magistrate of a district or province.

339 *'Other than apologizing for not being Asmodeus, what can I do?'*

Asmodeus (Hebrew, *Aschmedai*, 'the destroyer') was an evil spirit of Jewish demonology. In the book of Tobit, he was in love with Sara and destroyed each of her seven husbands in succession, appearing as a succubus on their bridal nights; hence, Asmodeus is known as the destroying demon of matrimonial happiness.[7/D]

Asmodeus

339 *'Initium sapientiae,' said Lymond absently, 'est timor Domini.'*

'The beginning of wisdom is fear of the Lord.'

339 *'You may look in vain for the sapientia, but the timor, I promise you, will be very much in evidence.'*

Sapientia is wisdom; timor is fear.

339 *'Wha sits maist high shall find the seat maist slidder.'*

> *The vain ascents of court,*
> *who will consider,*
> *Who sits most high shall find*
> *the seat most slidder (slippery).*

From *James V's Papingo* by Sir David Lindsay (c.1490-c.1555), an exhortation to the members of court to remember the higher the ascent, the greater and more grievous the downfall. *'Let not courtiership bedazzle your reason, for courts are but transitory things.'*

339 *'Or – Like to die mends not the kirk yard...'*

Scottish proverb; in Scots, to mend is to fill.

339 *'The intellect and its cultivation, as someone once said, bring a higher form of fertility and a nobler pregnancy into human life.'*

From Diotima's Speech in Plato's *Symposium*, wherein Socrates relates his instruction on the sober truth about love by the wise woman, Diotima of Mantinea.[8/D] Socrates believed love to be the principle which ranges from animal desire to hunger and thirst for wisdom, and in both the highest and lowest forms of love, the soul longs to beget the likeness of itself in others. 'True love is not the love of the beautiful for itself or for oneself, but it is love of the "birth of beauty" in others.'[9]

340   '*Did yon greetin' wean stop ye?'*

Scots dialect for 'yonder weeping child', here, indicating Will Scott.

340   '*It's nae loss: I'd have been sweir tae see ye leave, and me with nothing but my big wame on my mind from morning to night.*'

Scots dialect for , 'It's no loss: I'd have been reluctant to see you leave, and me with nothing but my big belly on my mind from morning to night.'

341   *Violence was the odour of Threave...*

Threave Castle by G. Cattermole, c.1834

In the beginning of the 15th century, the house of Douglas attained a level of power only scarcely inferior to the royal house of Stewart, so much so, it was said, 'nae man was safe in the country, unless he were either a Douglas or a Douglas man.'[10] William, the 6th Earl of Douglas, when only 14, succeeded to the head of the powerful family; their lands comprised two-thirds of Scotland south of Edinburgh, and many viewed them as the champions of Scotland.

In 1440, the young King James II, in an attempt to humble the overgrown power of the Douglases, invited the young earl and his brother to Edinburgh Castle; they were beheaded after a mock trial at what is now known as the Black Dinner. Several years later, William Douglas, 8th Earl of Douglas, returned to Scotland professing submission to King James II, yet he united almost one-half of Scotland against his sovereign. King James invited him, under safe conduct, to Stirling Castle, and urged him to disband those united with him. The Earl refused. In reply, King James stabbed him in the heart with his own hand, saying 'If you will not, then this shall!'[11]

The Earl's four brothers avenged his death by burning the town of Stirling, and civil war broke out between the king and the Douglases. William, 8th Earl of Douglas, kept a retinue of more than 1000 armed men at Threave, and it was the site of the murder of Sir Patrick MacLellan in 1452. Hostilities between the king and the 'Black' Douglases escalated in 1455, and the king was successful in routing the Douglases from several of their fortresses. Threave was the last of their strongholds to fall, after a long siege personally attended by the king.[12] The castle and its possessions were forfeited to the crown; and it was afterward transferred to the Maxwell family.

Threave Castle was built near the end of the 14th century by Archibald Douglas. Cruel oppression of his tenants and peasants earned him the execration and title of 'The Grim'[13]. The only access to the island on which the castle stands was by fording the river at the south end. The 40x60-foot tower was surrounded by a wall with round turrets at each corner. The entrance was through a gate tower, and the top of the drawbridge gave access to the second floor of the three-storey keep.[14]

341   *...the reception, fremescent to a degree...*

Fremescent (from Latin, *fremere*, make a low noise, roar, growl) is noisy and raging[15/D]; tumultuous; riotous.

343   *The Peine Forte et Dure was a perfectly valid punishment for silence: it used weights to achieve a gradual pressing to death.*

Peine forte et dure (French for 'hard and forceful punishment') was a method of torture used when a defendant stubbornly stood mute, refusing to plead either guilty or not guilty. The defendant was pressed to death as heavy weights were placed on his body; the practice was abolished in 1772.

Death of Giles Corey (1692) by Pressing

344 *'...you're another fool, playing Macarius with the lockjaw.'*

St. Macarius

St. Macarius the Elder of Egypt (c.300-390 AD) was the founder of a monastic community in the Scetic desert. He was falsely accused by a woman of deflowering her, for which Macarius was dragged through the streets and beaten as a hypocrite in the garb of a monk. He suffered the accusation in silence, even sending the woman what he earned. When the woman began her labour she lay in extreme anguish and could not deliver the child until she had named the true father.

345 *'I'd have held the Rose of Hamborough...'*

The Mary Rose of Hamborough, c.1546

The *Mary Rose* was a warship in the Tudor navy of King Henry VIII. While leading an attack on a French invasion fleet in 1545, she sank in the straits north of the Isle of Wight. The *Mary Rose* was one of the largest ships in the English navy, and one of the earliest ships to fire a broadside.

345 *...the girl showed no signs of anger with the jackanapes.*

A jackanapes is a conceited or impudent person. The term derives from 'Jack of Naples', which was applied to William de la Pole, 1st Duke of Suffolk (1396-1450), who was seen as an upstart from the merchant class. The city of Naples commonly exported exotic merchandise to England, including monkeys wearing leashes, which resembled the collar and chain on the de la Pole coat of arms, hence his derisive nickname.[16]

346 *'Ye leid, ye leid, ye filthy nurse,' said the prisoner pleasantly.*

From the Scottish ballad, *Gil Morrice.*

346 *'Manus loquacissimae – it's pantomime all right.'*

Manus loquacissimae: talkative, elegant hands

Pantomime is a musical-comedy theatrical production, a popular form of entertainment in ancient Greece and later, Rome. The pantomime actor did not speak on the stage, but acted with gestures, movements, and attitudes. The movements were rhythmic, like those in a ballet.

346 *'Ye kale-heided coddroch!'*

A coddroch (or codroch, from Gaelic *cod*, from Latin, *con*, with, and *droch*, bad, evil, wicked mischievous; *or* from the Irish Gaelic, *cudar*, the rabble) is an idle person of a low class; rustic; one who is dirty or slovenly; *or* one who is miserable, ugly, and detestable.

347 *...and he was left alone with initium sapientiae and the Master of Culter.*

'Initium sapientiae' is the beginning of wisdom.

347 *With the face of a Della Robbia angel, Lymond spoke.*

*Altar detail of Tobias and the Angel Raphael
by Andrea della Robbia, c.1475*

Della Robbia was a family of artists known for their work in glazed terra-cotta. Luca della Robbia (c.1399-1482), in his early years, executed important and exceedingly beautiful works in marble and bronze, known for their grace of attitude and beauty of expression. In his later years, he produced enamel-covered terra-cotta reliefs of exquisite beauty, including many of the Madonna and angels. His principal pupil was his nephew, Andrea della Robbia (1425-1525), who created a large number of reliefs of the Madonna and Child, distinguished for their 'extreme beauty of pose and sweetness of expression'[17]. Five of Andrea's sons worked with their father, and carried on the Robbia fabrique; one of his sons, Girolama (1488-1566) spent nearly forty years in service to the French Royal family as an architect and sculptor.

348 'In a day of gimgrack cannibalism and snivelling atrocities...'

Gimcrack is tawdry, fantastic; strange, curious.

348 'I'm used to being taken for a cross between Gilles de Rais...'

Gilles de Montmorency-Laval, Baron de Rais (1404-1440), was the central figure in a 15th-century *cause célèbre*. He distinguished himself under Charles VII, was a companion-in-arms of Joan of Arc, and was made marshal of France at the age of 25. The hero of France, however, was ultimately revealed as the heinous sexual murderer of 140 children and a practitioner of the Occult. He was condemned and executed for his atrocious crimes.[18/D]

Gilles de Laval, sire de Rais by Éloi Firmin Féron, 1835

348 '...like duck's meat in a ditch...'

Duck's meat is the Lemna plant, which grows in ditches and shallow water, and serves as food for ducks and geese. Also know as duckweed, which first appeared in *Opening Gambit: The swimmer, collared with duckweed, grounded, shook himself...*

348 '...into your imagination and sphacelate in your insufferable vanity.'

To sphacelate is to mortify, as flesh; to become gangrenous; or, to decay, as bone.

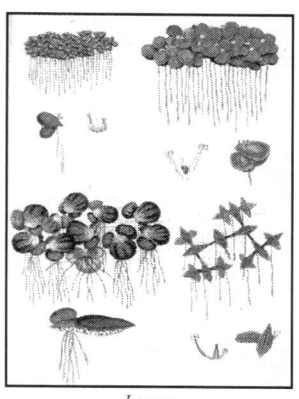

Lemna

349   '...with that bantling-brained romantic done up in an oatsack?'

Bantling (corrupted from German, *bänkling*, bastard, from *bank*, bench; a child begotten on a bench, and not in the marriage-bed) was a term for a young child, but carrying with it a shade of contempt.

349   ...he held himself lightly and easily, the poised Roc pitying the elephant.

The Roc was an enormous legendary bird of prey. In the 13th century, Marco Polo wrote, 'It was for all the world like an eagle, but one indeed of enormous size; so big in fact that its quills were twelve paces long and thick in proportion. And it is so strong that it will seize an elephant in its talons and carry him high into the air and drop him so that he is smashed to pieces; having so killed him, the bird swoops down on him and eats him at leisure.'

350   'What, then? Retreat underground into hebetude...'

Hebetude is a state of being dull or lethargic.

350   'I scotch the dragons.'

To scotch is to put an end to; crush; stamp out; foil.

350   'You know all about the law of talion...'

The law of talion (from Latin, *talis*, such), or the law of retaliation, was a mode of punishment established by Mosiac law (Leviticus 24:20), in which the punishment inflicted on the criminal corresponded precisely to the injury inflicted on the victim, as an 'eye for an eye' or a 'tooth for a tooth'.

350   'You're a master...of the art of apposite punishment.'

Apposite is strikingly appropriate and relevant; apt.

350   'And teach me to sing re, my fa, sol, and when I fail, to bob me on the noll.'

> Princess of youthè can ye sing by rote?
> Or 'Shall I sail with you' o' fellowship assay?
> For on the book I cannot sing a note.
> Would to God it would please you some day
> A ballad-book for me to lay,
> And learnen me to sing, 'Re, mi, fa, sol'!
> And, when I failè, bob me on the noll.

From *The Bowge of Court* by John Skelton (1460-1529), an allegorical poem about the vices and dangers of court life. Bowge (French, *bouche*, court rations) is the right to eat at the king's table.

350 *'...and I am left, as it happens, singing ut to Johannes...'*

The seven-note diatonic musical scale was developed in the 11th century: ut, re, mi, fa, sol, la, si. 'Ut' was changed in 1600 to 'do' by musicologist Giovanni Battista Doni. *Ut queant laxis* was a Gregorian chant in honor of Saint John composed by the monk Guido D'Arezzo to teach students the original solfeggio phonetics for learning music.

> *Ut queant laxis resoare fibris,*
> *Mira gestorum famuli tuorum,*
> *Solve polluti labii reatum*
> *Sancte Iohannes*

> > *So that your servants may,*
> > *With loosened voices,*
> > *Resound the wonders of your deeds*
> > *Clean the guilt from our stained lips,*
> > *O Saint John.*[19]

350 *'I have licked you like the cow Audhumbla from the salt of your atrocious upbringing...'*

In Norse mythology, Auðumbla is the cow from whose udders flowed the milk which nourished the first created being, the giant Ymir. Out of the salty ice, she licked the being Búri. From the Icelandic *Prose Edda, The Trick of Gylfi*:

> *Then said Gangleri: 'Where dwelt Ymir, or wherein did he find sustenance?' Hárr answered: 'Straightway after the rime dripped, there sprang from the cow called Audumia; four streams of milk ran from her udders and she nourished Ymir.'*
> *Then asked Gangleri: 'Wherewithal was the cow nourished?' And Hárr made answer: 'She licked the ice-blocks, which were salty; and the first day that she licked the blocks, there came forth from the blocks in the evening a man's hair; the second day, a man's head; the third day the whole man was there. He is named Búri.'*

Auðumbla, 18th century MS

351 'Conjure up Shamanism and the Black Mass if you like.'

Shamanism is the superstitious religion of the Turanian races of Siberia and northeastern Asia, consisting in a belief in evil spirits, and the necessity of averting their malign influence by magic spells and rites, or forcing them into obedience by the spells of the *shamans*.[20/D] The

Siberian Shaman (from the Sanskrit *çramana*, a Buddhist ascetic or mendicant) works his cures by magic, and averts sickness and death by incantations.

The Black Mass was a ceremony celebrated during the Witches' Sabbath, a sacrilegious parody of the Catholic Mass. *Malleus Maleficarum*, a treatise on witches written in 1486, gives details relating to the supposed practices.

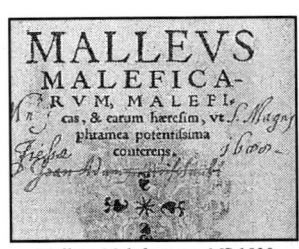

Malleus Maleficarum, MS 1520

351 'I don't want your coddled features singing Kassidas over me.'

Qaṣīda is a form of lyric poetry originating in pre-Islamic Arabia. It is a laudatory, elegiac poem of elaborate structure maintaining a single end rhyme throughout. It is often a public speech delivered as a eulogy in praise of a king or nobleman. The qaṣīda is respected as the highest form of poetry and as the special forté of the pre-Islamic poets. One of the most celebrated of Persian poets, Sádi (b.1184), a 'nightingale of songs'[21/D], was known for his *kassidas* ('odes', 'dirges').[22/D]

352 'Forth quenching go the starris, one by one ...'

> Forth quenching gan the starris, one by one,
> And now is left but Lucifer alone.
> And futhermore to blazon this new day,
> Who might discrive the birdis blissful bay?

From the translation of Virgil's *Æneid* by Gavin Douglas (c.1474-1522). Douglas, a member of the noble family descended from Sir James 'The Good' Douglas, wrote all of his poetry prior to the disaster of Flodden, when he lost his two older brothers, and he turned his attention to politics and the intrigues surrounding the life of his nephew, Archibald Douglas, 6th Earl of Angus. His major work was his translation of the *Æneid*, the first version of a Latin classic published in Britain. After his family fell from grace, Douglas fled to the court of Henry VIII. He died of the plague in London in 1522.

352 '...unless like Al-Mokanna you can cause moons to issue from our well...'

Hashim ben 'Ata (d.779), called *al-Moquanna*, 'The Veiled'[23/D]), posed as an incarnation of the Deity and led a rebellion in Khorasan. An arrow pierced one of his eyes; to hide his deformity he constantly wore a veil, although he told his followers it was to protect the beholder from the dazzling rays issued from his divine countenance. He deluded people into believing him a prophet with magic tricks, and was said to have caused the moon to issue from a deep well, for which he was called *Sàrinda Máh*, the Moon Maker. His rebellion failed; reduced to a choice between surrender and death, Mokanna preferred the latter choice, and he and his followers took poison.

352 *...jump like a rabbit over a somnolent game of prime...*

The Card Players by Lucas van Leyden, 1525

Prime (also, *Primero*) was a gambling card game dating from 1526. Originating in Spain or Italy, the game was a favourite in England during the reign of Henry VIII. *Primero* is directly related to modern-day poker.

354 *'...as free as Hosea's wife...'*

Hosea is the first of the minor prophets of the Hebrew Bible. According to the Book of Hosea, he represents the relation of Israel to God as that of a wife to her husband, and its apostasy as the faithlessness of a wife. These ideas are symbolically expressed and illustrated by Hosea's marriage to the unfaithful and depraved Gomer, who left Hosea and became the slave of her paramour. Yet Hosea is commanded by God to buy her back. This experience represents Israel's unfaithfulness and exile, and shows God bringing Israel back after the punishment of exile.

The Prophet Hosea
18ᵗʰ-century Russian ikon

354 *'..and yon three stookies littered in the passages with their heads dunted.'*

A stookie is a fool. Dunted is beaten; hence, blunted.

355 *'Well, Richard for all his flummery, worships his wife.'*

Flummery is meaningless or deceptive language; nonsense.

355 *'A woman is a worthy thing; they do the wash and do the wring.'*

From *In Praise of Women*, a secular song from the 14th or 15th century:

> *I am as light as any roe*
> *To praise women whereever I go*
> *To not praise women is a shame*
> *For a woman was thy dame*
> *Our Blessed Lady bears the name*
> *Of all women whereever they go.*
>
> *A woman is a worthy thing*
> *They do the wash and do the wring*
> *'Lullay, lullay,' she does thee sing*
> *and yet she has but care and woe.*
> *A woman is a worthy person*
> *She serves man both day and night*
> *There she puts all her might*
> *And yet she has but care and woe.*[24]   (Tr.L.R.)

355 *'With Wat it's sew Tibet, knit Annot and spin Margerie and no nonsense.'*

From *The Working Girls' Song* from *Ralph Roister Doister* by English playwright Nicholas Udall (1504-1556):

> *Pipe, merry Annot;*
> *Trilla, Trilla, Trillarie.*
> *Work, Tibet; work, Annot; work, Margerie;*
> *Sew, Tibet; knit, Annot; spin, Margerie;*
> *Let us see who will win the victory.*

355 *'...he carried off all the prizes at Kilwinning?'*

Kilwinning is a town in North Ayrshire and a noted centre of archery. Its company of archers existed prior to 1488, and once a year in mediæval times a grand exhibition was held, including the papingo shoot. The sport of archery continues in Kilwinning today: the annual papingo shoot is held on the grounds of the old abbey on the first Saturday in June.

360   *...shivered the bog orchis...*

The Bog Orchis (*Malaxis paludosa*) grows in bogs in the Northern Hemisphere. Its flowers are greenish-yellow and its leaves bear a fringe of tiny bulbils.

360   *'The little squirrel, full of business.'*

From *The Kingis Quair* by King James I of Scotland (1394-1437). 'In this poem the king describes his days of unhappy boyhood, his embarkation for France, his cruel and unjust seizure by the English, and his imprisonment at Windsor. He bewails his long captivity in a foreign land, and his lonely and inactive

Malaxis paludosa

existence, shut out, in the vigour of youth, from all the enterprise and enjoyment of life, while even the lower animals live in freedom, every one after its kind.'[25]

> *The lion king with his mate the lioness*
> *The panther like unto the emerald*
> *The little squirrel full of business,*
> *The slow ass, the drudger beast of pain,*
> *The nice ape, the warlike porcupine*
> *The piercing lynx, the lovely unicorn,*
> *That voids venom with his ivory horn.*[26]

(Tr.L.R.)

361   *'Strike on, strike on, Glasgèrion.'*

From *Glasgèrion,* a Mediæval ballad about a prince and his love. After playing his harp before a king, he and the king's daughter arrange a tryst. Glasgèrion naps, telling his servant to wake him in time for his meeting. The servant goes in his stead and rapes the princess. She learns the truth and kills herself; Glasgèrion kills his servant, and then kills himself.

> *Glasgèrion was a king's own son,*
> *And as a harper he was good,*
> *He harped in the king's chamber,*
> *Where the cup and candle stood.*
> *And so did he in*
> *the queen's chamber,*
> *Till the ladies waxed wood.*

And then spoke the king's daughter,
And these words thus said she:
Said, 'Strike on, strike on, Glasgèrion,
Of thy striking do not cease,
There's never a stroke come over your harp
But it gladdens my heart within.' [27]   (Tr.L.R.)

361 *'Prophète de malheur, babillarde...'*

'Prophet of doom, babbling...'

From the fable, *The Swallow and the Little Birds*:

The swallow's warning voice was heard again:
My friends, the product of that deadly grain,
Seize now, and pull it root by root
Or surely you'll repent its fruit.
False, babbling prophetess, says one,
You'd set us at some pretty fun
To pull this field a thousand birds are needed,
While thousands more with hemp are seeded...
'Tis thus we heed no instincts but our own;
Believe no evil, till the evil's done.

361 *'Of Paradise ne can I not speak properly, for I am not there.'*

From *The Travels of Sir John Mandeville*:

Of Paradise ne can I not speak properly. For I was not there. It is
far beyond. And that forthinketh me. And also I was not worthy.
But as I have heard say of wise men beyond, I shall tell you with
good will.

To forethink is to repent; to regret.

361 *'–But sicker than Rudel.'*

Seigneur de Blaye Jaufré Rudel (fl.1130-1150),
one of the great troubadours, is known for his
songs of *amor de lonh*, 'far-away love'. Rudel,
a noble prince of Blaye, became enamored with
Countess Hodierna of Tripoli, without seeing
her, after hearing of her grace and beauty from
the pilgrims of Antioch. He wrote many songs
to her with beautiful melodies and simple
words. In his desire to see her, he became a

Rudel dying in the arms of Hodierna
13ᵗʰ century MS

crusader and set to sea. He became ill and was taken to an inn in Tripoli, a dying man. The countess, upon hearing the news, rushed to his bedside and took him in her arms. He praised God for having let him live long enough to see her, and then died in her arms. He was buried with great honour; on the same day, overwhelmed with sorrow, she became a nun.

361 *...freshly dressed and anointed...with delicate things of sweet smell.*

From *The Travels of Sir John Mandeville:*

> *And the soldan hath four wives, one Christian and three Saracens, of the which one dwelleth at Jerusalem, and another at Damascus, and another at Ascalon; and when them list, they remove to other cities, and when the soldan will he may go to visit them. And he hath as many paramours as him liketh. For he maketh to come before him the fairest and the noblest of birth, and the gentlest damosels of his country, and he maketh them to be kept and served full honourably. And when he will have one to lie with him, he maketh them all to come before him, and he beholdeth in all, which of them is most to his pleasure, and to her anon he sendeth or casteth a ring from his finger. And then anon she shall be bathed and richly attired, and anointed with delicate things of sweet smell, and then led to the soldan's chamber; and thus he doth as often as him list, when he will have any of them.*

362 *'Cryand with many a piteous peep...'*

From *The Tale of the Paddock and the Mouse* by Robert Henryson (c.1425-c.1500). 'In strength, and sometimes even in sublimity of painting, in pathos and sweetness, in the variety and beauty of his pictures of natural scenery, in the vein of quiet and playful humour which runs through many of his pieces, and in that fine natural taste...he is altogether excellent.'[28]

> *Upon a time, as Æsop could report,*
> *A little Mouse came till a river side;*
> *She might not wade, her shankis were sae short:*
> *She could not swim, she had nae horse to ride:*
> *Of very force behoved her to bide;*
> *And to and fro beside that river deep*
> *She ran, cryand with many piteous peep.*

362 *'The Scot, the Frencheman, the Pope and heresie, overcommed...'*

From *Toxophilus* by Roger Ascham:

> *Rejoice England, be glad and merry,*

Truth overcomes thy enemies all,
The Scot, the Frenchman,
the Pope, and heresy,
Overcome by Truth, and evermore you shall
Through Christ, King Henry,
the Book and the Bow,
All manner of enemies, quite overthrow.[29]　　　　　(Tr.L.R.)

362 *'And as for Scottishe men and Englishe men be not enemyes by nature...'*

From *Toxophilus* by Roger Ascham:

> *But to let Textor and the Scots go: yet one thing would I wish for the*
> *Scots, and that is this, that seeing one God, one faith, one compass*
> *of the sea, one land and country, one tongue in speaking, one*
> *manner and trade in living, like courage and stomach in war, like*
> *quickness of wit to learning, hath made England and Scotland both*
> *one, they would suffer them no longer to be two: but clean give over*
> *the Pope, which seeks no other thing (as many a noble and wise*
> *Scottish man knows) but to feed up dissension and parties between*
> *them and, procuring that thing to be two, which God, nature, and*
> *reason would have one.*
>
> *How profitable such an atonement were for Scotland, both*
> *Johannes Major and Hector Boetius which wrote the Scots*
> *Chronicles do tell, and also all the gentlemen of Scotland with the*
> *poor commonality, do well know: So that there is nothing that stops*
> *this matter, save only a few fears, and such like, which with the dregs*
> *of our English Papistry lurking now among them, study nothing else*
> *but to brew battle and strife between both people: Whereby only they*
> *hope to maintain their Papistical kingdom, to the destruction of the*
> *noble blood of Scotland, that then they may with authority do that,*
> *which neither noble man nor poor man in Scotland yet knows. And*
> *as for Scottish men and English men be not enemies by nature, but*
> *by custom: not by our good will, but by their own folly: which should*
> *take more honour in being coupled to England, than we should take*
> *profit in being enjoined to Scotland.*[30]　　　　　(Tr. L.R.)

362 *'Whether I profess the "damnable opinions of the great heretic Luther"?'*

In July 1538, the Parliament of Scotland passed a law which referred to an act of 1525, against the 'damnable opinions of the great heretic Luther'[31].

362 *'I echo like a mynah, that's why.'*

The myna (Hindustani, *mainā*, a starling) is a bird native to the islands of the East Indian archipelago. It is easily domesticated, and can learn to whistle, sing, and imitate the human voice.

362   'But your man Panter has been in Paris all the same...'

David Panter (d.1558) was a principal secretary of state under James V, and was ambassador of Scotland at the French court for seven years. After a life of distinguished service, he died at Stirling in October 1558.

362   ...with little trace of the dilettante manner.

Dilettante (from Latin, *delectare*, to delight) is showing frivolous or superficial interest; often used disparagingly to indicate only the desultory interest of a dabbler.

363   'Religion and cupidity are on your side.'

Cupidity (from Latin, *cupiditās*, desiring, from *cupere*, to long for, desire) is an eager or inordinate desire to possess something, especially wealth or power.

365   'The sliding joy, the gladness short; the feigned love, the false comfort.'

The Scots poet William Dunbar (c.1450-1520) moralizing *'on the brevity of existence, the shortness and uncertainty of all ordinary existence, and the wickedness and woes of mankind.'*

> This wavering world's wretchedness
> The failing and fruitless business,
> The misspent time, the service vain,
>   For to consider is ane pain.
>
> The sliding joy, the gladness short,
> The feigned love, the false comfort,
> The sweir abade, the slightful train,
>   For to consider is ane pain.
>
> The suggared mouths, with minds therefra,
> The figured speech, with faces tway;
> The pleasing tongues, with hearts in plain,
>   For to consider is ane pain.

366   'What!' said Gideon dryly. 'Put such a singer in the soup?'

From the fable *The Swan and the Cook*:

> The pleasures of the poultry yard
> Were by the swan and gosling shared.
> The swan was kept there for his looks,

The thrifty gosling for the cooks, —
The first the garden's pride, the latter
A greater favorite on the platter.
They swam the ditches, side by side,
And oft in sports aquatic vied,
Plunging, splashing far and wide,
With rivalry ne'er satisfied.
One day the cook, named Thirsty John,
Sent for the gosling, took the swan,
In haste his throat to cut,
And put him in the pot.
The bird's complaint resounded
In glorious melody ;
Whereat the cook, astounded
His sad mistake to see,
Cried, 'What! put such a singer in my soup!
As if a paltry gander from the coop!
No, no ; I'll never cut a throat
That sings so sweet a note.'
     Tis thus, whatever peril may alarm us,
     Sweet words will never harm us.

366   'But will your wife, almighty Mohammet...'

Mohammet is a variant spelling of Muhammad, the founder of Islam and a messenger and prophet of God.

2. Shah Mat

Shah Mat is the Persian origin of 'check mate', or to put the king in such a position he is unable to escape.

366   ...dressed with her usual éclat...

Éclat (French, *éclater*, burst forth, from Old French, *esclater*, to shine, *s'esclater*, burst) is brilliancy of effect; splendour; magnificence.

368   'We could manage stavesacre and dwale, with a little fool's parsley and half a thorn apple, stewed, with toadstools.'

Stavesacre is a highly toxic perennial plant; it is 'violently emetic and cathartic'[32]. The seeds contain delphinine, which has been used since

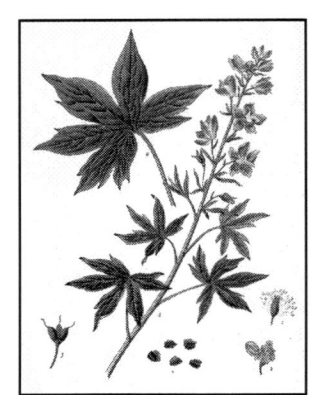

Stavesacre

262

antiquity to kill body-lice and other vermin.

Dwale (Anglo-Saxon, *dval,* erring, foolish, from *dvëlan,* to be dull, torpid) is a sleeping potion made with the deadly nightshade, *Atropa belladonna.* 'If you will follow my counsel, deale not with the same in any case, and banish it from your gardens and the use of it also, being a plant so furious and deadly; for it bringeth such as heave eaten thereof into a dead sleepe, wherein many have died.'[33]

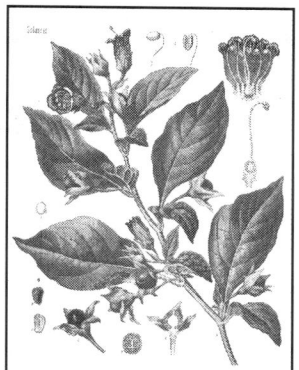

Dwale

Fool's parsley (*Æthúsa cynápium*), sometimes called Lesser Hemlock, is a poisonous annual herb closely resembling parsley. While less poisonous than hemlock, ingestion can be fatal. Its deleterious effects are thought to be due to the presence of *cyanpia* in its juice.

Common Thorn Apple (*Datúra stramónium*), a poisonous annual with foul-smelling foliage, has a long history of use for causing delirious states and even death. Every part of the plant is poisonous. A powerful narcotic, it produces a vivacious sort of intoxication; prior to causing stupor, it induces a state of wild delirium. The plant was thought to belong to the Prince of Darkness, the originator of all evil, and was used in ancient Pagan temples to induce ravings regarded as revelations from the gods.

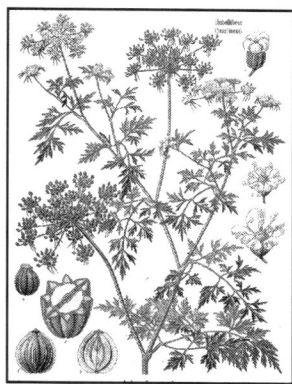

Fool's Parsley

368   '...*end of the passage with a chabouk.*'

A chabouk is a horse whip[34/D], used in the East to inflict punishment.

368   '...*preparing to recede into a gentle old age like Philemon and Baucis.*'

In Ovid's *Metamorphoses*, Philemon and Baucis, an old married couple, were the only ones to welcome disguised gods Zeus and Hermes. As a reward for their hospitality, the couple was granted a wish. They chose to remain together forever and when one of them died, the other would die as well. Upon their deaths, they were changed into a pair of

Common Thorn Apple

intertwining linden and oak trees.

369 *Slack by the palsied Behemoths, hands open, head thrown back...*

The behemoth (Hebrew, *b'hemōth*, 'great beast', possibly an adaptation of Egyptian, *p-ehe-mau*, literally, water-ox) is an animal described in the book of Job of the Hebrew Bible. Job 25: 15: *Behold now behemoth, which I made with thee, he eateth grass as an ox.*

369 *'I should rather be rancorous, too.'*

Rancorous is showing deep-seated resentment, implacably spiteful or malicious; intensely virulent.

369 *'...he's bleeding over Grandpa Gideon's oak chair like a Martinmas pig.'*

Saint Martin's Day, or Martinmas, is a feast day held on November 11th and is the traditional day for slaughtering fattened pigs for the winter. There is a Spanish saying, translated as, *'Every pig has its Saint Martin's Day'*, meaning every wrongdoer has his comeuppance.

369 *...a kind of barmecide feast of invalid diet...*

Barmecide is lavish or plentiful in imagination only, and thus disappointing. The term is an allusion to the story told in the *Arabian Nights*: the Barmecide family placed a succession of empty dishes before a beggar, pretending they contained a sumptuous feast, a fiction the beggar humorously accepted. Barmecidal is like the entertainment of the story; hence, unreal; a sham; a spurious gift.

370 *'Coals of fire.'*

Burning coals of fire has the purpose of cleansing from sin. Thus, to heap burning coals of fire on someone's head is to bring them to repentance so their sin may be forgiven. The expression 'heap coals of fire on his head' (Romans 12: 19-21) means to treat someone who wrongs you with extra kindness, in spite of their sin towards you.

370 *...and put up at Berwick Castle...*

Berwick first appears in the early part of the 12th century during the reign of Alexander I. Once a part of Scotland and the capital of the district of Lothian, the town was populous and wealthy and was the chief seaport of Scotland. The castle was once of considerable strength, and is the scene of innumerable military operations: it was repeatedly attacked, surprised, defended, burned and plundered, by both Scots and English.

Berwick-on-Tweed by J.M.W. Turner, c.1833

371 *'Sent Bowes and Gamboa out on Sunday night, and they burned around Edinburgh while Wilford and Wyndham went for Dalkeith.'*

Captain Pedro Gamboa, a Spanish officer, commanded troops in Scotland on behalf of King Henry VIII and Protector Somerset.

Sir James Wilford (1516-1550) was an English soldier who supervised the fortification at Lauder in April 1548, and was recommended by Lord Grey of Wilton for the command of the occupying force at Haddington. On 3 June 1548, Wilford and Thomas Wyndham captured Dalkeith Palace, burnt the town, and took James Douglas prisoner. Wilford wrote to Protector Somerset describing Haddington: 'The state of this town pities me both to see and to write it; but I hope for relief. Many are sick and a great number dead, most of the plague.'[35]

Thomas Wyndham (1508-1554) was an English vice-admiral and navigator. On Christmas Day 1547, he burnt Balmerino Abbey, and Elcho Nunnery on 29 December. He constructed a battery at Haddington called Wyndham's Bulwark. On 3 June 1548, he and James Wilford captured Dalkeith Palace.

371 *'Got the whole garrison – Douglas's wife, second son, lairds and Douglases in dozens, and cartloads of furnishings...'*

George Douglas was married to Elizabeth Douglas, the daughter and heir of David Douglas of Pittenreich. James Douglas (later, 4th Earl of Morton; 1516-1581) was the second son of Sir George Douglas of Pittenreich, Master of Angus. After the fall of Dalkeith Palace, he was taken as hostage to England, returning in 1550. Below is an account of the taking of Dalkeith, the stronghold of the 'crafty and able leader, George Douglas; who, after his old fashion, represented himself as favourably inclined'[36] to England:

> In accomplishing his purpose the English commander [Grey] imitated his [George Douglas's] own cunning. 'I pretend no manner of enmity against him but that still I had hope of his conversion, to breed in him such trust, that the less doubting, the sooner I might be revenged or get him into my hands.'[37]
>
> Trusting to these assurances, the Scottish baron lay secure, as he believed, in his castle; whilst Gamboa, a Spanish leader in the service of England, and sixty mounted hagbutteers, scoured and burnt the country in his neighborhood; but before the least intelligence could reach him, Captain Wilford, with six hundred foot and one hundred horse, had crossed the Esk, and pushing forward his advance, summoned the castle. Even then Douglas boldly encountered him at the head of his pikemen. By superiority of numbers, however, he was driven back through the postern. The English gained the base court after a desperate struggle, in which forty of the Scots were slain; and Wilford was proceeding to undermine and blow up the walls, when the garrison yielded without conditions. Much wealth was found in the place, as, according to Grey's account, 'all the country had brought their goods together, thinking that nothing could prevail against George's policy.'[38] He himself escaped; but his wife, eldest son the Master of Morton, afterwards Regent, the Abbot of Arbroath a natural son of Angus, Home the laird of Wedderburn, and many of the Douglases, fell into the hands of the enemy. To be thus overreached and entrapped in his own devices was particularly mortifying to this long-practiced intriguer, and seems to have sunk deeper into his spirit than the loss of either his wife or his castle.[39]

376   ...dispatched that day to the Archbishop of York...

In the Church of England, the Archbishop of York is second only to the Archbishop of Canterbury. Robert Holgate (c.1481-1555) served as Archbishop of York from 1545-1554.

II: The Ultimate Check

Caxton: Tract 3, Chapter 8

*The couriers and bearers of letters ought hastily and speedily
do deliver that commanded them without tarrying.
For their tarrying might annoy and grieve them that send them forth,
or else those to whom the letters are sent,
And turn them to right great damage and villany.[1]*

1. The Fast Moves

378 *A frangible and archaic courtesy reigned at Flaw Valleys.*

Frangible is liable to fracture; fragile; brittle.

379 *'...you feed them on honey cakes and forbid them to defend themselves.'*

Several ancient myths surround the rite of offering honey-cakes to appease sacred snakes. Ælian (c.175-235), Roman author and teacher, described the snake cult of the people of Epiros:

> *The people of Epiros sacrifice in general to Apolla. There is a grove dedicated to the god and it has a circular enclosure and within are snakes, playthings surely for the god. Now only the maiden priestess approaches them, and she is naked and brings the snakes their food. Now if they take their food kindly, that is taken to mean that there will be a plentiful year and free from disease; but if they frighten her and do not take the honey-cakes which she offers them, they portend the reverse.*

379 *'From cuticle to corium in four days.'*

267

The cuticle is the outermost layer of skin, or the epidermis. The corium is the deep inner layer of the skin, beneath the epidermis.

380 *'Yours aren't points, they're probangs.'*

A probang is a long, slender tool with a tufted end used for pushing obstructions down the throat. [2/D]

380 *'And I have drunk of Castalia as well as bathed in it.'*

In Greek mythology, Castalia was a fountain at the foot of Mount Parnassus, near the Temple of Apollo at Delphi. Those who visited the temple bathed their hair *rore puro Castaliæ* ('in the pure dew of Castalia'); those who needed purification from murder bathed their whole body. Its waters gave poetic inspiration to those who drank of it. The fountain is named for Castalia, who threw herself into the fountain to escape the pursuits of Apollo.

380 *'Grimalkin goes quavering back to the chimney piece.'*

A grimalkin is an old female cat.[3/D] In Scottish lore, a gremalkin is a faery cat who dwells in the Highlands.

380 *The long slender fingers tightened about the salt cellar...*

In the Middle Ages, salt was kept on the table in an elaborate dish as a status symbol. The social status of a guest was often measured by the distance at which a person sat from the salt cellar placed in the middle of the table. The phrases 'above the salt' and 'below the salt' derive from the custom of seating persons of higher rank closer to the salt cellar than those of lower rank.

Saltcellar made for Francis I by Benvenuto Cellini

380 *'...you may baulk me.'*

To baulk is to hinder, to impede, to frustrate; from the Gaelic, *bac*.

381 *'Pythonissa,' retorted Lymond, and unexpectedly smiled.*

Pythonissa is a witch or sorceress, a woman with the power of divination.[4/D] From the Latin 'python' meaning soothsayer, and also the pythonidæ, a type of snake. Pythons are ambush predators; they remain motionless in a camouflaged position and then strike suddenly and kill by constricting their prey until it dies of asphyxiation.

381 *Thus she was able to hear the sweet, preoccupied roulades of the lute...*

A roulade is a smoothly running passage of short notes uniformly grouped; an elaborate embellishment of several notes sung to one syllable. The lute, the premier solo instrument of the 16th century, is a plucked string instrument with a neck and a deep, round back.

The Ambassadors (detail)
by Hans Holbein the Younger, 1533

382 *'I can play the rebec as well.'*

Derived from the Arabic instrument *rehab* and the Byzantine lyra, the rebec was a bowed stringed musical instrument popular in the 15th and 16th centuries.

Gorgon, daughter of the gods Phorcys & Keto
MS, De Claris mulieribus by Boccaccio, 1374

382 *'And the recorder.'*

The recorder is a woodwind musical instrument popular in the 16th and 17th centuries. Renaissance recorders have a wide, almost cylindrical bore; they have powerful low notes, and are more responsive than other recorders.

382 *It was only* **L'homme armé**; *a tune Philippa had certainly heard...*

L'homme armé is a French secular song from the Renaissance.

> *The man, the man, the armed man,*
> *The armed man*
> *The armed man should be feared, should be feared.*
> *Everywhere it has been proclaimed*
> *That each man shall arm himself*
> *With a coat of iron mail.*

382 *There shall be mirth at our meeting.*

There sall be mirth at our meeting was a song common among the peasantry in the earlier half of the 15th century; reference is made to it in the last line of the 25th stanza *Of Peeblis to the Play* :

> *He flipped like one fatherless foal,*
> *And said, Be still, my sweet thing.*
> *By the Holy Cross of Peebles,*
> *I may not rest for greeting.*
> *He whistled and he piped both,*
> *To make her lighthearted that meeting:*
> *My bonny heart, how says the song,*
> *'There shall be mirth at our meeting.*
> *Yet.'* [5]
>
> (Tr.L.R.)

383 *'But try all three and you're a mountebank.'*

A mountebank is a hawker of quack medicine, a flamboyant charlatan, a boastful, unscrupulous pretender.

383 *'...because stultified talent is surely the ultimate crime against mankind.'*

To stultify (Latin, *stultus*, foolish, +*facere*, to make) is to make or cause to appear foolish; to reduce to foolishness or absurdity.

383 *'Like Paris, they have three choices.'*

In Greek mythology, the goddess Strife vengefully flung a golden apple inscribed

'To the Most Beautiful' among the three goddesses Hera, Athena, and Aphrodite. The mortal Paris was appealed to umpire the discord. Each attempted to bribe Paris: Hera offered a kingdom; Athena offered wisdom and skill in war; Aphrodite offered love of the world's most beautiful woman, Helen of Sparta. Paris accepted Aphrodite's gift of Helen. The Greek expedition to retrieve Helen in Troy is the mythological basis of the Trojan War.

The Judgement of Paris
by Lucas Cranach the Elder, c.1513

384   *'Or to hide behind the more outré of their pursuits...'*

Outré is excessive, or outrageous.

384 *'I might be able to gull the law.'*

To gull is to fool; cheat; deceive.

385 *...Gideon's stallion...printed with sharp cloisonné...*

Cloisonné (from French, *cloison*, a partition) is an ancient decorative technique, wherein the outlines of a design are formed by small bands of metal bent to shape and affixed to porcelain. The cells between the metal fillets are filled with enamel paste and vitrified by heat. The surface is then ground smooth and polished.

386 *...which met him at one of the biggins where they used to keep fodder.*

Example of cloisonné, c.800 AD

A biggins is a building, especially a house or cottage. Fodder is hay or feed for cattle and other livestock.

386 *...were like phantasmagoria...*

Phantasmagoria was a form of theatre invented in France in the late 18th century, which used a magic lantern to project images; thus, phantasmagoria is a series or medley of illusive or terrifying images, specifically a combination wherein one view dissolves or gradually merges into the next.

387 *'Dod, are ye wandered!'*

Phantasmagoria, c.1885

Wandered (Scots, *wander, waun(n)er*) is to be confused; bewildered; lost.

388 *He studied the wayward eyebrows, the falcate nose...*

Falcate (Latin, *falcatus*, bent, curved, hooked) is curved like a scythe or sickle; specifically applied in anatomy, zoology, and botany.

389 *'... before ye get that meagre that ye slip down the town stank.'*

Stank (Scots, from French *estaing*, and Gaelic, *staing*, a ditch; *staingichte*, entrenched) is a pool; an entrenchment filled with water for the defence of a fortress; a receptacle for water. Removal of the first letter becomes the English *tank*.

389 *Sir George Douglas's lodging was in the Lawnmarket.*

The Lawnmarket is one of a succession of streets which make up the Royal Mile, Edinburgh's main thoroughfare. It extends from the West Bow and Castle-Hill to St. Giles Church, and derived its name from stalls erected for the sale of linen. The area was long occupied by families of rank and opulence; for five centuries it was the highly aristocratic quarter of Edinburgh.

The Lawnmarket from the West Bow towards St. Giles Cathedral
by W.L. Leitch, c.1840

389 *...the price D'Essé had paid for his and Angus's continuing interest.*

André de Montalembert, Seigneur d'Essé (1483–1553) was a French nobleman and officer. In 1548, d'Essé was sent into Scotland with 6,000 men to support Regent Arran against England. D'Essé spoke at the parliament at Haddington in 1548, proposing the marriage of Queen Mary to the Dauphin of France. Haddington was occupied and fortified by the English and it was d'Esse who laid siege.

390 *'Do-to the book; quench the candle; ring the bell.'*

'Do to the book; quench the candle; ring the bell' are the closing words of the rite of excommunication, meaning the service book is closed, the candle put out, and the passing bell rung, as a sign of spiritual death.

2. The Tragic Moves

391 *Next morning Lymond, swordless, left Edinburgh's Bristo Port...*

There were six ports in the Flodden Wall, one of which was Bristo Port, built close to Greyfriars Kirk around 1515.

Bristo Port

392 *'...a black, brosy yin on a nice bay, and a swack, smert yin on a chestnut.'*

brosy:	stout and strong; well-built; well fed with brose
yin:	one; a certain person
bay:	horse with reddish-brown coat and black mane
swack:	of wits, quick, nimble
smert:	smart; quick, vigorous, skilled, clever
chestnut:	horse with reddish-to-brown coat with mane and tail of lighter color than coat

392 *'...they were that different: corbie and doo on the ane twig.'*

corbie: raven
doo: pigeon (dove)
ane: one
twig: branch

394 *Next day they reached Newcastle in the late afternoon...*

The Castle at Newcastle by Thomas Allom, c.1825

The Castle of Newcastle was a massive Norman fortress, built by Robert, eldest son of William the Conqueror (1028-1087), on his return from an expedition into Scotland. Named the New Castle in contrast to some more ancient fortress, the castle was more than 100 feet in height, its walls were 17 feet thick, and it stood three storeys tall.

> *The castle, or more strictly speaking, Keep of the original Norman edifice, which was once the stronghold of the Conqueror's representative – the fortress and often the abode of the Anglo-Norman kings – the palace of David, King of Scots, upon one invasion – the hall of state in which the mightiest sovereigns held their courts, sat in judgment, and maintained regal hospitality – in which King John conferred with William the Lion, King of Scotland, and Henry III with King Alexander – in which Edward I and Edward III held high festival and warlike council – fell into a state of dilapidation before the reign of James I of England.[6]*

394 *'...Wylstropp honoured the safe conduct and let them go...'*

Sir Oswold Wylstropp was stationed at Haddington in 1548 with Christofer Ellerkar. Earlier in 1547-48, Grey of Wilton 'lay Sir Oswold Wylstropp with 200 horse Jedworth and Roxburgh to annoy the Scots'[7].

394 *Now they were adrift on the Lammermoors...*

The Lammermoor Hills lie within East Lothian and Berwickshire, forming a southern screen to East Lothian. The range forms the vast triangular basin of the Tweed and overlooks the Scottish Lowlands. The Lammermoors are a curvature of 'wild and cheerless heights'[7] which subside into 'low rolling tablelands of bleak moor'[8]. Once clothed in forest, they are almost everywhere sprinkled with heather.

Lammermoor Hills, May 2007

397 *'...reduced to a state of crapulence for your purposes.'*

Crapulence is sickness caused by excessive eating or drinking.

400 *...the stalking, gem-cut line of the Wall ahead...*

Hadrian's Wall was a defensive fortification in Roman Britain, begun in 122 AD, during the rule of emperor Hadrian. The wall was the most heavily fortified border in the Empire, and its many gates served as custom posts; it extended west from the River Tyne to the shore of Solway Firth.

Fosse, from Latin, *fossa*, is a long narrow excavation, ditch or trench, especially in a fortification.

Hadrian's Wall near Greenhead Lough, Northumberland, October 2005

3. The Last Move

401 *'Adhesive as St. Anthony's pig.'*

St. Anthony the Great (251-356) is the patron saint of pigs; legend holds he was a swineherd who appeared with a pig which never left his side.

401 *'Qu'on lui ferme la porte au nez, il reviendra par les fenêtres.'*

'It's no good closing the door, he'll find entry through a window,' meaning old habits die hard.

From the fable, *The Cat Transformed into a Woman:*

Saint Anthony

> *In mockery of change, the old*
> *will keep their youthful bent.*
> *When once the cloth has got its fold,*
> *The smelling pot its scent,*
> *In vain your efforts and your care*
> *To make them other than they are.*
> *To work reform, do what you will,*
> *Old habit will be habit still.*
> *Nor fork nor strap can mend its manners,*
> *Nor cudgel-blows beat down its banners,*
> *Secure the doors against re-enter*
> *As through the windows it will enter.*

401 *'...your name will fly tetragrammaton round the world...'*

Tetragrammaton, from the Greek word meaning 'having four letters', refers to the name of the God of Israel used in the Hebrew Bible, transliterated to the Latin letters YHWH.

From *Pearl*, a Middle English dream vision, considered 'the most highly wrought and intricately constructed poem in Middle English'[10].

> *'O Pearl,' said I, 'in pearls adorned,*
> *Are you my Pearl, for whom I cried,*
> *For whom I grieved alone at night?*
> *Great yearning I have suffered*
>   *for thee in secret*
> *Since into the grass thou slipped away from me*
> *Gloomy, wasted, I am in pain,*
> *And thou in a life of pleasant light,*
> *In Paradise, a life unstrained with strife.*
> *What fortune has brought my jewel here,*
> *And cast me in this grief and great danger?*
> *For since we were separated and torn asunder,*
> *I am a joyless jeweller.'*

An explanation of the poem from *The Pearl: An Anonymous English Poem of the 14ᵗʰ Century* by C.G. Osgood:

> *First, there sounds prophetically, but faintly, the note of peace and triumph which later brings the poem to its final cadence. Then begins the prelude, wherein is shown the agonizing conflict of grief and doubt that raged in the poet's heart after the loss of his Pearl. Through the deep sleep that at length comes to his exhausted body and soul the poem issues into the first of its three great phases. The poet is almost dazed with the brightness of the strange land in which he awakes; gradually his mind begins to comprehend its surroundings, and he starts to range among the endless beauties of the place; more and more eagerly he goes forward, until at the shining brink of Paradise he pauses, straining his heart after the joys of the fairer land beyond. And here, without warning, his eyes fall upon his Pearl in all the bright glory of the heavenly life, yet sweet and maidenly in her graciousness towards him.*
>
>   *A moment of humbled embarrassment, then of ecstatic joy, and he thinks: 'Here is the solution of all my troubles; there is nothing left to dread, and everything to enjoy in this dearest of all companionships.' And he cries aloud to her in anticipation. But tenderly and gravely she rebukes him; such delights go not with his condition of sin and mortality. At once the old war in his soul springs up with new fury. 'God is unfair. There is nothing but misery in the world for me and all men. I cannot endure it!' Then more like a mother than a child, mingling transcendent pity with sternness, as did Beatrice when she melted the soul of her lover to contrition and*

obedience, the Pearl shows this sorrow-broken man how his trouble may become not an instrument of self-destruction, such as he is making it, but the very voice of God, quieting his soul, and revealing to him the vision of endless peace.

'And what,' he asks, 'is the nature of that peace which she has found?' First, she explains, it lies in the acceptance of God's way as not only inevitable, but kindest and best. Second, in unfailing gratitude for his goodness as a friend. Third, in utter freedom from the spirit of selfish competition, that we may enjoy pure delight in the happiness of our fellows. But all this is incomprehensible to one whose emotional experiences have been self-centred, and whose habit of mind, owing to his scholastic training, has been, after the manner of his times, formal and rationalistic. The maiden at first, therefore, concedes somewhat to his demand for logical proof; but with every point and sentence she mingles suggestions of feeling and rightness of heart, which slowly and subtly convince him, as he listens to her description of the blessed life. Less and less resistant, and more and more eager his questions become, until, at last, the need of question, and proof, and sympathy, is done away, and he is ready to behold with his own eyes the Beatific Vision. In the glory that then bursts upon his sight he hardly misses his Pearl, who has now withdrawn from him. Before him unfold in order the splendours of the Heavenly City, surpassing in beauty and number the imagination of man, and beyond the power of his unaided sense to receive.

Then, as in the earlier part of his dream all the joys of the Earthly Paradise were consummate in the visitation of the Pearl, so here through the higher glories of the Heavenly Paradise the poem rises to the apotheosis of the redeemed, of Christ the Lamb that was slain, and of his Bride rejoicing with perfect joy. Unutterable then the brightness, the purity, the adoration, the far-reaching sound of angels' song; ineffable the tenderness, the pity, the triumph of Christ himself; for ever happy and secure the Pearl in the fullness of eternal life. Beside himself with ecstasy, driven by one last selfish impulse, the poet forgets for an instant all that his visitant has taught him, and tries with hasty force to seize more than God has given him. A sudden shock of blindness and insensibility, and he gropes slowly back to his earthly life. For a moment he finds himself in the midst of his old sorrow, but only for a moment. Through his experience of the vision he has been born into a new life of peace, and service, and patient looking-forward to the dear and unbroken companionship that awaits him in the life to come.[11]

402 *'There aren't any dregs in my cup,' said Christian.*

Psalm 75:8 King James Version:

> *For in the hand of the Lord there is a cup, and the wine is red; it is full of mixture; and he poureth out of the same: but the dregs thereof, all the wicked of the earth shall wring them out, and drink them.*

403 *'Io son fatta da Dio, sua merce, tale ...'*

> *'I am the chosen of God. He will see*
> *That your suffering does me no harm*
> *That the flames of this fire never touch me.'*

From *Davina Commedia (The Divine Comedy, Inferno, Canto II, lines 91-93)* by Dante Alighieri (c.1265-1321), the poet's vision of Hell, Purgatory, and Heaven. Although expressed in sublime and exquisite poetry, with power and beauty of language, the poem aims not to delight, but 'to reprove, to rebuke, to exhort; to form men's characters by teaching them what course of life will meet with reward, what with penalty, hereafter "put into verse," as the poet says, "things difficult to think."'[12]

Illustration of Canto II, lines 70-71
by Gustav Doré, 1892

403 *'...stumbles on a glossa interlinearis...'*

A gloss is a translation or explanation of a word or phrase; a collection of such notes is a glossary. The *Glossa Interlinearis*, written in 1117, derived its name from the fact it was written over the words in the text of the Vulgate, a 4th-century translation of the Bible.

404 **Lymond:** *'This time you shall have music to sound in a high tower--'*
Christian: *'–So merrily that it was a joy for to hear, and no man should see the craft thereof ...'*

From *The Travels of Sir John Mandeville*, describing Paradise:

> *And he had made a conduit under earth, so that the three wells, at his list, one should run milk, another wine and another honey. And that place he clept Paradise. And when that any good knight, that was hardy and noble, came to see this royalty, he would lead him into his paradise, and show him these wonderful things to his disport, and the marvellous and delicious song of diverse birds, and*

the fair damsels, and the fair wells of milk, of wine and honey, plenteously running. And he would let make diverse instruments of music to sound in a high tower, so merrily, that it was joy for to hear; and no man should see the craft therof. And those, he said, were angels of God, and that the place was Paradise, that God had behight to his friends, saying Dabo vobis terram fluentum lacte et melle. (I will give you a land flowing with milk and honey.)

405 *...burst from the metempirical quills...*

In metaphysics, metempirical means beyond or outside the realm of experience; transcendental. 'The metempirical region is the void where Speculation roams unchecked, where Sense has no footing, where Experiment can exercise no control, and where Calculation ends in impossible Quantities.'[13]

405 *Jouissance vous donneray*
Mon amy, et vous méneray
Là où prétend
Votre espérance
Vivante ne vous laisseray
Encores quand morte seray
L'esprit en aura souvenance

> *Joy, dearest lover, thine shall be,*
> *And I shall lead thee tenderly*
> *Where hope would have thee seek thy pleasure;*
> *Alive I shall not part from thee,*
> *And still when death has come to me*
> *My soul its memories shall treasure.*[14]

From a chanson composed by Claudin de Sermisy (c.1490-1562), with lyrics by Clément Marot (1496-1544).

405 *...like Ulysses perhaps their ears were tingling with the music of the sirens.*

Ulysses, or Odysseus, was a legendary Greek king of Ithaca and one of the most celebrated heroes of the Trojan War. His adventures after the fall of Troy form the subject of the Homeric poem the *Odyssey*, in which he and his crew encounter the Sirens. In Greek mythology, the Sirens were dangerous and devious creatures who lured sailors to their deaths on the rocky shores of their island with their enchanting music and voices.

406 *...while he loosed his fierce elegies he had watched them...*

An elegy is a song expressive of sorrow or lamentation; or a mournful, melancholic, plaintive poem.

406 *...he was a primitive figure, of pantheistic and dreadful force.*

Pantheism equates God with the forces and laws of the universe.

408 *'Exposing her to public obloquy at Threave – that's another fact.'*

Obloquy (Latin, *ob,* against, + *loqui,* speak) is abusive language addressed to or aimed at another, or disgrace suffered as a result of abuse or vilification; shame.

410 *In a year he had become used to command: his father, after all, was within the most intimate circle of the Court; his grandfather was Archibald, second Duke of Argyll; his grandmother and his sister had borne sons to two kings.*

John Erskine, 5th Lord Erskine, *de jure* Earl of Mar (d.1552; Father of Tom Erskine) was married to Lady Margaret Campbell, daughter of Archibald Campbell, 2nd Earl of Argyll. In 1513, Erskine was appointed keeper of ten-year-old King James V and Stirling Castle. He traveled to England in 1535, to receive the Order of the Garter from King Henry VIII on James's behalf.

Archibald Campbell, 2nd Earl of Argyll (d.1513; Grandfather of Tom Erskine), was a Scottish nobleman and politician who rose to the position of Lord High Chancellor in Scotland. He was killed at the Battle of Flodden.

Tom's grandmother on his father's side was Isobel Campbell, wife of Robert Erskine, 4th Lord Erskine. His grandmother on his mother's side was Elizabeth Stuart, wife of Archibald Campbell, 2nd Earl of Argyll.

Lady Margaret Erskine (d.1572; Sister of Tom Erskine) was a mistress of King James V of Scotland, and mother of the most important of his illegitimate children, James Stewart, 1st Earl of Moray (c.1531-1570). Margaret is reported as being the favourite mistress of James. She married Sir Robert Douglas of Lochleven in 1527, but it was rumoured James considered seeking a divorce on Margaret's behalf and marrying her.

413 *'We are about to hold trial by combat...as if this were done in Scotland, in champ clos.'*

A trial by combat is a trial decided by a personal battle between the two parties involved in a dispute, with the idea God would give victory to the person in the right. The method was introduced into England by the Normans after 1066, and became obsolete several centuries before being formally abolished in 1818. *Champ clos* means 'closed field'.

Duel between Wilhelm Marshalk and Theodor Hashfield in Augsberg, 1409
MS illustration by Jörg Breu and Paulus Hector Mair, c.1544

414   *...the thin tempered rapiers with steel quillons and counterguard; the daggers with their thick, double-edged blades, twelve inches long.*

A rapier is a slender, sharply pointed, long-bladed sword characterised by a complex hilt, or guard, which provides protection for the sword hand. Quillons, also called the crossbar, are rods which extend perpendicular to either side of the blade, and are used for protecting the wielding hand and to deflect the sword of the opponent.

A dagger is a weapon similar to a sword, but shorter. In rapier fencing, a dagger is held in the fighter's off hand and used to make parries and attacks. During the Renaissance, the dagger was used as part of everyday dress.

Ancient swords, daggers,
and battle-axes

414   *Inside, the sun prinked and patterned the floor...*

To prink is to adorn oneself in a showy manner.

415   *'Since we are here,' said Lymond conversationally, 'why not pronounce something appropriate? "Eh bien, dansez maintenant?"'*

Fom the fable, *The Grasshopper and the Ant*, translated as *'Well, dance now!'* or *'You'd better practice dancing now!'*

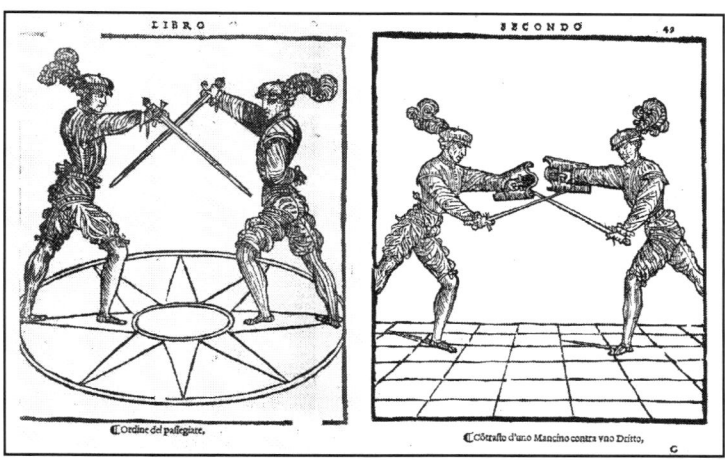

Manuscript illustrations from the premier fencing manual of the 16ᵗʰ century, Opera Nova dell 'Arte delle Armi by Achille Marozzo, 1536

415   *'Or, "We came both out of one womb: so shall we lie both in one pit"?'*

From *The Book of Three Quests* in *The Arthurian Tales*.

415   *'And there's "Brother, whi art thou so to me in ire?" – the killing of Abel, my dear: a mine of suitable commentary...'*

From *Mactatio Abel (The Killing of Abel)*, one of the thirty-two Towneley Mystery Plays. Believed to be the work of Augustinian friars, the plays were based on stories from the Bible and were performed, it is thought, on fair days. The object of the plays was to serve religion, but also to simply entertain.

415 *'Let us fight with sugar in our mouths like the litigating tailors of V--'*

This may possibly refer to the practice of 15th- and 16th-century Venetian fabric merchants of applying paste to their heaviest silk cloths, velvets and damasks. The gelatinous mixture was used to alter the density and disguise defects. There are several cases cited where Venetian merchants were sued because their cloths were altered.

415 *'Nature works in the...shortest way possible.'*

Aristotle in his fifth book of *Metaphysics* stated: *Nature works in the shortest way possible, and the straight line is the shortest of all.*

415 *'You're rolling about like a pear in a pottle.'*

A pottle is a small basket of fruit.[15/D]

415 *'His heart was light as leaf on tree, when that he thought on his--'*

From *The Pleasant History of Roswall and Lillian,* a mid-16th century Scottish romance. 'The title of *Roswall and Lillian* suggests a love-story, but the core of the tale is Roswall's release of the prisoners, their oath of perpetual friendship, and the way in which they fulfill it in his time of need.'[16]

416 *'He's* **twice** *the size of common men, wi' thewes and sinewes strong.'*

From *The Marriage of Sir Gawain*, an Arthurian ballad:

> *Hee's twyce the size of common men,*
> *Wi' thewes, and sinewes stronge,*
> *And on his backe he bears a clubbe,*
> *That is both thicke and longe.*

416 *'Reaping the eddish. Try the other side next time.'*

The eddish is the stubble remaining after mowing or reaping; the aftermath. Here, Lymond is mocking Richard for attacking his weak side.

417 *In the middle of an imbroccata he dropped his left hand...*

An imbroccata is a downward thrust over the opponent's rapier. In preparation for an imbroccata the arm is held vertically with the palm to the right and the rapier angled down at the opponent's face.

417 *...his eyes bitter as squill.*

Squill is a perennial herb with an acrid juice having a bitter taste. The Vernal Squill (*Scilla vérna*) grows in profusion in rocky pastures near the sea and is a frequent flower in the Orkney islands. Autumnal Squill (*Scilla autumnális*) is abundant on the rocks at St. Helen's, Isle of Wright. The bulbs of these plants are very acrid and furnish an active medicine with a bitter taste.

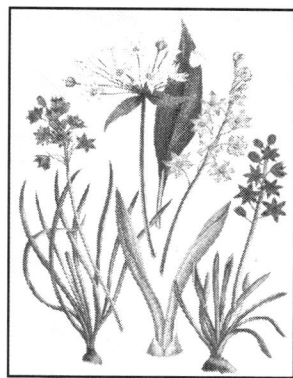

Squill

418 *...sparkling largo to larghetto...*

Largo is in a very slow tempo, slower than adagio and with great dignity. Larghetto is in a slow tempo, slightly faster than largo but slower than adagio.

419 *Tap, tap went the compound riposte...*

In fencing, the riposte (French for 'retort') is an offensive action, a counter-attack immediately following a parry.

420 *Corps à corps fighting was death to the Master now.*

Corps à corps is hand-to-hand fighting.

420 *..the blades in his hands swooping like the many scythes of Chronos...*

In Greek mythology, Cronus was the leader and youngest of the first generation of Titans. He is depicted with a scythe, the instrument used to castrate and depose his father, Uranus. During antiquity, Cronus was interpreted as Chronos, the personification of time. In the Renaissance the identification of Cronus as Chronos gave rise to Father Time wielding the harvesting scythe.

421 *'Handy Dandy prickly prandy, Richard...Which hand will you have?'*

From a popular nursery rhyme of the era:

> *Why loe heere we are both,*
> *I am in this hand, and hee is in that*
> *Handy dandy, prickly prandy,*
> *Which hand will you haue.*

422 *Lymond flew before them like a honey guide seducing a vespiary...*

A honeyguide is a bird which will deliberately lead humans directly to a bee colony so the bird can feed on the grubs left behind. A vespiary is a wasp colony.

422 *...his job was to prevent Osiris from being destroyed by brother Set.*

Osiris is the Egyptian god of the afterlife, while Set is his younger sibling, the god of darkness and chaos. In Egyptian myth, Set killed his brother Osiris for the throne.

424 *Affairs at the wicket...*

A wicket is a person-sized door set into a main gate door.

423 *...into the Alpine bosom of Hexham.*

Hexham from the West by Thomas Allom, c.1865

Hexham is an ancient market town situated on the crown of a considerable hill just below the confluence of the North and South Tynes, about 20 miles west of Newcastle. At the centre of the old town is an open and spacious market-square, once the most picturesque in England. Of the vale of Hexham it was said, 'Its harvests are the earliest, its trees have the richest foliage, and its landscape is the most diversified and interesting of any in Northumberland.'[17]

Hexham Market-Place by Thomas Allom, c.1835

425 *Both Acheson and his assailant...had been taken to the Abbey...*

Hexham Abbey Church, Northumberland

The Abbey and Cathedral Church of St. Andrew of Hexham was founded in the year 675 AD when Queen Etheldreda, wife of King Egfrid, granted land to St. Wilfrid, who built the church and monastery, said to surpass in beauty all the religious houses in England and no finer church 'could be seen on this side of the Alps'[18]. The abbey church prospered, and with increasing wealth came the desire to erect more beautiful and more extensive buildings; thus the original church was replaced by a new priory in the style of the 13th century; the church as it now stands dates from this period and is considered an impressive example of Early English church architecture.

425   *...he gave a passing nod to the Augustinian sense of proportion...*

> *To describe the emotions under which we survey this lofty memorial of olden piety and ancient art, would be a gratuitous undertaking. Some there are, who can recognize, in structures of this kind, nothing but a waste of human labour – an extravagance of skill. Yet, wherefore should we cast contumely on those ancient shrines which good men consecrated, and which time has hallowed? Why deprecate as vain and futile, all those rites and observances that tend to loosen the mind from the thrall of worldly pursuits – to calm and subdue the fluctuations of human passion – to draw a holy mystery around the sanctuary? Whatever unfavourable associations may be connected with their long history – a history embracing the casualties of seven centuries, and the actions of ten generations of men – cold is the heart that can enter their portals unaffected by feelings of piety and awe; and more deaf than the adder is that ear, which continues listless and wandering,*

> > *'When through the long drawn aisle and fretted vault,*
> > *The pealing anthem swells the note of praise.'[19]*

425   *On his right, a flight of steps rose into the wall...*

On the south end of the main transept is a stone gallery with a bold and imposing set of stone stairs, which served as the night stairs leading to the dormitory. The priory of Hexham was notorious for its laxity of discipline and its excesses; several canons were convicted of incontinence. In 1535, injunctions were imposed to thwart further abuses and emphasize chaste behavior: no canon was to associate with a woman of doubtful character; no women but mothers and sisters were allowed entry; and the doors were to be locked every night.

Hexham Church by Thomas Allom, c.1835
View looking south through the North Transept to the Night Stairs

Hexham Abbey Church, showing the Screen and North Transept

Hexham Abbey Choir, looking eastward

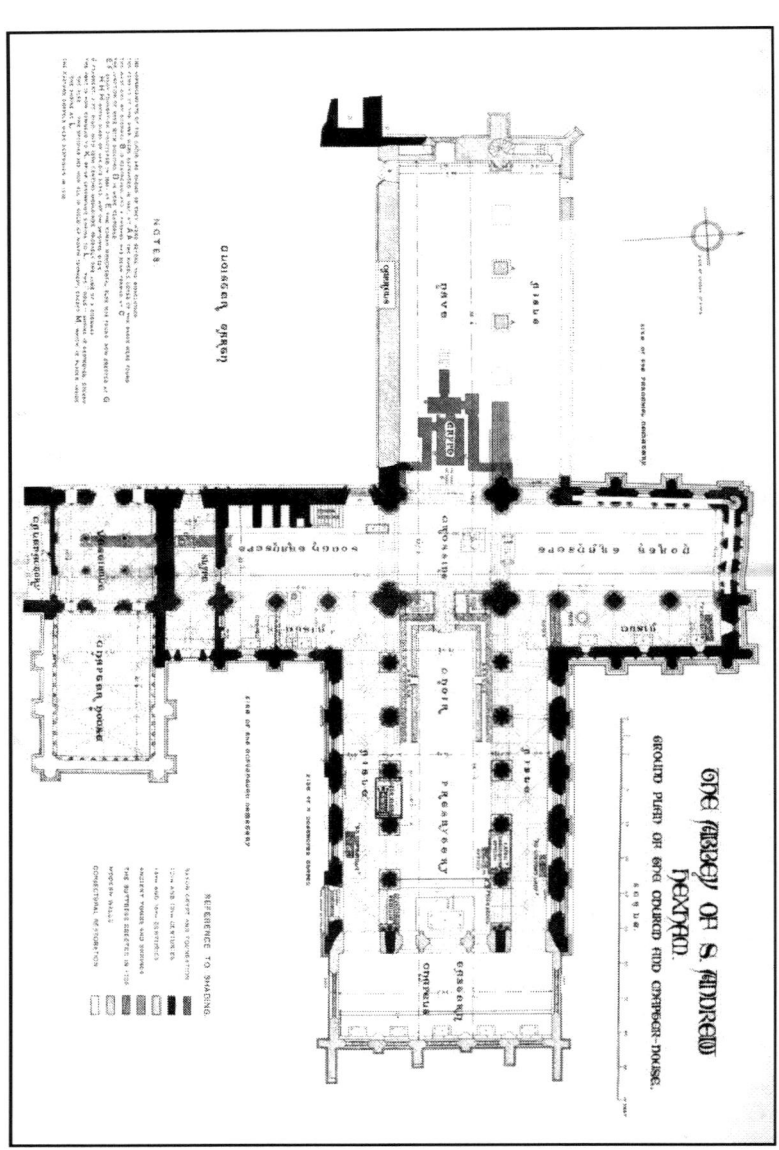

426 *'I can give you one name that you can't give me: cuckold, Lord Lennox!'*

Cuckold is the historic derogatory term for a man who has an unfaithful wife. Cuckolds were said to 'wear the horns', a reference to a stag beaten in battle yielding its mate to the victor. 'Cuckold' derives from 'cuckoo', a bird whose female mate is often promiscuous and is known to lay eggs in foreign nests to be fostered by unsuspecting strangers.

427 *...roughly as humble as Shishman, Emperor of the Slavs...*

Ivan Shishman (1371-1395) is the most prominent mediæval ruler in Bulgarian folklore. He is represented as a saint in the role of protector or as a heroic ruler who fought dragons and oppressors, facing overwhelming enemy forces. Ivan is depicted as a child (*second from the left*) in the 14th-century manuscript illustration, the *Tetraevangelia of Ivan Alexander*.

Tetravangelia of Ivan Alexander MS, 14th century

427 *...Brahma finding pest...*

In the Hindu religion, Brahmā is the universal Spirit, the impersonal and absolute divinity, the ground and cause of all existence. In later theosophy, he became personified as the Creator, and combined into a trimurti with Vishnu ('the Preserver') and Siva ('the Destroyer').

Braham, 18th century watercolour

427 *'Gushing Hippocrenes at every joint.'*

Hippocrene (derived from *hippos*, 'a horse', and *krēnē*, 'a fountain'), is a fountain on the slope of Mt. Helicon, sacred to the Muses and Apollo, and created from the hoof of Pegasus. Drinking its water brought forth poetic inspiration.

428 *'...lambs dutiful to the bellwether...'*

Bellerophon on Pegasus by Walter Crane, c.1893

A bellwether is something which serves to create or influence trends, or presage future happenings. The term is derived from the Middle English *bellewether* and refers to the practice of placing a bell around the neck of a castrated ram (a *wether*) who then led his flock of sheep. The movements of the flock could be noted by hearing the bell before the flock was in sight.

428 *'...bending like a springal towards the weightiest pocket?'*

A springal is an active, springy young man.

428 *'A Lennox pressed is a Dead Sea apple...'*

In mediæval times, a Dead Sea apple was the fruit from a mythical tree which grew where Sodom and Gomorrah once stood. Any traveller foolish enough to pick one of the apples would see it turned to smoke and ashes in his hand, a sign of God's eternal displeasure with those who succumb to physical temptation.

429 *'And where have you been, my billy...'*

From the ballad, *Billy Boy*.

429 *'...to the devil and back to have your beard combed?'*

Referring to the Scottish legend of goats visiting the devil daily to have their beards combed.[20]

429 *'Milked like a cow tree.'*

A cow-tree (*Brosimum Galactodendron*) is especially distinguished by its sap, a nourishing milk-like juice.

Brosimum Galactodendron

429 *'He was bearded like a Dammar pine...'*

A Dammar pine (*Agathis dammara*) is a species of evergreen tree; its adult leaves are very leathery and quite thick.

430 *...the catafalque with Acheson...*

A catafalque is a raised bier or platform used to convey a coffin during a funeral. They are often ornate.

Agathis dammara

430 *'I was to be driven into the nets since, unlike the beaver, my self-defence stops short of unserviceable gestures.'*

The beaver is hunted for its testicles, which are valued for medicine. When the beaver sees it cannot escape, it bites off its testicles and throws them to the hunter. The moral is if a man wishes to live chastely he must cut off all his vices and throw them in the face of the devil.

431 *'Are you known, do you imagine, as Zenobia?'*

Zenobia's Last Look on Palmyra
by Herbert Schmalz

Septima Zenobia (240-c.274), queen of Palmyra and one of the heroes of antiquity famed for her beauty, courage, intelligence, and masculine energy, refused a 'husband except for a king'[21/D]. During the reigns of Gallienus and Claudius, she was able to retain the throne of Palmyra independent of Roman power, and even compelled one attacking Roman general to retreat. When Aurelian became emperor, however, he marched against her, defeating her in two pitched battles, and then besieged her city of Palmyra. At this critical moment, Zenobia's courage failed her, and she attempted to escape, but was captured. Brought as a captive into the presence of emperor, who sternly demanded how she presumed to defy the power of Rome, she replied, with prudent policy, 'Because I disdained to acknowledge as my masters such men as Aureolus and Gallienus. To Aurelian I submit, as my conqueror and my sovereign.'[22]

Aurelian seized the wealth of the city and put to death her officers and advisors, but Zenobia was granted life. She was led in the triumphal procession of the emperor at Rome, adorned with jewels and almost fainting under the weight of gold chains. There are two widely divergent accounts of Zenobia's fate. One is she starved herself to death; the other is Aurelian presented her with an elegant villa at Tibur, where, with her two sons, she passed the rest of her life in comfort and splendour.

431 *'And al was conscience and tendre herte.'*

From *The Canterbury Tales: The Prioress & the Second Nun* by Geoffrey Chaucer.

432 *...their swords might be unbarrelled shooks.*

A shook is a set of pieces for making a cask or box, usually wood.

433 *'...teach you a lesson with some* ex cathedra *observations.'*

Ex cathedra, literally 'from the chair', is a theological term which signifies authoritative teaching, in particular definitions given by the Roman pontiff. The phrase *ex cathedra* occurs in the writings of the mediæval theologians, and in the discussions which arose after the Reformation in regard to papal prerogatives.

433 *...inexorable as Melpomene, turned like a dark flower to its killing...*

In Greek mythology, Melpomene ('the singing one'), one of the nine Muses, presided over Tragedy.

434 *'And died stinkingly martyred,' said Lymond...*

From *Why Come Ye Not to Court?* by John Skelton (1460-1529), which tells the tale of the case of Cardinal Balue, who advanced to Cardinal...

> *And, against all reason,*
> *Committed open treason,*
> *And against his Lord Sovereign,*
> *Wherefore he suffered pain,*
> *Was beheaded, drawn, and quartered,*
> *And died stinkingly martyred*
> *Lo! yet for all that*
> *He wore a Cardinal's Hat!*

Chapter III: Knight Adversary

Caxton: Tract 3, Chapter 5

And also it behooves them to first have cure of themselves,
and ought to purge from the self all abcesses and all vices,
and that they should hold themselves pure and ready for to help others.[1]

I. Strange Refuge

435 *...sent its voice across the river:* **Voce mea viva depello cuncta novica...**

Associated with ancient rituals, church bells often acquired a kind of sacred character. They were consecrated by a complete baptismal service, received names, had sponsors, were sprinkled with holy water, and anointed. Bells had mostly pious inscriptions, often indicative of a widespread belief in the mysterious virtue of their sound to drive away enemies, disperse storms, and extinguish fire. *Voce mea viva depello cuncta novica* ('With my living voice I drive away all hurtful things') is a mediæval inscription frequently found on bells in the west of England.

435 *...a blackened and doorless dovecote...*

A dovecote is a structure intended to house pigeons or doves. In Mediæval Europe, the possession of a dovecote was a symbol of status and power; only nobles had the privilege of *droit de colombier*.

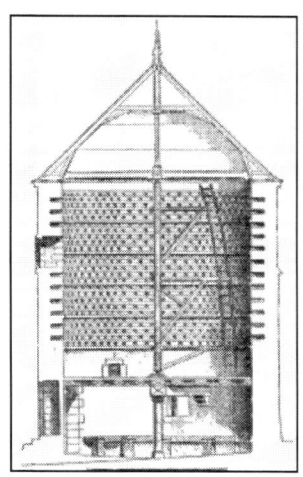

Dovecoat showing potence

435 ....*a tall and creaking potence, its revolving arms scanning the circles of tiered nests...*

A potence is a rotating ladder used to collect squabs. In the center of the cote, a pole rises from floor to roof, with two arms attached to it, one at the top and one at the bottom, which extend outward towards the wall. At the ends of these two extending arms is attached a ladder which then rotates around the outer edge of the cote, allowing a person to pull themselves around the interior to reach the nests.

Dovecote at Drylaw, East Linton by Robert Hope

438   ...*the scarred hands, the old whippings; the last degradation of the brand.*

Lymond's status on the galleys was between a formal slave and a convicted criminal who is legally reduced to slave-like status. In France, a galley slave who was a convicted criminal sentenced to work at the oar (*travaux forcés)* was branded with TF; a slave or prisoner of war (*galérien)* was branded with GAL. From *A History of Torture* by George Ryly Scott:

> *Of all the punishments which the Inquisition inflicted in the name of God, for sheer long-continued cruelty, nothing ever rivalled the treatment of the galley-slaves, who were flogged very nearly every day during the period they laboured at the oars...It was a fate worse than death. For, as everyone knew, it meant a life of the most terrible hardship man could possibly endure and yet continue to live; it almost inevitably entailed death long before the sentence was completed. It meant, in the majority of instances, that the victim was gradually whipped to death.*
>
> *Thus few ever survived the terrible ordeal. Of these few, one managed to put upon paper an account of the awful sufferings under*

the whip which the galley-slave was called upon to endure. This man was condemned for thirteen years' service as a galley-slave: 'Imagine,' he says, 'six men chained to their seats, naked as when they were born, sitting with one foot on a block of timber fixed to the footstool of the stretcher; the other lifted up against the bench before them, holding in their hands an oar of enormous size. Imagine them lengthening their bodies, their arms stretched out to push the oar over the backs of those before them; who are also themselves in similar attitude. Having thus advanced their oar, they raise that end which they hold in their hands, to plunge the opposite into the sea; which done, they throw themselves back upon their benches below, which are somewhat hollowed out to receive them. None, in short, but those who have seen them labour, can conceive how much they endure.'

This terrific labour was continued for ten, twelve and, on occasion, twenty hours at a stretch, the slaves stopping for nothing, not even in response to the calls of nature, not even to eat or drink, food being pushed into their mouths while they toiled at the oars. All the time, the lashing of the guards' whips continued, the bodies of the rowers streaming blood. No free man, says the writer of this horrifying account, could continue at an oar for a single hour. Under the spurs of cruelty and necessity man can perform almost superhuman tasks – for a time. And when flesh and blood could endure the strain no longer and the slave swooned in this seat (a very frequent occurrence) he was whipped mercilessly as long as his tortured body showed the faintest sign of life.

In addition to this daily flogging of the slaves at their work, the slightest insubordination or the most trivial offence was punished by whipping.[2]

438   'If you're waiting to preach in articulo mortis...'

In articulo mortis: at the moment of death

438   'But the fenestration seems fairly extensive.'

The word fenestration comes from the Latin word *fenestra*, for window; generally referring to an opening in a structure. In anatomy and entomology, it is the condition of having *fenestræ*, small orifices, openings, or short passages, such as a hole in a bone through which a nerve passes.

438   'Two chapters of Anatomia Porci and they think they're Avicenna.'

Anatomia Porci was an important document of mediæval medicine. Written during the first half of the 12th century, it is a description of the dissection of a pig, believed to be the animal whose internal structure most resembled that of man.

Abū ʿAlī al- usayn ibn ʿAbd Allāh ibn Sīnā (c.980-1037), known as Avicenna, was a Persian philosopher and physician, whose *Canon of Medicine* was a standard medical text in mediæval universities. The *Canon* includes five books: the first and second deal with physiology, pathology, and hygiene; the third and forth discuss methods of treating disease; and the fifth describes the composition and preparation of remedies. Avicenna was described as versatile, light-hearted, boastful, and pleasure-loving; his passion for women and wine was almost as well known as his learning. He wrote approximately 100 treatises on a wide range of subjects such as theology, philology, mathematics, astronomy, physics, and music.

Avicenna

438 *'...and drop you in the Billy Mire?'*

The Billy Mire was a bog near the Priory of Coldingham in Berwickshire. Ancient human bones and funeral cairns of the original Celtic inhabitants of the area were discovered there.

439 *'But try that too often, Master Haly Abbas Cat...'*

Ali ibn al-ʿAbbas al-Majusi (d.982-994), 'Haly Abbas', is one of the three most eminent Arab physicians of the Middle Ages, along with Razi and Avicenna. His seminal work, *Kitāb al-malikī* (*The Royal Book of All Medicine*) was the basis of the curriculum at mediæval Europe's prestigious medical schools, and along with other important Arabic medical texts it formed the curriculum of Western medical schools for hundreds of years. The *Kitāb al-malikī* emphasized the importance of the relationship between medicine and psychotherapy, and found a correlation between mental health and physical health, concluding, 'joy and contentment can bring a better living status to many who would otherwise be sick and miserable due to unnecessary sadness, fear, worry, and anxiety'[3].

440 *'Happy are the cicadas' lives.'*

Greek poet Xenarchus (1st century BC) noting only the male cicada sings:

> *Happy are the cicadas' lives*
> *for they have voiceless wives.*

Nuremberg Chronicle, MS 1493

440   'Grand Amour should be received royally...'

Grande Amoure (Great Love) is the central character in the allegorical poem *The Passetyme of Pleasure* by Stephen Hawes (d.1523), a popular English poet of the Tudor period. Its main motivation is the education of the knight, Grande Amoure, as he starts out his quest of La Bel Pucel at the suggestion of Fame. Accompanied by two greyhounds, Grace and Governence, he visits the Tower of Doctrine and Science, the Tower of Music, and the Castle of Chivalry. He arrives at the Castle of La Bel Pucel where he is met by Peace, Mercy, Justice, Reason, and Memory. The story goes on to tell of the coming of Age, and the evils of Avarice and Cunning, Contrition and Conscience, and Remembrance and Fame.

441   'I,' said Lymond plaintively, 'am the octogenarian who planted.'

From the fable, *The Old Man and the Three Young Ones:*

> *Un octogénaire plantait.*
> *Passe encor de bâtir; mas planter à cet âge!*

> *A man was planting at fourscore*
> *Three striplings, who their satchels wore.*
> *In building, cried, the sense were more;*
> *But then to plant young trees at that age!*
> *The man is surely in his dotage.*
> *Pray, in the name of common sense,*
> *What fruit can he expect to gather*
> *Of all this labor and expense?*

441   '...and your wife, thank God, is no marrow of mine.'

In Lowland Scots, marrow is one of a pair, a companion, a sweetheart, from the Gaelic *mar*, meaning like, similar. This word is applied to a lover or wedded partner, as one whose mind is the exact counterpart of the other, such as expressed in the Scottish proverb, *One glove or shoe is marrow to the other.*

441   'You can ask leading questions till you're cross-eyed as Strabo...'

Strabo (c.64 BC-c.24 AD) was a celebrated Greek geographer who traveled extensively, writing seventeen books describing Europe, Asia, Egypt, and Libya. His name (Greek, *Strabōn*) means 'squinty-eyed', hence, 'squinty' became a term used by the Romans for anyone whose eyes were distorted or deformed.

Nuremberg Chronicles, MS. 1493

442 'I could enact you Phoenissae-like tragedies...'

The *Phœnissœ* (*The Phoenician Women*) is a tragedy by the Greek dramatic poet Euripedes (480-406 BC), who sought to maintain the place of tragedy in the spiritual life of Athens by modifying its interests to meet the needs of his own generation. 'Could not the heroic persons still excite interest if they were made more real – portrayed with greater vividness and directness? And might not the less cultivated part of the audience at least enjoy a thrilling plot, especially if taken from the home-legends of Attica? Euripedes became the virtual founder of the romantic drama.'[4] The major themes of The *Phœnissœ* are the grief of banishment, patriotism, and the tragedy of innocents caught in the middle of war.

442 'I don't mind being calx in a columbarium...'

Calx is chalk or lime; the ash which remains after a substance is subjected to violent heat. There are several definitions for a columbarium which work within Lymond's statement: a) a dovecote or pigeon-house; b) one of the niches, or pigeon-holes within a dovecote; and c) a niche for a funeral urn containing ashes of the dead.

442 '...the doves will feed me and I shall rise and found Nineveh.'

Nineveh, a city on the banks of the Tigris River, was the capital of the ancient kingdom of Assyria. Ishtar, the chief goddess of Assyria, was the goddess of Nineveh. The emblem of the 'great mother', who fostered vegetation and agriculture and symbolised the fertility of the earth, was the dove.

The Mother-Goddess Ishtar

442 'Hic turtur gemit...'

'The dove moans...'

From *Carmen Æstivum (The Song of Summer)* a 10th-century composition from an MS known as the *Cambridge Songs*, thought to be the song book of a wandering scholar, the contents of which include fragments from Virgil, laments for dead emperors, sequences for Easter, a comedy, an impish tale, and love songs. The first strophe of *The Song of Summer* describes spring and birds; the third strophe is devoted to the nightingale[5]; and the sixth strophe focuses on the bee, a symbol of chastity in mediæval divinity.[6]

The sadness of the wood is bright
With young green sprays, the apple trees
Are laden, in their nests high overhead
Wood pigeons croon.

The doves make moan, deep throated sings the thrush,
The blackbirds flute their ancient melody;
The sparrow twitters, making his small jests
High underneath the elm.

The nightingale sings happy in the leaves,
Pouring out on the winds far carrying
Her solemn melody : the sudden hawk
Quavers in the high air.

The eagle takes his flight against the sun;
High overhead the lark trills in the sky,
Down dropping from her height and changing note,
She touches earth.

Swift darting swallows utter their low cry;
The jackdaw jargons, and clear cries the quail;
And so in every spot some bird is singing
A summer song.

Yet none among the birds is like the bee,
Who is the very type of chastity,
Save she who bore the burden that was Christ
In her inviolate womb. [7]

442   *'...drowning the groans of the Britons...'*

When Roman emperor Honorius recalled his troops, it left the Celtic population of Britain weak; they could not protect themselves from the Scots, the Picts, and the Jutes and Saxons who threatened to overrun the country. *The Groans of the Britons* (c.1440s AD) is the name given to the appeal made by government of the Britons to the Roman commander asking for help defending themselves. It read, in part: *'The barbarians drive us to the sea; the sea throws us back on the barbarians; thus two modes of death assail us, – we are either slain or drowned.'* [8]
Rome could not spare troops, so the Britons called upon the Jutes, a Germanic tribe, to aid in their defence against the Picts. 'The defenders became conquerors; and their example was followed by their more numerous kinsmen, the Angles and the Saxons, who in time subdued and settled all the Romanized part of the island. The Britons who survived were pushed back or reduced to serfdom, so that little trace of them is left in England which resulted from the conquest; on the other hand, Wales, Scotland, and Ireland remain Celtic.' [9]

442 *'An elephant's head riding on a rat –*
the symbol of prudence....'

In Hindu mythology, Ganesha is the god of
wisdom and prudence. The most popular of the
Brahmanic gods, he is invoked at the
commencement of almost every act, whether
religious or social. Ganesha is represented with
an elephant's head, riding upon a rat.

443 *Is this fraternall charitie,*
Or furious follie, quhat say ye?

From *The Satyre of the Three Estaitis* by Sir
David Lindsay:

Ganesha

> *All the princes of Almanie,*
> *Spain, Flanders, and Italy,*
> *This present year are all aflutter*
> *Some say their wages find daring bought,*
> *The pope, with bombard, speir, and shield,*
> *Has sent his army to the field.*
> *Saint Peter, Saint Paul, nor Saint Andrew,*
> *Resist never such an army, I trust.*
> *Is this fraternal charity,*
> *Or furious folly, what say ye?*[10]

(Tr.L.R.)

444 *'Pannage, my dear brother.'*

Pannage is an Old English law term for swine-food, i.e. beechnuts, acorns, etc.[11/D]

444 *'Wo worth your tedyus synne of lechery.'*

From *The Conversation of Swearers* by Stephen Hawes (d.1475-1523):

> *My words my prelates unto you do preach...*
> *The world has cast you in such blindness*
> *Like unto stones your hearts have hardened...*
> *Wo worth your hearts so planted in pride*
> *Wo worth your wrath and mortal ennui*
> *Wo worth sloth that does with you abide*
> *Wo worth also immeasurable gluttony.*
> *Wo worth your tedious sin of lechery,*
> *Wo worth you whom I gave free will*
> *Wo worth courtesy that does your soul spill.*[12]

(Tr.L.R.)

444 *'Oh, try somebody else's sudorific.'*

A sudorific (Latin, *sudor*, sweat, + *facere*, make do) is a drug which induces sweating.

446 *'The prickmadam chasing you?'*

Prickmadam is the name given to several species of sedum used as ingredients of vermifuge medicines used to expel intestinal worms.

446 *'I was getting tired of the John-go-to-bed-at-noon era.'*

Johnny-go-to-bed, or goats-beard (*Tragopogon pratensis*), is a weedy annual. Tea from the roots can be used internally to treat stomach pains and internal bleeding, and can be used externally to bathe swollen feet and rheumatic joints. The root ashes can be used to make a salve to rub into sores.

Sedum rupestre

447 *'The ant milking the mighty aphid.'*

Some species of ants 'farm' aphids, among the most destructive pests, by stroking them with their antennae, and eating the honeydew the aphids release.

447 *'...hailing you as their mighty Lar...'*

Lars Porsena (c.508 BC), 'the mighty Lar', was king of Clusium in Etruria. He marched on Rome with an Etruscan army on behalf of the Tarquins, who had previously been expelled from the ancient city. Porsena besieged the city, but on the appeal of Mucius Scævola, he chose to make peace. The legend is believed to veil Porsena's short subjugation of Rome, as is implied by Pliny and Tacitus.

Tragopogon pratensis

447 *Impaled shrikewise on his boulder...*

Shrikes are a family of bird known as 'butcher birds' because of their habit of catching insects

Lanius Sibiricus

and small vertebrates and impaling their bodies on thorns. This helps them tear the flesh into smaller fragments, and serves as a cache to return to uneaten portions at a later time.

447 'Nay, brother,' said Lymond, 'I wyll not daunce.'

From *Mankind*, a mediæval morality play written in the late 15th century, an allegory of Mankind's struggle between listening to his better judgement, as expressed by Mercy, and falling victim to the worldly temptations of Mischief, New Guise, Nowadays, and Nought, and the demonic Titivillus. Mankind is led astray, but discovers God's mercy is available to even the most abysmal sinner. The above line is spoken by the character Mercy.

447 ...inexorable, ruthless, dissecting, hygienic as burin or scalpel.

A burin (French, *burin*, engraver's tool) is an instrument for engraving made of hard steel, with a sharp beveled point.

448 ...rolled like the thunder of Götterdämmerung through the meadow.

Götterdämmerung ('Twilight of the Gods', from Old Norse, *Ragnarök*) is the final battle of the gods which brings about the end of the world. The term used in English refers to a disastrous conclusion of events; a collapse (as of a society or regime) marked by catastrophic violence and disorder.

451 It didn't enter the head of Sir James Wilford...

Sir James Wilford (1516–1550), known as the defender of Haddington, was raised an English soldier, and fought in the French war of 1544-1545. He fought at the Battle of Pinkie Cleugh in September 1547, and was knighted by Somerset at Roxburgh later the same month. He remained on the Borders and served with Lord Grey at the capture of Haddington, and was commander of the stronghold there. The allied Scots and French laid siege for eighteen months; Wilford's defence was called 'one of the most brilliant defences of the century'[13] and Wilford was described as 'such a one as was able to make of a cowardly beaste a courageous man'[14]. Early in 1549, however, when leading an attack on Dunbar Castle his men deserted him; he was wounded and taken prisoner. Exchanged later, he arrived at York in a weakened state; he died a year later at the age of thirty-five.

451 ...against the malefic glitter of French arms and the shiftless shuffle of the neighbourly Scot on his patellas.

Malefic is having or exerting a malignant force; evil; malicious. Patellas are kneecaps.

451   ...*insifflating the precious troops and horses...*

To insufflate is to blow or breathe into or on; to treat medically by blowing a powder, gas, or vapor into a bodily cavity. In religious and magical practice, insufflation and exsufflation are ritual acts signifying expulsion or renunciation of evil (the devil) or infilling or blessing with good (the Spirit or grace of God). Here, meaning Lord Grey was rallying the troops, breathing life into their campaign.[15]

452   ...*Villegagne quietly left Court...*

Nicolas Durand, Sieur de Villegagnon (1510-1571) was a commander of the Knights Hospitallers of St John. He was ordained a knight of the order in 1521; his uncle, Villiers de L'Isle-Adam, was Grand Master. He fought in the Mediterranean on behalf of the Order; in 1548, he commanded the French fleet charged with bringing Queen Mary from Scotland to France. After several missions on behalf of Scotland and the Knights Hospitallers, he led a French expedition to Brazil in 1555. His troops occupied an island off the coast of what is now Rio de Janeiro, called *Ilha de Villegagnon*.

Nicholas Durand,
Sieur de Villegagnon

452   ...*in July, the Scottish Parliament met...*

Haddington Church by Robert W. Billings, c.1847

On 7 July 1548, the Scottish Parliament convened at the Abbey of Haddington, a Franciscan church dating to the 12th or 13th century. Parliament agreed France should be entrusted 'with the jewel for which England had no equivalent'[16], and Queen Mary, likened 'to the Helena of the age, in whose cause there was no sovereign of Europe but would have been fond to embark with his subjects and allies, in the Trojan-like war, to be possessed of her envied beauty and consequential grandeur'[17] should be sent to France for marriage to the Dauphin.

454   *Abandoning sense, revenge, and the role of complacent dempster...*

Dempster is a Scots law term for the officer of a court who pronounced doom or sentence as directed by the clerk or judge.

455   *...in a deep and unlikely forme at the foot of the meagre willow.*

Forme is the Middle English spelling of *form*, retained in English and Scots usage among printers, and defined as an arrangement of type from which a page may be printed.

The willow tree (*Salix alba*) symbolises healing and the cycle of rebirth. According to old Celtic custom, planting willows on graves allows the spirits of the deceased to unite with the trees and live on, a vision of which is evoked by the image of Lymond nearly dead at the base of the willow.[18]

Salix alba

455   *...whined and ran blenching...*

To blench is to shy away, to shrink back from lack of courage; to give way.

455   *...dim breakwaters of burdock and furze.*

Burdock (*Acrium lappa*) is a biennial thistle. Its prickly burs easily catch on fur and clothing, and was the inspiration for Velcro. Furze (*Ulex europaeus*), or gorse, is a thorny evergreen shrub with beautiful yellow flowers. It is a common plant on the plains and hills of Great Britain.

455   *...in a yellow carpet of silverweed.*

Silverweed (*Potentilla anserine*) is a yellow-flowering plant with silvery, fern-like leaves valued for its powerful healing properties. It is one of Britain's most common flowers, growing in moist meadows and on the banks by the roadside.

455   *...it promised monts et merveilles...*

A direct translation of the phrase is 'the mountains and wonders'; an idiomatic translation is 'hope of wealth in all its glorious forms', from the fable *The Shepherd and the Sea:*

> *That one should be content*
> *   with his condition,*
> *And shut his ears to*
> *   counsels of ambition,*
> *More faithless than the*
> *   wreck-strewn sea, and which*
> *Doth thousands beggar*
> *   where it makes one rich –*
> *Inspires the hope of wealth,*
> *   in glorious forms,*
> *And blasts the same*
> *   with piracy and storms.*

Acrium lappa

455   *...when a man opening his eyes on the lentils and salt...*

'Lentils and salt' is a reference to the customary dish served in Jewish grief ceremonies, as prescribed in the Book of Lamentations, but with the irony that Richard, after praying over the meal of condolence, would open his eyes upon a living Lymond.[19]

456   *The empty calyx he was attacking...*

A calyx is the sepals of a flower forming the outer floral envelope which protects the developing flower bud; or a cuplike animal structure.

Ulex europaeus

456   *'...lie like a Gothamite fisherman.'*

In the tale of *The Twelve Fishermen of Gotham*, after a day fishing the twelve meet, and each tells a more fantastical story of his extraordinary day fishing, yet only one was able to return with one small fish, which the fisherman found floating dead upon the water.

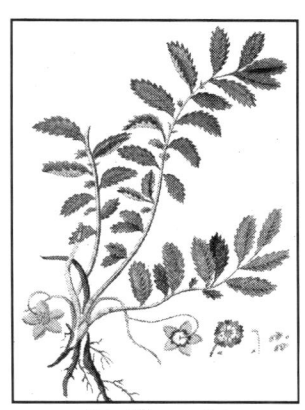

Potentilla anserine

458 *'I'm scunnered at washing bandages.'*

Scunnered is nauseated, disgusted, loathe.

459 *'Instead of surviving to bellow like a barghest?'*

A barghest (possibly from German, *berggeist*, 'mountain demon') was a legendary black dog with huge teeth and claws, portending death or bad fortune for the person to whom it appeared.

459 *'To my kinsmen I will truly, praying them to help me in my necessity...'*

From *The Summoning of Everyman*:

> *Alack! shall we thus depart indeed?*
> *Our lady, help, without any more comfort,*
> *Lo, Fellowship, forsaketh me in my most need:*
> *For help in this world whither shall I resort?*
> *Fellowship herebefore with me would merry make;*
> *And now little sorrow for me doth he take.*
> *It is said, in prosperity men friends may find,*
> *Which in adversity be full unkind.*
> *Now whither for succour shall I flee,*
> *Sith that Fellowship hath forsaken me?*
> *To my kinsmen I will truly,*
> *Praying them to help me in my necessity;*
> *I believe that they will do so,*
> *For kind will creep where it may not go.*
> *I will go say, for yonder I see them go.*
> *Where be ye now, my friends and kinsmen?*

460 *'One more skirl...'*

A skirl is a shrill cry; a high, shrill wailing tone.

460 *'Come, my friend, my brother most enteere; for thee I offered my blood in sacrifice...'*

From *The Testament* by John Lydgate of Bury (c.1370-c.1451):

> *Tarry no longer, toward thy heritage*
> *Haste on thy way,*
> *and be of right good cheer.*
> *Go each day onward on thy pilgrimage,*
> *Think how short time thou shale abidë here.*
> *Thy place is built above the starrës clear,*

None earthly place is wrought so stately wise.
Come on, my friend, my brother most enteere,
For thee I offered my blood in sacrifice.

460 'Erskine got the idea he was carrying out the Third Crusade, but all he carried out was me, the lord be thankit.'

The Third Crusade (1189-1192) was an attempt by European leaders to reconquer the Holy Land. It was mostly successful, but fell short of its goal of taking control of Jerusalem.

> *The Selkirk Grace:*
> *Some hae meat and canna eat,*
> *And some wad eat that want it;*
> *But we hae meat, and we can eat,*
> *Sae let the Lord be thankit.*

460 'Bury me at Leibethra, where the nightingale sings.'

After Orpheus lost his love, Eurydice, to the land of the Shades, he mourned her, expressing his sorrow through the songs of his lute.

> *As he sat one day near a river in the stillness of the forest, there came from afar an ugly clamour of sound. It struck against the music of Orpheus' lute and slew it, as the coarse cries of screaming gulls that fight for carrion slay the song of a soaring lark. It was the day of the feast of Bacchus, and through the woods poured Bacchus and his Bacchanates, a shameless rout, satyrs capering around them, centaurs neighing aloud. Long had the Bacchanates hated the loyal poet-lover of one fair woman whose dwelling was with the Shades. His ears were ever deaf to their passionate voices, his eyes blind to their passionate loveliness as they danced through the green trees, a riot of colour, of fierce beauty, of laughter and mad song. Mad they were indeed this day, and in their madness the very existence of Orpheus was a thing not to be borne.*
>
> *At first they stoned him, but his music made the stones fall harmless at his feet. Then in a frenzy of cruelty, with the maniac lust to cause blood to flow, to know the joy of taking life, they threw themselves upon Orpheus and did him to death. From limb to limb they tore him, casting at last his head and his blood-stained lyre into the river. And still, as the water bore them on, the lyre murmured its last music and the white lips of Orpheus still breathed of her whom at last he had gone to join in the shadowy land, 'Eurydice! Eurydice!'*
>
> *In the heavens, as a bright constellation called Lyra, or Orpheus, the gods placed his lute, and to the place of his martyrdom came the*

Muses, and with loving care carried the fragments of the massacred body to Leibethra, at the foot of Mount Olympus, and there buried them. And there, unto this day, more sweetly than at any other spot in any other land, the nightingale sings.[20/D] *For it sings of a love that knows no ending, of life after death, of a love so strong that it can conquer even Death, the all-powerful.*[21]

460 '...would make a dayfly feel like Enoch.'

Elijah & Enoch, 17th century

Enoch (Hebrew, *Hănōkh*, Dedication or Teaching) appears in Genesis as one of the ten Patriarchs who mark the passage of immense periods of time. After a life of 365 years, Enoch 'was not, for God took him'. A dayfly is an insect whose adult stage lasts but a few hours or a few days before it dies. Meaning even a dayfly's short life span would seem interminable if spent with Will Scott.[22]

460 '...in a voice like a Gadwall duck.'

The Gadwall duck has a loud, harsh voice.[23/D]

461 '...although you've bought the rights of fuel, feal and divot...'

The right of fuel, feal and divot was a legal right in Scotland:

> *The servitude of feal and divot is the right one has of turning up feals and divots [pieces of turf] from the surface of the servient tenement, and carrying them off, for that to his house, or for the other uses of the dominant tenement. Much like to this is the servitude of fuel, which is the right of raising turf or peats from the servient moss or peat land, for fuel to the inhabitants of the dominant tenement. Both of these servitudes imply a right to use the nearest grounds of the servient tenement, on which to lay and dry the turf, peats or feal; and to a way or passage by which they may be carried off to the dominant.*

462 '...making themselves into a clearing nut for other people's emotions.'

The Clearing-Nut (*Strychnos potatorum*) is a small tree abundant in India. The seeds of the tree are used for purifying water: the seeds are rubbed on the inside of a vessel, and muddy water put into it becomes clear, any impurities settling to the bottom.

463 '...lying at Coldingham.'

Coldingham is a village in Berwickshire. Its nunnery was the oldest in Scotland, founded as early as 661; the priory was founded in 1098. In 1544, the English occupied the priory as a fortification. The Earl of Arran attacked with an

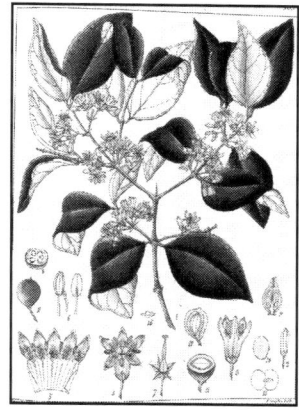

Strychnos potatorum

army of 8000 men, but retreated in a panic after battering the priory for a day and a half. Supposedly, the English left it in such a dilapidated state they set it on fire when they abandoned it.

Coldingham Nunnery by Francis Grose, 1789

463 *'...joining the two of you with the horse at Pease Burn...'*

Pease Burn is in the Scottish Borders near the southeast coast, approximately two miles from Cockburnspath. Pease Dean is a deep, thickly wooded ravine, once regarded as a natural barrier against invasion by the English. Described by an English officer under Somerset in 1547, Pease Dean was:

> *So steep be these banks on either side and deep to the bottom, that who goeth straight down shall be in danger of tumbling; and the comer up so sure of puffing and pain: for remedy whereof, the travellers that way, have used to pass it, not by going directly, but by paths and footways leading slopewise from the number of which paths, they call it the Peaths.*[24]

Pease-mouth by A.L. Collins, c.1912

463 *'A quick course of Udall would work wonders with this army.'*

Nicholas Udall (1504-1556) was the author of the play *Ralph Roister Doister*. Educated at Oxford, and headmaster successively at Eton and Westminster, he translated several works, including *Apophthegmatum opus* by Erasmus, *Anatomie* by Geminus, and, at the behest of the English queen dowager Katherine Parr, *The Paraphrases of the Gospels* by Erasmus.

463 *'Don't you think they need a lingua franca, poor things?'*

A lingua franca (Italian, literally, the Frank language) is a hybrid language containing elements of several different languages; an international dialect for communication between people not sharing a mother tongue.

463 *'...and Lord Shrewsbury with eleven thousand Englishmen...'*

Francis Talbot, 5th Earl of Shrewsbury, 5th Earl of Waterford, 11th Baron Talbot (1500-1560), spent most of his military career on the Scottish Borders. In 1542, he served under the Duke of Norfolk, and in 1544 was commander of the rear-guard of the Earl of Hertford's army. He was excused from attendance at the Battle of Pinkie Cleugh, but was part of the command of the Borders, along with Lord Grey, and the relief and fortification of Haddington. It was rumoured Protector Somerset entrusted the command to Shrewsbury with the sinister intent of seeing him ruined by his mistakes.

465 *...spouted venom like Loki's serpent.*

In Norse mythology, the god Loki is punished by being bound to a rock while a serpent drips venom over his face. His wife Sigyn collects the venom in a bowl but must empty the bowl periodically, leaving Loki to be splashed with venom and writhe in pain, thereby causing earthquakes.

465 *'Ellerkar, by God!'*

Sir John Ellerker was an English officer in service at Hume in February 1548.

467 *'Just so's your friends'll know where to send the siller to.'*

The Punishment of Loki
by Louis Huard

Siller is a Scots variant of silver.

2. One Loss is Made Good

469 *Quant compaignons s'en vont juer*
Ils n'ont pointe tou dis essouper...

From a ballade by Richard Loqueville (d.1418):

> *As companions go play (gamble)*
> *They have not always enough for supper*
> *No fat rabbits or roasted capon*
> *Once their money is gone.*[25]   (Tr.L.R.)

471 *'We honour Yeber-Abou-Moussah-Djafar-al-Sofi, the Master of Masters; Zosimus and Synesius; Trismegistus the Thrice Great; Olympiodorus, Philosopher to Petasius, King of Armenia; Nagarjuna who discovered distillation; and the blind Abu-Bakr-Muhammad-Ibn-Zakariyya-al-Razi...'*

Abū ʿAlī al- usayn ibn ʿAbd Allāh ibn Sīnā (c.980-1037), commonly known as Avicenna, is regarded as the most influential polymath of the Islamic Golden Age, and the father of modern medicine. He was also an astronomer, chemist, geologist, psychologist, scholar, theologian, logician, mathematician, physicist, Maktab teacher, and poet.

Zosimus of Panopolis, who lived near the end of the Hellenistic period (300 BC – 300 AD), is regarded as one of the earliest authentic alchemists. His alchemical theory focused on the idea a substance exists which can bring about transformation, instantaneously and magically. This 'tincture' was translated into

Avicenna

Latin as 'elixir', and then as the 'philosopher's stone'. To Zosimus, alchemy was a 'composition of waters, movement, growth, embodying and disembodying, drawing the spirits from bodies and binding the spirits within bodies'[26].

Synesius (c.373-414), a Greek bishop and diplomat, wrote several treatises on the subjects of philosophy, dream interpretation, and alchemy. According to Synesius, alchemy was a mental operation, independent of the science of matter: 'Take from them that living silver and you will make it the medicine or quintessence, the imperishable and permanent power, the bond of all elements which contained within itself the spirit which unites all things.'[27]

Hermes Trismegistus ('Thrice-Great Hermes'), the originator of alchemy in Egypt, is considered the patriarch of the art. Sometimes thought to be a combination of the Greek god Hermes and the Egyptian god Thoth, the Renaissance alchemists believed him to be a real person of antiquity and the author of the Hermetic writings. In *The Emerald Tablet*, he writes, 'I am called Hermes Trismegistus, possessing three parts of the philosophy of the world.' These three parts of the wisdom of the whole universe are, according to Hermes, alchemy, astrology, and theurgy.

Hermes Trismegistus

The identity of the Olympiodorus of alchemy is not positively known, and could be either Olympiodorus of Alexandria (c.495-570), a teacher of philosophy at the Alexandrian school, or Olympiodorus of Thebes (c.380-c.425), a Neoplatonist of the 5th century. In *The Philosopher Olympiodorus to Petasius, King of Armenia, on the Divine and Sacred Art of the Philosopher's Stone*, Olympiodorus provided particulars for several tinctures, and alluded to a tradition amongst the Greek alchemists to believe 'certain demons were jealous with regard to the making of some recipes'[28].

Nāgārjuna

Nāgārjuna (c.150-250) is considered to be the most important Buddhist philosopher after the historical Buddha himself. The founder of the Mādhyamaka school of Buddhism, and regarded by many of the Mahāyāna tradition as the 'Second Buddha', Nāgārjuna taught a philosophy of the 'middle way' (*madhyamaka*) between substance and solipsism, based around the central notion of 'emptiness' (*śūnyatā*). The purpose, therefore, of life, is not to strive towards a goal (i.e. enlightenment), but to uncover what one already is: the Buddha-nature of oneself.

Muhammad ibn Zakariyā Rāzī (865-925) was a Persian physician and alchemist. He was a prolific author, writing books on a variety of subjects including philosophy, religion,

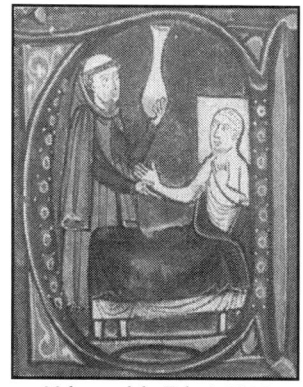

Muhammed ibn Zakariyā Rāzī

medicine (*al-Hawi* (*The Virtuous Life*) and a medical encyclopedia), and several books on alchemy, including the well-known *Al-Asrar* (*The Secret*) and *Sirr al-Asrar* (*The Secret of Secrets*).

471 '...that the imperfect metal, the crude substance of Saturn...'

The alchemists believed each planet governed a mineral; Saturn ruled lead.

471 'The Stone of the Wise. The Magisterium. The Universal Essence.'

Three alternative terms for the Philosopher's Stone.

472 '...and speak the words of the Emerald Table...'

The Emerald Table by Hermes Trismegistus is a short philosophical treatise which reveals the secret of the primordial substance and its transmutation, the nature of magic, and the creation of life and matter by one God. The translation given in *The Game of Kings* is from an Arab collection of commentaries of the early 12th century.

Hermetis Trismegisti, 1657

473 ...like the black underbelly of the ancient Chaos himself...

In ancient cosmology, Chaos (Greek, χάος, empty space, abyss, from χαίνειν, to gape, to open widely) signified the vacant, infinite space which existed before all things, or the confused mass out of which the ordered creation of the universe was formed into the *kosmos*.

475 ...and goffered the gutter mud...

To goffer is to treat a lace edge or a frill with heated irons in order to crimp or flute it. From French *gaufrer*, 'to stamp with a patterned tool', from *gaufre* 'honeycomb'; from Middle Low German *wāfel*, 'waffle'.

475 Against the red western sky the outline of the Pentland hills...

The Pentland Hills begin about three miles southwest of Edinburgh and extend southward for sixteen miles towards Biggar. About 1825, Lord Cockburn wrote of the Pentlands: 'There is not a recess in their valleys, nor an eminence on their summits, that is not familiar to my solitude. One summer I read every word of

Tacitus in the sheltered crevice of a rock (called 'My Seat') about 800 feet above the level of the sea, with the most magnificent of scenes stretched out before me.'[29]

The Pentlands

476 *'Kittle cattle, women, kittle cattle: but its wersh and wae without them.'*

Kittle cattle is a term meaning touchy, unpredictable; to puzzle, perplex; or a group of people who are difficult to manage and inclined to be capricious, as in the Scots proverb, *'Women are kittle cattle, and the mair ye rin after them the mair they flee awa'.*

476 *...opened out like girasol to the sun.*

A girasol is a sunflower (*Helianthus tuberosus*). In Greek legend, the beautiful water-nymph Clytie would watch, with eyes of love, the sun-god Apollo drive his flaming chariot across the heavens. She was so enamoured she sat for days, never taking her eyes from him, yet Apollo never cast a look upon her. The gods took pity on her, and rooted her limbs into the earth, and changed her face into a flower with the disk and the rays of the sun she so dearly loved. It is said the flower still contains the soul of the nymph, for it faces the sun as it rises

Helianthus tuberosus

and turns its head on its stalk to follow the sun through the day and faces it still as it sets.

479 *'This isn't an act of expiation.'*

Expiation is the act of atoning for a sin or wrongdoing; making satisfaction for an offense, by which guilt is removed and the necessity of punishment is canceled.

481 *...she sat in her high chair like Demeter about to breakfast on Pelops...*

In Greek mythology, Demeter (Greek, *gē meter*, 'Earth-Mother') was the patroness of agriculture and of fruits. Her daughter, Persephone, was abducted while gathering flowers by Aïdoneus, god of the underworld. Demeter abandoned Olympus to wander the earth among men in search of her daughter.

While Demeter was grieving, Tantalus, a son of Zeus, prepared an offering to the gods in order to test their omniscience. He killed his son Pelops, cut him into pieces, making his flesh into stew, which he then fed to the gods. Demeter, lost in grief, absentmindedly accepted the offering and ate Pelops's left shoulder. The other gods sensed the plot and refrained from eating the body. Pelops was reassembled and brought back to life, his shoulder replaced with one of ivory.

Demeter

Pelops

IV: Baring

Caxton: Tract 4, Chapter 2

Wherefore the nobles and the peoples
having been set in their proper places...
They that have been set on the other side keep the Queen.
And thus they keep all the strength and firmness of the kingdom.[1]

1. Remiss

Baring, or bare king, is when a player is left with only the King, his other fifteen pieces having been captured. In Royal Chess, this results in an automatic win for the opponent. In modern chess, a bare king situation can play to a stalemate. If both players are left with a bare king, the game is drawn.

483   ...and had heard Carrick Pursuivant...

The Carrick Pursuivant was one of six pursuivants in Scotland, the others being Kintyre, Unicorn, Dingwall, Bute, and Ormond. A pursuivant regulated heraldry, had criminal jurisdiction in heraldic matters, and would raise proceedings against those who improperly usurped armourial bearings. The punishment for usurpation of arms was severe, including fines, imprisonment, and the issue letters denouncing a person as a rebel. The letters would be announced by three blasts of a horn, thus becoming known as 'letters of the horn'.

Cpt. G.S.C. Swinton,
March Pursuivant of Arms, c.1904

483 *...at the Cross six years before charging and warning the traitor...*

The Mercat Cross was where merchants gathered, public announcements and proclamations were read, and executions performed. Edinburgh's current Mercat Cross was assembled in 1885, incorporating parts of the 15ᵗʰ-century original.

The Mercat Cross, Edinburgh

483 *Twice they had summoned the absent Lymond to the diet of his libel.*

Both 'diet' and 'libel' are Scots law terms. A diet is a meeting or session of court to deal with a specific case or step in the legal process. Libel is a formal statement of charge, stating the grounds on which prosecution is brought.

484 *...sentence of fugitation was passed, making him a rebel and an outlaw.*

Fugitation is a Scots law term for a judicial declaration of outlawry.

484 *...carrying the date in her breast like an aposteme.*

An aposteme is an abscess; a swelling filled with purulent matter.

484 *...under the vacant survey of alabaster and murrhine.*

Alabaster is a dense, translucent, white or tinted gypsum, used as an ornamental stone for ecclesiastical decoration and for rails of staircases and halls. It was used to make delicate cups and vases once prized by the Romans.[2]

487 *'Romanies can only be controlled by their King.'*

The Romani, more commonly called Gypsies (from the word 'Egyptian', though their origin was India), probably came to Britain in the 15ᵗʰ century after achieving wide dispersal throughout Europe. A nomadic people of swarthy appearance known for skill with horses, metalwork, music, and fortune-telling, they have nevertheless been a persecuted minority throughout their history. Romanies have their own language and largely rely on internal government, laws, and traditions, many of which are kept secret from outsiders. Historically, they travelled in caravans, making the rounds of country fairs and carnivals to trade their wares. Romani, also called Travellers in many places, were looked upon with scorn and suspicion in Lymond's time, and are often still discriminated against today.[3]

487 *'I have your charter chest at Midculter.'*

A charter chest is a repository for family papers and documents, such as charters and deeds. It is particularly Scottish.

488 *'I keep my chest in the strongroom of this house.'*

A strongroom is a vault built into the structure of a building, used to secure valuables.

2. The Queen Moves to Her Beginning

493   *Rumour of the hurried Assize had reached the streets by midday...*

An Assize is a session of court for the trial of civil and criminal cases.

493   *...the Lawnmarket...*

The Lawnmarket from St. Giles, 1825

493   *...from the Butter Tron ...*

A tron was a weighing machine in the marketplaces of the burghs of Scotland, used to weigh goods for taxes and commerce. Some burghs had more than one tron, often for different weights. Edinburgh had a butter tron located at the head of the West Bow, and a salt tron located further down the Royal Mile.

The Weigh-House

The Lawnmarket, from the site of the Weigh-House, 1825

493   ... *to St. Giles was thick with people.*

St. Giles Cathedral, named for the patron saint of Edinburgh, dates from the 14th century, although it was extensively restored in the 19th century.

The High Church of St. Giles

493   ...*the prisoner, taken out through the Castle postern...*

A postern is a secondary door or gate in a castle, often in a concealed location allowing inconspicuous entry or exit.

The Old Tolbooth by A. Nasmyth

The Tolbooth was located on the Royal Mile near the west door of St. Giles Cathedral. It housed meetings of the Estates, the Court of Sessions, and the Provost. It was also used as Edinburgh's main gaol and site for judicial torture and execution. A permanent platform was built so the mob could view beheadings and hangings. The exterior had jougs attached (iron collars chained to the wall placed around an offender's neck) and there were spikes to hold body parts of those convicted. The heads of the executed were often displayed for long periods after the execution. Regent Morton's head was affixed there for 18 months, following his execution in 1581.

493 *...someone with no religious intent started up the 109ʰ Psalm...*

Psalm 109 is noted for containing some of the most frighteningly severe curses in the Bible, including : *Let there be none to extend mercy unto him: neither let there be any to favour his fatherless children;* and, *Let his posterity be cut off; and in the generation following let their name be blotted out.*

493 *'Deus laudem meam ne tacueris...'*

The first lines of Psalm 109: *'Hold not thy peace, O God of my praise.'*

494   *...short Crawford and big Foulis and Lauder of St. Germains...*

Sir David Lindsay, 9th Earl of Crawford (d.1558), was a Scottish noble and member of Parliament.

Sir James Foulis of Colinton (d.1549) was a Scottish judge who served as a member of Parliament, a founding member of the College of Justice, the Privy Council, and private secretary to King James V. In 1543, he was a commissioner sent to negotiate the marriage between Queen Mary and Prince Edward.

Henry Lauder, Lord St. Germains (d.1561), was Lord Advocate of Scotland.

494   *Glencairn... and Keith, the Earl Marischal... Methven, Queen Margaret's withered widower; Marjoribanks; Hugo Rig and the President of the Court of Session, Bishop Reid of Orkney...*

Alexander Cunningham, 5th Earl of Glencairn (d.1574), was amongst the first of the Scots nobility to concur with the Scottish Reformation.

William Keith, 4th Earl Marischal (1506-1581), fought at the Battle of Pinkie Cleugh, and was thought to support the marriage of Queen Mary to Prince Edward.

Henry Stewart, 1st Lord Methven (1495-1552), was Master of the Scottish Artillery and the third husband of Margaret Tudor.

Thomas Marjoribanks was one of ten advocates appointed to Lords of the Court of Session. In 1535, he was appointed advocate 'for the puir'[4] and became Lord Provost of Edinburgh in 1540, representing the city in the Parliament of Scotland.

Master Hugo Rig was a commissioner in the Scottish Parliament.

Robert Reid (d.1558) was educated at St. Andrews; after receiving his degree, he further studied at university in Paris. Under James V he was sent on several embassies to England. On 1 February 1548, he was named president of the court of session.

502   *'Non minime ex parte, Mr. Lauder.'*

Non minime ex parte: In no small degree on the part of

502   *'If we may separate the facts from the faculae we seem to have this.'*

Facula (plural: faculæ) is Latin for 'little torch', literally 'bright spot'. It is a bright spot or veined patch on the sun's photosphere.

503 *'...until 1544 was employed on travaux forcés in the French galleys.'*

A sentence of forced labor was a punishment of detention accompanied by work. A French galley slave was either a convicted criminal sentenced to work at the oar: *travaux forcés*, 'forced labor', branded with TF; or a slave or prisoner of war, *galérien*, branded with GAL.

The French Galley La Réale, c.1604

504 *'...I stayed with him as secretary and general amanuensis...'*

An amanuensis is one who writes from dictation; a copyist; a secretary.

504 *'Dod, he's never been known by man to pook a penny before now.'*

To pook is to pluck; twitch; tug.

507 *'The girl was no light o' love.'*

Light-o'-love is a term for a prostitute, or paramour, derived from the title of a dance tune. A light or wanton woman, or a woman inconsistent in love, was called a light-of-love.

509 *A macer, hurrying from Lord Culter's side...*

A macer is a Scots law term for an officer attending the Courts of Session and Justiciary. They were servants of the court with the duty to preserve silence, execute orders of the judges, act as messenger, and execute warrants.

510 ...*Colinton caught Oxengang's eye...*

Nicholas Crawford of Oxengangs was a Scottish judge and founding member of the College of Justice in 1532. He held the office of Lord Justice Clerk, the second most senior judge in Scotland, from 1524-1535.

510 *'Dod, d'ye need a dub and whistle?'*

A dub-and-whistle is a pair of instruments played by a single player: a three-hole pipe with one hand and a small drum with the other.

Triumph des Scipio, detail,
by Andrea Mantegna, c.1500

511 *'...up to the oxters in evidence...'*

The oxters are one's armpits.

511 ...*of the Old Man at Boulogne...*

The Tour de l'Orde was a Roman lighthouse overlooking the port of Boulogne-sur-Mer in northern France. The occupying English force called it the Old Man. A new fort built between the Old Man and Boulogne in 1454 was called the Young Man. Thought to have been built by Caius Caligula to commemorate his victories, the lighthouse served as a beacon for Channel sailors until the 'gaining sea upon the cliff destroyed it in 1644'[5].

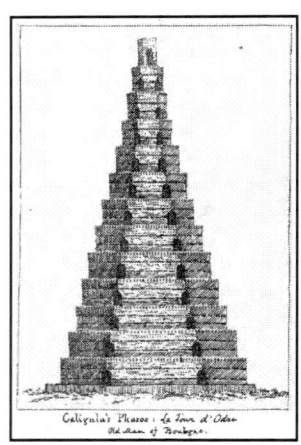

Old Man of Boulogne

512 *'If you'd offered me...Helen of Troy...'*

In Greek mythology, Helen of Troy was the daughter of Zeus, the personification of grace and loveliness, and so beautiful hers was the face that 'launched a thousand ships'. After her abduction by Paris, her husband mustered all of the Greek princes to avenge the wrong, which resulted in the 10 years' Trojan War.

512 *He had seen these tarots...*

Tarot (Italian, *tarocco*) are cards in a deck used for trick-taking card games. The basic rules for the various games first appeared in 1425. The

The Abduction of Helen by Raoul
Lefevre, MS 1495

cards were created for gaming purposes; later, they came to be used for divination.

512   *The four suits were commonplace enough: the artist had reserved his fantastic brushes for the figured cards.*

The card images displayed below are of the Visconti-Sforza tarot deck, printed in approximately 1451. The surviving cards, valued for their beauty and detail of design, were executed in precious materials and depict members of the Sforza and Visconti families in period garments and settings. The four suits in the deck are Cups, Staves, Coins, and Swords.

Visconti-Sforza Deck: Aces of Coins, Cups, Staves, and Swords, 1451

512   *The Bateleur, the Empress, the Pope, l'Amoureux and le Pendu, Death and Fortitude, the Traitor, the Last Judgment itself, all shared a grotesque camaraderie of the paintpot.*

Le Bateleur, L'Imperatrice, Le Pape, L'Amoureux

The Juggler, *Le Bateleur*, is the practitioner of stage magic, the mountebank, the sleight-of-hand artist. The Empress, *L'Imperatrice*, is often associated with Venus, the goddess of beautiful things and love. Her shield bears an eagle, the heraldic device of the Holy Roman Empire. The Pope *(Le Pape)* is a timeless power which gives legitimacy to the secular political power: he has no direct authority but is unassailable. As shown in the presence of the faithful, he is a man of influence and relationships, rather than titles and official responsibilities. The Lovers *(L'Amoureux)* represent relationships and choices, the uncertainty of which path to take: easy pleasures and desires, or virtue and its harshness. Love is seen as an ordeal: it is not enough to achieve a high position, it is still necessary to have the moral resources to remain so. Does one remain stable and self-assured, or will one reject what is already attained for short-lived pleasures?

La Pendu, La Mort, La Force, Le Jugement

The Hanged Man *(Le Pendu)* symbolises self-sacrifice, lack of interest in worldly things, altruism, and the overthrow of a current situation via a personal decision. Death *(La Mort)* implies an end, possibly of a relationship or interest, and an increased sense of self-awareness. The threatening weapon is borrowed from Saturn, equated with the Greek god Chronos. In the Middle Ages the sickle became a symbol of destructive power, or that of death. The horse is a reference to the four horsemen of the Apocalypse, one of which symbolises death. Fortitude (*La Force*) symbolises courage and moderation in attitude toward pain and danger, with neither being avoided nor actively wanted. The Last Judgement *(Le Jugement)* symbolises transformation and renewal, and listening to one's inner voice and the guidance of angels. The Gospel of Matthew is the source for the depiction of the Last Judgment: the dead, awakened by angels blowing trumpets, come out of their tombs, naked.

513 *'Sine lucro friget ludus is a family motto.'*

'No gaining, cold gaming.'

513 *'...but we're a gey practical nation.'*

'Gey' is a humorous Scots synonym for very; fairly; considerably.

513 *Palmer, unoffended, glinted the butter-tooth in his direction...*

A butter tooth is a broad fore-tooth[6/D], one of the two middle incisors of the upper jaw. Here, meaning Palmer's wired tooth.

516 *'After three days in the Tower. Not very preferential.'*

The Tower of London is a fortress and former royal residence on the banks of the River Thames in London. Erected by William the Conqueror in 1076 and completed by his son Rufus, various additions were made by succeeding monarchs until it assumed its 16th-century shape with a solid Norman keep and an inner wall with twelve towers, protected by a strong outer wall surrounded by a deep moat. The most romantic and the most pathetic incidents of its history are connected to its prisoners, and even sovereigns themselves were captives within its walls.

The Tower of London
from the Poems of Charles, Duke d'Orléans
MS, late 15th century

516   *'The Earl of Glencairn died last year...'*

William Cunningham, 4th Earl of Glencairn (c.1490-1548), was a Scottish nobleman and soldier. The grandson of Archibald Douglas, 5th Earl of Angus, he was one of the principal adherents of the English Court in Scotland. He accepted a pension from Henry VIII, and was allied with Lennox until 'the old fox and his cub'[7] defected at a critical moment for Lennox. Glencairn, along with Angus, supported the queen-regent against Henry, and at a Parliament held in Edinburgh they were both formally absolved of treason. Glencairn died March 1547, while receiving a French pension for loyalty to the alliance between Scotland and France.

516   *'Lord Maxwell two years ago...'*

Robert Maxwell, 5th Lord Maxwell (1493-1546), was knighted by James IV on the field at Flodden. For his assistance in escaping the captivity of the Earl of Angus, King James V rewarded Maxwell with a portion of the lands forfeited by Angus. At the Battle of Solway Moss, Maxwell was one of the nobles who attempted to restore order amongst the troops. He was captured, but soon returned to Scotland after paying a ransom and signing a bond to aid the English king, by force if necessary, in his scheme for a marriage of Prince Edward with Queen Mary. In 1546, having affirmed he only made terms with Henry VIII in fear of his life, he received a remission, and was made chief justice of Annandale and appointed Warden of the West Marches. He died 9 July 1546.

516   *'...and Mr. Robert Erskine at Pinkiecleugh.'*

Robert Erskine (d.1547) was the eldest son of John Erskine, 4th Lord Erskine; he thus held the title of Master of Erskine until his death at the Battle of Pinkie Cleugh. His brother, Tom, then succeeded him as Master of Erskine.

516   *'...are my misfortune, not my fault.'*

From *The Essays of Michel de Montaigne*, discussing the Roman senator and historian Tacitus (56-117 A.D.):

> *He needs no excuse for having approved the religion of his time, according to the laws enjoined, and to have been ignorant of the true; this was his misfortune, not his fault.*

Michel de Montaigne

Michel Eyquem de Montaigne (1533-1592) was a French Renaissance essayist. From his own remarks, he was familiar with the French court, and saw Queen Mary during her stay in France, and greatly admired her.

517 *'Europe's most Christian Bachelor and I had nothing in common.'*

'Europe's most Christian Bachelor' refers to King Henry VIII of England, and alludes to the invalidity of his marriage to Catherine of Aragon. The title of Most Christian King was a title of the Kings of France owing to the long and distinctive relationship of France with the Catholic Church. Under Charles VII the title was recognised as a hereditary and exclusive title of the kings of France. Pope Julius II, allied with Henry VIII of England from 1510-1513, considered transferring the title to the English monarch, but the drafted Papal brief was never issued.

518 *'...the lady asked for Gardington as her dot?'*

In civil law, dot is a woman's dowry, the property she brings upon the marriage to her husband, either formally settled in writing or secured in the marriage contract, as under dotal rule.

519 *'Dod, look at him: his een glinting like a coo with the yellows.'*

'Een' are the eyes; a coo is a pigeon; and the yellows is a disease.

520 *Like the face of many-eyed Indra...*

In Hindu mythology, Indra is the most lauded god in the Vedic pantheon, the mighty ruler of the firmament, god of the clear sky, lord of the elements and the thunder-god. He is often represented painted with eyes all over his body, thus called Sahasraksh, 'The Thousand Eyed'.

521 *The room in David's Tower was suffocatingly crowded...*

David's Tower, one of the principal buildings in Edinburgh Castle, was built as a royal residence in the 1370s by King David II. The 10-storey building was revolutionary when it was built, becoming a model for accommodation and fortification into the 16th century. It contained 'a spacious hall and rose to a height of more than 40 feet above the present precipice, which threw its shadows on the loch 200 feet below'[8]. A vault in the tower below the king's residence was used as a state prison for important prisoners, who enjoyed relatively comfortable conditions. David's Tower was reduced to a heap of debris in the Lang Siege of 1573.

521 *The colletic stare of guards...*

Colletic is agglutinate; having cause to adhere, as with glue.

521 *...on the sweating, subsaltive hands and on the grinning tarots.*

Subsultive is moving by fits and starts[9/D]; bounding and leaping; spasmodic.

521 ...the impious Papess...the jeering Fool...

La Papessa represents reflection, mental work and analysis, and everything related to education, training, and learning. It is thought *La Papessa* of the Visconti-Sforza tarot deck is a depiction of Sister Manfreda, a member of the Vistonti family, a nun of the Umiliata order who was elected Pope by a small sect of Guglielmites at the beginning of the 14th century. She was burned at the stake as a heretic by the Inquisition.

The Fool, *Il Matto*, represented one who stood outside the social order of mediæval life: the lunatic, the homeless, one cast adrift and left to beg on the street, yet clever Fools could find themselves a niche in the courts of the day to provide comedy and entertainment.

La Papessa

522 '...I'll have them skint off the superior Sassenach dowp o' ye...'

skint:	skinned
Sassenach:	Scots term for an English person (from the Latin *saxonēs*, Saxons)
dowp:	buttocks; bottom end of something; seat of the pants

522 'Quum infirmi sumus, optimi sumus, I see.'

When we are sick, we are at our best, or most virtuous.

From *The Anatomy of Melancholy:*

Il Matto

Sickness is the mother of modesty, puts us in mind of our mortality; and when we are in the full career of worldly pomp and jollity, she pulleth us by the ear, and maketh us know ourselves. Pliny calls it the sum of philosophy: 'If we could but perform in our health, which we promise in our sickness.' Quum infirmi sumus, optimi sumus.
For 'what sick man' (as Secundus expostulates with Rufus) 'was ever lascivious, covetous, or ambitious? He envies no man, admires no man, flatters no man, despiseth no man, listens not after lies and tales.' And were it not for such gentle

remembrances, men would have no moderation in themselves, they would be worse than tigers, wolves, and lions: who would keep them in awe? 'Princes, masters, parents, magistrates, judges, friends, enemies, fair or foul means cannot contain us, but a little sickness (as Chrysostem observes) will correct and amend us.'

Gaius Plinius Cæcilius Secundus (c.61-c.113), known as Pliny the Younger, was the Latin author of *Panegyric on Trajan* and his *Epistolæ*. Having lost his father at a young age, his guardian was Verginus Rufus, who twice held the office of consul. The tenth book of *Epistolæ* contains correspondence between Pliny and Trajan, including a letter regarding the early Christians, in which he describes the religion as a 'perverse and extravagant superstition'[10].

522   *...from his numb cataphract...*

A cataphract (Greek, *kataphraktēs*, fully covered, protected, fully armored; from *kata*, fully, completely, and *phrass-ein*, to enclose, protect) was a form of heavy armour, which covered both rider and horseman. It also means a protective bulwark or covering.

522   *'Quod purpura non potest, saccus potest, Mr. Lauder.'*

'Sackcloth and ashes did that which purple robes and crown could not effect.'

From *The Anatomy of Melancholy:*

Emperor Maximilium I
by Hans Burgkmair, 1508

Faith, hope, repentance, are the sovereign cures and remedies, the sole comforts in this case; confess, humble thyself, repent, it is sufficient. Quod purpura non potest, saccus potest, *saith Chrysostom; the King of Nineveh's sackcloth and ashes did that which his Purple Robes and Crown could not effect...*

John Chrysostom (c.347-407) was Archbishop of Constantinople. He is known for his eloquence and his denunciation of the abuse of authority, both ecclesiastical and political.

St. John Chrysostom of Antioch
Cathedral of Hagia Sophia

522 *'But I prefer my truth flat and not concamerate...'*

Concamerate is to arch over; to vault.

522 *'... even with the most dulcet spring of famous rhetoric in spate beneath.'*

Stephen Hawes (c.1475-c.1523), a popular English poet during the Tudor period, addressing John Lydgate of Bury (c.1370-c.1451), an English monk and poet:

> *O master Lydgate, the most dulcet spring*
> *Of famous rhetoric, with ballad royal.*[11]   (Tr.L.R.)

During the 15th and 16th centuries it was believed rhetoric was honeyed speech exhibited at its best in the works of poets. The best example of rhetoric of the period is believed to be *The Pastime of Pleasure* by Hawes.

522 *'...or the combined keys of Tucker and Schertz's treasure houses...'*

Lazarus Tucker and Erasmus Schertz, money lenders from Antwerp, were the principal suppliers of funds to the English treasury on behalf of Protector Somerset.

524 *'I wouldna say yes to a drink of water on the lip of Gehenna...'*

In Jewish and Christian tradition, Gehenna is the place of the 'fire which cannot be put out', a place of constant torment reserved for the wicked. Gehenna was originally the name of a valley south of Jerusalem where Canaanites burned human sacrifices to tribal gods. When the Israelites returned from captivity, they considered the site a place of abhorrence, and kept fires burning there continuously for the destruction of waste and refuse. The name became synonymous with Sheol or Hell.

525 *'Are you calling my son a debauchee?'*

A debauchee is a man who leads a life of reckless drinking, promiscuity, and self-indulgence.

525 *'That boy,' bellowed Sir Wat, 'was a shilpit, shiftless, shilly-shallying gomerel before he met up with Francis Crawford.'*

shilpit:	puny; thin; weak-looking
shiftless:	lacking ambition or purpose; lazy
shilly-shally:	hesitate, vacillate, unable to come to a decision
gomerel:	slow-witted or stupid person

525   *'...or a fight than any finnicking ninny...*

Finicking is persnickity, over-dainty, adorned with trifling articles. A ninny is a sap, a fool, a simpleton.

525   *'...that stayed at home and got wed at St. Cuthbert's...*

St. Cuthbert's Church, also known as the 'West Kirk', was located beyond the Edinburgh city walls and stood at the west end of the Nor' Loch, close to the base of Castle Rock. The parish was the oldest and wealthiest in Edinburgh; the first church was constructed soon after the death of St. Cuthbert in 687 AD. The church suffered severe damage during the siege of Edinburgh Castle in 1689 and was taken down in 1775, eventually being replaced with the present building.

St. Cuthbert's Church and the Nor' Loch

526   *The carrying, escharotic voice was thick with sheer cold fury...*

Escharotic is caustic; corrosive.

526   *'...but Mr. Lauder, all heat and no light, like hell-fire, is not like that.'*

The darkness of hell-fire is a traditional part of the Christian image of hell. In *The Parson's Tale* by Geoffrey Chaucer (c.1340-1400), Hell is described as dark, including the fires:

The cause why that Job calleth hell the land of darkness,
understandeth that he clepeth it land or earth, for it is stable and
never shall fail: and dark, for he that is in hell hath default of light
material: for certes the dark light that shall come out of the fire that
ever shall burn, shall turn him to pain that is in hell, for it sheweth
him to the horrible devils that him torment.

526   '...but instead he counted on me to wreck your amour propre...'

Amour propre is self-love, self-esteem; feelings of excessive pride.

527   'I understand the damned limmer's got stuck somewhere....'

A limmer is rascal; a villain; a scoundrel.

528   ...and Lord Culter rose, purposeful and solid as Ebenezer.

Eben-Ezer ('stone of help') is the standing stone erected by Samuel of the Bible after God helped the Israelites defeat the Philistines.

529   ...through the harsh Orcadian pastures of Bishop Reid's imagining.

Orcadian refers to the Orkney Islands.

529   Of these bright phrases, forged and concatenated, would emerge the gyves which tomorrow would snap into place.

Concatenate is to link together; to unite in a series or chain. A gyve is a shackle or fetter, especially for the leg.

531   'It's an opulent word, a mighty key to a royal Cloud-Cuckoo-Land.'

From *The Birds* by Aristophanes (c.448-385 BC), considered the greatest comic playwright of ancient Athens. In the play, Piethetairos and his friend Euelpides persuade the birds to build a city – Cloud-Cuckoo-Land – in mid-air to establish their sovereignty, cut off the gods from men, and intercept men's offerings to them; their plan succeeds. The term has come to mean an impossibly ideal realm.

532   '...will make its recommendation to the Three Estates...'

The Three Estates was the Parliament of Scotland. The broad social order of hierarchy in the Middle Ages was distinguished as the three estates: the First Estate is the clergy, the Second Estate is the nobility, and the Third Estate is the commoners, or burghers.

533   *...the thatched gables and uncertain slates and the dancetté roofs...*

Dancetté is an architectural molding with a zigzag pattern, also known as a chevron molding.

533   *...the light beat down on a swaying corymb of heads...*

A corymb is a flat-topped flower cluster, from the Latin, *corymbus.*

534   *His feet were on le chemin royal de la vie...*

The word Tarot is made from two Egyptian words: *Tar* meaning *royal* and *ot* meaning *road.* Thus, Tarot means *the royal road of life,* or *le chemin royal de la vie.*

534   *He had the World...*

Meant to be placed as the penultimate card in the sequence, the World followed the other celestial spheres: the Star, the Moon, and the Sun, completing the cosmos. The card itself is a symbol of completion.

534   *...his two tarrochi nobili ...*

The *tarrochi nobili* consist of a juggler, an empress, an emperor, a pope, and a lover wooing his mistress, each counting five points.

Le Monde

535   *Scott sat like a marmorean and gently smiling Buddha...*

Marmorean, or marmoreal, is resembling marble.

535   *'...and in and out of Clinton's boats...'*

Edward Fiennes de Clinton, 1ˢᵗ Earl of Lincoln (1512-c.1584), was an English nobleman and Lord High Admiral. He married (c.1530) Elizabeth Blount, the former mistress of Henry VIII and mother of his illegitimate son Henry Fitzroy, Duke of Richmond. Clinton served in the Royal Navy against French and Scottish naval forces from 1544 to 1547, and was knighted for his participation in the storming of Edinburgh. He commanded the English fleet during the invasion of Scotland and provided naval artillery support at the Battle of Pinkie Cleugh.

537 *'Your young catachumen played tarocco all night...'*

A catachumen is one receiving instruction in the principles of Christianity.

537 *'These are stormy petrels...'*

The stormy petrel is a sea bird thought to warn sailors of oncoming storms.

539 *'...I am not to be divided into four pieces tomorrow.'*

In the 15th century, the punishment for treason was to be 'hanged, drawn, and quartered'. The convicted was drawn (dragged by the tail of a horse), hanged (to a point just shy of death), emasculated, disemboweled, beheaded, and quartered (anciently, while alive and by being pulled apart by the limbs tied to four horses; latterly, post-beheading by chopping). The remains were often displayed in prominent places across the country.

Execution of Hugh Despenser
Froissart's Chronicles, MS c.1470s

539 *'No appointment with Apollyon.'*

Apollyon ('The Destroyer') is the king of torments and the angel of the bottomless pit.

539 *The Culters' house in Bruce's Close...*

Bruce's Close is the original name of what is now called Warriston's Close, which leads off the High Street near St. Giles towards the Nor' Loch.

Bruce's Close

540 *...where for nine hours she had once sat and watched Davie Lindsay mock the Three Estates before the Three Estates, and the Crown before the Crown.*

Ane Pleasant Satyre of the Thrie Estaitis by David Lindsay (1490-1555) was presented in two forms: the first as an interlude performed indoors before James V at the Royal Palace of Linlithgow in 1540, the second performed in open air at Fifeshire, and then again on the Greenside Playfield, Calton Hill, Edinburgh on 12 August 1554. The Queen Dowager, Mary of Guise, was present at the performance.

Sir David Lindsay

The Satire of the Three Estates...was acted before as refined an audience as could then be assembled. The king and queen, the ladies and nobles of the court, with the spiritual estate, were present, and yet its coarseness and licentiousness is extreme, and on many subjects its wit of such a kind as to preclude all quotation. Yet Lindsay wrote in the character of a professed reformer of manners; but, if its grossness and vulgarity give us a low picture of the morality or delicacy of the age, the boldness of the author, and the liberality or folly of the audience, are equally conspicuous. The representation took place before the king, with his favorite ministers and advisers, yet it lashes his youthful excesses, and their profligate and selfish devices, with unsparing severity. It was performed in the presence of the bishops and clergy, and before an immense multitude of the people, the burgesses, the yeomen, the poor labourers, and tacksmen, and yet it exposes with a poignancy of satire, and a breadth of humour which must have made the deepest impression, the abuses of the Catholic religion, the evils of pluralities and non-residence, the ignorance of priests, the grievances of tithes, the profligacy of the prelates, and the happy effects which would result from a thorough and speedy reformation. Hitherto what had been written against these excesses had never reached the people; it was generally shut up in a learned language, which they did not understand; if composed in English, there were few printing-presses to multiply books, or if printed, the great body of the people could not read them. But Lindsay, when he wrote a play in a language of the people, and procured permission to have it acted before them, at once acquired a moral influence over the times, and gave a strength and edge to his satire, which probably neither the king, the clergy, nor the author himself contemplated. Had it been otherwise, it is difficult to believe that the prince or prelates would have suffered, or any author have dared the trial of such an experiment.[12]

540   *The Lang Gait and Gabriel's road, unlit; and few and distant lights from Broughton and Silver Mills and Kirkbraehead and Canon Mills.*

The Lang Gait is present-day Princes Street, part of Edinburgh's New Town begun in 1760. Princes Street was the outer edge of the original city, facing Edinburgh Castle. During the construction of the New Town, the polluted waters of the Nor' Loch were drained and the area converted into the Princes Street Gardens.

Gabriel's Road was once a narrow country path, 'along which some venerable citizens still remember to have wended their way between green hedges that skirted the pleasant meadows and cornfields of Wood's Farm, and which was in days of yore a favourite trysting place for lovers, where they breathed out their tender tale of passion beneath fragrant hawthorn.'[13]

Broughton was a small, isolated village about a mile from the city of Edinburgh. It had its own courthouse and tolbooth (c.1582), several stone mansions and many thatched cottages. The town supposedly supplied the garrison of Edinburgh Castle.

Broughton Mills, 1852

Silver Mills was a tiny district north of Edinburgh, near the Water of Leith. It was settled to refine the silver ore mined near Livingston.

Canon Mills was a village at the northern edge of town, located close to the water of Leith, where the canons from the Abbey of Holyrood brought their grain to be ground.

542   *'My God, M. le maître, you have done us an injury...'*

M. le maître: Monsieur the Master

542   *'La reine douairière is generous.'*

La reine douairière: the Queen Dowager

CHARACTERS

The following is an alphabetical listing of the characters, identifying each as historical or fictional, and with a few basic facts. More information for each of the historical figures is provided in the guide, in the order in which they appear in the text.

BEATON, Janet
> Historical: 1519-1569
> Lady of Branxholme and Buccleuch
> Third wife of Sir Walter Scott of Buccleuch

BULLO, Johnnie
> Fictional: a gypsy, one of Lymond's band of mercenary soldiers

CRAWFORD, Eloise
> Fictional: younger sister of Richard and Francis, who died at the age of 13 in a gunpowder explosion at the convent of St. Mary's in Dec. 1542

CRAWFORD, Francis of Lymond
> Fictional: brother of Richard and Eloise
> Master of Culter

CRAWFORD, Gavin
> Fictional: deceased husband of Sybilla
> 2nd Baron Culter of Midculter Castle

CRAWFORD, Mariotta
> Fictional: Irish wife of Richard
> Lady Culter

CRAWFORD, Richard
> Fictional
> 3rd Baron Culter of Midculter Castle
> Oldest brother of Francis and their deceased sister, Eloise

CRAWFORD, Sybilla
> Fictional: mother of Richard, Francis, and Eloise
> Dowager Lady Culter
> Widow of Gavin Crawford, the 2rd Baron Culter

CROUCH, Jonathan
> Fictional: prisoner of war
> Former officer in the Royal household of Princess Elizabeth

DOUGLAS, Archibald, 6ᵗʰ Earl of Angus
Historical: c.1489-1557
6ᵗʰ Earl of Angus
Ex-husband of Margaret Tudor, widow of King James IV
Father of Margaret Douglas
Eldest brother of Sir George Douglas

DOUGLAS, Sir George
Historical: d.1552
Master of Angus
Brother of Archibald Douglas

DOUGLAS, Sir James of Drumlanrig
Historical: d.1578
7ᵗʰ Baron of Drumlanrig
Brother-in-law of Archibald Douglas; uncle of John Maxwell

DOUGLAS, Lady Margaret, Countess of Lennox
Historical: 1515-1578
Wife of Matthew Stewart, the 4ᵗʰ Earl of Lennox
Daughter of Margaret Tudor and Archibald Douglas
Niece of King Henry VIII of England
Mother of Henry Stewart, Lord Darnley (1545-1567)

ERSKINE, Thomas, Master of Erskine
Historical: dates unknown
Third son of John Erskine, 4ᵗʰ Lord Erskine (d.1555)

FLEMING, Lady Janet ('Jenny') of Boghall Castle
Historical: 1502-1562
Illegitimate daughter of James IV of Scotland
Widow of Malcolm Fleming, 3ʳᵈ Lord Fleming
Aunt and governess to Mary, Queen of Scots

GREY, William, 13ᵗʰ Baron Grey de Wilton
Historical: 1508-1562
Lord Lieutenant of the North Parts for England

GUISE, Mary of
Historical: 1515-1560
Widow of King James V (1512-1542)
Mother of Mary, Queen of Scots (1542-1587)
Member of the powerful French de Guise family

HAMILTON, James, 2nd Earl of Arran
Historical: c.1516-1574
Governor of Scotland

HARVEY, Samuel
Fictional
Former officer of the Royal household of Princess Mary of England

HERRIES, Lady Agnes
Historical: c.1534-1594
Daughter and heir of William Herries, 3rd Lord Herries (d.1543)

HUNTER, Sir Andrew of Ballagan
Fictional
Son of Catherine Hunter

HUNTER, Catherine
Fictional
Mother of Sir Andrew Hunter of Ballagan

LAUDER, Henry of St. Germains
Historical: d.1561
Lord Advocate to the Queen

MATTHEW, Turkey
Fictional
Mercenary Soldier

MAXWELL, John, Master of Maxwell
Historical: dates unknown
Second son of Robert Maxwell, 5th Lord Maxwell (1493-1546)

PALMER, Sir Thomas
Historical: d.1553
English soldier and engineer
Brother of Sir John 'Buskin' Palmer

STEWART, Christian
Fictional
God-daughter of Lady Jenny Fleming

STEWART, Mary, Queen of Scots
Historical: 1542-1587
Only surviving legitimate child of King James V

SEYMOUR, Edward

Historical: 1506-1552
1st Duke of Somerset
Lord Protector of England (1547-1549)
Also known as 'the Protector' and 'Protector Somerset'
Uncle of King Edward VI of England (1537-1553)

WHARTON, Thomas, 1st Baron Wharton

Historical: 1495-1568
English soldier and nobleman
Captain of Carlisle
Warden of the Western Marches

WHARTON, Sir Henry

Historical: d.1550
English soldier
Second son of Thomas Wharton

SCOTT, Sir Walter of Branxholme and Buccleuch

Historical: 1495-1552
Noted Border reiver and 'inveterate English hater'
Husband of Janet Beaton
Father of Will Scott of Kinkurd (by his first wife)

SCOTT, Sir William of Kinkurd

Historical: d. 1552
Second son of Sir Walter Scott and his first wife Elizabeth Carmichael
Heir of Sir Walter Scott

SOMERVILLE, Gideon of Flaw Valleys

Fictional
Former officer of the Royal household of Princess Mary

SOMERVILLE, Kate

Fictional
Wife of Gideon Somerville

SOMERVILLE, Philippa

Fictional
Daughter of Gideon and Kate Somerville

STEWART, Matthew, 4th Earl of Lennox

Historical: 1516-1571
'Franco-Scot turned English'
Husband of Lady Margaret Douglas
Father of Henry Stewart, Lord Darnley

THE GAME OF KINGS

1547	*1547*	
		OPENING GAMBIT: THREAT TO A CASTLE
011	August	'*Lymond is back.*' - Lymond overhears a conversation between Mungo Tennant, Wat Scott of Buccleuch, and Tom Erskine - Lymond crashes Sybilla's party for her new daughter-in-law, Mariotta, and sets fire to Midculter
		PART I: THE PLAY FOR JONATHAN CROUCH

035	10th September
	Saturday
		PART I: CHAPTER I: TAKING *EN PASSANT*
		1. The English Opening:
		   - The Battle of Pinkie Cleugh
		   - Will Scott joins Lymond's band of men
		2. Pins and Counterpins
		   - Lymond and Scott meet Lennox and Wharton at Annan
		3. Capture of a King's Pawn
		   - Lymond meets Richard; challenges him to a match at the Wapinshaw Popinjay

059	September	PART I: CHAPTER II: BLINDFOLD PLAY - Christian Stewart rescues a memory-deprived Lymond behind Boghall Castle - Lymond regains his memory. Christian helps him escape; Tom Erskine arrives at Boghall - Christian offers to find the location of Jonathan Crouch via Tom Erskine; Lymond refuses her help

074	Friday 24th September Saturday	**PART I: CHAPTER III: MORE BLINDFOLD PLAY: THE QUEEN MOVES TOO FAR** - Christian moves to Bogle House (at Stirling) with the Culters to care for the Queen - Tom Erskine visits the Scottish court in hiding at Inchmahome Priory - Lymond visits the little Queen and teaches her a rhyme - Christian meets with Lymond
086	25th September Sunday 26th September	**PART I: CHAPTER IV: SEVERAL MOVES BY A KNIGHT** 1. Mishap to a Queening Pawn - Richard saves Agnes Harries (13) from drowning 2. A Knight Wins an Exchange - Sir Andrew Hunter negotiates for the purchase of Jonathan Crouch from Sir George Douglas - Richard invites Agnes to come watch him at the Papingo Shoot - Sir George, the Earl of Angus (Archibald Douglas), and Sir James Douglas plot and scheme
096		**PART I: CHAPTER V: CASTLING** 1. Capture of Some Advancing Pieces - Will Scott watches and learns and contemplates taking control of men from Lymond - Lymond returns from a night at the Ostrich with information about the supply train to Hume 2. Sudden Danger for a Passed Pawn - Lymond's band attack the supply train - Will Scott infiltrates Hume only to be imprisoned - Don Luis Fernando de Cordoba y Avila to the rescue!
120	mid-October	**PART I: CHAPTER VI: FORCED MOVE FOR A MINOR PIECE** - Lymond blackmails Sir George Douglas for Jonathan Crouch - Jonathan Crouch held at Ballaggan Keep with Dame Catherine Hunter (mother of 'Dandy' Hunter) - Lymond captures Jonathan Crouch

212	late December	PART II: CHAPTER III: FRENCH DEFENCE
		1. Touching and Moving
		  - a pregnant Mariotta learns about Lymond's past from Dandy Hunter
		2. A Queen's Knight Fails Signally to Adjust
		  - Richard goes to Perth to discover who ordered the glove

	Christmas Eve Christmas Day	- John Maxwell meets Agnes Harries
1548	*1548*	

	last Friday in January	PART II: CHAPTER III: FRENCH DEFENCE
		3. Another Royal Lady Enters the Game
		  - Lord Wharton, Gideon Somerville, Lord Grey, and Margaret Douglas meet at Castle of Warkworth
		  - Lymond meets with Maxwell

		PART III: THE PLAY FOR SAMUEL HARVEY

241	early February	PART III: CHAPTER I: BITTER EXCHANGE
		1. Offer of a Pawn is Discussed
		  - Lymond and George Douglas negotiate
		2. Brief Return to Home Squares
		  - Buccleuch and Will meet; Richard intervenes

	5th February Sunday	- Lymond chastises Will - Janet Buccleuch introduces their newest child, a girl, to Wat

258	early February	PART III: CHAPTER II: THE QUEEN'S PROGRESS BECOMES CRITICAL
		1. A New Pawn Is Taken
		  - Tom Erskine proposes to Christian
		  - Mariotta tells Richard about the jewellery from Lymond; packs and leaves Midculter
		  - Maxwell, Douglas, Buccleuch and Culter overthrow Wharton & Lennox

	21ˢᵗ February
	Tuesday
		2. But Proves to Be Covered
		  - Lymond kidnaps Margaret Douglas; she tries to bribe him
		  - Lymond quarrels with Will; drinks him under the table
		  - Mariotta loses the baby

288	early March	PART III: CHAPTER III: MATE FOR THE MASTER
		1. A Bereft Knight is Checked by His Own Side
		  - Richard is imprisoned after a terrible row with Sybilla (and disobeying the Dowager Queen)
		  - Lymond spurns Mariotta
		  - Lady Herries marries John Maxwell
		  - Lymond meets with Christian to thank her; Christian becomes affianced to Tom Erskine
		  - Buccleuch, Culter, and Hunter plan the taking of Lymond and the rescue of Will Scott

309	19 April
	21 April
		PART III: CHAPTER IV: CONCERTED ATTACK
		1. The Four Knights' Game
		  - Sir George renegotiates with Lymond for Will Scott; no exchange for Harvey
		  - Mariotta recovers at the convent Midculter
		  - Lymond coordinates ambush at Heriot; kidnaps Gideon Somerville
		  - Gideon agrees to arrange meeting between Lymond and Harvey

	end of May	2. The Pinning Move - Sybilla tells Janet Buccleuch about the plan to trap Lymond at the ruined convent

	23rd June	3. The Last Move (continued) - Hexham Abbey with Lord Grey, Lord Wharton, Matthew Lennox, and Margaret Douglas - Lymond kills Acheson at Hexham Abbey - Tom Erskine escapes with a badly injured Lymond - Richard remains with Lymond at the dovecote as Erskine takes troops back to Scotland
435		PART IV: CHAPTER III: KNIGHT ADVERSARY 1. Strange Refuge
	late June	- Richard nurses Francis back to health
	7th July	- After 6 days, Lymond breaks; attempts suicide; begs Richard to kill him - Scottish Parliament gives their consent to the marriage of MQoS to the Dauphin of France - Richard has a change of heart and begins preparations to get Lymond out of Scotland
	16th July	- Haddington: Scots forces join French troops to storm the town but are driven away by cannon fire - Lymond captured by Scots and taken to Edinburgh for trial 2. One Loss is Made Good - Sybilla busts Johnnie Bullo's Philosopher's Stone charade at Midculter - Richard returns to Midculter, reconciles with Mariotta
483		PART IV: CHAPTER IV: BARING 1. Remiss
	1st August	- Lymond is summoned to appear in Court on 8th August 1548 - Sybilla confronts Dandy Hunter at Ballaggan - Judicial Committee calls Lymond to appear the day before the date set for trial 2. The Queen Moves to Her Beginning
	7th August	- The Preliminary Hearing is held; the case against Lymond is presented - Will Scott plays tarot with Tommy Palmer for the Harvey confession
	8th August	- Lymond is exonerated of all charges against him and is reunited with Sybilla

		LYMOND'S BACK STORY
	September 1513	Battle of Flodden Field - 17-month-old James V is crowned King of Scotland after his father is killed in battle.
	1542	*1542*
517 518	24th November through early December	Battle of Solway Moss - After losing the battle, many members of the Scottish nobility are captured and taken to London. - Lymond spends three days in the Tower and then is placed under house arrest in the home of Sir George Douglas. - Lymond is seduced by Margaret Douglas and learns of secret plans of King Henry.
518	8th December 14th December	- Mary is born of James V and Mary de Guise. - James V dies; Mary becomes Queen of Scots. - At the death of James V, King Henry VIII switches tactics: instead of ransoming his Scottish prisoners, he releases the influential Scottish nobles after demanding their oath of fealty in supporting the marriage between his son, Prince Edward, and Queen Mary. As a younger son, Lymond was not asked to sign.
	December	- While remaining under house arrest in London, Lymond writes a letter to the Scots describing the stash of gunpowder stored at the convent at St. Mary's, in order to keep it from the English. - The letter is intercepted by the English. Forged instructions as an addendum to the letter implicate Lymond as a traitor, suggesting the English blow up the store of gunpowder. - Lymond's younger sister, Eloise (aged 13), and several nuns die in the ensuing explosion. - The Scots discover Lymond's letter next to the body of an English soldier.

December	- In an attempt to divert attention away from the real culprit, the English begin spreading the rumour Lymond is a spy, having shared intelligence prior to the battle of Solway Moss, and about the stash of gunpowder at the convent - Further fueling the evidence of Lymond's traitorous behaviour, King Henry gives Lymond the manor of Gardington 'for services rendered'; Lymond refuses the gift.
December	- For his protection, the English move Lymond from London to Calais. - Lymond is 'accidentally' captured by the French near Calais. - He is sent as a criminal to the galleys where he slaves 'at the oar'.
1543	*1543*
January	Lymond serves as a slave on the galleys from December 1542 until September 1544.
March	Lymond encounters Matthew Lennox, traveling from France aboard the galley.
1ˢᵗ July	Treaty of Greenwich is signed, contracting the marriage of Prince Edward and Queen Mary.
1544	*1544*
6ᵗʰ July	- After being rejected as a husband by Mary de Guise, Matthew Lennox marries Margaret Douglas, niece of King Henry VIII. He becomes a naturalized English citizen, and receives the property of Temple Newsam. - Lennox returns to Scotland on behalf of England, while his wife Margaret remains in London.
September	- Lymond escapes the galleys at Dumbarton, supposedly with the aid of Matthew Lennox. The galley was bringing gold and arms from France to Mary de Guise. Lennox absconds with the gold.

October	- Lymond serves as secretary to Lennox at Dumbarton from October through April 1545. - During this time, Lymond travels to Midculter but is rejected by Gavin. Note: Gavin dies violently 'in the field' sometime after this event and before August 1547
1545	*1545*
6th February	- Margaret Douglas gives birth to her first child, 7 months after marrying Lennox (the child dies in November 1545).
March	- Lymond continues to serve as secretary to Lennox at Dumbarton. - Margaret conceives Henry, Lord Darnley (born December 7th, 1545).
May	- Lennox leaves Scotland; at some point, Lennox puts a price of 1000 crowns on Lymond's head (GOK-p045). - Lymond goes to work for Wharton at Carlisle, taking a portion of the Queen Dowager's gold from Lennox. - Lymond works for Wharton from May until August/September.
August/September	- While employed with Wharton, Lymond leads 3 small raids. On his fourth raid, Lymond deliberately throws the raid, causing significant damage to the English. - Lymond leaves Wharton on the night of the fourth raid and goes to continental Europe. - Wharton threatens to gut Lymond publicly (GOK-p045).
September-December	- Lymond secretly returns some of the Queen Dowager's gold and uses a portion of it to assemble a group of mercenaries and an intelligence service.

November 7ᵗʰ December	- Margaret's first son dies. - Margaret gives birth to Henry, Lord Darnley.	
1546		*1546*
January to September	- Lymond in continental Europe for the fighting season of '46 with his mercenary troop.	
October/ November	- Lymond returns to Scotland with a few mercenaries, a portion of the Queen Dowager's gold, and profits from his mercenary troop. He creates a band of outlaws who engage in 'all manner of vice'.	
1547		*1547*
June	- Lymond goes to the Low Countries.	
August	'Lymond is back.' Lymond returns to Scotland and The GAME of KINGS begins.	

OPENING GAMBIT

1. Cessolis: Tract Four, Chapter 2. Translation by Laura Lee Caine.
2. Jenny Adams. *William Caxton, The Game and Playe of the Chesse* (Medieval Institute Pub., 2009).
3. Ibid.
4. Ibid.
5. Grant, James. *Cassell's Old and New Edinburgh* (London: Cassell, Petter, Galpin, 1880): 35.
6. Ibid.
7. Mackie, Charles. *Castles, Palaces, and Prisons of Mary of Scotland* (London, 1850): 106.
8. Ibid.
9. Ibid.
10. *American*, q.v. 'Battle of Flodden Field,' quoting Sir Walter Scott.
11. *DNB*, q.v. 'James Hamilton, 2ⁿᵈ Earl of Arran and Duke of Châtellerault.'
12. Browne. *History of Scotland, Vol. 2*: 12.
13. Gairdner, James, *et al*, editors. *Letters and Papers, Foreign and Domestic, of the Reign of Henry VIII, Vol. 19, Part 1* (London: Mackie, 1903). 10 April 1544. 314. Privy Council to Hertford.
14. Grant, James. *Cassell's Old & New Edinburgh* (1880): 118-119.
15. Ibid.
16. Ibid.
17. Grant, James. *Cassell's Old & New Edinburgh* (1880): 118-119.
18. Ibid.
19. *Chambers*, q.v. 'Columba, St.'
21. Jenkins, O. *The Student's Handbook of British and American Literature* (Murray, 1891): 23-24.
21. *Chambers*, q.v. 'Alcuin.'
22. Fraser, Antonia. *Mary, Queen of Scots* (New York: Dell Publ. Co., 2009): 303.
23. Ibid.
24. *Chambers*, q.v. 'University.'
25. *Eminent Scotsmen*, q.v. 'Lyndsay, Sir David.'
26. *DNB*, q.v. 'Lyndsay, Sir David.'
27. *Chambers* q.v. 'Lyndsay, Sir David.'
28. *DNB*, q.v. 'Lyndsay, Sir David.'
29. Chambers, q.v. 'John Calvin.'
30. Ibid.
31. *Chambers*, q.v. 'Martin Luther,' quoting Ranke.
32. *Chambers*, q.v. 'Martin Luther.'
33. *Chambers*, q.v. 'Desiderius Erasmus.'
34. *Chambers*, q.v. 'Pierre Terrail, seigneur de Bayard.'
35. Ibid.
36. DD – National Library of Scotland Archive #12135/36.
37. Entry by Jaime Jacobs.
38. *Britannica*, q.v. 'Lucius Apuleius.'
39. *Chambers*, q.v. 'Lucius Apuleius.'
40. *Britannica*, q.v. 'Lucius Apuleius.'
41. DD – NLS Arc. 12135/34
42. Tytler, Patrick Fraser. *Lives of Scottish Worthies, Vol. 3* (London: John Murray, 1831): 76-88.
43. Tr. L.R.
44. Entry by Jaime Jacobs.
45. *Gazetteer*, q.v. 'Branxholm.'
46. *Scottish Nation*, q.v. 'Fleming.'
47. 'Giant Cabbage.' *This is Jersey* ,quoting Farmer's Magazine, Vol. IV. 1836.
48. Translation courtesy of Victoria Saccenti.
49. Interpretation courtesy of Victoria Saccenti.
50. Tr. L.R.
51. *Britannica*, q.v. 'John Lydgate.'
52. Ibid.

CHAPTER I: TAKING *EN PASSANT*

1.   Caxton: Tract 3, Chapter 7. Tr. L.R.
2.   Lawson, J. *Historical Tales of the Wars of Scotland, Vol. 2*. Tytler quote. (Fullarton, 1852): 126.
3.   Quote by Patten, Ibid, 129.
4.   *Gazetteer*, q.v. 'Annan' quoting Miller.
5.   *Gazetteer,* q.v. 'Annan.'
6.   *DNB*, q.v. 'Matthew Stewart, 4th Earl of Lennox.'
7.   *American,* q.v. 'Langland, William.'
8.   *Britannica*, q.v. 'Henryson, Robert'.
9.   Translation by Laura Lee Caine.
10. *American*, q.v. 'Dunbar, William.'
11. *Britannica*, q.v. 'Dunbar, William.'
12. *Wikipedia,* q.v. 'Heliogabalus.'
13. Translation by Laura Lee Caine.
14. *Scottish Nation*, q.v. 'Bellenden, John.'
15. Translation courtesy of Elizabeth Ramsey.
16. *Chambers*, q.v 'Varro, Marcus Terentius.'
17. Ibid.
18. *American*, q.v. 'Paracelsus.'
19. Lockhart, W. 'Historical Notes Relating to Branxholme.' *History of the Berwickshire Naturalists' Club* (Alnwick, 1887): 426.
20. Ibid.
21. *DNB*, q.v. 'Stewart, Matthew, 4th Earl of Lennox.'
22. Irving, David. *The Lives of the Scotish Poets* (Edinburgh: Oliver & Boyd, 1810): 372.
23. *DNB*, q.v. 'Wharton, Thomas, 1st Baron Wharton.'
24. Dale, Bryan. *The Good Lord Wharton: His Family, Life, & Bible Charity* (London: Congregational Union of England and Wales): 11-24.
25. *DNB*, q.v. 'Wharton, Thomas, 1st Baron Wharton.'
26. Ibid.
27. Dale. *The Good Lord Wharton: His Family, Life, & Bible Charity*: 11-24.
28. Davidson, Alan. 'Wharton, Thomas (c. 1495-1568), of Wharton and Nateby, Westmoreland, and Healaugh, Yorks.' *The History of Parliament 1509-1558*. Published 1982.
29. *Academic Dictionaries and Encyclopedias*, q.v. 'Thomas Wharton, 1st Baron Wharton.'
30. Tr. L.R.
31. Tr. L.R.
32. Commentary by Jaime Jacobs.
33. Ibid.
34. *DNB*, q.v. 'Douglas, Lady Margaret, Countess of Lennox.'
35. Tr. L.R.
36. Tr. L.R.
37. Kindrick, Robert L *The Testament of Cressied: Introduction* (Medieval Institute Pub., 1997).
38. Conrad, Laura, editor. *Drinking Songs* (2 September 2002). CC-ASA.
39. Boucher, Robert. *The Kingdom of Fife: Its Ballads and Legends* (Dundee: J. Leng, 1899): 155.

CHAPTER II: BLINDFOLD PLAY

1.   Caxton: Tract 4, Chapter 3 (misidentified as chapter 2 in original).
2.   MacCulloch, J.A. *The Misty Isle of Skye* (Edinburgh: Oliphant Anderson & Ferrier, 1905): 32.
3.   Tr. LR.
4.   'Blaw-i'-my-lug'. Mackay, Charles. *Dictionary of Lowland Scotch.*
5.   Mallory, Sir Thomas. *Le Morte d'Arthur, Vol. 1* (London: J.M. Dent, 1908): 44.
6.   Ibid, 27.
7.   Tr. L.R.
8.   Tr. L.R.
9.   Tr. L.R.
10. Lydgate, John. Bergen, Henry, ed. *Lydgate's Fall of Princes* (Carnegie Inst. of Washington, 1923).
11. *Chambers*, q.v. 'Nibelungenlied.'

12. 'Paradise of the Desert Fathers.' *Encyclopedia Coptica: Orthodox Church of Egypt.* January 2006.
13. Tr. L.R.
14. Laing, David. *Early Popular Poetry of Scotland...Vol. 2* (London: Reeves & Turner, 1895): 254.
15. Riddy, Felicity. *Sir Thomas Malory* (Netherlands: E.J. Brill, 1987): 81-83.
16. Stevenson, K. *Chivalry and Knighthood in Scotland: 1424-1513* (Boydell Press, 2006): 149-150.
17. Tr. L.R.
18. *Scottish Nation*, q.v. 'Douglas, Gavin.'
19. *DNB*, q.v. 'Douglas, Gavin.'
20. Mallory, Sir Thomas. *Le Morte d'Arthur, Vol. 1* (London: J.M. Dent, 1908).
21. Commentary by Jaime Jacobs.
22. Reese, Gustav. *Music in the Renaissance.* (New York: Norton & Co. 1954): 318.
23. Bostock, John, and H.T. Riley, trans. *The Natural History of Pliny, Volume II* (G. Bell, 1890): 244.
24. Burton, Richard F. *The Book of the Thousand Nights and a Night, Vol. 1* (Burton Club, 1885): 15.

CHAPTER III: MORE BLINDFOLD PLAY

1. Caxton: Tract 4, Chapter 3.
2. Dun, P. *Summer at the Lake of Monteith* (Glasgow: J. Hedderwick, 1866): 5-6.
3. Tr. L.R.
4. Tr. L.R.
5. Explanation by Jaime Jacobs.
6. *Britannica*, q.v. 'Publius Ovidius Naso.'

CHAPTER IV: SEVERAL MOVES BY A KNIGHT

1. Caxton: Tract 2, Chapter 4.
2. Ovid. Miller, Justus Frank, trans. *Ovid, Vol. 3, Metamorphoses* (Harvard U. Press, 1916): 36-38.
3. Ramage, Crauford Tait. *Drumlanrig Castle and the Douglases* (Dumfries: J. Anderson, 1876): 36.
4. *Gazetteer*, q.v. 'Drumlanrig,' quoting Pennant (1772).
5. *DNB*, q.v. 'Douglas, Margaret, Countess of Lennox.'

CHAPTER V: CASTLING

1. Caxton: Book 3, Chapter 8. Tr.L.R.
2. Tr. L.R.
3. Tr. L.R.
4. Billings. *The Baronial and Ecclesiastical Antiquities of Scotland, Vol. 1* (T.N. Foulis, 1909): 60-61.
5. Translations by Jaime Jacobs and Laura Lee Caine.
6. *Tytler's Scottish Worthiies, Vol. 3*: 81.
7. *Gazetteer*, q.v. 'Cowthally.'
8. *Scottish Nation*, q.v. 'Seton'; Tr. L.R.
9. *Scottish Nation,* q.v. 'Seton.'
10. *Britannica*, q.v. 'Dunbar, William.'
11. Tr. L.R.
12. DD – NLS. Acc.12135/36.
13. *Gazetteer,* q.v. 'Roxburgh.'
14. *Gazetteer*, q.v. 'Hume.'
15. Grey, Arthur, Lord of Wilton. Egerton, Sir Philip de Malpas Grey, ed. *A Commentary on the Services and Charges of William Lord Grey of Wilton, c. 1557* (London: Camden Society, 1847).
16. *DNB*, q.v. 'Howard, Henry, Earl of Surrey.'
17. *DNB*, q.v. 'Grey, Sir William, 13th Baron Grey de Wilton.'
18. *DNB*, q.v. 'Dudley, John, Earl of Warwick.'
19. *Gazetteer*, q.v. 'Eildon Hills.'
20. Ibid.
21. Translation assistance by Victoria Saccenti.

CHAPTER VI: FORCED MOVE FOR A MINOR PIECE

1. Cessolis: Tract 4, Chapter 7. Translation by Jaime Jacobs.
2. *Chambers,* q.v. 'Melrose Abbey.'

3. Wright, *History of Scotland, Vol. 1* (1900): 163.
4. Tytler, *The History of Scotland, Vol. 5* (1866): 15.
5. *Gazetteer*, q.v. 'Dalkeith.'
6. Jones, V.S. Vernon. *Aesop's Fables; A New Translation* (London: W. Heinemann, 1912).
7. DD – NLS. Acc. 12135/36.
8. Ritson, J. *Robin Hood, A Collection of All the Ancient Poems...Vol. 1*(London: J. Nimmo, 1887).
9. Duncan, Edmonstoune. *The Story of Minstrels* (London: Walter Scott Publ. Co., 1907): 89-91.
10. Tr. L.R.
11. Ramage, Crauford Tait. *Drumlanrig Castle and the Douglases* (Dumfries: J. Anderson, 1876).
12. DD – NLS. Acc. 12135/34.
13. Guest, C. *The Mabinogion, from the Welsh of the Llyfr Coch O Hergest* (B. Quaritch, 1877): 233.
14. *Britannica*, q.v. 'Mary I, Queen of England.'
15. Ibid.

CHAPTER VII: A VARIETY OF MATING REPLIES

1. Cessolis: Tract 4, Chapter 6.
2. Translation courtesy of Maria Elena Alonso-Sierra.
3. Tr. L.R.
4. Lang, David. *Early Popular Poetry of Scotland, Vol. 1* (Reeves, 1895): 169-174.
5. Tytler. *The History of Scotland, New Edition, Vol. V*: 13.
6. Commentary by Jaime Jacobs.
7. Tr. L.R.
8. Comments by Jaime Jacobs.
9. Translation courtesy of Jaime Jacobs.
10. Translation and explanation courtesy of Maria Elena Alonso-Sierra.
11. Jerome. *De Viris Illustribus*; quoting Hegesippus, 5th book, *Commentaries*. Wikipedia, q.v. 'James the Just.'
12. Commentary by Jaime Jacobs.
13. *American*, q.v. 'François Rabelais.'
14. Ibid.
15. *Chambers*, q.v. ' François Rabelais.'
16. Ibid.
17. Translation courtesy of Victoria Saccenti and Maria Elena Alonso-Sierra.
18. Tr. L.R.
19. Ross, John,. *The Book of Scottish Poems: Ancient and Modern* (Edinburgh Publ. Co., 1878): 234.

PART TWO: THE PLAY FOR GIDEON SOMERVILLE

CHAPTER I: SMOTHERED MATE

1. Caxton: Tract 3, Chapter 6.
2. DD – NLS Acc.12135/34.
3. DD – NLS Acc.12135/24.
4. Rait, R.S. *Royal Palaces of Scotland* (London: Constable & Co., 1911): 284.
5. Mackie, Charles. *Castles, Palaces, and Prisons of Mary of Scotland:* 4-11.
6. Ibid.
7. Ibid.
9. Tr. L.R.
9. Tr. L.R.
10. Gassner, John. *Medieval & Tudor Drama* (H. Leonard Co., 1987): 205-206.
11. *Chambers,* q.v. 'Dunbar, William.'
12. DD – NLS Acc.12135/34.
13. Doran, D. *The History of Court Fools* (London: R. Bentley, 1858): 10-11.
14. Translation courtesy of Maria Elena Alonso-Sierra.
15. *Scottish Worthies*, Vol. 3: 84.
16. Gazetteer, q.v. 'Tweed.'
17. *Chambers*, q.v. 'Pike *(Exos lucius).*'
18. DD – NLS. Acc.12135/36.

CHAPTER II: DISCOVERED CHECK

1. Caxton: Tract 3, Chapter 3.
2. *Britannica*, q.v. 'Henry Cornelius Agrippa von Nettesheim.'
3. *Chambers*, q.v. 'Henry Cornelius Agrippa von Nettesheim.'
4. Philalethes, Eirenaeus. *Collectanea Chemica: Alchemy and Hermetic Medicine* (Elliott, 1893): 116.
5. *Wikipedia,* q.v. 'Midas.' Quote from *In Rufinem* by Claudian.
6. Tr. L.R.
7. Tr. L.R.
8. Commentary by Jaime Jacobs.
9. Ibid.
10. *American*, q.v. 'Valeria Messalina.'
11. DD – NLS. Acc.12135/37.
12. DD – NLS. Acc.12135/36.
13. DD – NLS. Acc.12135/36.
14. *Century*, q.v. 'Casuistry.'
15. Child, Francis J. *English & Scottish Ballads, Vol. 1* (Boston: Houghton, Osgood, 1880): 29.

CHAPTER III: FRENCH DEFENCE

1. Caxton: Tract 3, Chapter 2.
2. Thank you to Elizabeth Holden for identifying Cellini as 'yon Italian fellow'.
3. Britannica, q.v. 'Benvenuto Cellini.'
4. Commentary by Jaime Jacobs.
5. Percy, Thomas, ed. *Reliques of Ancient English Poetry, Vol. 2* (London: Lewis, 1839): 105-121.
6. Ibid.
7. Wright. *History of Scotland, Vol. 1: 48.*
8. *Scottish Nation, Vol. 3*: 396.
9. *Gazetteer*, q.v. 'Logie Parish.'
10. Campbell, James. *Balmerino and its Abbey* (Edinburgh: Wm. Blackwood & Sons, 1894): 236-239.
11. Ibid.
12. Mackenzie. *The History of Scotland* (1902): 285-288.
13. Ibid.
14. *Britannica*, q.v. 'James IV.'
15. Rait. *Scotland*: 128.
16. *Chambers*, qv. 'James IV.'
17. *Britannica*, q.v. 'Stephen Hawes.'

PART III: THE PLAY FOR SAMUEL HARVEY

CHAPTER I: BITTER EXCHANGE

1. de Cessolis: page 41 (Tract 4, Chapter 5). Translation by Jaime Jacobs.
2. Tr. L.R.
3. Gazetteer, q.v. 'Tantallon.'
4. Translation and explanation courtesy of Elizabeth Ramsey.
5. Commentary by Jaime Jacobs.
6. Masson, Rosaline. *Edinburgh* (London: A & C Black, 1907).
7. Tytler, Vol. 5. P117.
8. *Chambers*, q.v. 'Pico della Mirandola.'
9. Ibid.
10. *Britannica*, q.v. 'Pico della Mirandola.'

CHAPTER II: THE QUEEN'S PROGRESS BECOMES CRITICAL

1. Caxton: Tract 3, Chapter 5.
2. *Britannica*, q.v. 'Petronius.'
3. Commentary by Jaime Jacobs.
4. DD – NLS. Acc.12135/37.

5.   DD – NLS. Acc.12135/37.
6.   DD – NLS. Acc.12135/37.
7.   Commentary by Jaime Jacobs.
8.   Ibid.
9.   DD – NLS. Acc.12134/34.

CHAPTER III: MATE FOR THE MASTER

1.   de Cessolis: Tract 4, Chapter 5.
2.   DD – NLS. Acc.12135/37.
3.   Commentary by Jaime Jacobs.
4.   Ibid.
5.   DD – NLS. Acc.12135/27.
6.   DD – NLS. Acc.12135/34.
7.   Van Orden, K. *Music, Discipline, and Arms in Early Modern France* (U. Chicago, 2005): 21.
8.   DD – NLS. Acc.12135/34.
9.   Commentary by Jaime Jacobs.
10. Ibid.
11. Udall, Nicholas. *Ralph Roister Doister* (London: Early English Drama Society, 1907).
12. Wart & Trent.*The Cambridge History of English and American Literature, Vol. 5* (Putnam, 1907).
13. *Chambers*, q.v. 'John Skelton.'
14. Ibid.
15. *Wikipedia*, q.v. 'Epaminondas.'
16. Commentary by Jaime Jacobs.
17. Ibid.
18. *Chambers*, q.v. 'Michael Scot.'
19. *Britannica*, q.v. 'Michael Scot.'
20. Commentary by Jaime Jacobs.
21. 'Sotie.' *Oxford Companion to French Literature* (Oxford University Press, 2005).

CHAPTER IV: CONCERTED ATTACK

1.   Caxton: Tract 1, Chapter 3.
2.   *DNB*, q.v. 'Sir Thomas Palmer.' Tr. L.R.
3.   Commentary by Jaime Jacobs.
4.   *DNB*, q.v 'Sir Robert Bowes.'
5.   Commentary by Jaime Jacobs.
6.   DD – NLS. Acc.12135/37.
7.   Commentary by Jaime Jacobs.
8.   Ibid.
9.   Translation courtesy of Jaime Jacobs.
10. *Britannica*, q.v. 'John Heywood.'
11. DD – NLS. Acc.12135/37.
12. *Chambers*, q.v. 'Polycarp.'
13. DD – NLS. Acc.12135/37.
14. Tr. L.R.
15. Allen, P.S. *The Age of Erasmus* (Russell & Russell, 1963): 106-107.
16. Lecky, W. *History of European Morals from Augustus to Charlemagne, Vol. 2* (Longmans, 1890):
     241; DD – NLS Acc.12135/36.
17. DD – NLS. Acc.12135/34.

PART IV: THE END GAME

CHAPTER I: TWICE TAKEN

1.   Caxton: Tract 4, Chapter 1.
2.   Bateson, Edward. *History of Northumberland, Vol. 11* (Newcastle-Upon-Tyne: A. Reid,1893).
3.   Ibid.
4.   Ibid.
5.   Gunderscheimer, Werner L. *The Italian Renaissance* (U.of Toronto Press, 1993): 105.

6.   Alchinm Linda. 'Greek Fire.' Middle-Ages.org.uk. 20 Sep. 2012.
7.   DD – NLS. Acc.12135/34.
8.   DD – NLS. Acc.12135/34.
9.   Bryan, William Lowe. *Plato the Teacher* (New York: Charles Scribner's Sons, 1897).
10.   *Gazetteer*, q.v. 'Douglas Castle.'
12.   Ibid.
12.   DNB, q.v. 'James Douglas, 9th Earl of Douglas.'
13.   Fraprie, Frank Roy. *The Castles and Keeps of Scotland, Illustrated* (Boston: Page, 1907): 376-378.
14.   Ibid.
15.   DD – NLS. Acc.12135/37.
16.   Explanation courtesy of Jaime Jacobs.
17.   *Britannica*, s.v. 'Della Robbia.'
18.   DD – NLS. Acc.12135/36.
19.   Translation by Matthew D. Thibedault. 2008. CC-ASA.
20.   DD – NLS. Acc.12135/37.
21.   DD – NLS. Acc.12135/37.
22.   DD – NLS. Acc.12135/37.
23.   DD – NLS. Acc.12135/34.
24.   Tr. L.R.
25.   Mackenzie. *The History of Scotland*: 203.
26.   Tr. L.R.
27.   Tr. L.R.
28.   *Scottish Worthies, Vol. 3*: 76.
29.   Tr. L.R.
30.   Tr. L.R.
31.   Lefferts, M. *Catalogue of a Splendid Collection of English Literature* (D. Taylor & Co., 1902): 7.
32.   Grieve, Maud. *A Modern Herbal*. 1931.
33.   Pratt, Anne. Quoting Gerarde. *Flowering Plants of Great Britain, Vol. 2* (Warne, 1905): 272-273.
34.   DD – NLS. Acc.12135/34.
35.   Wikipedia, q.v. 'James Wilford.' *Calendar State Papers Scotland, Vol. 1* (1898): 165-166.
36.   *Tytler. History of Scotland, Vol. IV.*
37.   *Letter from Grey to the Protector, 12th June 1548 or 23 April 1548.*
38.   *Letter from Grey to Protector, June 4 1548.*
39.   *Tytler. History of Scotland, Vol. IV.*

CHAPTER II: THE ULTIMATE CHECK

1.   Caxton: Tract 3, Chapter 8.
2.   DD – NLS Acc.12135/37.
3.   DD – NLS Acc.12135/37.
4.   DD – NLS Acc.12135/34.
5.   Tr. L.R.
6.   Timbs, J. *Abbeys, Castles, and Ancient Halls of England & Wales, Vol. 3* (Warne, 1872): 367-369.
7.   *Calendar of State Papers relating to Scotland and Mary, Queen of Scots 1547-1603, Vol.1.* Edited by Joseph Bain (1898): 57 (entry number 120, Jan 5, 1547).
8.   *Gazetteer*, q.v. 'Lammermuir Hills.'
9.   Ibid.
10.   Bishop, Ian. *Pearl in Its Setting: A Critical Study...* (Oxford, 1968).
11.   Osgood, C. G. *The Pearl: An Anonymous English Poem of the 14th C.* (Translator, 1907): ix - xiv.
12.   *Britannica*, q.v. 'Dante Alighieri.'
13.   G.H. Lews, Probs. Of Life and Mind. I. i. §15.
14.   Reese, Gustav. *Music in the Renaissance* (New York: Norton & Co., 1959): 291-295.
15.   DD – NLS Acc.12135/34.
16.   Rickert, Edith. *Early English Romances: Romances of Friendship* (Chatto & Windus, 1908).
17.   Rose, T. *Westmoreland, Cumberland, Durham, & Northumberland* (London: Fisher, 1835).
18.   Hinds, Allan B. *A History of Northumberland, Volume III: Hexhamshire, Part I* (A. Reid, 1896).
19.   Rose, T. *Westmoreland, Cumberland, Durham, & Northumberland* (London: Fisher, 1835): 70.
20.   Commentary by Jaime Jacobs.

21. DD – NLS. Acc.12135/36. In her notes, Dorothy wrote, *'Zenobia refused husband except for a king.'* LR: I was unable to verify with any source, but utilised the statement within the entry as it may assist one in analysing Lymond's statement.

22. Jameson, Anna. *Memoirs of Celebrated Female Sovereigns, Vol. 1* (New York: Harper, 1840): 62.

CHAPTER III: KNIGHT ADVERSARY

1. Caxton: Tract 3, Chapter 5.
2. Ryley, George Scott. *The History of Torture Throughout the Ages* (Kessinger Pub., 1940): 190-191.
3. *Wikipedia*, q.v. 'Ali ibn al-'Abbas al-Majusi.'
4. *Britannica*, q.v. 'Euripedes.'
5. Warren, F.M. *The Troubadour "Canso" and Latin Lyric Poetry*. Modern Philology. Vol. 9, No. 4 (April 1912), pp. 469-487.
6. Waddell, Helen. *Mediæval Latin Lyrics* (New York: H. Holt & Co., 1929): 322.
7. Ibid: 142-143.
8. Botsford, G. W. *A History of Rome for High School and Academies* (Macmillan, 1901): 321-322.
9. Ibid.
10. Tr. L.R.
11. DD – NLS. Acc.12135/37.
12. Tr. L.R.
13. *DNB*, q.v 'Wilford, Sir James.'
14. Ibid.
15. Commentary by Jaime Jacobs.
16. Miller, James. *Lamp of Lothian, or The History of Haddington* (Haddington: Sinclair, 1900): 31.
17. Ibid.
18. Commentary by Jaime Jacobs.
19. Commentary by Jaime Jacobs.
20. DD – NLS. Acc.12135/36.
21. Lang, Jean. *A Book of Myths* (New York: G. P. Putnam's Sons): 40-41.
22. Commentary by Jaime Jacobs.
23. DD – NLS. Acc.12135/38.
24. Miller. *Lamp of Lothian: The History of Haddington* (1900): 28.
25. Tr.L.R.
26. Miller. *Lamp of Lothian: The History of Haddington* (1900): 28.
27. Thompson, C.J.S. *Alchemy and Alchemists* (Mineola: Dover Publications, 2002).
28. Ibid.
29. *Gazetteer*, q.v. 'Pentland Hills.'

CHAPTER IV: BARING

1. Caxton: Tract 4, Chapter 2.
2. DD – NLS. Acc.12135/37.
3. Entry by Jaime Jacobs.
4. *Wikipedia*, q.v. 'Clan Majoribanks.'
5. Puckle, John. *The Church and Fortress of Dover Castle* (Oxford: J. Henry & J. Parker, 1864): 8-10.
6. DD – NLS. Acc.12135/38.
7. *DNB*, q.v. 'William Cunningham, 4th Earl of Glencairn.'
8. *Gazetteer*, q.v. 'Edinburgh. The Castle.'
9. DD – NLS. Acc.12135/34.
10. *Britannica*, q.v. 'Gaius Plinius Cæcilius Secundus.'
11. Tr. L.R.
12. Tytler. *Lives of Scottish Worthies, Vol. 3*: 237-238.
13. Grant, James. *Cassell's Old and New Edinburgh, Vol 2*: 117.

All end-notes marked with a 'D' (i.e. [1/D]) indicate a note from a file in the Dorothy Dunnett Archives at the National Library of Scotland.

All fables quoted are from *The Fables of La Fontaine* translated by Elizur Wright, Jr. (Boston: Sanborn, Carter, & Brazin, 1856).

BIBLIOGRAPHY

Adams, Jenny. *William Caxton, The Game and Playe of the Chesse* (Medieval Inst. Pub., 2009).

Aikin, John, and John Frosts. *The Works of the British Poets* (Philadelphia: Wardle, 1845).

Aikin, Lucy. *Memoirs of the Court of Queen Elizabeth* (London: Longman, 1819).

Alchin, Linda. 'Greek Fire.' Middle-Ages.org.uk. 20 September 2012.

Allen, David G., and Robert White. A. *Subjects on the World's Stage: Essays on British Literature of the Middle Ages* (University of Delaware Press, 1995).

Allen, P.S. *The Age of Erasmus* (Russell & Russell, 1963).

Allibone, Samuel Austin. *A Critical Dictionary of English Literature* (1859).

Almond, Philip C. *Heaven and Hell in Enlightenment England* (Cambridge U. Press, 2009).

Amours, F.J. *Scottish Alliterative Poems in Riming Stanzas* (Edinburgh: Blackwood, 1897).

'Anatomy of a Rapier.' *Western Martial Arts*. 13 Nov. 2008.

Anderson, Joseph. *Scotland in Pagan Times* (Edinburgh: D. Douglas, 1883).

Anderson, William. *The Scottish Nation* (Edinburgh: A. Fullarton, 1877).

André, Mary. *La Chambre des Dames* (Paris: Boivin, 1922).

Angel, H.R. *The Book of Chess* (New York: D. Appleton, 1858).

Anonymiana, or Ten Centuries of Observations (London: J. Nichols, 1818).

Anthon, Charles. *A Classical Dictionary* (New York: Harper, 1848).

Arber, Edward. *The Dunbar Anthology, 1401-1508* (London: H. Frowde, 1901).

Arber, Edward. *The Surrey & Wyatt Anthology, 1509-1547* (London: H. Frowde, 1901).

Arber, Edward. *An English Garner, Vol. 3* (London: A. Constable, 1895).

Arnot, Hugo. *The History of Edinburgh* (Edinburgh: T. Turnbull, 1816).

Ascham, Roger. *English Works: Toxophilus, &c.* Edited by William Wright (Cambridge U. Press, 1904).

Ashley, Kathleen M. *Mankind* (Kalamazoo: Medieval Inst. Pub., 2008).

Ashton, John. *The History of Gaming in England* (London: Duckworth, 1898).

Association for Renaissance Martial Arts (arm.org).

Aubry, Pierre, *Trouvères and Troubadours*, (New York: G. Schirmer, 1914).

Ausonius, Decimus Magnus. *Ausonius, Vol. 2*. Translated by H. Evelyn-White. (W. Heineman, 1919).

Baikie, James. *Peeps at Many Lands: Ancient Assyria* (London: A. & C. Black, 1916).

Bain, Joseph. *Calendar of State Papers Relating to Scotland and Mary, Queen of Scots, 1547-1603* (Edinburgh: H.M. General Register House, 1898).

Balmerino and its Abbey (Edinburgh: W. Blackwood, 1894).

Bannatyne, George. *Ancient Scottish Poems* (Edinburgh: A. Murray, 1770).

Bartlett, W.H. *Ports, Harbours, Watering-Places of Great Britain* (J. Virtue: 1840).

Bartsch, Karl. *Altfranzösische Romanzen und Pastourellen* (Leipzig: Vogel, 1870).

Bateson, Edward. *History of Northumberland* (Newcastle-Upon-Tyne: A.Reid,1893).

Beale, Thomas W. *The Oriental Biographical Dictionary* (London: W. Allen, 1894).

Beatson, Robert. *A Political Index to the Histories of Great Britain & Ireland* (London: Longman, 1806).

Beattie, William. *Scotland, Illustrated* (London: G. Virtue, 1838).

'Beaver.' *The Medieval Bestiary*. Web. 15 January, 2011.

Belanger, Michelle. *Dictionary of Demons: Names of the Damned* (Llewellyn Pub. 2010).

Bell, Robert. *Ancient Poems, Ballads and Songs of England* (London: J.W. Parker, 1857).

Bell, William. *A Dictionary and Digest of the Laws of Scotland* (Edinburgh: Bell & Bradfute, 1861).

Benham, Sir William. *A Book of Quotations, Proverbs and Household Words* (J.B. Lippincott Co., 1907).

Benham, William. *The Tower of London* (London: Seeley & Co., 1906).

Berdan, John Milton. *Early Tudor Poetry, 1485-1547* (New York: Macmillan, 1920).

Bergen, Henry. *Lydgate's Fall of Princes, Part III* (Washington: Carnegie Institute, 1923).

Berwickshire Naturalists' Club. *History of the Berwickshire Naturalists' Club, 1885-1886* (1887).

Billings, Robert W. *Baronial and Ecclesiastical Antiquities of Scotland* (London: Blackwood, 1845).

Black, A. & C. *Black's Picturesque Tourist of Scotland* (Edinburgh: A. & C. Black, 1857).

Black, George Fraser. *Scottish Charms and Amulets* (Edinburgh: Neill and Co., 1894).

Bostock, John. *The Natural History of Pliny, Volume II* (London: G. Bell, 1890).

Boucher, Robert. *The Kingdom of Fife: Its Ballads and Legends* (Dundee: J.Leng, 1899).

Botsford, George. *A History of Rome for High Schools and Academies* (MacMillan, 1901).

Boyden, Edward A. *The Anatomical Record, Volume 11* (New York: A.R. Liss, 1917).

Bradley, A.G. *The Gateway of Scotland* (London: Constable & Co., 1912).

Bradley, A.G. *The Romance of Northumberland* (Chicago: A.C. McClurg & Co., 1909).
Breul, Karl. *The Cambridge Songs: A Goliard's Song Book* (Cambridge University Press, 1915).
Brewer, E. Cobham. *Etymological & Pronouncing Dictionary of Difficult Words* (London: Ward, 1882).
Brewer, E. Cobham. *Brewer's Dictionary of Phrase & Fable* (London: Cassell,1890).
Brians, Paul. *Reading About the World* (Harcourt Brace Custom Books, 1998).
Brittain, F. *Medieval Latin and Romance Lyric to A.D. 1300* (Cambridge U. Press, 1937).
Britton, John. *A Dictionary of Architecture & Archaeology* (London: Longman, 1883).
Brown, Keith M. *Records of the Parliaments of Scotland to 1707* (St. Andrews, 2012).
Brown, P. Hume. *Early Travellers in Scotland* (Edinburgh: D. Douglas, 1891).
Brown, P. Hume. *History of Scotland* (Cambridge: University Press, 1899).
Brown, P. Hume. *A Short History of Scotland* (Edinburgh: Oliver & Boyd, 1908).
Brown, P. Hume. *Scotland in the Time of Queen Mary* (London: Methuen & Co., 1904).
Brown, P. Hume. *Surveys of Scottish History* (Glasgow: J. Maclehose, 1919).
Brown, Thomas. *Dictionary of the Scottish Language* (London: Simpkin & Marshal, 1845).
Brown, William. *Select Views of the Royal Palaces of Scotland* (Edinburgh: Cadell, 1830).
Browne, William H. *The Taill of Rauf Coilyear* (Baltimore: John Hopkins Press, 1903).
Bryan, William L. *Plato the Teacher* (New York: Charles Scribner's Sons, 1897).
Buchanan, George. *The History of Scotland*. Translated by James Aikman (Glasgow: Blackie, 1827).
Burns, Robert. *Poems, Chiefly in the Scottish Dialect* (Edinburgh: T. Cadell, 1793).
Burton, Robert. *Anatomy of Melancholy* (Philadelphia: J.W. Moore, 1847).
Burton, Robert. *Anatomy of Melancholy* (London: J. Nimmo, 1886).
Burton, Robert. *Anatomy of Melancholy* (London: Vernor & Hood, 1801).
Burton, Robert. *Anatomy of Melancholy* (London: Chatto & Windus, 1881).
Burton, R. F. *The Book of the Thousand Nights and a Night, Vol. 1* (Burton Club, 1885).
Calliope: a Selection of Ballads Legendary & Pathetic (London: Suttaby, Evance, 1808).
Campbell, Lord Archibald. *Records of Argyll* (Edinburgh: W. Blackwood, 1885).
'Campvere.' Encyclopedia 123. Web.
Cardonnel, Adam de. *Picturesque Antiquities of Scotland* (London: 1788).
Carlisle, Nicholas. *A Topographical Dictionary of Scotland* (London: G. & W. Nicol, 1813).
Capo Ferro, Ridolfo. *Great Representations of the Art and Use of Fencing* (Sienna, c.1610).
Carels, Peter E. *Eulenspiegel and Company Visit the Eighteenth Century* (Modern Language Studies, Vol. 10, No. 3, Autumn, 1980).
Carr, Alexander A. *A History of Coldingham Priory* by (Edinburgh: A. & C. Black, 1836).
Cessolis, Jacobus de. *The Buke of Ye Chess* (Auchinleck Press, 1898).
Chalmers, George. *The Life of Mary, Queen of Scots* (London: J. Murray, 1822).
Chambers, Robert. *Biographical Dictionary of Eminent Scotsmen* (London: Blackie, 1872).
Chambers, Robert. *Cyclopædia of English Literature* (Boston: Gould, Kendall, 1847).
Chambers, Robert. *Chamber's Encyclopædia of Universal Knowledge* (London: Chambers, 1901).
Changeri, Heather. 'The Virgin & the Unicorn.' *White Rose Garden*. 2007. Accessed 2011.
Chappell, William. *Old English Popular Music* (London: Chappell, 1893).
Charter and Other Documents Relating to the Royal Burgh of Stirling, A.D. 1124-1705 (Glasgow, 1884).
Chaucer, G. *The Canterbury Tales of Geoffrey Chaucer*. Translated by P. Mackaye (Duffield, 1914).
Chaucer, Geoffrey. *Troilus and Criseyde* (Project Gutenberg, 2008): lines 1806-1813.
Chaucer, Geoffrey. *Canterbury Tales of Chaucer, Volume III.* Edited by George Gilfillan (Nichol, 1860).
Cheviot, Andrew. *Proverbs, Proverbial Expressions, & Popular Rhymes of Scotland* (A. Gardner, 1896).
Child, Francis James. *English & Scottish Ballads* (Boston: Houghton, Osgood, 1880).
Chisolm, Hugh. *Encyclopædia Britannica, 11th Edition* (Cambridge Univ. Press, 1910).
Choi, Charles. 'Ancient 8-foot Sea Scorpions Probably Were Pussycats.' *Live Science*. 30 Dec. 2010.
Clark, Donald. *Rhetoric and Poetry in the Renaissance* (New York: Columbia U. Press, 1922).
Cleveland, Charles D. *A Compendium of English Literature* (Philadelphia: Biddle, 1852).
'Coals of Fire.' *Pearls in a Nutshell*. Web. 11 June 2007.
Cochran-Patrick, R.W. *Mediæval Scotland* (Glasgow: J. Maclehose & Sons, 1892).
Collection Des Anciens Alchimistes Grecs, Vol. 1 (Paris: Georges Steinheil, 1887).
Connie. 'My Own Dog Tooth Violets.' *Notes from a Garden*. Web. 22 March 2008.
Conrad, Laura. *Drinking Songs*. Web. 2 September 2002.
Cook, Arthur. *A Book of Dovecotes* (London: T.N. Foulis, 1920).
Cook, A.B. *Zeus: A Study in Ancient Religion* (Cambridge Univ. Press, 2010).
Cook, William. *The Chess Primer* (London: Smart & Allen, 1880).
Cornish, F. Warre. *Chivalry* (London: Swan Sonnenschein, 1908).

Cowan, Samuel. *The Ancient Capital of Scotland* (London: Simpkin, 1904).

Cowan, Samuel. *Life of Princess Margaret, Queen of Scotland, 1070-1093* (Mawson, 1911).

Cowan, Samuel. *The Lord Chancellors of Scotland* (Edinburgh: W. Johnston, 1911).

Cowan, Samuel. *The Last Days of Mary Stuart* (Philadelphia: J.B. Lippincott, 1907).

Cowan, Samuel. *Mary Queen of Scots* (London: Sampson Low, Marston & Co., 1901).

Cowan, Samuel. *The Royal House of Stuart* (London: Greening & Co., 1908).

Cowan, Samuel. *Three Celtic Earldoms: Atholl, Strathearn, Menteith* (MacLeod, 1909).

Craik, Sir Henry. *English Prose: Selections with Critical Introductions, Vol. 1* (Macmillan, 1916).

Crane, Walter. *The Frog Prince and Other Stories* (George Rutledge, 1874).

Crockett, W.S. and James C. Law. *Sir Walter Scott* (London: Hodder & Stroughton, 1903).

Crockett, W.S., *Abbotsford, painted by William Smith, Jr.* (London: A. & C. Black, 1903).

Crockett, W.S. *The Scott Country* (London: Adam & Charles Black, 1905).

Croker, T.C. *Fairy Legends and Traditions of the South of Ireland* (J. Murray, 1828).

Cummings, Robert. *Marchetto Cara.* Web. Allmusic.com.

Curzon, Lord of Kedleston. *War Poems and other Translations* (London: John Lane, 1915).

Dale, Bryan. *The Good Lord Wharton* (London: Congregational Union of England & Wales, 1906).

Dalzell, Tom. *New Partridge Dictionary of Slang and Unconventional English* (Taylor & Francis, 2006).

Davies, J. C. *Folk-lore of the West and mid-Wales* (Aberstwyth: Welsh Gazette, 1911).

Davidson, Alan. *The History of Parliament 1509-1558.* Web. 1982.

Della Casa, G. *Galateo of Manners and Behaviours: A Renaissance Courtesy Book* (G. Richards, 1914).

A Description of England and Wales (London: Newbery & Carnan, 1769).

Dictionary of the Scottish Language (Edinburgh: J. Sawers, 1818).

Ditchfield, P.H. *The Counties of England, their story and Antiquities* (G. Allen, 1912).

Doran, Dr. *The History of Court Fools* (London: Richard Bentley, 1858).

Douglas, Gavin. *The Poetical Works of Gavin Douglas.* Edited by John Small (W. Patterson, 1874).

Douglas, Sir George. *A History of the Border Counties* (Edinburgh: Blackwood, 1899).

Douglas-Irvine, Helen, and R. S. Rait. *Royal Palaces of Scotland* (Constable, 1911).

Drummond, William. *Genealogy of the Most Noble and Ancient House of Drummond* (Glasgow, 1889).

Drysdale, William. *Auld Biggins of Stirling: Its Closes, Wynds, and Neebour Villages* (E. MacKay, 1904).

Drysdale, William. *Old Faces, Old Places, and Old Stories of Stirling* (E. MacKay, 1898).

Drysdale, William. *Old Faces, Old Places, and Old Stories of Stirling, 2nd Series* (E. MacKay, 1899).

Dugdale, James. *The New British Traveller* (London: J. Robins, 1819).

Dun, P. *Summer at the Lake of Monteith* (Glasgow: J. Hedderwick & Son, 1866).

Dunbar, William. *The Poems of William Dunbar.* Edited by David Laing (Edinburgh: Laing, 1834).

Duncan, Edmonstoune. *The Story of Minstrels* (London: Walter Scott Publ. Co., 1907).

Dyboski, Roman. *Songs, Carols, & Other Miscellaneous Poems* (Early English Text Society, 1907).

Earl of Hertford's Expedition Against Scotland, 1544 (Edinburgh: Goldsmid, 1886).

'Edinburgh Castle Uncovered: Exploring the Ruins of David's Tower.' Scotsman.com. 4 February 2011.

Egan, Pierce. *Grose's Classical Dictionary of the Vulgar Tongue* (London: Sherwood, Neely, 1823).

Erskine, John. *An Institute of the Law of Scotland, Volume 1* (Edinburgh: Law Society of Scotland, 1824).

Evans, Thomas. *Old Ballads: Historical and Narrative* (London: R. H. Evans, 1810).

Farmer, John S. *The Summoning of Everyman* (London: Gibbings & Co., 1906).

Farmer, Lydia Hoyt. *The Girl's Book of Famous Queens* (New York: T.Y. Crowell, 1887).

Ffoulkes, Charles J. *Inventory and Survey of the Armouries of the Tower of London* (London: 1916).

'Field Guide to The Second Shepherd's Play.' Folger Shakespeare Library. Web.

Fleming, J.S. *Old Nooks of Stirling* (Stirling: Munro & Jamieson, 1898).

Fleming, John, and John Wilson. *The Lakes of Scotland* (Edinburgh: A. Fullarton, 1839).

Fleury, Jean, ed. *Rabelias et son œvre, II* (Paris: Didier et Ce, 1877).

Ford, Robert. *Auld Scots Ballants* (Paisley: A. Gardner, 1889).

Forsyth, Robert. *The Beauties of Scotland* (Edinburgh: T. Bonar & J. Brown, 1805).

Foster, Edward E. *Sir Amadace* (Kalamazoo: Medieval Institute Publications, 1997).

Foster, J.J. *The Stuarts* (New York: Dickinsons, 1907).

Foster, John. *The Legend and Shrine of Saint Triduana* (British J.of Opthamology, 1953).

Foster, Joseph. *Members of Parliament of Scotland* (1882).

Fowler, H.W. *Concise Oxford Dictionary of Current English* (Clarendon Press, 1911).

Fraprie, Frank Roy. *The Castles and Keeps of Scotland* (Boston: L.C. Page & Co., 1907).

Fraser, Antonia. *Mary, Queen of Scots* (New York: Delta, 2001).

Fraser, William. *The Dukes of Albany and Their Castle of Doune* (Edinburgh, 1881).

Fraser, William. *Elphinstone Family Book of the Lords Elphinstone, Balmerino, and Coupar* (1897).

Fraser, William. *The Scotts of Buccleuch* (Edinburgh: 1878).

Fraser, William. *The Book of Carlaverock* (Edinburgh, 1873).

Froude, James Anthony. *History of England from the Fall of Wolsey to the Death of Elizabeth, Vol. 5* (New York: Scribner, Armstrong & Co., 1881).

Fulleylove, John, and Arthur Poysner. *The Tower of London* (A. & C. Black, 1908).

Gassner, John. *Medieval & Tudor Drama* (Milwaukee: H. Leonard Co., 1987).

Geddie, John. *The Royal Palaces, Historic Castles, and Stately Homes of Great Britain* (Schulze, 1913).

Gibbon, Edward. *Decline and Fall of the Roman Empire* (Dublin: W. Hallhead, 1788).

Gibson, William Sidney. *Descriptive and Historical Notices of Some Remarkable Northumbrian Castles, Churches, and Antiques* (London: W. Pickering, 1848).

Glick, Thomas. *Medieval Science, Technology, and Medicine* (New York: Taylor, 2005).

Goodrich, C.A. *Webster's Compete Dictionary of the English Language* (G. Bell, 1886).

Goodman, Kenneth S. *The Game of Chess* (New York: Vaughan & Gomme, 1914).

Grandgent, Charles H. *Publications of the Modern Language Association of America, Vol. 18* (Modern Language Association, 1903).

Grant, James. *Cassell's Old and New Edinburgh* (London: Cassell & Co., 1887).

Grant, William. Dixon, James M. *Manual of Modern Scots* (Cambridge U. Press, 1921).

Graves, Robert. *The Crowning Privilege: Collected Essays on Poetry* (Doubleday, 1956).

Green, Robert F. *Chess* (London: G. Bell & Sons, 1905).

Green, Samuel G., and T. Faulkner. *Scotland, Illustrated.* (New York: Hurst & Co., 1800).

Grey, Arthur. *A Commentary on the Services and Charges of William Lord Grey of Wilton.* Edited by Sir Philip de Malpas Grey Egerton (London:Camden Soc., 1847).

Grieve, Mrs. M. *A Modern Herbal.* Web. Botanical.com

Groome, Francis H. *Ordnance Gazetteer of Scotland* (Edinburgh: T. C. Jack, 1885).

Grose, Francis. *Glossary of Provincial and Local Words Used in England* (Smith, 1839).

Grose, Francis. Clark, Hewson. *Lexicon Balatronicum: A Dictionary of Buckish Slang, University Wit, and Pickpocket Eloquence* (London: C. Chappell, 1811).

Grose, Francis. *The Antiquarian Repertory* (London: Francis Blyth, 1775).

Grose, Francis. *The Antiquities of England and Wales* (London: S. Hooper, 1782).

Grose, Francis. *The Antiquities of Scotland* (London: Hooper & Wigstead, 1797).

Grose, Francis. *Military Antiquities* (London: T. Egerton, Whitehall, & Kearsley, 1801).

Grose, Francis. *A Treatise on Ancient Armour and Weapons* (London: S. Hooper, 1786).

Grote, George. *A History of Greece* (J. Murray, 1850).

Grove, Sir George. *Dictionary of Music and Musicians, A.D. 1450-1889* (Macmillan, 1880).

Guest, Lady Charlotte. *The Mabinogion, from the Welsh of the Llyfr Coch O Hergest* (B. Quaritch, 1877).

Guiley, Rosemary E. *The Encyclopedia of Demons and Demonology* (Facts on File, 2009).

Gundersheimer, Werner L. *The Italian Renaissance* (University of Toronto Press, 1993).

Haberman, Charles. *The Catholic Encyclopedia* (New York: Encyclopedia Press, 1907).

Hagar, George J. *The New Supreme Webster Dictionary* (New York: Adair & Petty, 1919).

Hall, S.C. *The Baronial Halls & Ancient Picturesque Edifices of England* (Willlis, 1858).

Hallen, A.W. Cornelius. *The Scottish Antiquary* (Edinburgh: A. Constable, 1886).

Halliwell-Phillips, James O. *Popular Rhymes and Nursery Tales* (London: J. Smith, 1849).

Halsall, Paul. *Medieval Sourcebook: Geoffrey Chaucer (d.1400).* Prologue. Web. August 1996.

Hardy, James. 'The Pike as a Scottish Weapon.' *The Berwickshire Naturalists's Club. Vol. 11, 1885-1886* (Alnwick: 1887).

Harrison, Jane E. *Themis: A Study of the Social Origins of Religion* (CUP Archive 1927).

Harrison, Wilmot. *Memorable Edinburgh Houses* (London: Oliphant, Anderson, 1898).

Harshome, Charles. *Memoirs Chiefly Illustrative of the History and Antiquities of Northumberland* (London: Bell & Daldy, 1858).

Haselhurst, S. Rennie. *Northumberland* (Cambridge: The University Press, 1913).

Hawes, Stephen. *The Pastime of Pleasure: an Allegorical Poem.* Edited by Thomas Wright (London: The Percy Society, 1846).

Hazlitt, William C. *English Proverbs and Proverbial Phrases* (Reeves & Turner, 1907).

Hemingway, Samuel B. *English Nativity Plays* (New York: Henry Holt, 1909).

Henderson, Thomas F. *A Little Book of Scottish Verse* (London: Methuen, 1899).

Henderson, Thomas F. *James I and VI* (New York: Goupil & Co., 1904).

Henderson, Thomas F. *Scottish Vernacular Literature* (London: David Nutt, 1898).

Henryson, Robert. *The Poems of Robert Henryson, Volume 2.* Edited by G. Smith (Blackwood, 1906).

Henryson, Robert. *The Poems of Robert Henryson.* Edited by William Metcalf, (Paisley: Gardner, 1917).

Herd, David. *Ancient and Modern Scottish Songs, Heroic Ballads, Vol. 2* (Edinburgh: Dickson, 1776).

Herkless, Sir John. *Cardinal Beaton, Priest and Politician* (Edinburgh: Blackwood , 1891).

Herries, Lord (J.Maxwell, and J. Maxwell, 5th & 8th Lord Herries). *Historical Memoirs of the Reign of Mary Queen of Scots.* Edited by Robert Pitcairn (Edinburgh: 1836).

Highland, J.D. *Frog Went a-Courtin', or, 'A Frog He Would a-Wooin' Go.* Web. 2007.

Hill, G.F. 'Notes on Italian Medals-XXVI On the Technique of Renaissance Medal.' *The Burlington Magazine for Connoisseurs*, Vol. 15, No. 74 (May, 1909).

Hilliard Ensemble. *Love Among the Ruins.* Web.

Hinds, Allan B. *A History of Northumberland, Vol. 3* (Newcastle-upon-Tyne: Reed, 1896).

Hislop, Alexander. *The Proverbs of Scotland* (A. Hislop & Co. 1868).

History of Dumfries and Galloway (Edinburgh: Wm. Blackwood, 1896).

History of the Abbey, Palace, and Chapel-Royal of Holyroodhouse (J. Gall, 1825).

Hodgson, John Crawford. *A History of Northumberland, Vol 4* (A. Reed & Co., 1897).

Hoffer, L. *Chess* (Philadelphia: D. McKay, 1937).

Holme, Charles. *Old English Mansions* (London: The Studio, 1915).

Home, Beatrice. *Peeps at Royal Palaces of Great Britain* (London: A. & C. Black, 1913).

Hopkins, Arthur John. *Alchemy, Child of Greek Philosophy* (Columbia Univ. Press, 1934).

Huebner, Lisl Meredith. 'Myrrh's Bitter Tears of Sacrifice.' *Herbalisl.* 1 Dec 2010.

Hulme, Frederick E. *Natural History, Lore and Legend* (London: Bernard Quaritch, 1895).

Hume, David. *The History of the House and Race of Douglas and Angus* (London: Mortimer, 1820).

Hume, Martin A.S. *Chronicle of King Henry VIII of England, Vol.25* (G. Bell, 1889).

Hunnewell, James F. *England's Chronicle in Stone* (London: J. Murray, 1886).

Hunnewell, James F. *The Lands of Scott* (Boston: James R. Osgood & Co., 1871).

Hunter, Thomas. *Woods, Forest, and Estates of Perthshire* (Perth: Henderson, 1883).

Hunter, William. *Biggar and the House of Fleming, 2nd ed.* (Edinburgh: Paterson, 1867).

Huson, Paul. *Mystical Origins of the Tarot* (Inner Traditions, 2004).

Hutchinson, Andrew F. *The Lake of Menteith: Its Islands and Vicinity* (E. Mackay, 1899).

Hyatt, Alfred H. *The Charm of Edinburgh* (Philadelphia: G.W. Jacobs, 1913).

Innes, Cosmo. *Lectures on Scotch Legal Antiquities* (Edmonston & Douglas, 1872).

Innes, Cosmo. *Scotland in the Middle Ages* (Edinburgh: Edmonston & Douglas, 1860).

Irvine, David. *The Lives of the Scotish Poets* (Edinburgh: Oliver & Boyd, 1810).

Irving, Joseph. *The Book of Scotsmen* (Paisley: A. Gardner, 1881).

Jacobs, Joseph. *More English Fairy Tales* (New York: G.P. Putnam's Sons, 1894).

James I. *The Works of James the First, King of Scotland.* Edited by William Tytler (G. Clark, 1827).

James I. *The King's Quair: A Poem.* Edited by Walter W. Skeat (Edinburgh: Blackwood, 1884).

Jameson, Anna. *Memoirs of Celebrated Female Sovereigns, Vol. 1* (Harper, 1840).

Jamieson, James. *Select Views of the Royal Palaces of Scotland* (Edinburgh: Cadell, 1930).

Jamieson, John. *An Etymological Dictionary of the Scottish Language* (Paisley: A. Gardner, 1879).

Jammer, Max. *Concepts of Force* (Courier Dover Publ., 1957).

Jastrow, Morris. *Aspects of Religious Beliefs and Practices in Babylonia and Assyria* (Putnam, 1911).

Jastrow, Morris. *Religion of Babylonia and Assyria* (London: Ginn, 1898).

Jeffrey, A. *The History and Antiquities of Roxburghshire* (Jedburgh: Easton, 1855).

Jenkins, Oliver. *The Student's Handbook of British and American Literature* (Baltimore: Murray, 1891).

Jerningham, Hubert E. H. *Norham Castle* (Edinburgh: William Paterson).

Johnson, Samuel. Walker, John. *Johnson's English Dictionary* (Boston: N. Hale, 1835).

Johnstone, C.L. *Historical Families of Dumfriesshire and the Border Wars* (Dumfries: Anderson, 1889).

Jones, Charles. *The Edinburgh History of the Scots Language* (Edinburgh Univ. Press, 1997).

Jones, V.S. Vernon. *Aesop's Fables; A New Translation* (London: W. Heinemann, 1912).

Jones, W. *Studies of Chess* (London: S. Bagster, 1814).

Jowett, B. *The Dialogues of Plato, Vol. 1* (New York: MacMillan, 1892).

Johnson, James. *The Scots Musical Museum* (Edinburgh: 1771).

Jusserand, Jean Jules. *The Romance of a King's Life* (London: T.F. Unwin, 1896).

Keddie, William. *Edinburgh & Glasgow to Stirling* (Glasgow: MacLure, 1873).

Kelly, James. *A Complete Collection of Scottish Proverbs* (London: Rodwell, 1818).

Kindrick, Robert L. *Orpheus and Eurydice* (Medieval Institute Publications, 1997).

Kindrick, Robert L. *The Poems of Robert Henryson* (Kalamazoo: Medieval Inst. Pub. 1997).

Kindrick, Robert L. *The Testament of Cresseid* (Kalamazoo: Medieval Institute Publ.1979).

Klausner, David N. *The Castle of Perseverence*, (Kalamazoo: Medieval Inst. Pub. 2010).

Knight, Charles, *Old England: A Pictorial Museum* (London: James Sangster & Co., 1845).

Knight, Charles. *Old England: A Pictorial Museum* (London: J. Sangster & Co., 1860).
Knox, James. *The Topography of the Basin of the Tay* (Edinburgh: A. Shortreed, 1831).
Kuhff, Phillipe. *Les Enfantines du 'Bon pays de France'* (Paris: Sandoz, 1878).
Kuhn, Sherman. *Middle English Dictionary* (Ann Arbor: Univ. of Michigan Press, 1981).
Kuper, K. *Poetry and Drama: Literary Terms and Concepts* (Britannica Educ. Publ., 2012).
Laing, David. *Early Metrical Tales* (Edinburgh: W. & D. Laing, 1826).
Laing, David. *Early Popular Poetry of Scotland and the Northern Border* (London: Reeves, 1895).
Laing, David. *The Poetical Works of David Lyndsay.* Edited by J. Small (Edinburgh: Paterson, 1879).
Land, Andrew. *Aucassin et Nicolette* (T.B. Mosher, 1909).
Lang, Jean. *A Book of Myths* (New York: G.P. Putnam's Sons, 1915).
Lang, Jean. *A Land of Romance: The Border: Its History and Legend* (London: Jack, 1910).
Langland, William. *The Vision and Creed of Piers Ploughman.* Edited by T. Wright (Reeves, 1887).
Langland, William. *The Vision of Piers the Plowman.* Translated by W. Skeat (London: A. Moring, 1905).
Lawson, John Parkers. *Historical Tales of the Wars of Scotland, Vol. 2* (Edinburgh: A. Fullarton, 1852).
Lawson, John P. *Historical Tales of the Wars of Scotland* (Edinburgh: A. Fullarton & Co., 1839).
Lecky, William. *History of European Morals from Augustus to Charlemagne* (London: Longmans, 1890).
Lefferts, M.C. *Catalogue of a Splendid Collection of English Literature* (Taylor, 1902).
Lescarbot, Marc. *Lescarbot: The History of New France*(Toronto: Champlain Soc., 1907).
Leslie, Mary. *Historical Sketches of Scotland, in Prose & Verse* (1900).
Leyden, John. *The Complaynt of Scotland, written in 1548* (Edin.: A. Constable, 1801).
Lewis, C.S. *English Literature in the 16th Century* (Oxford: Clerenden Press, 1944).
Lewis, Samuel. *A Topographical Dictionary of Scotland* (London: S. Lewis, 1846).
Lindvall, T. *Surprised by Laughter, Revised and Updated: The Comic World of C.S. Lewis* (Nelson, 2012).
Littell, Eliakim. *Littell's Living Age, Volume 43* (Boston: Littell, Son & Co., 1883).
Lodge, Edmund. *Illustrations of British History, Biography, and Manners in the Reigns of Henry VIII, Edward VI, Mary, Elizabeth, & James I* (London: J. Chidley, 1838).
Longman, F.W. *Chess Openings* (London: Longmans, Green, & Co., 1870).
Lot-Borodine, Myrrha, *Le Roman Idyllique au Moyen Age* (Paris: A. Picard, 1913).
Low, W.H. *A History of English Literature, 1485-1580* (London: W.B. Clive & Co., 1913).
Luminist Manifestio. 'Ophites.' The Luminist League, 2012.
Lydekker, R. *Hertfordshire* (Cambridge University Press, 1909).
Lydgate, John. *Lydgate's Fall of Princes.* Edited by Henry Bergen (Carnegie Inst. of Washington, 1927).
Lytton, Baron E. B. *The Last of the Barons, Volume 1* (London: George Routledge, 1889).
MacArthur, Margaret. *History of Scotland* (New York: Henry Holt & Co., 1874).
MacDonald, George. *The Roman Wall in Scotland* (Glasgow: J. Maclehose & Sons, 1911).
Macdonald, T.D. *Celtic Dialects: Gaelic, Brythonic, Pictish* (Stirling: E. MacKay, 1903).
MacGibbon, David. *Castellated & Domestic Architecture of Scotland* (Edinburgh: D. Douglas, 1889).
Mackay, Charles. *A Dictionary of Lowland Scotch* (London: Whittaker & Co, 1888).
MacKenzie, James D. *Castles of England, Vol. 2* (New York: MacMillan Co., 1896).
MacKenzie, James. *The History of Scotland* (London: T. Nelson & Sons, 1869, 1902).
Mackie, Charles. *The Castles, Palaces, & Prisons of Mary of Scotland* (London: 1850).
MacLeod, Mary. *Honour & Arms: Tales from Froissart* (New York: Dodge Pub., 1910).
MacLeod, Iseabail. Cairns, Pauline. *The Essential Scots Dictionary* (Edin. U. Press, 2004).
MacPherson, A. *Webster's Etymological Dictionary* (London Cassell, Petter,1869).
Maidment, James. *Analecta Scotica* (Edinburgh: Thomas G. Stevenson, 1834).
'Madder: Our Natural Dyestuff.' Web. Azerbaijan Rugs. 2013.
Maine, G.F., and Cecile Walton. *The Castle of Edinburgh* (Edinburgh: G.F. Maine, 1920).
Mallory, Sir Thomas. *Le Morte d'Arthur* (London: J.M. Dent, 1908).
Manly, John Matthews. *Specimens of the Pre-Shakespearean Drama* (Boston: Ginn).
Mann, Jill. *Chaucer and Medieval Estates Satire* (Cambridge University Press, 1973).
Manual, D.G. *Dryburgh Abbey* (Edinburgh: Wm. Blackwood & Sons, 1922).
Marshall, George W. *The Genealogist* (London: George Bell & Sons, 1880).
Marshall, John J. 'The Dialect of Ulster.' *Ulster Journal of Archaeology* (Ulster Arch. Soc., 1902).
Marshall, H.E. *Scotland's Story* (London: T. Nelson & Sons, 1907).
Martine, John. *Reminiscences of the Royal Burgh of Haddington* (J. Menzies, 1883).
Masson, David. *Edinburgh Sketches & Memories* (Edinburgh: A. & C. Black, 1892).
Masson, Rosaline Orme. *Three Centuries of English Poetry* (London: Macmillan, 1876).
Masson, Rosaline. *Edinburgh.* Painted by John Fulleylove (London: A. & C. Black, 1907).
Masson, Rosaline. *Peeps at Many Lands: Edinburgh* (London: A. & C. Black, 1910).

Masson, Andrew S. *A Picture of Stirling: A Series of Eight Views* (Stirling: Hewit: 1830).

Maxwell, Herbert. *A History of the House of Douglas* (London: Freemantle & Co., 1902).

Mayhew, A.L. Skeat, Walter. *A Concise Middle English Dictionary* (Clarendon, 1888).

McCall, Hardy. *The History & Antiquities of the Parish of Mid-Calder* (Edinburgh: R. Cameron, 1894).

McConnochie, Alexander I. *Bennachie* (Aberdeen: D. Wylie & Son, 1890).

McGraw, J. 'The Life and Legacy of Hermes Trismegistus.' *Alchemy Journal, Vol. 3, No. 4.* Aug. 2002.

Mead, William E. *Selections from Sir Thomas Malory's Morte d'Arthur* (Ginn,1901).

Miller, Hugh. *Geology of Bass Rock* (New York: R. Carter, 1952).

Miller, James. *Lamp of Lothian, or The History of Haddington* (Haddington: W. Sinclair, 1900).

Miller, David. *Arbroath & Its Abbey* (Edinburgh: T.G. Stevenson).

Millar, John Hepburn. *A Literary History of Scotland* (London: T. Fisher Unwin, 1903).

Molà, Luca. *The Silk Industry of Renaissance Venice* (John Hopkins U. Press, 2000).

Monahan, Patricia. *The Encyclopedia of Celtic Mythology and Folklore* (Infobase Publishing, 2004).

Montaigne, Michel Eyquem de. *The Complete Works of Michel de Montaigne.* Translated by William Hazlitt (London: J. Templeman, 1842).

Morton, James. *The Monastic Annals of Teviotdale* (Edinburgh: W.H. Lizars, 1832).

Mosely, C. *English Renaissance Drama* (Humanities-ebooks.co.uk, 2007).

Motherby, Robert. *Pocket Dictionary of the Scottish Idiom* (Konisburgh: 1826).

Muir, T.S. *Ecclesiological Notes on Some of the Islands of Scotland* (D. Douglas, 1885).

Muirhead, George. *The Birds of Berwickshire* (Edinburgh: David Douglas, 1889).

Müller, Friedrich Max. *Contributions to the Science of Mythology, Volume 1* (London: Longmans, 1897).

Mueller. Janel. *Katherine Parr: Complete Works and Correspondence* (Univ. of Chicago Press, 2011).

Mummy, Kevin. *The Groans of Britons: Toward the British Civitates Period, ca. 406-455 C.E.* Journal of the History Students at San Francisco State Univ. Vol. XI. 2002.

Murray, Sir James. *The Dialect of the Southern Counties of Scotland* (London: Philological Soc. 1873).

Needham, Mark. 'Medieval Abbeys and Monasteries.' *TimeRef.com Medieval Timeline Reference.* Web.

Nelson, Arthur. *The Tudor Navy: the Ships, Men, and Organization, 1485-1603* (Naval Inst. Press, 2001).

Nelson-Burns, Lesley. 'Lord Rendel.' Web.

New Display of the Beauties of England (London: R. Goadby, 1776).

New Statistical Account of Scotland (Edinburgh: W. Blackwood & Sons, 1845).

Newbery & Carman. *A Description of England & Wales* (London: Newbery, 1769).

Newton, J. 'The King Isn't Dead After All! The Real Meaning of Shah Mat.' *Goddess Chess.* Sep. 2003.

Nimmo, William. *The History of Stirlingshire* (London: Hamilton, Adams, 1880).

Nisbet, Alexander. *A System of Heraldry* (Edinburgh: Wm. Blackwood, 1816).

Norris, Herbert, *Tudor Costume and Fashion* (NewYork: Dover Pub. 1997).

O'Day, Rosemary. *The Routledge Companion to the Tudor Age* (Routledge, 2010).

Og, Eogan."Insulting Song: (Bon Joure a Vous!).' *The Merry Rose Tavern.* 1998. Web.

Olcott, Charles S. *The Country of Sir Walter Scott* (Boston: Houghton Mifflin Co., 1913).

Old English Ballads (London: Ward & Lock, 1864).

Oliphant. *A Child's History of Scotland* (London: T. Fisher Unwin, 1895).

Oliver, J. Rutherford. *Upper Teviotdale and the Scotts of Buccleuch* (Hawick: W. & J. Kennedy, 1887).

Oman, C.W.C. *The Art of War in the Middle Ages* (Oxford: B.H. Blackwell, 1885).

Opie, Iona and Peter. *The Oxford Dictionary of Nursery Rhymes* (Oxford U. Press, 1951).

Original Historical Description of the Monastery and Chapel Royal of Holyroodhouse (Edinburgh: 1829).

Orr, James. *The International Standard Bible Encyclopedia* (Chicago: Howard-Severance Co., 1915).

Osberg, Richard H. *The Poems of Laurence Minot, 1333-1352* (Medieval Institute Publications, 1996).

Osgood, Charles G. *The Pearl: An Anonymous English Poem of the 14th Century* (The Translator, 1907).

Ovid. *Ovid, in 6 Volumes. Vol 3, Metamorphoses.* Translated by Frank J. Miller (Harvard Press, 1916).

Ovid. Allen, J.H. *Selections from Ovid, chiefly the Metamorphoses* (Boston: Ginn, 1890).

Oxford Companion to French Literature. *'French Romances et Pastourelles of the 12th and 13th centuries.'*

Palmer, Sean B. *'Will-O'-the-Wisp', The Earth's Anomalous Lightforms.* Web. 2012.

'Paradise of Desert Fathers.' *Encyclopedia Coptica: The Orthodox Church of Egypt.* 2006.

Pardon, George F. *A Handbook of Chess* (London: Routledge, 1860).

Parkinson, David. *Gavin Douglas, The Palis of Honoure: Introduction* (Medieval Institute Pub., 1992).

Paton, James. *Scottish History & Life* (Glasgow: J. Maclehose & Sons, 1902).

Paton, James. *Scottish National Memorials* (Glasgow: J. MacLehoe, 1890).

Patterson, Robert. *Introduction to Zoology* (London: Simms & McIntyre, 1854).

Paul, James Balfour. *The Scots Peerage* (Edinburgh: David Douglas, 1905).

'Peg-a-Ramsey.' Speak the Speech. *Twelfth Night Notes* (04 July 2008).

Pennant, Thomas. *A Tour in Scotland* (Chester: J. Monk, 1771).

Penny, George. *Traditions of Perth* (Perth: Dewar, Sidey, *et al.*, 1836).

Percy, Thomas. *Reliques of Ancient English Poetry*. Edited by Henry Wheatley (London: Lewis, 1939).

Perfect, William. *Annals of Insanity, 5th edition* (London: W. Perfect, 1800).

Philador, A.D. *Studies of Chess* (London: S. Bagster, 1814).

Philalethes, Eirenaeus. *Collectanea Chemica: Being Certain Select Treaties on Alchemy and Hermetic Medicine* (London: James Elliott & Co., 1893).

Phin, John. *The Shakespeare Cyclopædia* (New York: Industrial Publ. Co., 1902).

Pietersma, Albert. *The Apocryphon of Jannes and Jambres the Magicians* (Brill, 1994).

Pinkerton, John. *Scotish Poems* (London: John Nichols, 1792).

Pliny the Elder. *The Natural History of Pliny*. Translated by J. Bostock and H.T. Riley (G. Bell, 1892).

Poems Chiefly in the Scottish Dialect (J. Colerick, 1801).

Pollard, Alfred W. *15th Century Prose and Verse* (A. Constable & Co., 1903).

Pollard, A.F. *Tudor Tracts, 1532-1588* (Westminster: Constable, 1903).

Pratt. Anne. *The Flowering Plants &c. of Great Britain* (London: Frederick Warne, 1873).

Prioreschi, Plinio. *A History of Medicine: Volume V: Medieval Medicine* (Omaha: Horatius Press, 2003).

Prizer, William, and Villa I. Tatti. *Marchetto Cara at Mantua: New Documents on the Life and Duties of a Renaissance Court Musician*. Musica Disciplina, Vol. 32. 1978.

Puckle, John. *The Church & Fortress of Dover Castle* (Oxford: J. Parker, 1864).

Purdie. Rhiannon. '*Roswall and Lillian*, the "Lord of the Learne" and the Study of Medieval Romance and the Early-Modern Ballad.' Journal of the Northern Renaissance. Issue 4 (2012) – Natio Scota.

Purucker, G. de. *Theosophical Path Magazine, January to June 1931* (Kessinger, 2003).

'Quant compaignons s'en vont juer.' Medieval Music Databse. La Trobe U. Library, 2003.

Rabelais, Francois. *Rabelais: The Five Books and Minor Writings*. Translated by W. Smith (Watt, 1893).

Radford, Edwin, and Mona A. Radford. *Encyclopedia of Superstitions* (Kessinger, 2004).

Raine, James. *The Priory of Hexham* (Durham: Surtees Society, 1864).

Raine, James. *The Towneley Mysteries* (J.B. Nichols, London, 1836).

Rait, Robert S. *Royal Palaces of England* (London: Constable & Co., 1911).

Rait, Robert S. *Royal Palaces of Scotland* (London: Constable & Co., 1911).

Rait, Robert S. *Scotland* (London: A. & C. Black, 1911).

Ralston, Michael E. 'The Traditions of the Harrowing of Hell in Piers Plowman' (Master's Thesis, Texas Tech University, 1976).

Ramage, Crauford T. *Drumlanrig Castle and the Douglases* (Dumfries: Anderson, 1876).

Ramsey, Allen. *The Ever Green: Being a Collection of Scots Poems* (Glasgow: J. Cameron, 1724).

Reed, Edward Bliss. *English Lyrical Poetry* (New Haven: Yale University Press, 1912).

Reese, Gustav. *Music in the Renaissance* (New York: W.W. Norton & Co. 1954, 1959).

Reinfeld, Fred. *The Art of Chess* (New York: Dover Publ., 1958).

Rhys, Ernest. *Everyman with Other Interludes: Including Eight Miracle Plays* (London: J. Dent, 1909).

Riddy, Felicity. *Sir Thomas Malory* (Netherlands: E.J. Brill, 1987).

Ridpath, George. *The Border-History of England & Scotland* (London: T. Cadell, 1776).

Ripley, George, and C.A. Dana. *The American Cyclopædia* (New York: Appleton, 1879).

Ritson, Joseph. *Robin Hood, A Collection of All the Ancient Poems, Songs and Ballad* (J. Nimmo, 1887).

Robinson, Mairi. *Concise Scots Dictionary* (Edinburgh University Press, 1999).

Role, Richard (of Hampole). *The Pricke of Conscience*. Edited by Richard Morris (Berlin: Asher, 1863).

Ronald, James. *Landmarks of Old Stirling* (Stirling: Eneas Mackay, 1899).

Rose, Thomas. *Beauties of Westmoreland, Cumberland, Durham, and Northumberland* (H. Fisher, 1835).

Royal Commission on Ancient and Historical Monuments & Constructions of Scotland. 7th Report with Inventory of Monuments and Constructions in the County of Dumfries (Edinburgh: 1920).

Rudel, Jaufré. *Chansons de Jaufré Rudel*. Edited by Alfred Jeanroy (Paris, 1915).

Russell, John. *History of England* (Philadelphia: Hogan & Thompson, 1838).

Rutherford, O. *Upper Teviotdale and The Scotts of Buccleuch* (Hawick: Kennedy, 1887).

Ryley, George Scott. *The History of Torture Throughout the Ages* (Kessinger, 1940).

Salisbury, Eve. *Select Secular Lyrics of the 14th & 15th Centuries* (Medievel Institute Publications, 2002).

Sanders, Paul D. *Lyrics and Borrowed Tunes of the American Temperance Movement* (University of Missouri Press, 2006).

Saunders, Corrine, ed., *A Companion to Medieval Poetry* (Wiley-Blackwell, 2010).

Schmid, Angelyn. 'The Wizard Lady of Branxholme.' *Seduced by History*. Web. 2011.

Schmitdz, Leonard. 'Pantomime.' University of Chicago. 2009.

Schmidt, Michael. *Lives of the Poets* (Knopf, 1999).

Scots Observer, Vol. 3: From November 28, 1889 to May 17, 1890 (Edinburgh University Press, 1890).

Scott, Sir Walter. *The Lay of the Last Minstrel.* Edited by David H. Radcliffe (Virginia Tech Center for Applied Technologies in the Humanities).

Scott, Sir Walter. *Minstrelsy of the Scottish Border* (Edinburgh: Ballantyne & Co., 1810).

Scott, Sir Walter. *Marmion.* Edited by William J. Rolfe (Boston: Tickner & Co., 1885).

Scott, Sir Walter. Laing, David. *The Bannatyne Manuscript* (Hunterian Club, 1896).

Scott, Sir Walter. *Scotland* (New York: Peter Fenelon Collier & Son, 1900).

Scott, Sir Walter. *Provincial Antiquities of Scotland* (Edinburgh: R. Cadell, 1834).

Scott, Sir Walter. *Historical Illustrations of the Prose & Poetical Works of Sir Walter Scott* (Till, 1834).

Scott, Sir Walter. *Illustrations: Landscape, Historical, and Antiquarian to The Poetical Works of Sir Walter Scott* (London: Charles Tilt. 1834).

Scott. Sir Walter. *Poetical Works of Sir Walter Scott* (Edinburgh: Cadell, Whittaker, 1833).

Scott, Sir Walter. *Scotland* (New York: Peter Fenelon Collier & Son, 1901).

Scott, Sir Walter. *Border Antiquities of Scotland and England* (London: Longman, 1814).

Scottish Historical Review, Vol. 10 (Glasgow: J. Maclehose & Sons, 1913).

Scottish Tourist (Edinburgh: Stirling, Kennedy, & Co., 1842).

Setton, Kenneth M. *The Papacy and the Levant (1204-1571), Vol. 1* (American Philosophical Soc., 1976).

Sharpe, R. Bowdler. *Hand-book to the Birds of Great Britain* (London: E. Lloyd, 1896).

Shaw, William. *Galic and English Dictionary* (London: W. & A. Strahan, 1780).

Shearer's Guide to Stirling, Dunblane, Callander, The Trossachs, and Loch Lamond (Shearer, 1895).

Shearer's Stirling: Historical & Descriptive (Stirling: R.S. Shearer & Son, 1897).

Shepherd, Meg. 'Idyllic Romance.' *Medieval France: An Encyclopedia.* Edited by W. Kibler (1995).

Shipley, Joseph Twadell. *The Origins of English Words* (Johns Hopkins U. Press, 1984).

Sidgwick, Frank. *Everyman: A Morality Play* (London: A. H. Bullen, 1902).

Sidgwick, Frank. *Ballads of Romance & Chivalry* (London: A.H. Bullen, 1903).

Sierra, Joaquin, de la. 'Medieval Torture.' *Medieval Times and Castles.* Web. 2008.

Silverstein, Theodore. *English Lyrics before 1500* (Northwestern University Press, 1971).

Singer, Samuel W. *Researches into the History of Playing Cards* (London: Triphook, 1816).

Skeat, Walter W. *A Glossary of Tudor and Stuart Words* (Oxford: Clarendon Press, 1914).

Skelton, John. *Magnificence, A Moral Play.* Edited by Robert L. Ramsay (London: Kegan, 1906).

Skelton, John. *John Skelton: Selected Poems.* Edited by Gerald Hammond. (Routledge, 2003).

Skelton, John. *Poetical Works of John Skelton.* Edited by Alexander Dyce (London: T. Rodd, 1843).

Skene, William F. *John of Fordun's Chronicle of the Scottish Nation* (Edinburgh: Edmonston, 1872).

Small, John. *Select Remains of the Ancient Popular & Romance Poetry of Scotland* (Blackwood, 1885).

Small, Andrew. *Interesting Roman Antiquities Recently Discovered in Fife* (Edinburgh: Anderson, 1823).

Smeaton, Oliphant. *The Story of Edinburgh* (London: J.M. Dent, 1905).

Smeaton, Oliphant. *Edinburgh and Its Story* (London: J.M. Dent, 1904).

Smith, J.C. *A Book of Verse from Langland to Kipling* (Oxford: Clarendon Press, 1921).

Smith, G. Gregory. *Specimens of Middle Scots* (Edinburgh: Blackwood & Sons, 1902).

Smith, John. *Galic Antiquities* (Edinburgh: C. Elliot, 1780).

Smith, William. *Dictionary of Greek & Roman Mythology* (Boston: Little, Brown, 1870).

Spence, Lewis. *Myths & Legends of Babylonia and Assyria* (New York: Stokes, 1916).

Spottiswoode, John. *Liber S. Marie de Dryburgh* (Edinburgh, 1847).

Stace, C. *The Golden Legend: Selections by Jacobus de Voragine* (Penguin, 1998).

Stair-Kerr, Eric. *Stirling Castle: Its Place in Scottish History* (Glasgow: MacLehose, 1913).

Standing, Percy C. *Memorials of Hertfordshire* (London: Bemrose, 1905).

Stark, J. *Biographia Scotica: or, Scottish Biographical Dictionary* (Edin.: Stark, 1805).

Stark, John. *Picture of Edinburgh* (Edinburgh: Fairbairn & Anderson, 1821).

Stephen, Leslie. *Dictionary of National Biography* (London: Smith, Elder, & Co., 1885).

Stevenson, Burton. *Home Book of Verse, American and English, 1580-1918, Vol. 1* (Holt, 1915).

Stevenson, Joseph. *Illustrations of Scottish History: 12th – 16th centuries* (Maitland Club, 1834).

Stevenson, Karen. *Chivalry and Knighthood in Scotland: 1424-1513* (Woodbridge: Boydell, 2006).

Stratman, F. H., and H. Bradley. *A Middle English Dictionary* (Oxford U. Press, 1891).

Stewart, Michael. 'People, Places, & Things: Battle of Frogs and Mice.' *Greek Mythology: From the Iliad to the Fall of the Last Tyrant.* Web. 2005.

Strong, Sir Archibald Thomas. *A Short History of English Literature* (H. Milford, 1921).

Studer, Paul. *Le Mystère d'Adam: an Anglo-Norman Drama* (Manchester Univ. Press, 1918).

Sylvester, Louise, and Jane A. Roberts. *Middle English Word Studies* (Boydell, 2000).

Tacitus. *Annals of Tacitus, Translated into English.* Translated by Alfred J. Church (MacMillan , 1906).

Taylor, James. *The Pictorial History of Scotland* (London: J.S. Virtue, 1859).

Taylor, J.W. *Historical Antiquities of Fife* (Edinburgh: Johnstone, Hunter, & Co., 1875).

Taylor, W.C. *The Student's Manual of Ancient History* (London: John W. Parker, 1845).

'Theatre in England – Miracle Plays of the 15th Century and Their Performance.' 1902. *Old and Sold: Turn-of-the-Century Wisdom for Today*. Web.

Thompson, Charles J.S. *Alchemy and Alchemists* (Dover Pub., 1932, 2002).

Thornton, Percy M. *The Stuart Dynasty* (London: Wm. Ridgway, 1890).

Tillotson, John. *Album of Scottish Scenery* (London: T.J. Allman, 1860).

Timbs, John. *Abbeys, Castles & Ancient Halls of England & Wales* (London: Warne, 1872).

Tompkins, Herbert W. *Hertfordshire* (London: Methuen, 1903).

Turnbull, Robert. *The Genius of Scotland* (New York: Robert Carter, 1847).

Turnbull, William B. *Calendar of State Papers on the Reign of Edward VI, 1547-1553* (Longman, 1857).

Turner, Janet K. 'On the Emerald Tablet of Hermes.' *Alchemy Journal, Vol. 3, No. 4*. 2002.

Tytler, Patrick Fraser. *The History of Scotland* (Edinburgh: Wm. P. Nimmo, 1866).

Tytler, Patrick Fraser. *Lives of Scottish Worthies* (London. J. Murray, 1831).

Udall, Nicholas. *Ralph Roister Doister*. (London: Early Engllish Drama Society, 1907).

Van Orden, Kate. *Music, Discipline, and Arms in Early Modern France* (Univ. of Chicago Press, 2005).

Verberg, John. 'Dovecotes of Old England, Wales, and Scotland.' Web.

Victoria & Albert Museum. Historical notes to Toothpick Case. Museum #M.1:1,2-2010.

Vredeveid, Harry. *The Poetic Works of Helius Eobanus Hessus, Vol. 3* (Brill, 2012).

Waldie, George. *History of the Town and Palace of Linlithgow* (Linlithgow: Waldie, 1868).

Walford, Edward. *Antiquary: A Magazine Devoted to the Study of the Past*. Vol. 18.

Walker, Greg. *John Skelton and the Politics of the 1520s* (Cambridge U. Press, 1988).

Walker, Greg. *Medieval Drama: An Anthology* (Blackwell, 2000).

Walsh, William S. *American Notes and Queries, Vol. 4* (Phila.: Westminster Publ., 1890).

Walters, Henry Beauchamp. *Church Bells of England* (London: Henry Frowde, 1912).

Walters, Kerry. *Godlust: Facing the Demonic, Embracing the Divine* (Paulist Press, 1999).

Ward, A.W. *Cambridge History of English and American Literature* (Cambridge Univ. Press, 1907-1921).

Watt, L. Maclean, and Robert L. Stevenson. *The Hills of Home* (London: T.N. Foulis, 1914).

Webster, David. *A Topographical Dictionary of Scotland* (Edinburgh: P. Hill, 1819).

Webster, Noah. Webster's New Modern English Dictionary (Chicago, 1922).

Weir, Alison. *The Six Wives of Henry VIII* (New York, Grove Press, 2000).

Weirter, Louis. *The Story of Edinburgh Castle* (London: George G. Harrap & Co., 1913).

Westerhoff, Jan C. *The Stanford Encyclopedia of Philosophy* (Fall 2010 Edition).

Wharton, Edward Ross. *The Whartons of Wharton Hall* (Oxford Univ. Press, 1898).

White, Lynn, Jr. *Viator: Medieval and Renaissance Studies, Vol. 1* (University of California Press, 1971).

White. Walter. *Northumberland and the Border* (London: Chapman & Hall, 1859).

Whitney, W. *Century Dictionary: An Encyclopedic Lexicon of the English Language* (Century, 1904).

Wiggins, Alison. *Stanzaic Guy of Warwick* (Medieval Inst. Publ., 2004).

Wilhelm, James. *Lyrics of the Middle Ages* (Garland Publishing, New York, 1990)

Williams, W. H. *Skelton: A Selection for the Poetical Works of John Skelton* (London: Isbiter, 1902).

Wilson, John M. *The Imperial Gazetteer of Scotland* (Edinburgh: A. Fullarton, 1868).

Wilson, Sir Daniel. *Memorials of Edinburgh* (Edinburgh: Hugh Paton, 1848).

Wilson, George. *The Annals of the Glover Incorporation, 1300-1905* (Perth: Hay, 1905).

Wilson, Sir James. *Lowland Scotch* (London: Oxford University Press, 1915).

Wilson, Sir James. *The Dialect of Robert Burns* (Oxford University Press, 1923).

Woolnoth, William. *Ancient Castles of England & Wales (*London: Longman & Co., 1825)

'Women Warriors – The Sarmatians.' *Silkroad Foundation*. 2012.

Wordsworth, William. *The Poetical Works of William Wordsworth* (Clarendon Press, 1947).

World of Chaucer (The): Medieval Books and Manuscripts: Boccaccio De Casibus Virorum Illustrium. Special Collections Department, Library, University of Glasgow.

Worts, F.R. *A Gallery of Master Historians* (New York: E.P. Dutton, 1900).

Wright, Elizur, Jr. *Fables of La Fontaine* (Boston: Sanborn, Carter, & Brazin, 1856).

Wright, Joseph. *The English Dialect Dictionary* (London: H. Frowde, 1898).

Wright, Thomas. *The History of Scotland* (London Printing & Publishing Co., 1850).

Yeats, W. B. *Fairy and Folk Tales of the Irish Peasantry* (London: Walter Scott, 1888).

Yonge, Charlotte Mary. *The Monthly Packet of Evening Readings*. Series VI; Vol. 86. Part 509, July-December 1893 (London: A.D. Innes & Co., 1893).

Young, Franklin K. *The Major Tactics of Chess* (Boston: Little, Brown, & Co., 1898).

concatenate: 529
Contra Vitam Recti Moriemur: 138
coo: 519
corbie: 392
corium: 379
cormorant: 124
corn powder: 105
coronoch: 082
Corps à corpes: 420
corybantic: 166
corymb: 533
counterpane: 062
counterstrophe: 028
cow-tree: 428
Cowthally Castle: 101
cocks of Cramond: 083
crapulence: 397
creel: 015
Cronus: 420
crotchet: 068
Cryand with many a piteous: 362
Crying the coronoch on high: 082
cuckold: 426
cuckoo flower: 331
Cuckow and the Nightingale: 159
cuddie: 288
Cunningham, William: 516, 494
cupidity: 363
curling: 141
Cyrus II : 331
d'Esse, Seigneur: 389
dagger: 414
Dalkeith Castle: 120
dammar pine: 429
Damnable opinions of ... Luther: 362
dancetté : 533
David's Tower: 521
de Valois, Marguerite: 051
De los alamos vengo, madre: 027
Dead Sea apple: 428
Death of Arthur, The: 063
Death: 512
debauchee: 525
Deceit deceiveth: 063
decorticate: 255
decumbiture: 295
defecto de boca: 113
Deid: 063
dell'Altissimo, Cristofono: 254
Demeter: 481
dempster: 454
Devil's Bath : 042
Dichon: 333
diet 483
dilettante: 362
discovered check: 189
dishes: 054
disinter: 121
disticha: 208

Do-to the book:390
Dod: 151
dogtooth violet: 013
dolphin: 271
Domino Quod-Libertarius: 322
doo: 392
dorcus: 334
dorter: 174
dot: 518
Douglas, Gavin: 066, 351
Douglas, Margaret : 050
Douglas, Sir James: 178, 371
Douglas, George : 075, 371
Douglas, Archibald : 050
dovecote: 435
dowp: 522
Dragon's Blood: 191
Drama: 026
Dronken, dronken, y-dronken: 185
Drumlanrig, 7th Baron of: 178
dub-and-whistle: 510
duck's meat: 348
ducks and drakes: 081
Dudley, John : 107
Duke of Exeter's daughter: 273
Dumbarton Castle: 258
Dumyat: 228
Dunbar, William: 039, 051, 172, 365
dunt: 064
dunted: 354
dwale: 368
Ebenezer: 528
Echo: 157
éclat: 366
eddish: 416
Edinburgh Castle: 012
een: 519
Eh bien, dansez maintenant?: 415
Eidons: 107
Eldorado: 241
elegiac distich
elegy: 406
elegy: 086
Elephant's head riding, An: 442
Ellerker, Sir John: 465
embarazar: 113
embouchure 288
Emerald Table: 471
Empress: 512
en passant: 035
En mai au douz tens nouvel: 068
Enoch: 460
Epaminodas: 303
epithalamics: 086
epopee: 304
Erasmus: 322
Erskine, Robert: 516
Erskine, John : 077, 410
Erskine, Lady Margaret: 410

IMAGES

Printed in Great Britain
by Amazon